MULTICULTURALISM AND RELIGIOUS IDENTITY

Multiculturalism and Religious Identity

Canada and India

EDITED BY

Sonia Sikka and Lori G. Beaman

McGill-Queen's University Press

Montreal & Kingston · London · Ithaca

© McGill-Queen's University Press 2014

ISBN 978-0-7735-4374-4 (cloth)
ISBN 978-0-7735-4375-1 (paper)
ISBN 978-0-7735-9220-9 (ePDF)
ISBN 978-0-7735-9221-6 (ePUB)

Legal deposit third quarter 2014
Bibliothèque nationale du Québec

Printed in Canada on acid-free paper that is 100% ancient forest
free (100% post-consumer recycled), processed chlorine free.

McGill-Queen's University Press acknowledges the support of
the Canada Council for the Arts for our publishing program.
We also acknowledge the financial support of the Government
of Canada through the Canada Book Fund for our publishing
activities.

Library and Archives Canada Cataloguing in Publication

Multiculturalism and religious identity : Canada and India /
edited by Sonia Sikka & Lori G. Beaman.

Includes bibliographical references and index.
Issued in print and electronic formats.
ISBN 978-0-7735-4374-4 (bound). – ISBN 978-0-7735-4375-1 (pbk.). –
ISBN 978-0-7735-9220-9 (ePDF). – ISBN 978-0-7735-9221-6 (ePUB)

1. Multiculturalism – Canada. 2. Cultural pluralism – Canada.
3. Religious pluralism – Canada. 4. Multiculturalism – India. 5.
Cultural pluralism – India. 6. Religious pluralism – India. I. Sikka,
Sonia, 1963– editor II. Beaman, Lori G. (Lori Gail), 1963–, editor

HM1271.M836 2014   305.800954   C2014-902914-4
                                              C2014-902915-2

This book was typeset by True to Type in 10.5/13 Sabon

Contents

Introduction   3
LORI G. BEAMAN AND SONIA SIKKA

PART ONE   MODELS OF SECULARISM

1 Multiculturalism and Religious Pluralism in Canada:
Intimations of a "Post-Westphalian" Condition   33
PETER BEYER

2 Religious Diversity and Multicultural Accommodation   55
GURPREET MAHAJAN

3 State, Religious Diversity, and the Crisis of Secularism   76
RAJEEV BHARGAVA

4 Secularism: A Possible Gandhian Reconstruction   95
BINDU PURI

5 Lessons from the Management of Religious Diversity in Chinese
Societies: A Diversity of Approaches to State Control   120
ANDRÉ LALIBERTÉ

PART TWO   MULTICULTURALISM AND RELIGION

6 Justice, Diversity, and Dialogue: Rawlsian Multiculturalism   153
ASHWANI PEETUSH

7 The Normativity of Inclusion and Exclusion:
Should Multiculturalism Encompass Religious Identities?   169
GORDON DAVIS

8 What Can Weberian Sociology Tell Us About Multiculturalism and Religion?   189
ELKE WINTER

PART THREE   RELIGIOUS MAJORITIES

9 The Ayodhya Dispute: Law's Imagination and the Functions of the Status Quo   211
DEEPAK MEHTA

10 Laws of General Application: The Retreat from Multiculturalism and Its Implications for Religious Freedom   236
LORI G. BEAMAN

11 Theism and the Secular in Canada   253
SOLANGE LEFEBVRE

PART FOUR   PROBLEMS OF RECOGNITION

12 The Limits of Multiculturalism in Contemporary India   275
SHAIL MAYARAM

13 An Exploration of Multi-Religiosity within India: The Sahebdhani and the Matua Sects   301
SIPRA MUKHERJEE

14 The Difference "Difference" Makes: Jainism, Religious Pluralism, and Identity Politics   318
ANNE VALLELY

15 Religion Education in a Multicultural Society   333
SONIA SIKKA

16 Doing Caste, Making Citizens: Differing Conceptions of Religious Identities and Autonomy in Hindu Law   353
GOPIKA SOLANKI

Conclusion   381
SONIA SIKKA AND LORI G. BEAMAN

Contributors   393

Index   399

MULTICULTURALISM AND RELIGIOUS IDENTITY

Introduction[1]

LORI G. BEAMAN AND SONIA SIKKA

In recent years the question of the legal and social place of religious beliefs, practices, and values has attained increasing prominence within liberal democratic societies. On the one hand, liberal societies are deeply committed to the principle of respect for religious freedom, and to the protection of individual rights against the dangers posed by democratic majoritarianism. On the other hand, they are avowedly secular, raising concerns about the compatibility of religious and secular values, as well as about the potential erosion of secular values if religion is granted too much space, or the wrong kind of space, within public and political life. Also at play is fear of religious extremism and the violence it can engender. In Western countries especially, this fear has primarily targeted faith communities positioned as religious and cultural others, and fused with worries, not always well-founded, about the integration of these others within the cultural fabric of the nation. At the same time, many Western nations have seen a backlash against "multiculturalism," perceived as encouraging and allowing "them" to retain too much of their distinctness from "us."

With this context in mind, the present volume seeks to examine various aspects of the political recognition and management of religious identity in Canada and India. It asks whether, how, and to what extent religion can be included within commitments to multiculturalism, interpreting the latter as a political model that seeks to evolve legislative and social policies permitting groups within a state to retain and express their distinct identities while participating in the common public life of a wider society. Its approach is interdisciplinary, drawing on a range of expertise in religious studies, law, philosophy, and social science, and blending broader theoretical and normative reflections with close case studies. We believe that this is the best way to approach the subject of religious diversity if the goal is to achieve a level of understanding that could serve as an adequate basis for formulating social and political policies. One requires here a close knowledge of contexts, processes, and histories, and in tandem with this knowledge an ability to discern social, legal, and political patterns with an orientation toward normative principles and desired outcomes.

Given these requirements, however, the challenge for comparative analyses on this subject is that few single authors currently possess the expertise needed to undertake individual comparative studies between Canada and India. We have therefore not demanded such comparisons from the individual contributors to this volume. With a few exceptions, the chapters collected here focus on either India or Canada, but address themes that have parallels in the other country. That is the only way to begin the conversation, we feel, so as to generate the kind of information and dialogue needed for sophisticated and well-informed comparative work between the two nations. Consequently, in the remainder of this introduction we identify and explain the common themes around which the chapters are organized, while drawing attention to the quite different settings in which they take shape.

A comparison of India and Canada on multiculturalism and religious identity may not at first seem likely to prove highly fruitful, given the differences between the two countries. India contains over a billion people, insignificant levels of immigration, and a very long history of profound cultural and religious diversity. By contrast, Canada is far less populous, contains a sizeable immigrant population, and until recently was predominantly Christian (apart from indigenous peoples, whose religions and cultures were excluded from the idea of the nation for most of its short history). In addition, the model of multiculturalism that originated in Canada was largely designed to address the situations of national minorities and immigrant communities.[2] It was not intended to cover religious identities directly, although it has often done so due to inevitable overlaps between the categories of culture and religion. The framework of multiculturalism may not, therefore, accurately capture the social and historical reality of India, where regional and linguistic diversities cannot readily be divided into majorities and minorities, and where cultural differences are not the result of recent patterns of immigration.[3] One needs to be aware as well that the Indian version of secularism has always involved the recognition of distinct religious identities.[4]

Both countries, however, confront the basic question of how to make room for religious identity and diversity within a national framework, in a manner that is fair and helps to minimize conflict. Canada and India have both struggled to determine the forms of differential legislation and policy that such accommodation legitimately requires, and face the problem of balancing these efforts at accommodation with a respect for individual rights and freedoms, as well as with the search for a common national identity and moral consensus.[5] Majority dominance has been problematized in Canada, too, where it assumes the priority of a particular community that then has the task of making "reasonable accommodations" for others. Yet the enactment of social policy has had to take into account the disadvantages and insecurities faced by minority groups, with special protections being put into place where necessary, a consideration certainly relevant to the situation of religious minorities in India.[6] Furthermore, while it has been argued (with some justification), that religion is too deeply a part of the social fabric in India to be separated from other categories,[7] this difficulty also arises in other countries. In Canada, the interweaving of religion and culture is perhaps most easily visible in the character of certain minority communities, including indigenous ones. But religious traditions are also reflected in the majority culture, where they tend to be less clearly visible because they are taken for granted: in festivals, symbols, and holidays, in the structure of the work day and the work week, and, indeed, in presuppositions about the appropriate place of religion in relation to private and public life.[8]

The place of religion within the multicultural paradigm has only recently begun to receive the scholarly, as well as practical and political, attention that it deserves. In the past, religion and religious identity were generally not thematized as specific topics in works on multiculturalism. Rather, religious identity was treated as a part of cultural identity, without an appropriate effort being made to isolate and investigate in detail the precise problems raised by the positioning of religion as a basis for multicultural recognition.[9] It is now being recognized that the latter problems are socially urgent ones, in need of rigorous and independent treatment. The existing scholarly literature on the subject, however, has tended to concentrate mainly on the European situation, addressing issues pertaining to the accommodation of new religious minorities, especially Muslims, within European nation-states.[10] Relatively little work has been done on the intersection between religion and multiculturalism in Canada or other non-European countries committed to some variety of multiculturalism. Indeed, Will Kymlicka has identified this lack of attention to religion as a serious lacuna in multicultural theory, noting that we still do not have a good framework to decide which religious demands are legitimate.[11]

Exploring the ways in which India and Canada frame and respond to religious diversity may offer some clues as to how best to work through the quagmire of multiple identities, differences, and similarities presented by multicultural populations. Untangling some of the complexities of both countries, particularly in a global context that renders nation-state boundaries more fluid and more irrelevant than they perhaps ever have been, has offered us a unique opportunity to reflect on a number of issues, including how to recognize religious identities without essentializing them, how to unmask religious hegemonies, how to think about justice in the face of rich diversity, both formally and at an everyday level, and how to assess multiculturalism and the possibility of its decline using two very different vantage points. These issues are more urgent than ever as we move into an era marked by fear of the religious other, the rise of neoliberalism and the decline (perhaps) of multiculturalism.

Recognizing religious identities without essentializing them is a challenge for all liberal democracies as they struggle to give voice to religious minorities. Religious identities also pose challenges for civil society as religious difference is worked through or negotiated in day-to-day life. Preconceived notions about religious identities can overshadow these interactions, resulting sometimes in misunderstanding, resentment, a failure to recognize, inequality and injustice. In the current context of fear of fundamentalism and extremism, which has some legitimate basis given acts of violence, how can religious liberty be as unbounded as possible? And how can preconceptions be replaced with nuanced understandings of religious identities that leave space for the complexity of lived religion?

The influence of religious majorities, which in both Canada and India play an important role in framing the context in which these discussions take place, should not be underestimated. Although neither Canada nor India has a religious establishment, both do have dominant religions that risk imposing hegemony. Each nation-state has, moreover, a unique history that creates a complex social context in which religion is defined, recognized, and managed. Canada's peculiar arrangement might be described as a quasi-establishment through its constitutional preservation of funding for Protestant and Catholic schools, and its recognition of the "supremacy of God" in the *Charter of Rights and Freedoms*, which has had some interesting implications for religious minorities. At the very least it has sent a sometimes not so subtle message that Canada is a Christian country, although what this means when religious practice is somewhat muted is not always entirely clear. Social institutions, though, are embedded with Christian practices, from the celebration of Christian holidays to the swearing of oaths on the bible in court. An added layer of complexity enters the picture when Quebec is considered. A Roman Catholic establishment until the Quiet Revolution, the mostly negative reaction to that period of its history has impacted on present day approaches to religious freedom in that province and distinguishes it to some degree from the rest of Canada, especially in its rejection of the "Canadian" notion of multiculturalism.

The Indian case is quite different, as the Indian subcontinent has never been dominated by a single religion. It has been home to a vast number of religious groups, some of which can be categorized as "Hindu" from a later perspective, and many of which cannot. It is the birthplace of Buddhism, and parts of the subcontinent experienced substantial periods of Buddhist rule. Jainism and Sikhism are also indigenous religions, as are many so-called tribal religions. Islam first arrived in India in the seventh century through trade, and northern India fell under Muslim rule in the twelfth century, which lasted until the advent of British colonialism in the late eighteenth century. The latter resulted in Christianity becoming not only an important minority religion in itself, but a significant influence on other religions within India. Independence from British rule was accompanied by partition of the country along religious lines, with massive transfers of population and appalling levels of violence.

This history is essential to understanding the contemporary Indian context. The Indian constitution specifically recognizes the equality of all religions and grants them an equal measure of freedom. This is largely what "secularism" means in India, and it responds to the actual religious plurality of the subcontinent over its long history. The religious tensions so clearly visible at the time of partition, however, have by no means disappeared from the scene, as witnessed by the resurgence of Hindu ethnonationalism, mobilized especially against Muslims, over the 1980s and early 1990s. The construction of India as a Hindu nation, and of Hinduism as a single religion defined by a set of sacred texts and a fixed system of beliefs, began in the nineteenth century in the context of colonialism. It continues to be deployed in India by the Hindu Right, who are willing to include India's indigenous religions – Buddhism, Jainism, Sikhism – within a nation defined as Hindu (not that these groups necessarily wish to be so included), but who position Christianity and Islam as "foreign." Ironically, then, a kind of discourse about religious diversity involving the concepts of native and foreign, of us and them, has become a serious force in Indian politics, even though it does not properly represent the character of religion, and the relations between religious groups, over the course of India's history.

Given this situation, one might question the value of some elements in Western descriptions of diversity, and paradigms of diversity management, in relation to India. One might also ask whether there are contrasting Indian strategies from which nations like Canada might learn. It is reasonable to pose these questions in terms of finding an appropriate model of multiculturalism for each country. Granted that while Canada defines itself – demographically, legally, and ideologically – as a multicultural nation, India does not. It remains the case that India contains an immense diversity of peoples who must figure out how to live together peacefully. To this end, India's secular constitution imagines peaceful co-existence of difference much as does Canada's. Globally, however, there is an emerging trend toward if not outright rejection, then de-emphasis of multiculturalism as an approach that celebrates diversity without privileging one culture over others. Although this decline has been much debated, the overall tone has been one of a shift to a dominant culture model which sees "others" fitting in. This move is especially evident in Europe, but can also been seen as an emerging trend in Canada, and has been precipitated by a fear of the specifically religious other. And similar moves have been made in India against Muslims constructed as "other." It is worth comparing these reactions against forms of policy, law, and civil practice supporting diversity, and considering possible solutions.

One of the core debates forming the backdrop of discussions of multiculturalism is the extent to which a given society is secular. This problem raises a set of complex questions that remain to be resolved. The meaning of the word "secular" is contested, as is the very idea that society has become secular. The idea of the post-secular has been given some currency thanks to the work of Habermas, although, as Beckford points out, its usefulness in resolving any of the debates is doubtful. In short, as Beckford and others argue, the idea of the post-secular assumes that there once was a secular, which is itself a contentious foundational idea.

It is not easy to unpack the level to which any society can be said to be secular, or to which secularism exists within it as a project or reality. For example, in a Western context, it might be argued that the existence of a state church results in a less secular society than one in which there is no established church. Yet, if we compare the United Kingdom and the United States in this regard it should be obvious that this conclusion does not hold. Similarly, Denmark (for example) has a state church to which most Danes belong, but who do not actively participate in religious activities in the context of the state church. When we read a Canadian court declaring that "we live in a secular nation" we must simultaneously think about the preamble of the *Charter of Rights and Freedoms* that acknowledges both the rule of law and the supremacy of God, as well as the constitutional protection for Protestant and Roman Catholic schools.

In India, there is no state religion, and secularism is enshrined within the Indian constitution. However, the secularity of the Indian state from its inception has been defined less in terms of separation from religion than as even-handed treatment of religions. As in other liberal democracies, the Indian constitution contains provisions guaranteeing non-discrimination on the basis of religion (Article 15), freedom to practice and propagate religion (Article 25), and freedom for communities to manage their own religious affairs (Article 26). But it adds to this last provision a clause that would not prevent the state from "providing for social welfare and reform or the throwing open of Hindu religious institutions of a public character to all classes and sections of Hindus" (25.2b), where the category of "Hindu" is explicitly intended to include Sikhs, Jains, and Buddhists. A separate article abolishes untouchability (Article 17). In the years following independence, moreover, the Indian government intervened to enact reforms to Hindu personal laws, although it was reluctant to do so in the case of the corresponding Muslim laws for fear of evoking the distrust and resentment of a minority it could not be confident of representing. Such measures implicitly acknowledge the extent to which religion is deeply embedded in the social fabric of communities, and cannot be tidily separated from other spheres. One cannot have social justice while permitting the practice of untouchability, for instance, which involves very serious forms of discrimination in access to the most basic resources, including housing, education, employment, food, and water.

On the ground in India, what it means for the state to be "secular" is hotly contested, as is the interpretation of the constitutional guarantees pertaining to religion. Historically, India's religious traditions have been characterized by a great deal of fluidity and interaction, and some have argued that Hinduism is innately plural in its attitude toward other faiths.[12] Whether or not this is true, the alleged deep pluralism of Hinduism has been exploited by the Hindu Right to oppose conversion, on the grounds that efforts at conversion are incompatible with the view that all religions are equal. Although there are undeniably some political motives behind this opposition, there is also a genuine paradox here, at least from the perspective of the substantive belief in religious pluralism that characterizes some varieties of Hinduism.[13] One can see why, from that perspective, there would be a problem with granting equal recognition to the beliefs and practices of all religions, if the beliefs and practices of some religions involve a belief in their superiority over others. At the same time, there are fundamentalist factions within India's various religions that are not committed to this pluralistic view of religion, let alone to the syncretic interaction that has been a feature of India's religious traditions in the past. These co-exist in India with a powerful current of anti-religious views, influenced by Marxist critiques of religion as well as by modernist notions of religion as a relic of the past, bound to disappear as human societies progress. This is a widespread position among the Indian intellectual classes, and from its perspective, secularism means as little religion as possible in the public sphere.[14]

Thus, the idea of secularism requires a complex genealogy that is country specific as well as a broader analysis in terms of global trends, assuming such a thing is discernable at all. Recognizing this, the literature on secularism has burgeoned during the past decade. Long a topic of interest for sociologists of religion, they focused primarily on secularization and whether in fact the influence of religion, or lack thereof, was empirically measurable.[15] Political science was slower to take up the discussion, mostly because religion was largely absent from political theory generally, but in recent years many political theorists have engaged with the notion of secularism,[16] and the idea of political secularism, or the extent to which and how the state engages with religion has been of primary concern.[17] Although there is sometimes a tendency to translate *laïcité* into secularism, this compromises the social and cultural specificity of the former concept, which largely resides in France and to some extent in Quebec. France is widely acknowledged as the most fervently secular Western nation, progressively banning religious symbols first from schools and now from the public sphere. Quebec may follow suit, although the Bouchard-Taylor Commission recommended *laïcité ouverte*, a topic discussed more fully in Lefebvre's chapter in this volume. In addition, as mentioned earlier, the notion of the "post-secular," to name a condition inherited after the demise of modern Western secularism, has been introduced by Habermas (2008) and probably most effectively challenged by Beckford (2012).

It is certainly evident from these discussions that the presence or absence of secularism cannot be easily summarized in statements such as "we live in a secular society." We might begin with the observation that a consideration of majority religious presence is key to thinking about the ways in which religion is embedded in social structure. Thus, for example, in the case of the Danes, lack of contemporary participation in church rituals cannot lead to the conclusion that society is secular, for Lutheranism is embedded in the very social structure of that society. That is also the case for Roman Catholicism and Protestantism in Canada. This observation does not deny the presence of other religions, or the possibility of their influence, but a long majority religious history impacts on the ways in which social institutions such as the law, health care, and education are structured. This leads to another observation: that the idea of the secular should be considered in relation to specific social spheres. It is also useful, however, to think about the possibility of broader trends that transcend nation-states. If we observe shifts across countries with common dimensions, what can this tell us about religion, the secular, and multiculturalism? The chapters in the first section of this volume by Peter Beyer, Gurpreet Mahajan, Rajeev Bhargava, Bindu Puri, and André Laliberté address these issues.

Historical peculiarities lay the foundation for both multiculturalism and diversity. In the Canadian context, for example, tolerance and recognition of differences between Christianities set the stage for the contemporary approach to religious diversity. Despite the constitutional and legislative recognition of multiculturalism, Canada resembles India in that, as Beyer points out in his chapter "Multiculturalism and Religious Pluralism in Canada: Intimations of a 'Post-Westphalian' Condition," these post–Second World War shifts that have resulted in massive immigration and the significant weakening of the denominational system have been "less a description of a new state of affairs than a symptomatic indicator of the abandonment of older understandings without as yet the clear institutionalization of a different regime." Interestingly, this multicultural demography with ambiguous institutional and ideological direction bears a striking resemblance to Indian multiculturalism.

While it is important to pay attention to these peculiarities, they can also be understood as part of a more global picture. It is this global perspective to which Beyer calls our attention with his development of the idea of post-Westphalianism, a description that develops an alternative narrative to post-secularism and calls into question the religious/secular distinction itself. Since religion was intimately involved in the original Westphalian arrangement, it follows that post-Westphalianism also contains implications for religion. Beyer challenges the idea of a prevailing secularism, noting the ways in which religious establishments, or dominant religious patterns, infiltrated the nation-state order. The new (post-Westphalian) order, though, is better understood as a rebalancing than a complete transformation or break. Beyer identifies four intimations of the post-Westphalian condition: "the decline or volatility of national religions, the decentring of religious authority and authenticity, the more thorough transnationalization of religions, and the increasing contingency of civil religions or state secularisms." In his discussion Beyer draws on research results'from his Canadian Immigrant Youth project to provide empirical evidence for these intimations. The discussion has interesting implications for multiculturalism in that Beyer found no evidence that a civil religion exists as a substitute or alternative to religious commitment. The fluidity of multiculturalism, then, may simply be one sign of the move to post-Westphalianism.

What, though, does this new era hold for religious minorities? How do shifts in understanding of secularism impact on the ways in which people practise their religions? Is there a relationship between religious freedom and secularism? The relationship between secularism and multiculturalism can also impact on religious freedom and religious minorities. If multiculturalism extends to include religious practices, then religious minorities will be protected in societies that value, either formally or informally, multiculturalism. However, multiculturalism is not the only value (as it has been described by Canadian courts) at play. Gender equality and freedom from discrimination on various grounds, including sexuality, are also core values that come into conflict with religious freedom from time to time. Secularism becomes, in this context, a means for sorting through these conflicts.

Taking as her starting point two models of secularism, described as "rigid" and "open" secularism, Gurpreet Mahajan considers the implications of these two models for religious minorities and freedom of religion in "Religious Diversity and Multicultural Accommodation." Drawing on the Bouchard-Taylor Commission Report from Quebec, Mahajan considers the implications of open secularism for religious minorities. She concludes that although open secularism attempts to balance the four principles of secularism – moral equality of all persons, freedom of conscience and belief, separation of religion and politics, and state neutrality – it may ultimately fail in its attempt to "accommodate" religious minorities. In fact, Mahajan concludes that secularism in any form may not be able to accommodate the claims of religious minorities in liberal democracies. This is so, she argues, because religious minorities have shifted from claiming equality (acceptance of their practices that are like those of the majority) to making claims based on the importance of the practices in relation to their own way of life or identities, whether or not they bear any resemblance to majority practices. Liberal anxieties about the individual continue to shadow religious freedom in the West.

These anxieties do not exist to the same extent in India, primarily because space has been made for the freedom of religious communities with the expectation that religion would have a public presence. Secularism in this context, then, was not separated from politics or the public, and the state was expected to intervene to ensure peaceful co-existence and protection from intra-religious oppression for the vulnerable. In India, in other words, it is equality of groups rather than equality of individuals that has been the guiding principle of secularism. Each model brings its own challenges, but each is interwoven with secularism and multiculturalism.

What is quite clear as we have worked our way through discussions of secularism is that how this concept is defined or imagined varies from country to country, but also within social spheres. Thus, for example, public space may contain particular expressions of secularism, multiple religious presences, or none. So too with education, the law, and the state. The separation of church and state is one expression of secularism, in one realm. The multiple ways that religion is intertwined with the lives of everyday citizens or not are complex and require detailed consideration of what we mean both by "the secular" and "religion." As mentioned above, the differentiation of these two spheres and the artificiality of that distinction has been rendered especially visible by the post-Westphalian condition. What though of the state and its relationship to religion?

Rajeev Bhargava turns his attention to this topic in the discussion of principled distance in his chapter, "State, Religious Diversity, and the Crisis of Secularism." For Bhargava, this "best practice" located outside of the dominant Western models of church-state relations warrants sustained attention. It is time, he argues, to focus on models that exist outside of the United States and France to seek out other ways of imagining the manner in which states can relate to religion. The key goal is to avoid or eliminate inter-religious and intra-religious domination. Like Beyer, Bhargava identifies increased immigration and diversity together with de facto if not formal establishments as setting the stage for a crisis in secularism in Western states, or perhaps revealing that it has never existed to the extent imagined in the first place. Inter- and intra-religious domination have not been resolved by Western secularism. The Indian model, which, as noted by Mahajan, includes recognition of the importance of religious communities, begins with an assumption of deep religious diversity rather than diversity as an "add-on" to a majority religion. In this model, the separation of church and state is not assumed, but rather the state is expected to intervene to address inequalities, both of an inter- and intra-religious nature. Again, religions in India are expected to exist in the public sphere, and the state is expected to protect their right to be present. The state is not expected to treat everyone the same, but rather can treat groups differently depending on context, need, and the injustice experienced. Although Bhargava does not name it as such, this substantive approach to equality promises to achieve equality in a manner that Western models such as that of France or the United States cannot. Thus the challenge posed by Bhargava, Beyer, and Mahajan is to see the secular with new eyes, rethinking the ways in which boundaries are drawn around the sacred and the secular to move toward a new model – in the case of Beyer, one that is reflective of global realities, and for Bhargava and Mahajan, one that explicitly reshapes notions of equality away from explicitly Western ideals that frame equality primarily in individualist terms.

The inextricability of the religious from society as a challenge to the existence of a "pure" secularism is most often presented as the intertwining of the religious and secular realms such that they can never exist separate and apart. As such they are ideal types, existing not in reality but as frameworks within which analysis is conducted. Much less frequently discussed are the ways in which the religious and the secular are melded in the same individual or group. In other words, very often it is imagined that one is either secular or religious.

Bindu Puri takes up the challenge of sorting through the controversy surrounding Gandhi's position on secularism in her chapter "Secularism: A Possible Gandhian Re-construction." On one side of the debate are those who would wish to view his position as anti-secularist, and on the other those who argue that Gandhi was a secularist. Somewhat paradoxically, Gandhi insisted that religion and politics could not be separated, but that religion and the state must be separated. Thus, engagement with politics was a moral duty, or politics was understood as service rather than power. However, Gandhi also believed that religious communities should not receive state financial support. Puri engages with both Bhargava and Mahajan's ideas about Indian secularism, challenging the idea that there is a clear divide between Western and Indian notions of secularism. In the end, she proposes that there may be the possibility of reconciling the idea of principled distance and Gandhian secularism, but that it is contingent on the believer retaining the right to make private judgments in the religious domain. Perhaps more important, though, Puri argues that the notion of principled distance could benefit from an engagement with Gandhi's ideas to move to a more substantive idea of "the good." Gandhi's unique approach, which recognized both the importance of the religious community (a theme that runs through the discussions of India in this section) and the moral responsibility of the individual, requires a careful working through of any state approach to religion.

Finally, in this section, we step outside the Canada-India comparison to explore the Chinese case. This might seem to be an odd move in a volume primarily dedicated to a comparison of India and Canada. However, the Chinese cases highlight one of our core arguments: that Western models of diversity, multiculturalism, and state engagement offer only a narrow window of interpretation. In "Lessons from the Management of Religious Diversity in Chinese Societies: A Diversity of Approaches to State Control," André Laliberté contrasts the approaches to religious diversity adopted by the seemingly hyper-secular state of the People's Republic of China, and the more liberal policies of the Republic of China (Taiwan). Laliberté's analysis offers a challenge to the idea, sometimes advanced in India, that culture necessitates a particular relation between the state and religion, and a particular attitude toward religious diversity. He points out that China, like India, has always been characterized by deep religious diversity, and that its history reveals a variety of approaches to the management of this diversity, including periods of considerable tolerance that contrast sharply with the authoritarian secularism of the Cultural Revolution, when religion appeared to be banished from public view. The very different approaches adopted by the People's Republic of China and by Taiwan, moreover, reveal that China's religious traditions do not give rise to a political culture predisposing the state to a particular model of either secularism or multiculturalism in its chosen method of managing religious diversity.

A second question addressed in this volume is that of the nature, scope, and legitimacy of multiculturalism itself, as a normative paradigm. What needs do multicultural policies seek to address, and how fairly do they address these needs in comparison with policies grounded in commitments to individual equality and non-discrimination? Some of multiculturalism's critics have seen it as an unnecessary distraction at best, and, at worst, as working against the kind of political equality that justice genuinely demands. A popular image of multiculturalism, moreover, advanced mainly by its detractors, depicts it as positing discrete and homogeneous units called "cultures," and bestowing upon them the sort of autonomy rights that are otherwise reserved, in a liberal society, for individuals, or granting to these "cultures" something analogous to a national right of self-determination. Multiculturalism, interpreted in this manner, raises fears about group rights potentially trumping individual rights, as well as about nations fragmenting into a collection of ethnic and cultural subunits whose members do not interact, with the threat of social disintegration that such a condition entails. Motivated by such concerns, theorists like Seyla Benhabib, Anthony Appiah, and Jeremy Waldron have proposed varying forms of cultural cosmopolitanism as an alternative to what they see as the flawed principles, as well as the moral and political dangers, of multiculturalism (Benhabib 2002, 2006; Appiah 2005, 2006; Waldron 1992, 2000).

As has been pointed out by many political theorists and analysts in defence of multiculturalism, however, this image does not fairly represent the fundamental principles on which multiculturalism is based, the implementation of multicultural polices in the countries where these principles have been adopted or the results of that implementation.[18] Multiculturalism as a theory does not suppose that the various kinds of groups with which it deals are internally uniform and mutually distinct, nor does it produce ethnic enclaves and work against social cohesion. Furthermore, in Canada, the birthplace of multiculturalism as an official political policy, recognition of group identities, whether of national minorities or of immigrant groups, has always been premised on the view that individual rights need to be protected. In this context, certain basic rights have been considered non-negotiable while others may be balanced against collective histories, practices, and aspirations. Moreover, as Phil Ryan (2010) has demonstrated, much of the media-driven backlash against multiculturalism in Canada has been based on straightforward errors about matters of fact.

Questions nonetheless remain about what can and should be included within the forms of recognition that multiculturalism endorses, about what kind of conversation a "multicultural" conversation is, and about the relation between the category of "culture" and other diversity categories, such as race, employed in theoretical, public, and political discourses concerned with justice. The chapters by Ashwani Peetush, Gordon Davis, and Elke Winter take up these kinds of questions, relating them to religion in particular. Peetush's chapter, "Justice, Diversity, and Dialogue: Rawlsian Multiculturalism," begins by proposing that the normative architecture Rawls provides in his later work is more open to an intercultural and inter-religious dialogue with various non-Western communities, such as the First Nations, than are other liberal approaches. But it goes on to challenge Rawls' conception of overlapping consensus as political rather than comprehensive, criticizing the idea that dialogue and discussion concerning issues of justice must necessarily, as a matter of principle, exclude philosophical and religious reasons. The problems posed by such exclusion are compounded, Peetush argues, in a colonial context where the voices of non-Western communities have been marginalized and their self-understandings consistently denigrated for centuries.

Gordon Davis argues, on the other hand, for caution about certain kinds of religious views, and for limits on the ways in which these are socially recognized. In "The Normativity of Inclusion and Exclusion: Should Multiculturalism Encompass Religious Identities?," he points out that the doctrines of some religious communities involve deep ethical exclusion, claiming for instance that not all fellow citizens in society are fellow citizens in the "City of God." Once we take seriously problems related to religious associations having such an exclusionary soteriology, Davis suggests, a surprising implication may be that some societies, including Canada, are less suited to multicultural programs that would include religion than are societies with a different religious and spiritual landscape, such as India.

In "What can Weberian sociology tell us about multiculturalism and religion?," Elke Winter proposes that our current understanding of the apparent clash between multiculturalism as a normative framework of society-building on the one hand, and religious identities on the other, would benefit from an approach that (a) favours a highly dynamic and relational view of religious group formation, and (b) situates religious identities within unequal power relations without denying the "rationality" of religiously motivated actions. Drawing upon Weber's sociology of interethnic relations, she argues that multiculturalism should be conceptualized as an overarching principle that allows one to address the multiple forms of discrimination associated with nationalist closure. Because the latter historically favours some groups – and their cultures, religions, phenotypical features, and views of society – over others, this principle is needed.

The chapters in the third section of this volume by Deepak Mehta, Lori G. Beaman, and Solange Lefebvre examine the issue of religious majorities. Despite de facto legal recognition of multiculturalism in the case of Canada, and legal recognition of the rights of religious minorities in India, the existence of a religious majority cannot be underestimated in its influence on the social structure. Although Bhargava draws a line between these majoritarian impulses, framing diversity in India as deep diversity and in the West as an add-on, the line may not be so clean, for certainly the strong presence of Hinduism in India means that diversity there too is fragile, and can become an "add-on," even though it was not so historically. How, then, is the relationship between religious minorities and majorities negotiated both in law and between people in day-to-day life? What role does law play in mediating disputes, and does majoritarian religious culture infiltrate legal reasoning?

The opening lines of Deepak Mehta's chapter on the Ayodhya dispute (the use of a site as temple and/or mosque) perfectly capture what is at stake in those cases that come before the law: "It is at once a contest over property, historical and archaeological interpretation, cultural tradition, and the place of Muslims in India." Such is often the situation when legal claims are staked, and we need only turn to the Lautsi case, a recent decision from the European Court of Human Rights, to see that control of symbols in space, cultural tradition, and the place of religious groups are part and parcel of legal decisions on religion. In other words, there is often much more involved in religion cases than would first appear. Mehta's argument – that law is focused on restoring or preserving the status quo rather than on justice – has applicability in many situations where minority religious groups come into conflict with majority traditions. Mehta brings an additional twist to the analysis, though, by arguing that the idea of the status quo is also fluid, constructed, and deployable by all sides. Thus it is not simply a majority imposing its will on the minority, but rather a consideration of the ways in which power relations unfold in the particular social context, paying particular attention to the historical moment. As Mehta argues, embedded in these power relations is the inextricable link between the political and religion. As the dispute enters into the legal world, it is framed by it, to the extent that law then misrecognizes the religious world.

Law is a double-edged sword: while it can reframe issues to the detriment of religious groups, law can also act as a beacon or protector of religious freedom and the protection of religious expression. This can happen through particular constitutional guarantees as well as through court interpretations of cases that come before them. Thus law can provide guidance for those who are working through religious difference on a day-to-day basis. Such guidance can work to prevent inequality and discrimination, at least in theory. However, law can also send the opposite signal through the way it characterizes religious groups and religious claims.

Lori G. Beaman argues in her chapter "Laws of General Application: The Retreat from Multiculturalism and Its Implications for Religious Freedom" that religious freedom has undergone a transformation in Canada, but that that is part of a larger picture that includes a shift in law's approach to multiculturalism as a value and ideology to a demographic reality that the court is entrusted to aid the state in managing to the end of an imagined cohesive society. Further, the reframing of claims related to religious freedom from a broadly imagined, substantive equality to one in which religious groups are requesting exemptions re-positions the dominant narrative in Canada as one of formal equality rather than substantive or deep equality. Formal equality models the *laïcité* approach of France, which largely ignores the structural advantages for majoritarian religious groups. This flat model of equality is also emerging as the preferred model in Quebec. Whether the more tenuous position of multiculturalism as a Canadian value is linked to this less expansive approach to religious freedom remains to be seen.

The language employed both by law and in public discourse is critical to the ways in which religious minorities are imagined – are they part of society, or outside of it, asking for "special favours?" Two of the dominant modes of talking about religious diversity and religious difference position religious minorities in a "less than" position. Both tolerance and accommodation frame the negotiation of difference such that religious majorities maintain a hierarchical advantage. Particularly important in the Canadian context is the Bouchard-Taylor Commission and its subsequent report. Although Quebec is the focus of the commission and report, the discussions about the report reflect debates occurring not only in Canada, but in India and Europe.

Solange Lefebvre considers the Bouchard-Taylor Report and the position of its authors in some detail in her chapter, "Religion in the Public Arena: Case Studies." She points out that the report raises the important issue of how much religion should be present in the public square, and concludes that there are no simple answers to this question. The tension in Quebec between multiculturalism, which is outright rejected by the report, and *laïcité*, which is adopted in a modified form of *laïcité ouverte* ("open laicity") by the authors, is revealed within the report itself and by the submissions to the commission during its public hearings. *Laïcité ouverte* has been an attempt to move away from the banishment of religious symbols from the public sphere, such as that found in France, to a policy that is accepting of some public presence for religion and some diversity. For Bouchard and Taylor, the importance of individual involvement in working out religious difference is paramount and the law and the state's involvement secondary. Lefebvre's discussion, though, highlights the ways in which the traditional religion of Quebec, Roman Catholicism, is intertwined with Quebec culture, to the extent that even when the report recommended the removal of the crucifix from the walls of the National Assembly, the members of the assembly voted unanimously to keep the crucifix. In contradistinction to this is the vehement opposition from some quarters to *laïcité ouverte*, with some arguing that Quebec should be like France – unequivocally adopting the model of *laïcité*. This complex picture illustrates the difficulties in simplistic descriptions of majority or minority religious cultures and highlights the need for nuanced analyses.

Last but far from least, we take up problems posed by the model of "recognition." The ostensible purpose of policies of recognition is, as the word itself suggests, the acknowledgement and due accommodation of collective identities that are already present. This suggests that the identities in question are merely there to be discerned, and that the policies themselves have no impact on their formation. As noted earlier, though, one common objection against multiculturalism has been that it is premised on the existence of well-defined and mutually distinct identity units, which does not accurately reflect the reality of cultural groupings. While the idea of multiculturalism that forms the target of such critiques is sometimes a caricature, it is true that political recognition of a group requires at least enough definition and distinctness to permit identification of that group. This fact, intrinsic to the very character of recognition, poses a problem in the case of identities that do not fit any one of the social categories that may be devised for the purposes of political accommodation, or that happen to have become customary in a given society for complex and often contestable reasons.

In addition, the implementation of social and political policies involving the recognition of collective identities of various sorts – linguistic, religious, racial, to name only a few – can have a *productive* impact on the formation of those identities. By offering legal and material benefits to the recognized groups, such policies may incentivize (usually inadvertently) the formation of precisely the sorts of rigid and exclusionary identities whose existence critics of multiculturalism have wanted to challenge. The problem of essentialism, in this context, is not only that the character of cultural and other social identities cannot be properly captured through simple, single definitions, but also that policies requiring the definition of groups may promote the production of identities that are simpler and more singular than they otherwise would have been. Internal homogeneity and separation from others may be advanced and policed, moreover, by dominant segments within a group, as well as by political actors with their own agenda. This process can have serious costs for members of the group who do not conform, and do not wish to conform, to the character and values of the group so defined. Such costs are usually carried by vulnerable members of the group, and women may be especially victimized because they are so often positioned as the primary bearers of culture/ tradition.

The chapters in the fourth section by Shail Mayaram, Sipra Mukherjee, and Anne Vallely draw attention to these issues as they affect the cases of various religious groups in India. Shail Mayaram's "The Limits of Multiculturalism in Contemporary India" draws on two constellations of events suggesting the limits of Indian multiculturalism, as well as secularism: Kashmir and the region affected by "tribal" (Maoist) insurgency. The chapter argues that the deep diversity of Indian civilization, comprising intercultural fluidity, multiple religious belonging, and enclaved cosmologies has not been adequately recognized by the Indian state. Sipra Mukherjee, in "An Exploration of Multi-religiosity within India: The Sahebdhani and the Matua Sects" also uses case studies to examine the limits of multiculturalism, noting that any policy of "multiculturalism," official or unofficial, requires the delineation of identities, and that the discourse related to recognizing diversity in India has accepted certain multiplicities while rejecting others. Smaller sects lying in the liminal spaces between religions are left unnamed, encouraging the policy of recognition to gloss over their separateness and to include them within the boundaries of the dominant religions. Over time, this can lead to homogenization of the community, with smaller groups being swallowed up by the larger cultures/faiths.

Anne Vallely traces a related process with respect to the Jain community in "The Difference 'Difference' Makes: Jainism, Religious Pluralism, and Identity Politics." In this case, Vallely demonstrates policies of recognition, combined with a wish to make Jainism relevant as a world religion, have led some Jains to define themselves against a larger religious group and to resist being swallowed up by it. For much of Jain history, Vallely notes, being "a follower of the Jina" (from which the designation "Jain" was derived in the nineteenth century), was not necessarily predicated upon an ideological exclusion of non-Jain ideas and practices. Within contemporary Jainism, however, a robust identity politics is at play that makes use of an exclusionary ideological discourse.

Yet it would be wrong to conclude from the problematic features of collective recognition that the acknowledgement of group identities such as "culture" should simply be abandoned. Collective identities are real, and they matter to the individuals belonging to them. Consequently, for pragmatic purposes, identity categories are indispensable. They pick out highly significant aspects of social reality, ones not captured in the language of individual rights. For all the hazards they pose, therefore, one cannot do away with the policies recognizing communities of experience if we aim to advance genuine social equality. True equality requires that the rights of minorities be respected against the inevitable biases and pressures of the majority, that diverse communities within a nation be given appropriate degrees and types of representation and/or autonomy, and that historical and present wrongs affecting specific communities be made visible so that these communities may benefit from ameliorative measures.

Consequently, rather than jettisoning policies involving the recognition of group identities, we need to consider ways in which such policies may be designed and appropriated so as to avoid, or at least minimize, the problems of essentialism and ossification. Sonia Sikka's analysis, in "Religion Education in a Multicultural Society," suggests that education about religion is one way to counter these problems in the case of religious identities, and that such education is necessary to ensure a non-superficial respect for minority religions. In multi-religious societies, Sikka argues, citizens should not only be informed about the content and history of religions, but should understand that religious doctrines are evolving, and subject to contestation and reform. Her chapter examines the principles of Quebec's Ethics and Religious Culture program as providing a possible model for religion education in a diverse society.

Gopika Solanki's chapter, "Doing Caste, Making Citizens: Differing Conceptions of Religious Identities and Autonomy in Hindu Law," adds an element to the dialectic of individual versus group rights by pointing to the potentially positive role of community agency in democratizing internal structures, promoting equality, and preventing the ossification of group boundaries. In view of the question of whether multiculturalism is antithetical to gender equality, Solanki focuses on the recognition of religious family laws in India, as these shape gender roles as well as ethnogender identities and subjectivities within the family, and impact on the distribution of resources within the family. She investigates this issue by assessing the Indian state's policy of legal pluralism in the governance of the conjugal family in religious family laws. Her study offers a valuable counterpoint to the tendency, in much of the existing feminist literature on multiculturalism, to see the legal recognition of community rights as always a threat to women's autonomy and to gender equality.

Thus, in relation to the intersection between religion and multiculturalism, the chapters in this volume seek to offer new insights on a number of general questions. What are the principles of political secularism, and do they conflict with the recognition of religious identity within a multicultural framework? What is required for the appropriate inclusion of religion within the paradigm of multiculturalism? How does the fact that there is a majority religion in a nation impact on the decisions of the state, as well as of communities attempting to negotiate their religious identities in relation to the state? What dangers are posed by definitions of religious identity for the purposes of legal and political "recognition," and how might these be mitigated? Does such recognition inevitably disadvantage women, given the traditionally inegalitarian character of gender relations within many religions?

Because they are couched in the language of multiculturalism, the precise formulation of some of these questions may better reflect the historical trajectory of Canada than of India. As we have stressed, however, the underlying problems being addressed are ones that the two countries share. A conversation across the commonalities and differences between Canada and India on such points can therefore aid in understanding the character of religion and religious identity, while expanding our imagination of fair solutions to the difficulties posed by religious diversity. While differences in context must be taken into account, comparative politics may enable us to examine the outcomes of a variety of policies and social trends, and see possible futures in one another's present.

With these goals in mind, the intention of this volume is to focus equally on Canada and India and by doing so to challenge the assumption that North Atlantic countries have developed the best models for diversity management. Indeed, some of the chapters on India problematize these models, which have been exported to other countries, in ways that might not readily occur to researchers familiar only with Canadian (or for that matter North American and European) contexts. For example, unlike most of the Western literature on the political recognition of religious groups, Gopika Solanki's chapter, "Doing Caste, Making Citizens," examines the *interaction* of communities with laws designed to recognize them. While this topic rarely gets raised in Western discussions, it is highly relevant to feminist concerns about religion and gender equality. Other examples include the contributions by Anne Vallely and Sipra Mukherjee on the very tangible impacts of policies of recognition on groups in India that had not previously defined themselves as rigidly distinct from "other" religious communities. These two chapters, addressing the historical self-definitions of particular religious communities in India, raise profoundly important questions about the dangers of enacting policies based on a certain view of what "religions" are and should be. Such questions are also pertinent to Western countries, but they cannot be adequately captured within the terms of current Western models for the management of religious and other forms of diversity, such as "multiculturalism," "interculturalism," "cosmopolitanism," "secularism," or "post-secularism."

The chapters by Bhargava and Mahajan, moreover, examining secularism and multiculturalism within the Indian context, emphasize the importance of applying these models in manner appropriate to the differing histories and current realities of different nations. In addition, they suggest that such adaptations have lessons to offer Western nations, too, and that the flow of ideas here should not be a one-way traffic. Thus, while this volume begins with the idea of multiculturalism as a possible model for managing religious diversity, it does not end there. Rather, it deliberately allows for the identification and highlighting of issues that could lead to revisions of current Western frameworks for conceptualizing religious identity and diversity, and for the development of alternative visions.

A single volume cannot possibly do justice to the full range of topics relevant to the theme of managing religious diversity, nor can it cover significant developments in every region of Canada and India. This volume certainly does not pretend to offer a comprehensive overview of either Canada or India by region. Both countries are vast geographically, as well as regionally complex at many levels, including religious composition. In India, for instance, the historically constituted religious identities and inter-group relations of Kashmir are not those of Bengal or the northeast or Tamil Nadu or Odissa. Different regions contain very different constructions and admixtures of Hindu, Muslim, Christian, Jain, Sikh, and Buddhist, as well as a host of religious communities that fit into none of the official categories employed within governmental procedures. Moreover, divisions of governmental and legislative powers lend further jurisdictional complexity to matters in both countries. Education, for example, is under provincial jurisdiction in Canada, meaning that the ethics course developed in Quebec to respond to the "problem" of education about religion is indeed a Quebec solution.

We have therefore chosen to focus on a few centrally important themes in each country, to give a sense of the wide range of comparative possibility and the potential for future engagement at a more comprehensive level. With respect to India, important topics for future comparative work (and ones very prominent in discussions within India itself), include anti-conversion laws in a number of Indian states,[19] the situation of Dalits (members of communities formerly designated as lower caste or "untouchable") (Sikka 2012; Manohar 2010) and the complex, contested social/political/religious identities of Adivasis or "tribal" communities in regions like the northeast.[20] In Canada, the presence of religion in the public sphere will continue to attract debate, as will education about religion as a response to religious diversity. The formation of a state-sponsored office of religious freedom, and indeed the very discourse of religious freedom as an international human rights platform is also emerging as a contested issue that takes on even more importance in the comparative discussion in light of Indian anti-conversion laws.

While our discussions in this volume are inevitably selective and cannot cover all of these specific topics, they have broader implications affecting the appropriate formulation of approaches and agendas for further academic and policy research. We examine some of these implications in a brief conclusion.

NOTES

1 We are grateful for funding from the Social Sciences and Humanities Research Council's Aid to Workshops and to the University of Ottawa's Faculty of Arts Research and Publications Fund for the workshop "Multiculturalism and Religious Identity," held at the University of Ottawa on 23–25 September 2010. We would also like to thank the contributors to the volume for their intellectual contributions and for their patience as we brought this volume to press. We would like to express our deep gratitude for the editorial assistance provided by Marianne Abou-Hamad, Tess Campeau, and Heather Shipley. We would like to extend our thanks to the anonymous reviewers for their extremely helpful comments that helped to sharpen the arguments of this volume. We are also grateful to our editor Jacqueline Mason who has been unwavering in her support for this volume. Lori G. Beaman would like to acknowledge the ongoing financial support from her Canada Research Chair in the Contextualization of Religion in a Diverse Canada and from the Religion and Diversity Project. Sonia Sikka would also like to acknowledge funding from her Social Sciences and Humanities Research Council Standard Research Grant.

2 This fact is reflected in the philosophical formulations of the model in Canada; for instance, Charles Taylor's (1994) now classic essay, "The Politics of Recognition" and Will Kymlicka's major earlier works on the subject, *Liberalism, Community and Culture* (1989) and *Multicultural Citizenship* (1995).

3 Kumkum Sangari (1999) therefore rejects the Western "multiculturalist" paradigm as fundamentally unsuitable for India. But another approach is to develop a model of multiculturalism that will be sensitive to the realities of the Indian situation, as Gurpreet Mahajan (e.g., 2005) seeks to do.

4 In this respect, a number of authors have stressed the difference between Indian and Western models of secularism. A well-known example is Thomas Pantham (1997).

5 For a survey of the problems India faces in making such accommodations for identities of various types, with a focus on religious communities see Mahajan (1998).

6 This point is usually recognized even in analyses ultimately seeking to transcend the majority-minority structure (e.g., Prakash 2007, 187).

7 Such an argument has been made by T. N. Madan (1998), among others.

8 Kymlicka (1998, 46–9) therefore speaks of "fair terms of integration," involving policies of accommodation based on a recognition that many existing practices naturally, albeit unintentionally, advantage the religion(s) of the majority.

9 This is even true of Bhikhu Parekh's (2006) *Rethinking Multiculturalism*, which includes discussion of many religious practices.

10 That is, for instance, the topic of an important collection of essays published in 2009, *Secularism, Religion and Multicultural Citizenship*, edited by Levey and Modood.

11 Statement made in a 2009 public lecture, according to a report by Dennis Gruending (2009).

12 As Anwar Alam (2007, 37–8) points out, however, Indian versions of Islam have also been eclectic and plural.

13 Cossman and Kapur (1999, 72) ignore this difficulty when they state that "the Hindu Right does *not* equally respect all religions: since not all religions are as tolerant as Hinduism, then, not all religions are worthy of equal respect."

14 For an example expressing this position see Vanaik (1997).

15 Jose Casanova (1994, 2007a, 2007b, 2009); Rodney Stark (1985 (with William Sims Bainbridge), 1999); Steve Bruce (2002); Appleby (2011); Hurd (2008); Sullivan, Yelle and Taussig-Rubbo (2011); Feldman (2000); Asad (2003), and many others weighed in on this question.

16 Examples include Jürgen Habermas (2008), Charles Taylor (2007), and William Connolly (2000).

17 This is a concern that Bhargava takes up in this volume. Other interesting engagements with the notion of the secular and secularization are found in the works of Calhoun, Juergensmeyer and VanAntwerpen (2011); Asad, Butler, Mahmood, and Brown (2009); Bender and Taves (2012); Jakobsen and Pellegrini (2008).

18 See Kymlicka 2011.

19 For an overview, see Osuri 2012.

20 This subject is immensely complex. Aspects of it are examined by Bhaumik 2004; Subba, Pthenpurakal and Puykunnel 2009; Longkumer 2010, among many others.

REFERENCES

Alam, Anwar. 2007. "Political Management of Islamic Fundamentalism: A View from India." *Ethnicities* 7 (1): 30–60.

Appiah, Anthony Kwame. 2005. *The Ethics of Identity*. Princeton University Press.

– 2006. *Cosmopolitanism: Ethics in a World of Strangers*. New York: W.W. Norton.

Appleby, Scott R. 2011. "Rethinking Fundamentalism in a Secular Age." In *Rethinking Secularism*, edited by Craig Calhoun, Mark Juergensmeyer, and Jonathan VanAntwerpen, 225–247. Oxford: Oxford University Press.

Asad, Talal. 2003. *Formations of the Secular: Christianity, Islam, Modernity*. Stanford: Stanford University Press.

Asad, Talal, Judith Butler, Saba Mahmood, and Wendy Brown. 2009. *Is Critique Secular?: Blasphemy, Injury, and Free Speech*. Berkeley: The Doreen B. Townsend Center for the Humanities.

Beckford, James A. 2012. "SSSR Presidential Address Public Religions and the Postsecular: Critical Reflections." *Journal for the Scientific Study of Religion* (51) 1: 1–19.

Bender, Courtney, and Ann Taves, eds. 2012. *What Matters?: Ethnographies of Value in a Not So Secular Age*. New York: Columbia University Press.

Benhabib, Seyla. 2002. *The Claims of Culture*. Princeton University Press.

– 2006. *Another Cosmopolitanism*. Oxford University Press.

Bhaumik, Subir. 2004. "Ethnicity, Ideology and Religion: Separatist Movements in India's Northeast." In *Religious Radicalism and Security in South Asia*, edited by Satu P. Limaye, Robert G. Wirsing, and Mohan Malik, 219–44. Honolulu: Asia-Pacific Center for Security Studies.

Bruce, Steve. 2002. *God is Dead: Secularization in the West*. Malden: Blackwell Publishing Ltd.

Calhoun, Craig, Mark Juergensmeyer, and Jonathan VanAntwerpen, eds. 2011. *Rethinking Secularism*. Oxford: Oxford University Press.

Casanova, José. 1994. *Public Religions in the Modern World*. Chicago: University of Chicago Press.

– 2007a. "*Secular, Secularizations, Secularisms*." http://blogs.ssrc.org/tif/2007/10/25/secular-secularizations-secularisms/.

– 2007b. "Rethinking Secularization: A Global Comparative Perspective." In *Religion, Globalization and Culture*, edited by Peter Beyer, and Lori Beaman, 101–120. Leiden: Koninklijke Brill NV.

– 2009. "The Secular and Secularisms." *Social Research: An International Quarterly* 76 (4): 1049–1066.

Connolly, William E. 2000. *Why I Am Not a Secularist*. Minneapolis: University of Minnesota Press.

Cossman, Brenda, and Ratna Kapur. 1999. *Secularism's Last Sigh? Hindutva and the (Mis)Rule of Law*. Delhi: Oxford University Press.

Feldman, Stephen M., ed. 2000. *Law and Religion: A Critical Anthology*. New York: New York University Press.

Gruending, Dennis. 2009. "Will Kymlicka on Multiculturalism." Report on public lecture by Kymlicka delivered at the Congress of the Humanities, Carleton University, 27 May 2009. http://dennisgruending.ca /pulpitandpolitics/2009/ 06/02/will-kymlicka-onmulticulturalism/.

Habermas, Jürgen. 2008. "Notes on Post-Secular Society." *New Perspectives Quarterly* 25(4): 17–29.

Hurd, Elizabeth S. 2008. *The Politics of Secularism in International Relations*. Princeton: Princeton University Press.

Jakobsen, Janet. R., and Ann Pellegrini, eds. 2008. *Secularisms*. Durham: Duke University Press.

Kymlicka, Will. 1989. *Liberalism, Community and Culture*. Oxford: Oxford University Press.

– 1995. *Multicultural Citizenship*. Oxford: Clarendon.

– 1998. *Finding Our Way: Rethinking Ethnocultural Relations in Canada*. Oxford: Oxford University Press.

– 2011. "Multiculturalism in Normative Theory and in Social Science." *Ethnicities* 11 (1): 5–11.

Levey, Geoffrey Brahm, and Tariq Modood, eds. 2009. *Secularism, Religion and Multicultural Citizenship*. Cambridge: Cambridge University Press.

Longkumer, Arkotong. 2010. *Reform, Identity and Narratives of Belonging: The Heraka Movement in Northeast India*. London: Continuum.

Madan, T. N. 1998. "Secularism in Its Place." In *Secularism and Its Critics*, edited by Rajeev Bhargava, 297–320. Delhi: Oxford University Press.

Mahajan, Gurpreet. 1998. *Identities and Rights: Aspects of Liberal Democracy in India*. Delhi: Oxford University Press.

– 2005. "Indian Exceptionalism or Indian Model: Negotiating Cultural Diversity and Minority Rights in a Democratic Nation-State." In *Multiculturalism in Asia*, edited by Will Kymlicka, and Baogang He, 288–313. Oxford: Oxford University Press.

Manohar, Murali D. 2010. *Dalits and Their Religions*. New Delhi: Serials Publications.

Osuri, Goldie. 2012. *Religious Freedom in India: Sovereignty and (Anti) Conversion*. New York: Routledge.

Pantham, Thomas. 1997. "Indian Secularism and its Critics: Some Reflections." *The Review of Politics* 59: 523–40.

Parekh, Bhikhu. 2006. *Rethinking Multiculturalism*, 2nd ed. New York: Palgrave Macmillan.

Prakash, Gyan. 2007. "Secular Nationalism, Hindutva, and the Minority." In *The Crisis of Secularism in India*, edited by Anuradha Dingwaney Needham, and Rajeswari Sunder Rajan, 177–188. Durham: Duke University Press.

Ryan, Phil. 2010. *Multicultiphobia*. Toronto: University of Toronto Press.

Sangari, Kumkum. 1999. "Which Diversity?" In *Multiculturalism: A Symposium on Democracy in Culturally Diverse Societies, Special Seminar* 484: 24–30.

Sikka, Sonia. 2012. "Untouchable Cultures: Memory, Power and the Construction of Dalit Selfhood." *Identities* 19(1): 43–60.

Stark, Rodney. 1999. "Secularization, R.I.P." *Sociology of Religion* 60 (3): 249–73.

Stark, Rodney, and William Sims Brainbridge. 1985. *The Future of Religion: Secularization, Revival, and Cult Formation*. Berkeley: University of California Press.

Subba, Tanka B., Pthenpurakal, J., and Shaji Joseph Puykunnel. 2009. *Christianity and Change in Northeast India*. New Delhi: Concept Publishing Co.

Sullivan, Winnifred F., Robert A. Yelle, and Mateo Taussig-Rubbo, eds. 2011. *After Secular Law*. Stanford: Stanford University Press.

Taylor, Charles. 1994. "The Politics of Recognition." In *Multiculturalism*, edited by Amy Gutman, 25–74. Princeton: Princeton University Press.

– 2007. *A Secular Age*. Cambridge: Harvard University Press.

Vanaik, Achin. 1997. *The Furies of Indian Communalism*. New York: Verso Press.

Waldron, Jeremy. 1992. "Minority Cultures and the Cosmopolitan Alternative." *University of Michigan Journal of Law Reform* 25: 151–93.

– 2000. "What is Cosmopolitan?" *Journal of Political Philosophy* 8 (2): 227–43.

PART ONE

Models of Secularism

1

Multiculturalism and Religious Pluralism in Canada: Intimations of a "Post-Westphalian" Condition

PETER BEYER

INTRODUCTION:
ASSESSING RELIGIOUS DIVERSITY IN CANADA

In various senses, Canada has always been a multicultural and religiously pluralistic place. An important conceptualization of these diversities, still valid today, arrived with the Europeans in the seventeenth century, one that they succeeded in institutionalizing over the subsequent centuries. This understanding includes the following notions:

- that religion is a distinct realm of social and personal life;
- that religion comes in multiple units called religions and in distinct subunits of those religions;
- that people also divide into somewhat analogous multiple collective units called by such names as peoples, nations, cultures, or ethnicities;
- that there exists a significant but by no means exclusive overlap between the religions and the collectivities, such that certain peoples will tend to "have" a certain religion or at least belong predominantly to one or very few religions (see Beyer 2006; Masuzawa 2005).

Although the understanding of religious and collective cultural diversity has had these basic characteristics, there has also been a significant evolution in its details. The French in the seventeenth century, especially after 1627, only recognized one religion, Christian Roman Catholicism, to the exclusion of all others. Moreover, they considered the Aboriginal peoples of Canada as peoples without religion but generally in need of one: theirs (E. Anderson 2007; Trigger 1985). The British conquest in the later eighteenth century introduced a variation on this orientation. The new colonial power sought to establish one variety of Protestantism, the Church of England, as the established religion of the colony, but for pragmatic reasons "tolerated" as a "religious minority" (demographically a majority at the time) the French Roman Catholics that they inherited, albeit with notable restrictions. Aboriginal peoples were still considered as without religion to the extent that they did not adopt a variety of Christianity. In light of continuous immigration from the United States and Great Britain into the nineteenth century, they also "tolerated" and then "recognized" an increasing Protestant variety. The result was that, by the middle of the nineteenth century, attempts to establish one variety of Christianity over others were abandoned (Moir 1967; Rawlyk 1990). This change still allowed for the restriction of what was recognized as part of the legitimate religious and cultural pluralities, however.

From about 1840 on, the British colony, and later the Canadian Dominion, established a consistent way of understanding and managing religious and cultural plurality that derived from this history. It replaced the idea of an established or state religion in terms of which all others were "tolerated minorities" with a denominational structure that went beyond toleration to the recognition of a delimited variety of religious identities and their corresponding organizations. Almost to exclusion, those so recognized were varieties of Christianity, whether Protestant or Roman Catholic. Cultural pluralism was also recognized, predominantly in terms of diverse European ethnicities, mainly French (Canadian) and British (Irish, English, Scottish). There were thus many religions, but they were almost all varieties of Christianity. There were many cultures, but they were almost all varieties of European identity. Another, more negative reflection of this understanding was the Indian Act of 1876, which institutionalized a policy of (paternalistically) eliminating Aboriginal religious and cultural identity, in effect declaring these to be subject to neither toleration nor recognition (Miller 2000).

This system of toleration and recognition was, of course, not without its frictions and corresponding conflicts. Above all, the conflicts between French-speaking Roman Catholics and English-speaking Protestants continued, eventuating in a widespread understanding in both these "solitudes" that the language and the religion in each case belonged together, Irish and Scottish Roman Catholics notwithstanding. Like all such classification systems, it strained under its own contingency. That said, it also proved to be remarkably stable, institutionalizing itself solidly in the minds of many Canadians, including much of the elite, as self-evident for more than a century. Only in the post–Second World War era have Canadians witnessed a gradual but highly significant shift.

The beginnings of the transition after 1945 are evident in a number of significant events. These include the repeal of laws excluding non-European immigrants, the gradual reversal of the culturally genocidal policies with respect to Aboriginal peoples who would be reborn as First Nations, the ferment in Quebec that led to the Quiet Revolution, the opening up of consistent, large-scale immigration from all parts of the world, and the gradual emptying out of the denominational system as evidenced in the large-scale abandonment, in all but declared identity, of the largest denominations by the majority of their adherents (Bibby 1993; Clark and Schellenberg 2006).

UNDERSTANDING AND PROBLEMATIZING
RELIGIOUS DIVERSITY IN CONTEMPORARY CANADA

The post-1970s era on which I am focusing can usefully be called the era of multiculturalism in Canada. Yet this multiculturalism is fraught with ambiguities; it is less a description of a new state of affairs than a symptomatic indicator of the abandonment of older understandings without as yet the clear institutionalization of a different regime.

On the surface, multiculturalism, as officially and informally understood in today's Canada, points to the recognition and even celebration of cultural differences, which includes religious differences. As in previous eras, the relation between cultural and religious diversity is close, but far from unambiguous, let alone isomorphic. This recognition and celebration, however, includes the assumption that the diversities will somehow express themselves as a unity; that one can and should be different in Canada, but that this difference should somehow be done in a harmonious and unified way. In a sense, the United Church of Canada, arguably the quintessential religious expression of the old denominational understanding of diversity, puts the contemporary general Canadian situation very succinctly. According to its post-1980s official and theological stance, the unity of this church consists in its diversity (see O'Toole et al. 1991). Correspondingly, a close look at what is officially meant by multiculturalism reveals a twin emphasis on the recognition of differences and on the integration of those differences into a single inclusive whole. Official multiculturalism policy aims to recognize differences by incorporating all these different people into the economic, social, cultural, and political power structure of the country. It does this without considering that such an incorporation of necessity implies the adumbration if not effective irrelevance of the differences that are to be included (cf. Citizenship and Immigration Canada 2010).

Another symptom of this qualified understanding of multiculturalism, and therefore religious pluralism, is the current and periodic debates about the "limits" of diversity. Talk of limits expresses an abiding uncertainty about the extent to which differences can be legitimately expressed and the range of identities that receive recognition. Embedded in these debates are some old implicit distinctions: between those differences that can be "reasonably" integrated and those that cannot; between those differences that are to be recognized, those that are to be only tolerated, and those that are unrecognizable (cf. Woodsworth 1909). Just as importantly, the discourses on limits imply a set of standards that determine these limits. This assumption, in turn, points to the likelihood that the uniformity will, in key ways, resemble one of the diversities, namely a particular culture and a particular religion, or at least a limited range of each, an oligopoly if not a monopoly. Given the temporal proximity of the previous era in which certain forms of Christianity and certain versions of Western European cultures were the explicit hegemonic standard to which all else had to conform, it would be surprising indeed if elements of this hegemony were not still operating implicitly in the uniformity in question (Beaman 2003). Its implicit operation, however, will mean that it will not be called by its religious and cultural name, for instance French Canadian Roman Catholicism or Anglo-Protestantism. Instead it will be expressed indirectly, such as in talk of "our values," the need for "social cohesion" (Ryan 2010), or the notion of "reasonable accommodation" where it is always understood which identities are being reasonable and doing the accommodating (Biles and Ibrahim 2005; Bouchard and Taylor 2008). A similar purpose is embedded in the insistence that Canada (or Quebec) is a secular society in which a form of secularism or laïcité provides the norm in terms of which the limits are to be determined. The secular, however, is only definable as the "other side" of the religious, and the norms of secularism, in whatever variation, therefore take on the function and often even the form of religion, as, for example, in the idea of civil religion.

The current circumstance of transition means that older understandings still operate implicitly, but it does not mean that they will always do so. What I wish to explore further in this chapter is the idea that to really think beyond our current transitional situation, into a time and a set of understandings that we can at best intimate but cannot as yet convincingly know, we have to look more radically at our current categories of understanding. That means not just undoing religious and cultural hegemony, but also examining much more critically the basic assumptions upon which that hegemony is based, namely the basic assumptions that I listed at the outset and, more importantly in terms of religion, the secular/religious distinction itself.

In order to accomplish such an examination, in what follows, I first return to the question of the historical development of the old understandings, only not just in the Canadian context, but globally. This I do under the notion that the old understandings express what I wish to call the Westphalian model for structuring religion, nation, and state. On the basis of that historical narrative analysis, I then consider the possibility of a transition to a different order of understandings through the idea of a post-Westphalian condition. I adopt the language of "post" precisely because we cannot yet know what this new condition will eventually be. If we could, we would be able to describe it positively rather than only in terms of what it is not. The post-Westphalian model, I argue, rests fundamentally in the questioning and transformation, not of the possibility of religious difference, but rather of the secular/religious distinction itself.

THE WESTPHALIAN MODEL OF RELIGION, NATION, AND STATE

The Peace of Westphalia of 1648 has commonly been marked as a key event in the millennium-long formation and expansion of the modern European state system (Tilly 1992). Among the provisions of its treaties was an emphasis on the sovereignty of a plurality of states over clearly defined territories, sovereignty that extended to matters of religion. At the same time, the formula, *cuius regio, eius religio*, "to whom the realm, his religion," established the dominance of one religion (Lutheran, Calvinist, or Roman Catholic versions of Christianity) in a given state, while permitting a limited "tolerance" of what we would today label "religious minorities" (see Christin 1997). The Peace of Westphalia was, after all, understood to be resolving a protracted period of religious conflict in central Europe, even if that conflict was just as much political, and included wars among and within rival political powers. The kind of institutional religious disunity (or pluralization) created in the sixteenth-century Reformation period came to be expressed through and overlaid onto the institutional political disunity (or pluralization) that had characterized western and central Europe since the end of the Roman Empire. Regarded from a somewhat different angle, the Westphalian treaties lent expression to the further development of the European political state system, especially through the idea of state sovereignty; but they did so as part of the parallel development of a European religious system. European elites were at this time also gradually consolidating ideas about religion that correspond to the features I listed at the outset of this chapter: it was a separate domain, and it expressed itself in the form of different religions and subdivisions of those religions (cf. Despland 1979; Harrison 1990). Behind the formula of *cuius regio, eius religio*, however, is the further understanding that religion is nonetheless fundamental to how people live their lives, to their societies; hence the protracted conflict that comes in the wake of religious disunity: it portends societal disintegration. Religion was not just a set of "beliefs and practices," it also identified entire collectivities and their societies in a foundational way: religion(s) defined peoples (cf. Boyarin 2007). The formula sought to resolve the conundrum by having the sovereign – and by extension the sovereign state – determine what would be the religion within his realm and therefore of the society that existed within its (arbitrary and precise) borders.

The Westphalian treaties were, of course, not some kind of denouement, but rather only a place marker along the way. Among subsequent developments, three were instrumental in completing what I am calling the Westphalian model of religion, state, and the relation between the two. These developments are the "nationalization" of states after the middle of the eighteenth century, the further institutional differentiation of polity as state, and religion as religions, and the globalization of the model to eventually encompass the entire world, with very few, if any, exceptions.

At the time of Westphalia, the sovereigns were just that: individual monarchical leaders, to a large extent linked with one another through the lineages that composed the European aristocratic strata. They were the sovereigns of realms, of territories, but not of peoples. Over the next two centuries, that changed as the idea of the nation-state gradually asserted itself. This notion followed a logic by which states came to be seen as the (necessary) expression of specific collectivities or nations. This was almost always on a one-to-one basis: one nation, one state. Although to some extent these national collectivities were longstanding (Smith 1986), they were also to a significant degree invented to fit the nation-state idea (Anderson 2006; Gellner 1983; Hobsbawm and Ranger 1983). On this understanding, however, since the "realm" of the Westphalian formula now "belonged" to the people, it is those people that came to be seen as sovereign over their territory and thus the control of the nation-state should be in "their" hands. The consequence for religion was that the religion of the nation had to be, in one form or another, the religion of the state; even though, as at the time of Westphalia, the differentiation of religion meant that the isomorphism of the two entities was frequently far from perfect and that religious structures also tended to follow their own logic and developments, in the process challenging, and not just reinforcing, the neat boundaries that the Westphalian formula assumed. The Roman Catholic Church presented an obvious example, but so did various Protestant movements like the Moravians, the Methodists, the Pietists, Mennonites, among others.

The increasing differentiation of state and religion in this context also found expression in various directions that sought the further "secularization" of the state. Of course, in European Christian eyes, the state had at least since the time of Augustine been the "secular" or "temporal" power, in contrast to the "religious" power, the Church; yet the two were until very late also considered to be intimately related, like two sides of a coin. The much clearer and further differentiation of state and religion in more recent centuries expressed itself in a greater distancing of the two, and this manifested itself in a fairly wide variety of "secularisms." For instance, some states, like Great Britain or the Scandinavian countries, maintained state religions but with ever greater toleration for other religions. Some states, like the United States or Canada with their denominational religious systems, instituted an official separation of state and religion with the tacit or explicit continuation of the dominance of one religion. Some states, like France or Turkey, officially marginalized religion, banning it from the "public sphere." And some states, like the Union of Soviet Socialist Republics (USSR) or the Peoples Republic of China (PRC) adopted anti-religious regimes that sought to suppress religion and replace it with some variety of substitute foundational ideology and sets of practices. Indeed, the assumption of the necessity of some sort of foundational regime that guaranteed social order continued under all these variations, whether through the continued established or "shadow" established religion, or through a "civil" religious ersatz that almost always bore striking resemblances to the religion or religious culture that had dominated in the particular state.

The development of the Westphalian model was not restricted to transformations on the side of polity. The Westphalian formula only made sense in the context of a reconceptualization and restructuring of religion along the lines of a differentiated domain that appeared in the form of a plurality of religions and their variants. The idea that different states could have different religions – and that different peoples/nations had different religions – implied a certain structural modelling of one with the other; most centrally in the parallel division of the political and religious systems into segmentary subunits: states and religions. So far has this been the case that, since the onset and then the globalization of this arrangement, subdivisions within religions have developed at least to some extent along national or state lines. The churches of various European states are obvious examples, for example, the Church of England, the Church of Sweden, the Bulgarian, Serbian, Russian, Romanian, Orthodox churches, etc. Even Roman Catholicism to an extent took on features of "national" variations. Analogous developments have occurred in Buddhism with notions such as Japanese, Thai, or Sri Lankan Buddhism, and in some Muslim countries such as Turkey, Iran, or Indonesia. And yet, as is evident from all these examples, the isomorphism is anything but straightforward or complete, especially in the sense that all the religions in question at the same time conceive themselves and are structured along "universal" lines, across national and other social boundaries. In addition, as already noted, numerous developments within these restructured religions have more or less entirely ignored their "national" faces, as is evidenced in the numerous "transnational" movements that have arisen within every one of them.

The final dimension of the development of the Westphalian model is its globalization. Much as the form of the modern nation-state was, with significant variation, adopted at least formally by most every state as it became part of the global system of nation-states, so did religion enter this expansion in accordance with the Westphalian model. In this case, however, it must be stressed that, much as the variations among the European states and their colonizer states in the Americas and Australasia were significant, rather more was this the case as modern states formed in the rest of the world during the late nineteenth and twentieth centuries. The ways that religion has been incorporated into various East Asian, Southeast Asian, South Asian, Middle Eastern, and African countries differ in important respects. Yet there are also strong commonalities, including the adoption and adaptation of the modern concept of religion and its division into religions; the recognition of more or less the same set of religions that count as religions; the acceptance in many cases that the people, the nation, and the national culture identify with a particular one of those religions all the way to the adoption of an official state religion; and the frequent construction of "civil" religions modelled on the dominant religion or the dominant traditional religious patterns of the particular state.

INTIMATIONS OF A POST-WESTPHALIAN CONDITION

The idea that the world today is experiencing a transition to a post-West-phalian condition or order is not new. In various disciplines like political science, for instance, it has become an established theme (see, e.g., G. L. Anderson 2007; Suter 2003). The role or place of religion, however, hardly ever comes up in these discussions, preoccupied as they are with "national" boundaries in the context of principles like nation, state, sovereignty, and self-determination. The involvement of religion in the historical development of the Westphalian model, however, should alert us to at least the possibility that any transition to a post-Westphalian order will also manifest itself in the domain of religion, including insofar as "national ideologies" or "civil religions" have functioned as a presumed foundation for social order even in self-declared secular states. In other terms, to the degree that the nation-state conceives itself as secular (and that secularity is a key aspect of the Westphalian order), passage to a post-Westphalian condition should alter the place of the secular/religious distinction in the self-definitions of both religion and state.

Possible features of a post-Westphalian order for religion have been present since the development of Westphalianism itself, simply because religion, even in its peculiarly modern differentiated institutional forms, was always more than "national" religion. The modelling was only partial. When speaking about a post-Westphalian condition for religion, we are therefore looking more at a rebalancing or restructuring of religion than something radically different. And that rebalancing should concern primarily the parallel, but only very partially isomorphic, segmentation of state and religion. What we are looking for is the undermining of a certain structural logic along the lines of "state ≈ nation ≈ people ≈ religion," where all four terms come to manifest themselves as plural and discrete segments. Although, logically, this transformation could include the dissolution of any or all these terms, that is probably very unlikely; no more likely than states or nations disappearing. The contingency of all their boundaries, however, will likely be much clearer.

In terms of when such a significant rebalancing may have begun to occur, the post–Second World War era suggests itself because this was also an era when "global," as opposed to "national," structures started to attain unprecedented prominence, leading eventually to talk of "globalization" (cf. Suter 2003). Even more, therefore, would we be looking at the post-1960s period, the time when the term globalization reached prominence; and, not coincidentally, the time that has seen first the apogee of the idea that we are living in an increasingly secular world, and then exactly the opposite, the equally "evident" idea that the current era is one of desecularization and religious resurgence. Turbulence, one might say, is a sign of changing conditions.

Turning now to possible intimations of a post-Westphalian condition for religion, four interrelated developments of this era may qualify: the decline or volatility of national religions, the decentring of religious authority and authenticity, the more thorough transnationalization of religions, and the increasing contingency of civil religions or state secularisms.

One of the oft-noted peculiarities of the "religious decline" in many, especially Western, countries since the 1960s is that this decline was usually measured in terms of the weakening of involvement in the large, national, or dominant religious organizations, mostly Christian ones. Those religious manifestations not implied by these organizations were ignored, deemed insignificant, or precisely the opposite: as the place to look for and the source of future religious "renewal" and "resurgence" (see, e.g., Stark and Bainbridge 1985; Wilson 1979). Concomitant with these changes, in an era of increasing post-colonialism, many of the newly emerging national states outside the rich Western countries witnessed the ascendancy of self-conceived secular nationalist ideologies, often on a socialist/communist basis that included the denigration of religion. National religion, one might say, had fallen upon hard times. Yet Westphalianism was not thereby simply eschewed: many of the national founding ideologies had strong "civil religious" characteristics, in particular the expressly socialist/communist ones, but also others such as Indonesian Pancasila, Israeli socialist Zionism, Turkish Kemalism, South African apartheid, or even Indian secularism. Therefore, as circumstances changed, including the effective elimination of the socialist/communist option at the beginning of the 1990s, longstanding nationalist religious directions could in a number of cases reassert themselves, much to the shock and surprise of many observers (Juergensmeyer 1993). Examples of these developments might include what has happened in Turkey, India, Iran, and Israel, among others (e.g., Arian 2005; Jaffrelot 1996; Keddie 2003; Yavuz 2006).

Another dimension, connected to the first, is the moving away of religious adherents from the institutional centres of religious authority and authenticity. Such de-centring can be physical as in the case of the sharply increased global migration of the second half of the twentieth century. Migrants usually carry their religious identities and religious ways with them. In the context of migration, however, they move away from their erstwhile religious centres – where their religion was often the nationally dominant religion and provided a context of immersion – to places where they have partially to re-invent and restructure their religions, whether as minorities or parts of majorities. The variants generated in these "diasporas," while usually in strong continuity with those of the "heartlands" that they have left, are nonetheless comparatively independent of the latter and thus admit of greater "deviation" or "hybridization" as well, including the cross-fertilization of religious currents from one country, from one part of the world, to any other (Beyer 1998). De-centring of religious authority and authenticity also describes a different trend, the tendency of a great many adherents to the religions to keep identifying, belonging, and practising, but increasingly in their own selective way, picking and choosing from among the official features of their religions, and often combining these with beliefs and practices formally outside those orthodoxies and orthopraxies. A number of concepts have gained prominence among observers of such trends, including "religion à la carte," religious "bricolage," "lived religion," "popular religion," "post-materialist religion," "spirituality," "spiritual but not religious," among others (Bibby 1987; Heelas et al. 2005; Hervieu-Léger 1993, 1999; Inglehart 1997; Luckmann 1967; McGuire 2008; Parker 1996). What they all indicate is that the institutional boundaries established by the various nationally dominant religions are, at the very least, no longer to be taken for granted as the primary determinants of authoritative and authentic religious form.

A further intimation of a post-Westphalian condition is the greater transnationalization of religions through religious movements and religious organizations that, while usually centred in one country or another, also have significant presence outside those areas. Like the other developments, this one is also a case of intensification of what has been a feature of the global religious system for quite some time. The post-war proliferation of international religious organizations is unquestionable, even if they are as yet still dominated by Christian organizations (Boli and Brewington 2007). Many of the so-called New Religious Movements that received so much attention in the 1970s and 1980s have this characteristic, often having their origins in one part of the world, but rising to prominence (or notoriety) in quite a number of others (cf. Richardson 2004). Yet this proliferation is not limited to these most visible examples. New and global religious movements seem to be appearing constantly and everywhere (Clarke 2006), in the process rendering the global religious field more complex and diverse both nationally and transnationally.

A final intimation concerns the visibly increased contingency of Westphalian civil religions as assertions of national purity and guarantors of social coherence. In the post–Second World War era, all forms of national identity that insist on "one" people and one religion or "civil religion" have been more or less suspect in light of the horrors perpetrated in their names during that war. At the very least, such visions have had a more difficult time being justified globally outside a particular country. In recent decades, this "suspicion" has expressed itself in a global discourse, often legitimated in universal human rights terms, which insists that any national vision must include provision for "minority rights," for the ability of people and groups who are not of the dominant culture, religion, race, etc., to be not just tolerated but treated with complete equality in all respects (see, e.g., Al-Azmeh and Fokas 2007). In other words, the newly institutionalizing expectation requires national visions to break with the Westphalian "one nation, one religion" formula. Toleration is no longer optional, and neither is equality. Instances where this does not obtain – such as the hard form of French *laïcité*, Hindu nationalism, and right-wing nationalist visions in countries like Turkey, Austria, the Netherlands, or Japan – are consistently subject to global criticism.

POST-WESTPHALIAN INTIMATIONS FROM RELIGION IN CANADA

A post-Westphalian condition is one in which the mutual modelling of state and religion loses its self-evidence, and thereby allows greater modelling along other lines, including perhaps modelling with respect to other institutional domains like art or economy. In Canada, as already noted above, the "state" side of this transformation has been materializing with the advent of multiculturalism in its shifting, ambiguous, and peculiar variant. It also manifests itself in two other ways. I am referring to the rise of Québécois "secular" nationalism in the post–Quiet Revolution era and to the emergence of Canada's Aboriginal populations as First Nations. In this regard, the relative delinking of religion and nation is also visible in current Canadian censuses: questions about official languages – the bilingualism dimension – are separate from questions about Aboriginal identity and status, which in turn are separate from questions about ethnicity, race (visible minority status), and religion. In other words, although there is some overlap in practice, the French/English diversity, the Aboriginal/non-Aboriginal diversity, and the multicultural diversity are separate and separated. The importance of this three-dimensionality for the issue at hand can be seen in how the ideas of nation and religion operate in them. Nation appears in two places: the Québécois consider themselves and are in effect recognized for the most part as a nation (read also: distinct society, distinct culture, founding people, etc.). The Rest of Canada (ROC), however, is not a nation. Binationalism (and biculturalism) as a concept or even as an ideal did not survive the transition of the post-1960s era because there is only one nation and it does not include all of Canada. What the ROC and, by extension, all of Canada *is* remains open, unarticulated, controversial, and ambiguous. The second appearance of the word nation is among Aboriginal peoples: they are First Nations, a designation that carries the same impulse to sovereignty (or self-determination) as nation does among many Québécois. Notably and by contrast, "nation" does not appear in the idea of bilingualism or in that of multiculturalism. Of equal significance is that religion appears, if anywhere, only under multiculturalism, and to some extent, in mirror image in the secularism attached to the idea of a Québécois nation. In the third dimension, that of First Nations, religion does not appear as a secularism or "civil religion," but also cannot quite be formulated as religion. Spirituality is more often the word that appears in its place, but then primarily to mark a difference, namely a non-differentiation of religion from nation/culture. Finally, although there is frequent reference in public discourse to Canada as a secular state, this does not amount to "civil religious" secularism, perhaps one of the reasons that the overt Quebec debates about accommodation and its limits or about "open secularism" (*laïcité ouverte*) remain implicit in the ROC. In this regard, it may be of some significance that people aspiring to positions of political power in Canada mostly do not talk about their personal religion at the risk of losing political credibility; and yet they do not therewith have to declare allegiance to a contrasting secularism. Religion, it seems, is just supposed to be irrelevant, or private. This too is a post-1960s development.

POST-WESTPHALIAN STRUCTURING OF RELIGION IN CANADA

I noted above that one symptom of the deconstruction of Canadian Westphalianism in the post-1960s era was the comparative voiding of the denominational structure that dominated the Canadian religious landscape from the mid-nineteenth to the mid-twentieth century. The apogee of that dominance was during the immediate post–Second World War period. After about 1965, in what has been interpreted as a period of rapid secularization, people gradually stopped going to church, stopped being members of churches, and even stopped identifying with denominations, but mainly in the mainline denominations, such as the Anglican and United Churches, that constituted Canada's Westphalian shadow establishment. The trend has been somewhat hidden in the case of the Roman Catholic Church because, until recently, the majority of its adherents were French Canadians. The national exceptionalism of Quebec has seen the maintenance of a "cultural Catholicism," one that retains little but the identification, in true Westphalian fashion. In fact, the Roman Catholic Church has been fully a part of this trend, such that, for instance, the continuing decline in regular participation among Canadian nominal Christians is today due largely to the persistence of that decline among Roman Catholics both inside and outside Quebec (Clark 2003). By contrast, the religious organizations that have not suffered this decline are mostly those that were never identified with the Westphalian mainline, groups like Pentecostals and Evangelicals. Where religion is "growing" it is outside the previous mainline, and largely as a result of immigration. It is in this sector, the religion of immigrants, that we see further expressions of a post-Westphalian reconstruction of religion.

In a research project carried out in Canada by myself and several colleagues between 2004 and 2008, we sought to discover, among other aims, how young Muslims, Buddhists, and Hindus who were of immigrant families but had grown up in Canada related to the religions of their heritage (see Beyer 2007, 2010; Ramji 2008a, 2008b). We wanted to know how they "did" religion, if at all. The results of this research are relevant in the current context in several ways. These young adults are an integral outcome of more recent transnational migration. Their inherited religions are by now thoroughly global and, in the case of Islam at least, have a long history of such globality; Islam also has a significant history of incorporation into Westphalian models in modern nation-states from Morocco to Indonesia. The construction of Hinduism in the nineteenth and twentieth centuries also occurred in tandem with the emergence of Westphalian nationalism in India, eventuating in three Westphalian states in South Asia, India, Pakistan, and Bangladesh. The relation of Buddhism to Sri Lanka and Sinhalese nationalism also falls under this rubric.

In Canada, however, Islam, Hinduism, and Buddhism are minority religions and most of their participants also belong to cultural minorities. They are born in diaspora but of heartland origins, and thus can be expected to exhibit in their own lives answers to the question of multiple centres of authenticity and authority. They are also among those who often have strong transnational connections through physical and electronic social networks. With respect to them, therefore, it is relevant to ask to what extent they do their religion in what I have been calling West-phalian and/or post-Westphalian modes.

Looking first at the Muslim participants, one of the more remarkable consistencies among this group is that they shared a strong sense of what constitutes Islam and religion. Most of them understood religion as a way of life centred on clear moral and ritual rules. Islam for them was expressly centred on the Five Pillars and on a corresponding moral code that featured caring for one's fellow humans and a personal disciplined life. Most of them were from moderately to highly practicing. Some were not active Muslims at all, but even these agreed on what constituted a "good Muslim." In significant majority, then, they converged on a widespread global model of Islam.

This Islam, however, was not centred in one place more than another. They stressed the global *ummah* and the oneness of Islam, but they refused to locate this Islam more in one country or region than another. In fact, a great many of them expressly distanced themselves from an association of their inherited, national culture with Islam; they also consistently criticized this melding in their parents. Correspondingly, relatively few of them felt that it would be easier being a Muslim in their country of origin or in another Muslim-majority country, as compared with Canada. Several of them went so far as to declare Canada a more conducive place for practising their religion than Muslim majority countries, where, as it were, a Westphalian religio-nationalism would be enforced on them.

A number of prevalent features corresponded to this basic position. With respect to religious authority and authenticity, almost all of them declared that they, as individuals, were responsible for understanding and finding true Islam. They could not and did not receive this as tradition, passed on by religious authorities or their families and simply carried on by them. In almost all cases, they felt that they had to reconstruct Islam for themselves using a variety of resources, including parents and relatives, direct consultation of the Qur'an and Hadith, and literature or Internet sources of all kinds. They looked for and found trusted sources, but they did this through their own critical faculties. They generally did not favour sources from one country over another. Their Internet sources were selected and used in an almost entirely de-localized manner. It was the quality of the source that mattered, not its location. In brief, their Islam was individually understood in a de-localized manner, even if they practiced in locally and also in community.

On the whole, these Muslim young adults felt very comfortable living in Canada. They were well aware of being part of a religious and cultural minority, and many knew about or had experienced some discrimination or mistreatment as a consequence of looking different than the majority. Yet that minority status did not include considering themselves or being considered less Canadian. They insisted that, even if Canada was still a majority Christian country, and even if there was still evidence of a privileged status of Christianity over other religions, they and their religion of Islam belonged just as much – but not more – than any other. They almost all valued not just Canadian religious diversity, but made a positive assessment of religious pluralism as an inherent good, as a condition that enabled Islam rather than inhibiting it. Correspondingly, few saw themselves as "caught between two worlds"; more were able to live in several environments at once and were well practised in cultural and religious "code switching."

Perhaps one of the more notable features among this group of young Muslims is the virtually total absence of overt political Islam. Few indeed made any connection between religion and state, let alone between nation and state. This, of course, accords well with their valorization of religious pluralism and their conviction that Canada is a good place to practise Islam. Political Islam around the world, in spite of protestations to the contrary and the example of al Qaeda, is almost always centred in and for a particular state. These young Muslims did not make that connection and located genuine Islam away from any particular state or even the state in general.

Many of these observations about the Muslim participants in this research also apply to those of Hindu or Buddhist background. The assessments of Canada and the place of religion in Canada were very similar; Hindu and Buddhist participants stressed the individual as the locus of responsibility for understanding/constructing religion; they had little tolerance for politicized religion or the close association of state and religion. They were, however, quite different from the Muslims with respect to the role that religion played in their lives and how they related that religion to culture. Briefly put, they understood Hinduism and Buddhism very much in cultural terms, as distinct in principle from the cultures of their families, but not in actual practice. They recognized that being Hindu or being Buddhist was not necessarily the same thing as being, for instance, Indian or Chinese; but in their day-to-day lives they considered that which was Hindu was also Indian and that which was Buddhist was also Chinese. For the most part, in fact, they had little concrete knowledge of these religions, and few of them could be said to be regular practitioners of these religions except as part of their cultural practice. To the extent that they identified themselves as Hindus or Buddhists, they were much like the "cultural Christians" so common in the rest of the Canadian population, especially in Quebec. Unlike that population, they did not differentiate nearly as clearly between culture and religion in their heritage, nor did they exhibit a strong attachment to the countries where those cultures and religions were dominant. Put differently, they exhibited the Westphalian tendency to associate closely a people and its religion(s); but in post-Westphalian fashion, they abstracted that religio-culture from any state and did not express their cultural belonging in nationalistic terms. Correspondingly, although they were aware of being part of cultural/religious minorities in Canada, this was much more of a simple demographic observation than an evaluative one: they did not consider themselves minorities in the sense of belonging less, or being less "at home" in Canada than other people around them. While many of them also had experienced discrimination based on their ethnicity or perceived race, and while they generally acknowledged that Canada was still demographically a Christian and Euro-cultural country, this was just a fact, not a symptom of a Westphalian state of affairs. The majority of both groups was proud of their cultural heritage, sometimes of their Buddhist or Hindu religious heritage in that context. They felt that this should and could be as "Canadian" as anything else. They therefore thought that Canada was managing its diversity reasonably well, even though for most it could also do better.

Finally, in none of the three groups did one encounter the conviction that Canadian society needed religion, let alone a specific religion as the basis of a good society. For many of them religion was definitely the basis of their personal lives, but not for the society as a whole. Even the most religious accepted that other people could be of other religions or of no religion at all. Not surprisingly, therefore, even among the many non-religious there was little insistence that some kind of civil religious equivalent, let alone an articulated secularism, had to provide unity for all the religions and cultures that constitute Canadian diversity. That aspect of the Westphalian logic seemed to me more or less completely absent.

CONCLUSIONS

Questioning Westphalian and post-Westphalian constructions of religion is a way of exploring in what directions we are headed with respect to religion. Are we witnessing the progressive deconstruction of religion and religions as systematic institutional entities? Are we heading even further down the road of the individualization of religion? Or are we, as a result of these reconstructions, heading down the road of a more religious world? My argument has been to say yes and no to all of these questions. Deconstruction may be happening, but it is more a matter of loosening the hold of Westphalian assumptions about religion. This loosening may allow "the religions" to appear less solid and less necessary as the primary form that religion must take, but this does not mean that alternative forms are taking over. A "spiritual revolution" (Heelas 2002) is consistent with the continuation of "strong religion" (Almond, Appleby, and Sivan 2000). If deconstruction is happening, then so is reconstruction. Individualization, undoubtedly a real trend, is the other face of reconstruction: as the old forms become less dominant, the individual perspective offers a way of looking at religion without having to adopt those old forms as the standard of what counts as religion. The change of optic reflects more the greater difficulty of observing self-evidently in the old ways than it does a necessarily real shift of religion from the institutional and collective to the individual and "private." And finally, whether we are inhabiting a more or less religious world may be a question that reveals more about the insecurity of the observer in his or her old assumptions than it does any measurable change in degree of religiousness, whatever this latter may mean.

If the thesis of an incipient post-Westphalianism does not provide a clear answer to such questions, that may not be the most important conclusion. The post-Westphalian thesis, in pointing to the contingency of substantive religious forms, also indicates the contingency of assumed religious function. Undoing Westphalian self-evidence means that it is less and less possible to take for granted that, whatever form religion (and state) takes, it no more provides the foundation, or, in Parsonian mode, the integrative and latent pattern maintenance functions of society, than any other institution. Religion can be structured to be foundational and integrative, or not. It is not necessarily the basis of social cohesion, the guarantor of meaning, or the prophylactic against corrosive anomie. In the post-Westphalian condition, religion can appear and can be non-foundational; and if it is deemed to continue to represent the whole, then the whole will be just another part. And that includes "the secular" and "civil religion."

All these observations would, of course, apply to the Canadian case as well. What is striking here is how the ambiguity inherent in the policy and ideal of multiculturalism may be a way of signalling the gradual shift from Westphalian to post-Westphalian circumstances, both of the nation and of religion(s). The concern in Quebec with seeing its own society as one characterized by secularism or *laïcité*, even if an "open" secularism, and the need in Quebec to distinguish the interculturalism of its province from the multiculturalism of the ROC, when in the details they appear to be more or less exactly the same thing; these are Quebec's attempts to assert its difference as a nation and as a society. Yet these attempts are also symptomatic of the greater Westphalianism that still prevails in Quebec as opposed to the ROC. The contrast between Quebec and Canada is itself an intimation of post-Westphalian turbulence. Carrying further this idea that in the ROC the reason that the Westphalian dog does not bark is that she has lost her voice, we arrive at the possibility that Canada is on the way to becoming a society in which religion is not on an inevitable decline, as in the more rigid meanings of the word secularization, but that, rather, as exemplified in the attitudes and behaviours of the participants in the immigrant youth research project, religion can remain and become important for a great many people, but it is structuring itself away from the characteristics enjoined by the Westphalian model. This does not mean privatization of religion in the sense that it ceases to have a public presence and a public influence. Rather, it means that religion is on the way to a restructuring that removes it as the self-evident provider of societally foundational knowledge, values, structures, and orientations. This of course means that the Canadian state is becoming less and less the secular echo of its religious foundation. The state becomes at the same time both more and less secular in that it ceases to see itself as foundational, even as it continues to provide collective regulation and collectively binding decisions. The state ceases to operate in any meaningful way in terms of the secular/religious polarity. Only from the perspective of religion is the state now secular; the state no longer identifies in terms of that dichotomy. It is in this sense that Canada, or more precisely the Canadian state, in a post-Westphalian condition, becomes more secularized even as religion is given greater freedom to restructure itself along different, and of course also the same, lines as before. The latter, however, will henceforth have to be done without the collusion and perhaps even the recognition of the state. But all this remains to be seen. For the moment the idea of post-Westphalianism stays at the level of intimations, of what it is not, and far less in the realm of a positively identifiable situation.

REFERENCES

Al-Azmeh, Aziz, and Effie Fokas, eds. 2007. *Islam in Europe: Diversity, Identity and Difference*. Cambridge: Cambridge University Press.

Almond, Gabriel A., R. Scott Appleby, and Emmanuel Sivan, eds. 2000. *Strong Religion: The Rise of Fundamentalisms around the World*. Chicago: University of Chicago Press.

Anderson, Benedict. 2006. *Imagined Communities: Reflections on the Origin and Spread of Nationalism*. London and New York: Verso.

Anderson, Emma. 2007. *The Betrayal of Faith: The Tragic Journey of a Colonial Native Convert*. Cambridge: Harvard University Press.

Anderson, Gordon L. 2007. "A Post-Westphalian World and the Quest for Self-Determination." *International Journal on World Peace* 24(4): 3–10.

Arian, Asher. 2005. *Politics in Israel: The Second Republic*. 2nd ed. Washington: Congressional Quarterly Press.

Beaman, Lori G. 2003. "The Myth of Plurality, Diversity and Vigour: Constitutional Privilege of Protestantism in the United States and Canada." *Journal for the Scientific Study of Religion* 42 (3): 311–28.

Beyer, Peter. 1998. "The City and Beyond as Dialogue: Negotiating Religious Authenticity in Global Society." *Social Compass* 45: 61–73.

– 2006. *Religions in Global Society*. London: Routledge.

– 2007. "Can the Tail Wag the Dog? Diaspora Reconstructions of Religion in a Globalized Society." *Norwegian Journal of Religion and Society* 20 (1): 39–61.

– 2010. "Differential Reconstruction of Religions among Second Generation Immigrant Youth in Canada." In *Annual Review of the Sociology of Religion: Youth and Religion*, Vol. 1., edited by Giuseppe Giordan, 1–28. Leiden: Brill.

Bibby, Reginald W. 1987. *Fragmented Gods: The Poverty and Potential of Religion in Canada*. Toronto: Irwin.

– 1993. *Unknown Gods: The Ongoing Story of Religion in Canada*. Toronto: Stoddart.

Biles, John, and Humera Ibrahim. 2005. "Religion and Public Policy: Immigration, Citizenship, and Multiculturalism – Guess Who's Coming to Dinner?" In *Religion and Ethnicity in Canada*, edited by Paul Bamadat, and David Seljak, 154–177. Toronto: Pearson Longman.

Boli, John, and David V. Brewington. 2007. "Religious Organizations." In *Globalization, Religion and Culture*, edited by Peter Beyer, and Lori G. Beaman, 203–231. Leiden: Brill Academic Publishers.

Bouchard, Gérard, and Charles Taylor. 2008. *Building the Future: A Time for Reconciliation*. Quebec City: Gouvernement du Québec.

Boyarin, Daniel. 2007. *Border Lines: The Partition of Judaeo-Christianity*. Philadelphia: Univesity of Pennsylvania Press.

Christin, Olivier. 1997. *La paix de religion. L'autonomisation de la raison politique au XVIième siècle*. Paris: Seuil.

Citizenship and Immigration Canada. 2010. "Promoting Integration. Annual

Report on the Operation of the Canadian Multiculturalism Act, 2008–2009." Ottawa: Citizenship and Immigration Canada. Available at www.cic.gc.ca/english/multiculturalism/index.asp.

Clark, Warren. 2003. "Pockets of Belief: Religous Attendance Patterns in Canada." *Canadian Social Trends* 68: 2–5.

Clark, Warren, and Grant Schellenberg. 2006. "Who's Religious?" *Canadian Social Trends* 81: 2–9.

Clarke, Peter. 2006. *New Religious Movements in Global Perspective: A Study of Religious Change in the Modern World*. London and New York: Routledge.

Despland, Michel. 1979. *La religion en occident: Evolution des idées et du vécu*. Montreal: Fides.

Gellner, Ernest. 1983. *Nations and Nationalism*. Oxford: Basil Blackwell.

Harrison, Peter. 1990. *"Religion" and the Religions in the English Enlightenment*. Cambridge: Cambridge University Press.

Heelas, Paul. 2002. "The Spiritual Revolution: From 'Religion' to 'Spirituality'." In *Religion in the Modern World*, edited by Linda Woodhead, Paul Fletcher, Hiroko Kawanami, and David Smith, 357–377. London: Routledge.

Heelas, Paul, Linda Woodhead, Benjamin Seel, Bronislaw Szerszyinski, and Karin Tusting. 2005. *The Spiritual Revolution: Why Religion is Giving Way to Spirituality*. Oxford: Blackwell.

Hervieu-Léger, Danièle. 1993. *La religion pour mémoire*. Paris: Cerf.

– 1999. *Le pèlerin et le converti: La religion en mouvement*. Paris: Flammarion.

Hobsbawm, Eric J., and Terence O. Ranger. 1983. *The Invention of Tradition*. Cambridge: Cambridge University Press.

Inglehart, Ronald. 1997. *Modernization and Postmodernization: Cultural, Economic, and Political Change in 43 Societies*. Princeton: Princeton University Press.

Jaffrelot, Christophe. 1996. *The Hindu Nationalist Movement in India*. New York: Columbia University Press.

Juergensmeyer, Mark. 1993. *The New Cold War? Religious Nationalism Confronts the Secular State*. Berkeley: University of California Press.

Keddie, Nikki R. 2003. *Modern Iran: Roots and Results of Revolution*. New Haven: Yale University Press.

Luckmann, Thomas. 1967. *The Invisible Religion: The Problem of Religion in Modern Societies*. New York: Macmillan.

Masuzawa, Tomoko. 2005. *The Invention of World Religions*. Chicago: University of Chicago Press.

McGuire, Meredith. 2008. *Lived Religion: Faith and Practice in Everyday Life*. New York: Oxford University Press.

Miller, J. R. 2000. *Skyscrapers Hide the Heavens: A History of Indian-White Relations in Canada*. Toronto: University of Toronto Press.

Moir, John S., ed. 1967. *Church and State in Canada, 1627–1867: Basic Documents*. Toronto: McClelland & Stewart.

O'Toole, Roger, Douglas F. Campbell, John A. Hannigan, Peter Beyer, and John H. Simpson. 1991. "The United Church in Crisis: A Sociological Perspective on the Dilemmas of a Mainstream Denomination." *Sciences religieuses/Studies in Religion* 20 (2): 151–63.

Parker, Cristián. 1996. *Popular Relgion and Modernization in Latin America: A Different Logic*. Translated by Robert R. Barr. Maryknoll: Orbis Books.

Ramji, Rubina. 2008a. "Being Muslim and Being Canadian: How Second Generation Muslim Women Create Religious Identities in Two Worlds." In *Women and Religion in the West: Challenging Secularization*, edited by Kristin Aune, Sonya Sharma, and Giselle Vincett, 195–206. Aldershot: Ashgate Publishing.

– 2008b. "Creating a Genuine Islam: Second Generation Muslims Growing up in Canada." *Canadian Diversity / Diversité canadienne* 6 (2): 104–109.

Rawlyk, George A., ed. 1990. *The Canadian Protestant Experience, 1760–1990*. Burlington: Welch Publishing.

Richardson, James T., ed. 2004. *Regulating Religion: Case Studies from around the Globe*. New York: Kluwer Academic/Penum.

Ryan, Phil. 2010. *Multicultiphobia*. Toronto: University of Toronto Press.

Smith, Anthony D. 1986. *The Ethnic Origins of Nations*. Oxford: Basil Blackwell.

Stark, Rodney, and William S. Bainbridge. 1985. *The Future of Religion: Secularization, Revival, and Cult Formation*. Berkeley: University of California Press.

Suter, Keith. 2003. *Global Order and Global Disorder: Globalization and the Nation-State*. Westport: Praeger.

Tilly, Charles. 1992. *Coercion, Capital and European States, AD 990–1992*. Cambridge: Blackwell.

Trigger, Bruce. G. 1985. *Natives and Newcomers: Canada's "Heroic Age" Reconsidered*. Montreal & Kingston: McGill-Queen's University Press.

Wilson, Bryan. 1979. "The Return of the Sacred." *Journal for the Scientific Study of Religion* 18 (3): 268–280.

Woodsworth, J. S. 1909. *Strangers within Our Gates, or, Coming Canadians*. Toronto: F.C. Stephenson.

Yavuz, M. Hakan, ed. 2006. *The Emergence of a New Turkey: Democracy and the AK Party*. Salt Lake City: University of Utah Press.

2

Religious Diversity and Multicultural Accommodation

GURPREET MAHAJAN

Over the last three decades religious minorities, often immigrant populations, have raised a number of issues involving the accommodation of
their community practices in Western liberal democracies. Whether it is
the case of Sikhs with turbans asking for an exemption from wearing the
prescribed headgear in the Royal Canadian Mounted Police or at construction sites; Muslim girls wanting to wear the headscarf to school;
devout Muslim workers claiming time off on Friday afternoon to offer
the mandated special prayers; Sikh children seeking permission to carry
a small kirpan to school; communities (often Muslims and Jews) demanding availability of a particular kind of food (halal/kosher) in public
institutions like hospitals and schools, a separate prayer room in public
institutions, or a male driving instructor or a female gynecologist; religious communities are bringing into the public domain practices that
challenge the prevailing consensus. Western liberal democracies are, as a
result, being compelled to rethink the existing mode of social ordering
and justify why certain practices of religious minorities cannot, or should
not, be permitted in society.

Almost everywhere the strongest appeal for the accommodation of
these diverse sets of community practices has come from advocates of
multiculturalism. At one level this is somewhat puzzling because theorists of multiculturalism have traditionally defended diversity of cultures,
and the cultural communities that they focused on were, by and large, not
defined by their religious identity. In Canada particularly multiculturalists made a plea to accommodate the claims of the indigenous people and
the Francophone populations – communities that were, to use the words

of Will Kymlicka (1995, 10–25), "national" minorities. That is, people with a distinct "societal culture" (i.e., institutions, rules, and norms) who had lived on a given territory over a long period of time and saw that territory as their homeland (ibid.). Others, like Charles Taylor (1992, 1993), linked culture to language; since the ability to speak and to express one's thoughts and ideas was the basis of the social life of individuals as self-defining creatures, access to one's language was seen as a critical condition for the good life. Accordingly, the world created by a community of language users was seen as a cultural domain that had a special significance and value for its members. In underlining the need to protect and promote cultural diversity, these theorists were thus making a case for cultural communities of a distinct kind, and even though these communities adhered to a religion that was different from that of the majority, religion was not the reason for valuing their culture.

In brief, cultures and cultural communities that theorists of multiculturalism were talking about in the case of Canada were different from religious communities. Even when some theorists, like Joseph Carens (2000), Melissa Williams (1996), Avigail Eisenberg (2007), and Jeff Spinner (1994), addressed the issue of religious differences and what equal treatment meant for them, they did not make a case for special rights for these communities. In part this was because religious communities were not concentrated in a given territory, so such rights as the right to self-government (that was supported for the French population of Quebec or the indigenous people) could not be extended to them. At the same time, there was no attempt to make a case for separate representation for these religious communities. The plea was to accommodate the cultural difference that was expressed in their community practices by making exceptions to the prevailing rule or by expecting the market and society to be more accommodating in their practices regarding dress codes, holidays, work hours. Formal policies involving special institutional arrangements were suggested only for "national" and "cultural" minorities and not for different religious communities. The differences that religious minorities were bringing into the public domain were not the primary focus of multicultural theory in Canada.[1]

Yet, ideas when they enter into the public domain are open to different appropriations and applications. Theories of multiculturalism are no different in this respect. While in the past multiculturalists in Canada have explicitly underlined the need to recognize the diversity of cultures, the arguments they offered could be, and indeed with the passage of time they have been, used by different religious minorities to make a case for the recognition of their difference. Multiculturalism has emphasized the value of community membership. Against the prevalent liberal-individualist ethos, it has argued that personal identity is, to some extent, constituted by community membership, and that the latter also forms our context of experience. It shapes a person's conception of what is good and desirable, and structures his or her imagination. It is the lens through which others perceive us and relate to us. For these reasons community memberships are important. This meant that claims relating to these identities cannot be simply ignored or bracketed out of the public domain.

Once the value of community membership has been emphasized in the case of specific cultural communities, this argument can readily be applied to assert the significance of religious community for the individual. The case for acknowledging and accommodating the difference represented by religious communities is further reinforced by questioning the neutrality of the state. Against the liberal perspective, theorists of multiculturalism have argued that no state (not even the liberal democratic state) can be completely neutral. It has to have policies on such matters as the official language of the state, declaration of public holidays, marriage, abortion, inheritance, suicide, and euthanasia. On these questions the state cannot be completely neutral. Even more importantly, they argue that in most Western democracies policies on these subjects reflect the cultural orientation of the majority (see Parekh 1994a; Chaplin 1993). Most of the time minorities are not included in the deliberative process, so their preferences and norms are, by and large, ignored. For instance, the decision to declare Sunday as the weekly day off reflects the religious norms of the Christian community. As a result, it places some minorities, such as Jews and Muslims, at a disadvantage. While devout Christians can observe Sunday as the day of rest, devout Jews cannot as easily observe Sabbath on Saturday – something that is prescribed by their religion. Likewise, devout Muslims do not have the necessary time off to render their mandatory Friday afternoon prayers. Prevailing laws and policies in this way disadvantage minorities, and fairness demands that the cultural concerns of minorities also be accommodated in the public arena. If religious minorities are expected to assimilate or accept the prevailing general norms, this is, like forced segregation, a form of unacceptable discrimination (Kymlicka 1989).

The critique of liberal neutrality raises concerns of fair treatment, and the multicultural defence of the value of diversity further strengthens the claims of religious minorities. Most theorists of multiculturalism maintain that diversity of cultures is essential for fulfilling and deepening the liberal commitment to "revisability" (Kymlicka 1989, 58–64).[2] Exposure to other ways of organizing life and society is a precondition for critical self-reflection. It is therefore a valued good and has to be protected and cherished. If diversity is itself desirable, or if it is needed to minimize existing patterns of disadvantage and discrimination, then religious communities can readily make a case for the accommodation and protection of their difference.

Thus, even though theories of multiculturalism in Canada make a case for the accommodation of cultural minorities, the arguments they offer in support of cultural diversity can be used to make a case for the accommodation of the differences religious minorities bring into the public domain. However, the question remains – how should these religious differences be accommodated? Clearly strategies like those of self-governance rights that have been used to accommodate cultural minorities such as the Francophone population of Quebec or the indigenous people, cannot be extended to take care of religious minorities. So how should these minorities be accommodated? To the extent that the framework of secularism is used to minimize religion-related discrimination in most liberal democracies since the late nineteenth century, could it be used to accommodate the claims that are now coming from religious minorities in these societies?

Looking back at the role played by the ideology of secularism in extending the religious liberty of non-recognized faiths in Europe and America, invoking this framework for accommodating religious practices of minority communities in these societies remains a distinct possibility. The difficulty, however, is that in recent times the strongest resistance to the accommodation of the claims of religious minorities has been framed in the language of secularism, on the one hand, and gender equality, on the other. In France the wearing of religious symbols, in the form of different headgears (hijab in the case of Muslim girls, the turban in the case of Sikh boys, and the yarmulke in the case of Jews) was strongly opposed, and eventually prohibited in schools on the ground that it violates the commitment to *laïcité* that mandates the exclusion of religion from public institutions. Something akin to the idea of secularism was invoked here to keep religion out.[3]

On other occasions, concerns about gender equality have been raised to challenge the accommodation of religious community practices within liberal democracies. Feminist scholars like Susan Moller Okin (1994) have argued that since most communities fail to give equal position to women, protection of community practices or recognition to different cultural ways of life could easily reinforce structures that perpetuate the subordination of women.[4]

Although these doubts have been raised by invoking the principles by which secularism is defined, there are nevertheless some voices that continue to regard secularism as a viable and adequate framework for accommodating the claims of religious minorities in liberal democracies. This is, for instance, the position taken by the recent report on the reasonable accommodation of minorities in Quebec (Bouchard and Taylor 2008a). Bouchard and Taylor argue that the defining principles of secularism are the moral equality of all persons and the freedom of conscience and belief. From these two principles emerge the two other allied principles of separation and the idea of state neutrality. Separation of religion from the state is not therefore the crucial or necessary feature of secularism. It is only "rigid" secularism that insists on separation of religion from politics, and it is this form of secularism that does not allow for the accommodation of minorities. "Open" secularism, by comparison, seeks to balance the four principles in a way that freedom of conscience is protected without compromising the principle of moral equality of all persons or the commitment to neutrality. Hence, it takes on board concerns of individual liberty and gender equality while accommodating religious and cultural diversity.

In making this distinction between rigid and open secularism, Bouchard and Taylor draw upon the experience of India and several countries in Europe where religion was not formally disestablished – that is, countries where religion continues to have a presence in the public domain in a variety of different ways, such as the existence of religious political parties, state support to schools run by religious communities, or the inclusion of religious community members in specific policy-making bodies. Open secularism, in other words, acknowledges the place of religion in individual and social life. Hence, it offers space for considering, and even accommodating, the claims of religious minorities in liberal democracies like Canada, and Quebec in particular.

Bouchard and Taylor (2008a, 53–60) take up a number of demands made by different religious communities including dress codes; food requirements; requests for separate swimming classes, separate prayer rooms in schools, home health care services on Shabbat, female health care providers, the removal of the Christmas tree from the entrance of Montreal City Hall; objections to certain medical practices (such as the refusal of blood transfusion by Jehovas Witnesses); requests for the list of religious holidays to be more inclusive and for the right to cast the vote with the face fully covered. In these and other cases involving claims of religious communities/minorities, Bouchard and Taylor underline the need to adopt informal modes of accommodation based on the principle of secularism, rather than formal legal and juridical processes of arbitration (2008a, 241–68).

Attempting to balance the four principles of secularism – namely, moral equality of all persons, freedom of conscience and belief, separation of religion and politics, and state neutrality – suggests that the claims of religious minorities should be accepted when they do not conflict with basic constitutional norms, such as the commitment to gender equality, and the rights of others. Likewise, existing inequalities that are present (for instance, in the list of religious holidays) should be rectified, religious symbols (such as, the crucifix in the National Assembly, prayers in municipal council meetings, the Christmas tree outside council buildings) should be removed. Key public officials should not display any religious symbols or signs, and all other claims must be negotiated by the different parties in the spirit of reconciliation and reasonable accommodation.

The suggestions in the Bouchard-Taylor report are made in the spirit of open secularism and its commitment to equality and neutrality. Yet it is difficult to conclude that open secularism can, or does, successfully accommodate the claims of religious minorities. There is no doubt that open secularism creates a positive condition for the consideration of the claims of religious minorities, but the four principles that it aims to balance cannot easily be reconciled. If freedom of conscience asks us to accommodate the decision of the Jehovah's Witnesses to refuse certain medical procedures, then the rights of others, for instance, the right of the unborn child, may compel us to intervene and provide the required medical assistance, including blood transfusion, if needed. If freedom of conscience pushes us to accept the decision of some women to cover their face fully, then the concern for gender equality (which is a part of the general concern for the equality of all) tells us not to accept practices that emerge against the backdrop of women's subordination in the public domain. Similarly, while freedom of conscience allows us to uphold the right of all individuals to wear religious symbols, the concern for state neutrality suggests that public officials should refrain from displaying religious symbols. The four principles through which secularism is identified thus push in different directions. If minorities stress the element of religious liberty, liberal critics express anxieties on the ground that religious liberty limits our commitment to neutrality or the moral equality of all persons. Hence, disputes linger and an appeal to open secularism does not settle them.

To assist in this apparent impasse, Bouchard and Taylor (2008b, 25) suggest that societies should be willing to accommodate the claims of religious minorities when they place no additional costs on others and do not infringe on the rights of others. However, these limiting conditions are almost impossible to fulfill; indeed there are very few cases that would immediately meet these conditions. Even accommodating a person's right to worship may place costs on others. If, for instance, some provision was to be made to allow a person to offer prayers at a specific time of the day or the week, it would place some costs on others. Separate prayer rooms may need to be built and colleagues may have to make adjustments or do some extra work to take care of the time that, say, a Muslim teacher would be away in order to offer prayers on Friday afternoon. Even symbolic gestures, such as renaming public spaces, may entail some costs to the general public as the majority would need to reorient itself to the new set of significations. So if we are attentive to the conditions laid down in the report it may be difficult to even justify accommodations that have already taken place in Quebec and other parts of Canada. Indeed, the framework of secularism would not offer much space for the accommodation of the claims of religious minorities.

These difficulties that surface when considering claims of religious minorities in Quebec only get compounded and become more intractable when we take up other issues, such as those of polygamy and female circumcision. In such situations the paradigm of secularism does not offer much assistance. Open secularism helps insofar as it allows us to entertain the religion-backed claims of minorities instead of shutting the door upon them. It also enables us to say that bringing religious symbols into the public domain may not in itself be sufficient ground for dismissing these claims. This is not insignificant, but it is also not sufficient and it does not offer us a principle for determining what should or should not be permitted in the public domain.

In Western liberal democracies today, religious minorities are seeking public space and recognition for their community practices so that they may live in accordance with their religious beliefs and way of life. Secularism, understood as a commitment to the principles of moral equality of all persons and state neutrality, puts these practices to the test. Instead of accommodating these practices, secularism compels us to ask if they comply with these two principles. Since minority communities do not often endorse the liberal notion of individual autonomy that accompanies the principles of equal liberty for all and equal moral worth of all persons, most of their practices cannot be accommodated even through the framework of open secularism. Open secularism can therefore be at best an enabling condition but not a sufficient one for making space for the claims of religious minorities in contemporary liberal democracies.

There is another reason why secularism, in any form, may not be able to accommodate the emerging claims of religious minorities in liberal democracies. In the past, when the different frameworks of secularism were devised to minimize religion-related discrimination, the main concern of the minorities was equal treatment. That is, till the middle of the nineteenth century, religious minorities were denied the freedom that was enjoyed by the majority community or religion of the state. In that situation, minorities pleaded for equal, if not identical, treatment. They wanted the same degree of religious liberty so that they could openly build places of collective worship, access facilities and public resources available to the adherents of the state religion, enjoy the right to political participation, and be eligible to study in institutions of higher learning and receive state honours and awards.

The crucial consideration for religious minorities then was "same treatment" and in different ways the framework of secularism ensured this for them. In some societies, like the United States and France, equal or identical treatment was pursued by disestablishing religion and separating religion from the state and the political arena. The state, on the one hand, distanced itself from all religions and, on the other, extended to people of different religions and beliefs the same set of political rights and civil liberties. In other countries of Europe equal/identical treatment came in the form of recognizing minority religions, withdrawing legal forms of exclusion, and extending religious liberty to members of different religious communities. In England, for instance, the Church of England remained the official church of the state, but the penalties for not attending the official Church were withdrawn, the universities of Oxford and Cambridge were opened to the Catholics and the Jews, and these communities could openly assemble, pray, and preach their faith to their congregation. In Sweden the state recognized the Catholic Church in addition to the established Evangelical Lutheran Church. In Germany the state disestablished religion, but members of the Church continued to be represented in boards dealing with social and family matters. In Belgium, given the number of students who go to Catholic schools, the state provided subsidies to these schools, and indexed support to enrolment. Thus, equal treatment for members of different religious minorities was pursued in many different ways. The attempt in each case was to see that existing patterns of disadvantage faced by minority religions were minimized, if not eliminated. As the sources of disadvantages were in most cases formal exclusion and denial of state services and support, it was these elements that were corrected.

Today, citizenship rights have been granted to people of different religions, and religious minorities are raising a different set of issues in Western liberal democracies. The issue is not primarily of formal inclusion or removal of legal barriers in the exercise of religious freedom. There are still a few glaring issues involving unequal treatment (for example, the prohibition against the construction of minarets in Switzerland or the construction of structures that look like mosques in many cities in Europe, or the inability of minorities to administer their cemeteries), and in these instances minorities want, quite justifiably, the same treatment/opportunities as the majority within the operating framework of secularism itself. However, in a large number of cases minorities are raising a different issue. They are invoking the language of multiculturalism to ask for the accommodation of difference that is represented by religious minorities. In other words, religious minorities are seeking accommodation of their distinct religious and cultural practices not because similar practices have been accepted in the case of the majority, but because these practices express the commitment to a way of life that is valued by its members. Claims of this nature are exceedingly difficult to accommodate within the framework of secularism.

There are two reasons for this. One, in Western liberal democracies the process of secularization went hand-in-hand with the right to religious liberty. The different frameworks of secularism (those involving formal separation and disestablishment and those that extended religious liberty without separation), did not protect religious freedom because they valued religion or saw it as a valued source of identity. Rather they tried to minimize religion-related discrimination insofar as it violated the principle of equal liberty for all. Individual liberty was privileged and it is through this lens that other issues of disadvantage and discrimination were addressed. Two, the concern for accommodating religious and cultural diversity was preceded by the secularization of society and the marginalization of religion. The progress in science, Enlightenment rationality, and the liberal philosophy of individualism, along with the Protestant Reformation, challenged the authority of religion and considerably reduced its hold over individual and social life. Christianity – the dominant religion in these societies – was transformed from a religion of practices to a religion of faith and individual conscience; it took a form that made it almost like any other association in society. In the past the Church had played a critical role in the life of the individual by regulating such critical matters as marriage, divorce, burials, and education. Gradually, in most parts of Europe, by the mid-nineteenth century, the authority of the Church on these matters was severely curtailed if not almost taken away by the state. Even the vast amount of land and wealth held by the Church was taken away by the state. These measures collectively reduced the power of the Church (religion) in public and social life. On the one hand, it empowered the state to enact laws, including those relating to marriage and family, in a way that was more sensitive to the emerging concerns of individual autonomy and equality. On the other, it enabled the individual to have some space in social and religious affairs. It gave the individual greater voice and the option to exit. Christianity, as a consequence, was transformed from a religion exercising authority over the individual to a religion that was dependent in more ways than one upon congregation, and it attempted to speak for and take up the concerns of its congregations (Spinner-Halev 2005).

The commitment to religious freedom and liberty that became central to the secular, political imagination in the late nineteenth century came along with these changes in the nature and functioning of the Church and religious authority. Indeed, liberal tolerance was made possible by these crucial changes. Consequently, neither liberal tolerance nor the right to religious liberty offered a cover for all existing religious practices. As it was individual liberty that was the operative norm, the state intervened, time and time again, to ensure that practices violating the basic principles of equality were changed or disallowed; and even more importantly, that individual members had a say, a voice, in the decisions of the Church. Even when religious authority remained and was exercised, the Church became almost like a voluntary association, and it could not enforce its writ upon those who did not wish to be a part of its congregation. So it was the liberty of individuals that was protected even as the right to religious freedom was extended to all persons. The different frameworks of secularism shared in this history and understanding of tolerance and religious liberty. In other words, even though the notion of secularism aimed to minimize religion-related discrimination, it remained closely aligned with the concern for equality, including gender equality. It did not, indeed it could not, simply protect religious liberty or defend the religious against non-believers and atheists.

It is this link between secularism and the concern for equality and individual liberty that remains a limiting condition – one that resists the possibility of accommodating some of the claims of religious minorities.

While making demands for the accommodation of their difference, for instance, diversity of dress codes, or facilities to offer prayers in public institutions, communities point to the authority of religion and the sincerity of their claims. They back these claims by the argument that these practices are an intrinsic part of their religion and that individuals committed to that way of life should have the opportunity to live by these practices. In the process they give a special status to religion and religion-backed practices. Such practices are not just seen as defining a distinct way of life, they are seen also to be more sincere than other freely chosen ways of life that do not place a similar kind of obligation upon the state to accommodate them. This is an element that is frequently overlooked when the claims of religious minorities are sought to be accommodated through the framework of secularism.

It is this peculiar nature of the claims of religious minorities that has prompted some scholars, like Avigail Eisenberg (2007), to argue that the existing clauses dealing with freedom of conscience in the Canadian Constitution may offer greater possibility of accommodating the claims of religious minorities than the framework of secularism. Since the courts in North America have been more inclined to protect religious liberty against encroachment by other associations and agencies, both private and public, they are more likely to make space for the observance of diverse religious practices. This is certainly an option that can be explored; meanwhile the point that needs to be underlined is that accommodation of the diverse claims of religious minorities is only possible if diversity is valued in and for itself.

Valuing diversity in this form may raise concerns of gender equality and the fate of internal minorities. But multiculturalists often argue that these apprehensions may be addressed by activating processes of democratization within the community, or by giving individual members the right to exit. The former could make the voice of the marginalized members of the community count so that the decisions taken reflect the will of the community as a whole and not only its dominant sections (see Deveaux 2005). The latter would allow individual members space to disagree with and opt out of the community practices. If exit options of this kind exist, the individual is protected against the coercive imposition of the will of the community. In theory, both these strategies offer ways of protecting the individual and her liberty, but in actual practice they pose a number of difficulties. Few communities act as voluntary agencies that allow individuals to exit at will without incurring some costs, such as being excommunicated from the community; nor do marginalized sections feel free to deliberate as equals within an overall framework of inequality (Mahajan 2005). Hence, liberal anxieties about the fate of the individual remain. Nevertheless in a steadily globalizing world we have to learn to live with differences. This is necessary not only for affirming our commitment to fair treatment but also for fulfilling the minimum conditions of peace and well-being in society. If we are to rethink our past inheritances, overcome our fears and anxieties about the other, and nurture mutual trust, then we need to initiate ways of reaching out to others and drawing upon the experience of others. In lieu of searching for principles that enable accommodation of minorities, perhaps we should be willing to endorse strategies based on modus vivendi. At the same time, we can try to enrich our understanding by examining how others live with differences and cope with the challenges they confront. It is with this understanding that I now turn to the case of India.

The case of India is particularly interesting and relevant because religious claims that seek accommodation in Western liberal democracies, and which have been the subject of considerable debate and difference there, are in a way non-issues in India. Covering one's head, even the covering of the face by some women, wearing a turban, or other religious signs, such as the red thread around the wrist or a *tilak* on the forehead, have easily been accepted into the public domain. In the Nehruvian era (1950s and 1960s) there was some debate about such issues as key political leaders visited places of worship, but even then there were significant differences of opinion on this matter. And over a period of time the presence of religious signs in the public domain has been more or less accepted.[5] Claims about public holidays, and food-related prohibitions have either been accepted or, for different reasons, they are not matters of critical debate that require justification.

This is not to say that the rights of religious minorities have been protected in every sphere or that these communities have no lingering concerns and anxieties. On the contrary, security of life and property, protection against communal violence and misrepresentation or negative imaging of the community remain important concerns. But problems of accommodation that confront most Western liberal democracies today are not key issues of minority concern. This is not because these communities are far too vulnerable to raise religious and cultural claims. Rather it is the availability of space for the articulation of religious and cultural differences that has played a critical role in accommodating these community claims in the public domain. This space for the expression of differences has been created by two different sets of provisions – one relating to religious liberty and the other pertaining to the rights given to minorities to set up their own educational institutions. Collectively it is these provisions that valued diversity and recognized the vulnerability of minorities in the nation-state that made a crucial difference to the capacity of the system to accommodate differences.

When India gained independence, a significant section of the political leadership agreed that India would not be a Hindu state endorsing the religious and cultural identity of the majority community. Instead it would be home to people of different religions and they would each be treated as equal. So pronounced was the concern to include different religious and other cultural minorities that a few members lamented that the category of the citizen (and with it the rights of the individual as a citizen) was gradually being eclipsed by the overwhelming concern with community identities. This commitment remained even as the consensus on how religious communities should be accommodated changed considerably after the unprecedented scale of communal violence that followed the declaration of independence and the establishment of the new state of Pakistan. Perhaps the most important change was that the proposal for separate representation for minorities was set aside, but the deeper resolve to accommodate the religious and cultural claims of minorities remained steadfast. So community personal laws were protected and all communities enjoyed an equal degree of religious liberty.[6] The religious liberty granted to all religious communities, particularly in the form of the right to practise their religion, brought religion into the public domain. But even more importantly, it made space, in principle, for the practices of different religious communities in the public domain. Communities could take out processions on the streets, lacerate the body, sing and dance in the manner accepted by the community, wear a specific dress, or walk naked so long as it expressed the sincerity and commitment to a particular way of life that had a tradition and history.[7]

Supplementing the freedom of conscience and belief with the right to religious practice created room for the observance and pursuance of community practices. As I have argued elsewhere, the right granted to profess, propagate, and practice one's religion placed, at least implicitly, an obligation upon the state to remove obstacles that may hinder the observance of community practices (Mahajan 2008). In fact, when practices involve the coming together of a very large number of persons, the state is expected to ensure that basic facilities necessary for the occasion are provided. Today, in very many different ways the state facilitates the *hajj*, the pilgrimage to Amarnath and Mansarovar, the holy dip on the occasion of the *Kumbh*, the *Jaganath yatra*, to name a few. The point is that the Constitution makers operated with the understanding that religion will have a public presence; indeed it could not be, or was not to be, banished from the public sphere. So there was from the beginning space for the observance of different practices in the public domain. The public presence of religion and the visibility of religious signs and symbols was not a matter of deep concern. Indeed it was not seen as violating the spirit of secularism.

Secularism, it was assumed, entailed that the state must not endorse or align itself with a particular religion as that could be a source of disadvantage to some. Hence, the state was not to have any religion of its own nor was there to be any religious instruction in educational institutions administered and run by the state. But there was also no attempt to clearly separate the sphere of the religious from the public and the political. The state was expected to play a role not only in facilitating the smooth and uninterrupted observance of religious practices, it had a role to play in regulating what the Constitution referred to as the "secular" aspects of religious practices. Its interventions were also considered necessary for ensuring the peaceful coexistence of different communities, and, above all, for seeing that existing religious practices were not a source for oppressing and subordinating vulnerable groups, like women or lower castes, within a community. This was a framework that was markedly different from the notion of secularism that prevailed in America or even France. It was, if anything, much closer to the framework of secularism that structured the relationship between state and religion in many other parts of Europe. Most countries in Europe did not disestablish religion or build a wall of separation between the two; instead they became secular by extending recognition and religious liberty to people of different faiths. In India, too, secularism, as a way of ensuring equal treatment to all, guaranteed the same degree of religious liberty to all persons as members of different communities.[8] But there was an important difference even here – the reference was to equality between groups and through that to the ideal of diversity. It is this commitment to diversity that eventually made a crucial difference to the capacity to accommodate religious differences in the public domain.

Independent India was not making a concession to minorities in order to accommodate them in its midst. Instead, different populations, cultures, and languages were seen as being an integral part of India. It is this recognition that prompted the making of a framework that tried to give equal legal status to all communities and, along with it, the assurance that minority communities would not be compelled to assimilate into the culture of the majority. This was a significantly different starting point for dealing with issues of majority and minority: one where the issue was not of accommodation but of equal rights and equal status.

The centrality accorded to treating different communities as equal partners eventually emphasized, what may be called, equality of groups rather than equality between individual citizens. The political leadership of independent India saw religion-, caste-, and gender-based differences to be the major stumbling block, and it is these that they wanted to rectify in democratic India. Equality was to be ensured and, given the crucial role played by religious communities, it was equality between communities that was considered critical to the survival and growth of democratic India. The agenda of equality between groups/communities pushed in the direction of equal religious liberty for all and, in this larger framework, individual liberty became a secondary consideration. To put it in another way, in independent India the main concern was accommodating religious diversity and creating a framework in which different religious communities could be seen as equal. Relatively less attention was given to the authority exercised by religion over the individual.

In Europe, by comparison, the liberal journey began by challenging the control of religion over individual and social life. As crucial matters, such as marriage, divorce, burial, and education were freed from the control of the Church, space was made for the exercise of individual liberty and rights as equal citizens. This process of secularization did not take place in India, so even though the idea of non-discrimination on grounds of religion was accepted, this commitment to secularism was not accompanied by a focus on the individual. Thus, although the constitutional provisions relating to secularism included religious liberty along with the concern for the moral equality of persons (to borrow the phrase from Bouchard and Taylor 2008a), the latter was often taken to imply all persons as members of different communities rather than as individuals.

This pushed the concern for individual liberty into the background. Formally the constitution gave religious liberty to individuals but even here the emphasis on practices brought the community in very centrally. It was community practices and not individual interpretations of them that were protected. It was the vantage point of the community, its religious leadership and the textual authority that received weightage over the individual. This relative neglect of the liberty of the individual, and corresponding centrality accorded to the community and religious liberty, assisted the process of accommodating differences – particularly forms of difference that are seeking accommodation in most liberal democracies today. It yielded a different set of challenges relating to the protection of individual liberty and gender equality, but it certainly facilitated the accommodation of diverse practices.[9]

The willingness to accommodate has been further assisted by the implicit acceptance of the majority-minority framework. The process of constitution making in India began by acknowledging differences and minority vulnerability. Even though the final document did not explicitly speak of the rights of minorities (except when it came to the right to establish their own educational institutions), in the post-independence period a distinction was implicitly made between the majority and the minority. The government, for instance, decided to make changes in the personal codes of the majority – the Hindus – but not in the personal laws of other minority communities even though gender inequalities existed in each of them. Over the decades electoral considerations have accentuated this sensitivity toward minorities, and some political parties have been eager to accommodate the religious and cultural claims of religious minorities. The reasons for this eagerness to accommodate social and cultural practices vary, and there are also political parties who wish to anchor the state in the culture of the majority. Yet despite this, most political parties are keen to express their willingness to accommodate community claims, particularly when they are backed by religious sanction.

The space for religious diversity has been further expanded by the vast network of minority educational institutions. Educational institutions set up by minorities existed even before independence, and the Constitution of independent India created space for them by giving all minorities the right to establish and administer educational institutions of their choice. These institutions could impart religious education and create an environment that was conducive to the observance of community religious and cultural practices. Even more importantly, they could receive funds from the state, the only proviso being that there would be no compulsory religious instruction. The critical difference that institutions of this kind can make can be understood by turning to the experience of Quebec. As the Bouchard-Taylor report points out, Orthodox Jews, unlike the Muslim community, have been able to take care of many of their community-specific needs by establishing their own hospitals, eating places, and educational institutions. Muslims, who do not have similar options available to them, have had to pressure the government to accommodate their religious and cultural sensitivities in the public domain. Minority educational institutions have made a similar kind of difference in India. As they exist from the primary stage of school education to professional courses and degrees, they offer to community members (particularly the devout members) an opportunity to send their children to institutions where observance of their community practices is more or less assured. This has taken the pressure off the state and other allied public institutions while simultaneously providing space for the observance of specific religious and cultural practices by different communities, most of all the minorities.

The point that I wish to emphasize is that if India has successfully accommodated a range of different religious and cultural practices, it is not simply the peculiarity of the Indian framework of secularism that has made the key difference. A framework of secularism that protected religious liberty and gave all persons the right to practice their religion pushed in the direction of accommodation, but it is the commitment to protect diversity of religions and cultures, along with the belief that the presence of diversity is the crucial condition of equal treatment for all communities, that has made the biggest difference. If the government and the court have been reluctant to intervene in, restrict or prevent the observance of certain practices, it is because of this understanding of the link between diversity and equality. This is a form of multiculturalism, albeit quite different from its Western counterpart, which does not similarly value diversity of religions.

The centrality accorded to diversity within the framework of competitive electoral democracy allowed visibility to differences without these generating a sense of anxiety or fear about the other. Perhaps the co-presence of different communities over a long period of time had created a consciousness and acceptance of such differences; the constitutional provisions and values only granted a formal sanction to this way of thinking about the self and the other. It made the absence of homogeneity of form an acceptable and non-threatening norm of public life.

This mode of accommodation has however yielded a different set of problems, the most significant ones being the protection of individual liberty vis-à-vis the diktats of the community and equality for women. The state has dealt with the latter by providing exit options (that is, the option to marry under the Special Marriage Act instead of religious personal laws) and minority communities have attempted to reform their respective personal laws through internal initiatives. The task is far from complete and women's equality remains a lingering concern. However, there is an emerging consensus that gender-just laws must be made within the framework of diversity.[10] But the question of individual liberty still poses a challenge – one that the state and society have not been able to address within the present framework of diversity.

So there are challenges, albeit of different kinds, before each of these societies. One can neither ignore the need to accommodate diversity nor the equally compelling urge to protect individual liberty and equality for vulnerable groups like women. Given the different histories, the framework of diversity that emerged in India cannot be transplanted to Europe or North America, nor could one expect to do the same in reverse. Nevertheless, one can learn from each other's experience. Accommodation is an ongoing process and turning the gaze upon other ways of organizing social and political life is an important means of reconsidering one's anxieties and understanding the other.

NOTES

1 The story was a little different in England. Here multiculturalists addressed the concerns of immigrant populations. and invariably community practices anchored in a religious way of life became the focus of attention. Nevertheless, arguments favouring accommodation of religious minorities rarely used the language of special rights. Bhikhu Parekh, for instance, emphasized the need to view cultural and religious identities as constituting a relevant difference while applying laws, such that tattooing the cheeks of a child are not considered to be just another instance of causing physical harm or injury to the young. Taking up specific community practices, such as dress codes for nurses, polygamy, and wearing the turban, he examined whether liberal anxieties and resistance to the accommodation of these practices were justified. Besides highlighting some of the ways in which religious minorities are disadvantaged, and at times, unfairly treated in a regime that adheres to the principle of formal equality, he stressed the need to bring minority cultures into the public arena so that majority and minority interactions can minimize the anxieties and fears that are triggered by the presence of difference (Parekh 1994b). However, even as Parekh argued for the recognition and accommodation of the difference that came in with religious minorities, he did not make a case for granting special rights to immigrants/religious minorities.

2 That is, the capacity to reconsider and choose the ends a person wants to pursue.

3 While concerns for gender equality were raised when the issue of young girls wearing the headscarf to school was discussed, that concern was not the reason for prohibiting the use of religious symbols like the turban or the yarmulke.

4 Okin recognizes that even women within the majority community are often not treated fairly. For instance, women in monogamous marriage may suffer abuse and violence and in some cases they may not be, as Honig (1997) argues, better off than women in polygamous marriages. But this only means that this particular problem also has to be addressed. It does not imply that practices such as polygamy, which violate the principle of gender equality, should be accepted and permitted. One might also add here that the concern about gender equality applies equally to the practices of the religious majority; if the practices of minorities are foregrounded here it is only because the commitment to cultural diversity focuses on the accommodation of minorities.

5 Following the debates about the headscarf in the West, there have been in recent times a few cases of students being sent home or asked to leave school if they did not comply with the prescribed dress codes, but in most of these cases the school administration has regretted the decision, or apologized and taken the student back. The intervention of the state (usually the Central Government) and at times the National Minority Commission have ensured the accommodation of visible religious signs and difference.

6 Keeping in mind the concerns of different communities, the Constitution protected the right to profess, propagate, and practise their religion. It did not mention and formally give any community the right to convert. There were strong differences of opinion on this issue so even as conversion was not formally protected, it was also not prohibited. The right to propagate contained that ambiguity and space. Shortly after independence, individual states closed this space by initiating laws and eventually an amendment to the constitutional provision in the form of conditions of scrutiny that must be met before any conversion takes place (Seervai 1975).

7 Right to religious liberty is limited, among other things, by the concern for "public morality," but it still remains fairly extensive. For instance, exposing one's body or being naked publicly has been considered an offense when it simply represents the will of a person, but when it is part and parcel of a commitment to a religious way of life it is treated differently. This is just an example of the way that the right to religious practice has made space for different religious and cultural practices.

8 Religious liberty was of course subject to certain restrictions – namely, public order, morality, and health, and as was just mentioned, the state could also intervene to protect equality of all persons, particularly people belonging to the lower castes and women.

9 In North America and Europe certain practices and signs of religious difference, such as the wearing of the veil or female circumcision, are resisted on the ground that they are a sign of the subordinate position of women in

these cultures, or alternately, that they reflect the control of the community over the individual. Hence, practices that are seeking accommodation in Western Europe are put to the test of individual liberty and gender equality. These were not, and are not, however the limiting conditions in India. As the principle of equality of all communities takes precedence over both individual liberty and gender equality it allows for diversity of religious practices in the public arena.

10 Up until the 1990s feminist scholars and women's activists repeatedly reminded successive governments to fulfill the obligation, placed by the Directive Principles of State Policy, Part IV of the Indian Constitution, to formulate a Uniform Civil Code. The voices of the secularists also pushed in the same direction. It is only when this agenda of formulating a Uniform Civil Code was usurped by groups advocating majoritarian cultural nationalism that the demand was changed to having gender-just community personal laws. The ascendance of Hindu nationalist parties put the spotlight back on the value of diversity – a value that had been consciously pursued by the framers of the Indian constitution.

REFERENCES

Bouchard, Gérard, and Charles Taylor. 2008a. *Building the Future: A Time for Reconciliation*. Quebec City: Government of Québec.
– 2008b. *Building the Future: A Time for Reconciliation*. Abridged Report, Quebec City: Gouvernement du Québec.
Carens, Joseph H. 2000. *Culture, Citizenship, and Community: A Contextual Exploration of Justice as Evenhandedness: A Contextual Exploration of Justice as Evenhandedness*. Clarendon: Oxford University Press.
Chaplin, Jonathan. 1993. "How Much Cultural and Religious Pluralism?" In *Liberalism, Multiculturalism and Tolerance*, edited by John Horton, 32–49. London: Macmillan.
Deveaux, Monique. 2005. "A Deliberative Approach to Conflicts of Culture." In *Minorities within Minorities: Equality, Rights and Diversity*, edited by Avigail Eisenberg, and Jeff Spinner-Halev, 340–362. Cambridge: Cambridge University Press.
Eisenberg, Avigail. 2007. *Diversity and Equality: The Changing Framework of Freedom in Canada*, Vancouver: UBC Press.
Honig, Bonnie. 1997. "Complicating Culture." *Boston Review* October/November: 30–2.
Kymlicka, Will. 1989. *Liberalism, Culture and Community*. Oxford: Oxford University Press.

– 1995. *Multicultural Citizenship.* New York: Oxford University Press.

Mahajan, Gurpreet. 2005. "Can Intra-Group Inequality Co-exist with Cultural Diversity? Re-examining Multicultural Frameworks of Accommodation." In *Minorities within Minorities: Equality, Rights and Diversity*, edited by Avigail Eisenberg, and Jeff Spinner-Halev, 90–112. Cambridge: Cambridge University Press.

– 2008. "Religion and the Indian Constitution: Questions of Separation and Equality." In *Politics and Ethics of the Indian Constitution*, edited by Rajeev Bhargava, 297–310. Delhi: Oxford University Press.

Okin, Susan Moller. 1994. *Is Multiculturalism Bad for Women?* edited by Cohen, Joshua, Matthew Howard and Martha C. Nussbaum. Princeton, New Jersey: Princeton University Press.

Parekh, Bhikhu. 1994a. "Cultural Diversity and Liberal Democracy." In *Defining and Measuring Democracy*, edited by David Beetham. London: Sage.

– 1994b. "Equality, Fairness and the Limits of Diversity." *Innovation* 7(3): 298–308.

Seervai, H. M. 1975. *Constitutional Law in India: A Critical Commentary.* Vol.1. 2nd ed. Bombay: N. M. Tripathy.

Spinner, Jeff. 1994. *The Boundaries of Citizenship: Race, Ethnicity, and Nationality in the Liberal State.* Baltimore: Johns Hopkins University Press.

Taylor, Charles. 1992. "The Politics of Recognition." In *Multiculturalism*, edited by Amy Gutmann, 25–74. Princeton: Princeton University Press.

Taylor, Charles. 1993. *Reconciling the Solitudes: Essays in Canadian Federalism and Nationalism.* Edited by Guy Laforest. Kingston: McGill-Queen's University Press.

Williams, Melissa S. 1996. "Muslim Minorities in Liberal Democracies: The Politics of Misrecognition." In *The Challenges of Diversity: Integration and Pluralism in Societies of Immigration*, edited by Rainer Baubock, Agnes Heller, and Ari Zollberg, 157–186. Aldershot, England: Avebury Press.

3

State, Religious Diversity, and the Crisis of Secularism

RAJEEV BHARGAVA

Over the last three decades, secular states – states that are separated from religion – have come under strain virtually everywhere. It is hardly surprising then that political secularism, the doctrine that defends them, has also been subjected to severe criticism. Some scholars have concluded that this critique is ethically and morally so profound and justified that it is time to abandon political secularism. I reject this conclusion. I argue that the criticism of secularism looks indefeasible only because critics have focused on mainstream conceptions developed in largely religiously homogenous societies. It is time we shifted focus away from doctrines underpinning some Western secular states toward the normative practices of a wide variety of states, including the best practices of non-Western states such as India. Once we do this, we will begin to see secularism differently, as a critical, ethical, and moral perspective not against religion but against religious homogenization and institutionalized (inter- and intra-religious) domination. Of all available alternatives, secularism remains our best option to help us deal with ever-deepening religious diversity and the problems endemic to it.

I begin with the assumption that ethical reasoning must be both contextual and comparative. Given this, if we value freedom and equality and are sensitive to religion-related domination, then we must find theocratic states and states with established religions, which privilege one or some religions, to be morally and ethically defective. Such states perpetuate inter-religious and intra-religious domination.

CRISIS OF SECULAR STATES?

For a start, it is worth asking if secular states and their underlying ideology of political secularism are really under siege everywhere. Secularism was severely jolted with the establishment of the first modern theocracy in 1979 in Iran. By the late 1980s, Islamic political movements had emerged in Egypt, Sudan, Algeria, Tunisia, Ethiopia, Nigeria, Chad, Senegal, Turkey, Afghanistan, Pakistan, and even in Bangladesh (see Ahmed 1987; Kepel 1994; Mohsin 1999; Westerlund 1996).

Movements challenging secular states were hardly restricted to Muslim societies. Protestant movements decrying secularism emerged in Kenya, Guatemala, and the Philippines. Protestant fundamentalism became a force in American politics. Sinhalese Buddhist nationalists in Sri Lanka, Hindu nationalists in India, religious ultraorthodoxy in Israel, and Sikh nationalists in the state of Punjab in India, as well as some members of diasporic communities in Canada and Britain, began to question the separation of state and religion (Juergensmeyer 1994).

In short, Western conceptions of political secularism do not appear to have traveled all that well in other societies. What is surprising is that such conceptions and the secular states they underpin are coming under strain even in Europe where only some time back they were believed to be firmly entrenched and secure.

Why so? It is true that substantive secularization of European societies has also brought in its wake extensive secularization of European states. Regardless of their religious affiliation, citizens have a large basket of civil and political rights unheard of in religion-centred states, past or present. But still, two problems remain.

First, migration from former colonies and an intensified globalization have thrown together on Western public spaces pre-Christian faiths, Christianity, and Islam (Turner 2001). The cumulative result is unprecedented religious diversity, the weakening of the public monopoly of single religions, and the generation of mutual suspicion, distrust, hostility, and conflict. This is evident in Germany and Britain but was dramatically highlighted by the headscarf issue in France and the murder of filmmaker Theo van Gogh in the Netherlands shortly after the release of his controversial film about Islamic culture (see Bowen 2007; Buruma 2006; Freedman 2004; Barker 2004; Modood, Triandafyllidou, and Zapata-Barrero 2004).

Second, despite substantial secularization, the formal establishment of the dominant religion does little to bolster better intercommunity relations or reduce religious discrimination in several European states. As it turns out, the widespread belief of a secular European public sphere is a myth. The religious biases of European states have become increasingly visible with deepening religious diversity. European states have continued to privilege Christianity in one form or another. They have publicly funded religious schools, maintained real estates of churches and clerical salaries, facilitated the control by churches of cemeteries, and trained the clergy. In short, there has been no impartiality within the domain of religion, and despite formal equality, this religious inequality continues to have a far-reaching impact on the rest of society (Klausen 2005).

To repeat, the crisis of secular states in Europe is in part because the secular humanist ethos endorsed by many citizens is not fully shared, particularly by those who have newly acquired citizenship. Any further secularization along humanist lines is not likely to resolve the crisis of European secular states. Also, many of these states have formally or informally established a religion, and the establishment of a single religion, even of the weaker variety, is part of the problem not the solution.

Why is this so? What ethical loss might ensue in the movement from a secular state to one that grants more importance to religion? What is wrong if states abandon secularism and become more religion-centred? The short answer is that theocratic states and states with established religions perpetuate intra- and inter-religious domination. They have historically recognized a particular version of the religion enunciated by a church as the official religion, compelled individuals to congregate for only one church, punished them for failing to profess a particular set of religious beliefs, levied taxes in support of one particular church, and made instruction of the favoured interpretation of the religion in educational institutions mandatory (Levy 1994). In such cases, not only was there inequality among religions (Christians and Jews) but also among churches of the same religion. Societies with such states either were wracked by inter-religious or inter-denominational wars or persecuted minority religious groups.

States with substantive religious establishments have not changed with time; just consider Saudi Arabia (Ruthven 2002). Or consider Pakistan where the virtual establishment of the dominant Sunni sect has proved to be disastrous, even to Muslim minorities. For example, Ahmadis have been deemed a non-Muslim minority and therefore persecuted for calling themselves Muslims or using the word "mosque" to designate their place of worship (Malik 2002; Bhargava 2004). While Saudi Arabia and Pakistan are illustrations, surely the result would be the same if a Hindu state were established in India. This would be a threat to religious minorities but also to the plural and tolerant character of Hinduism itself and therefore to a large number of practicing Hindus. The "democratic" state of Israel suffers from the same problem. Once it was declared a Jewish state, it could not but exclude from its full scheme of rights and benefits its own Arab citizens, let alone other Palestinians.

To some extent, as mentioned above, this is also true of many European states with formally established religion. What, in the face of this imbroglio, are European states to do? Those reflecting on this crisis have at least four conceptions of secularism staring back at them. The four conceptions flow from the different ways in which the metaphor of separation in the phrase "separation of state and religion" is unpacked, the levels at which separation is sought, and the manner in which ends are conceived. The first of these conceptions is thoroughly immoral and unethical because it separates religion from the state precisely because of the ethical or moral restrictions that religions place on its ends (wealth, power).

MAINSTREAM WESTERN SECULARISMS: PART OF THE PROBLEM

The dominant self-understanding of Western secularism is that it is a universal doctrine requiring the strict separation (exclusion) of church/religion and state for the sake of individualistically conceived moral or ethical values. This dominant self-understanding takes two forms, one inspired by an idealized version of the American model of separation and the other by the equally idealized French model. Can European states be reinvigorated by these two forms of Western secularism? Could they then deal better with the new reality of the vibrant presence of multiple religions in public life and the accompanying social tensions? In what follows I argue that available mainstream *conceptions* of Western secularism are likely to meet neither the challenge of the vibrant public presence of religion nor of increasing religious diversity.

THE IDEALIZED FRENCH MODEL

Take first the idealized French conception. With this conception, the state must be separated from religion but the state retains the power to interfere in religion. However, religion is divested of any power to intervene in matters of state. In short, separation means one-sided exclusion. The state may interfere in religion to hinder or suppress it, or even to help religion, but in all cases only to ensure its control over religion. Religion becomes an object of law and public policy but only on terms set by the state. This conception arose in response to the excessive domination of the Church, encourages an active disrespect for religion, and is concerned solely with preventing the religious order from dominating the secular. It hopes to deal with institutionalized religious domination by taming and marginalizing religion altogether. This conception can help states to deal with aspects of intra-religious domination – which exists when some members of a religious community dominate members of their own religion (for example, anticlericalism in France). However, it has few resources to properly address inter-religious domination, when members of one religious community discriminate against, marginalize, or even oppress members of another religious community.

Why so? Because issues of radical individual freedom and citizenship equality arose in European societies *after* religious homogenization. The birth of confessional states was accompanied by massive expulsion of subject-communities whose faith differed from the religion of the ruler. Such states found some place for toleration in their moral space, but as is well known, toleration was consistent with deep inequalities and with humiliating, marginalized, and virtually invisible existence. The liberal-democratization and the consequent secularization of many European states helped citizens with non-Christian faiths acquire most formal rights. But such a scheme of rights neither embodies a regime of inter-religious equality nor effectively prevents religion-based discrimination and exclusion. Indeed, it masks majoritarian, ethnoreligious biases.

These biases are evident in different kinds of difficulties faced by Muslims. For example, in Britain a third of all primary school children are educated by religious communities, yet applications for state funding by Muslims are frequently turned down. As of now, there are 2–5 Muslim schools compared to 2,000 run by Roman Catholics and 4,700 by the Church of England (Bader 2007). Similar problems persist in other European countries (Modood, Triandafyllidou, and Zapata-Barrerro 2006). These problems are also manifest in the failure of many western European states to deal with the issue of headscarves (France), demands by Muslims to build mosques and therefore to properly practise their own faith (Germany, Italy), or to have proper burial grounds of their own (Denmark). In recent times, as Islamophobia grips the imagination of several Western societies (exemplified by the cartoon controversy in Denmark), it is very likely that their Muslim citizens will continue to face disadvantages on account of membership in their religious community (Bowen 2006; Freedman 2004; Barker 2004).

Some sections of European societies, both on the Right and the Left, are tempted to follow the French model largely because they have bought the view that "Islam is a problem" and the only way to straighten the devil is to use the coercive power of the state. But this would be self-defeating because it leaves formal and informal establishments of Christianity in these societies untouched. Besides, every attempt to further intervene in religions is likely to meet with resistance not only from Muslims but from non-Muslims too. Any reliance on this model is likely to exacerbate problems.

THE IDEALIZED AMERICAN MODEL

Can these European states turn to the American model? The idealized American self-understanding interprets separation to mean mutual exclusion. Neither the state nor religion is meant to interfere in the domain of the another. This mutual exclusion is believed necessary to resolve conflicts between different Christian denominations, to grant some measure of equality between them, but most crucially to provide individuals with the freedom to set up and maintain their own religious associations. Mutual exclusion is believed necessary for religious liberty and for the more general liberties of individuals. This strict or "perfect separation," as James Madison termed it (Levy 1994, 99), must take place at each of the three distinct levels of (a) ends, (b) institutions and personnel, and (c) law and public policy. Levels (a) and (b) make the state non-theocratic and disestablish religion. Level (c) ensures that the state has neither a positive relationship with religion –for example there should be no policy of granting aid, even non-preferentially, to religious institutions – nor a negative relationship with it. It is not within the scope of state activity to interfere in religious matters even when some of the values (such as equality) professed by the state are violated within the religious domain. Congress simply has no power on matters pertaining to religion (Levy 1994; Hamburger 2002).

This non-interference is justified on the grounds that religion is a privileged, private (non-state) matter, and if something is amiss within this private domain, it can be mended only by those who have a right to do so within that sphere. This, according to proponents of this view, is what religious freedom means. Thus, the freedom that justifies mutual exclusion is negative liberty and is closely enmeshed with the privatization of religion.

In my view, this model of secularism encourages the state to have passive respect for religion. Idealized American secularism has some resources to fight inter-religious domination (for instance, it necessitates the disestablishment of the dominant religion) but not to wage a struggle against other aspects of the inter-religious domination or against intra-religious dominations. Because the state is unable to facilitate freedoms or equality within religions, it forces people to exit from their religion rather than to press for intra-religious equality.

Both forms of Western secularism have persistent difficulties coping with community-oriented religions such as Roman Catholicism, Islam, and some forms of Hinduism and Sikhism that demand greater public presence and even official recognition for themselves – particularly when they begin to cohabit the same society. Moreover, they were not designed for societies with deep religious diversity. Both of these versions developed in the context of a single-religion society and to solve the problems of one religion, namely Christianity. Both understand separation as exclusion and make individualistically conceived values – individual liberty or equality between individuals or both – the ground for separation. Because of their diversity-resistant character and individualistic character, both these forms of Western secularism have become part of the problem afflicting secularism.

INDIAN MODEL OF SECULARISM

Are we caught then between ideologies that legitimate religious domination of the secular and forms of secularism that are unable to prevent forms of intra-religious or inter-religious domination? I believe it is possible to get out of this impasse because although theoretically less developed, there exists another model of secularism, one not generated exclusively in the West, which meets the needs of societies with deep religious diversity and also complies with principles of freedom and equality: the subcontinental or Indian model found loosely in the best moments of intercommunal practice in India and in the country's constitution appropriately interpreted. In India, the existence of deep religious diversity has ensured a conceptual response not only to problems within religions but also between religions. Without taking it as a blue print, the West must examine the Indian conception and possibly learn from it.

Several features of the Indian model are striking and relevant to wider discussion. First, multiple religions are not extras, added on as an afterthought, but present at the model's starting point as part of its foundation. Indian secularism is inextricably tied to deep religious diversity. Second, it has a commitment to multiple values like liberty, equality, and fraternity. These values are not conceived narrowly as pertaining to individuals, but interpreted broadly to cover the relative autonomy of religious communities and equality of status in society. This model also includes other more basic values such as peace and toleration between communities. It has a place not only for the right of individuals to profess their religious beliefs but also for the right of religious communities to establish and maintain educational institutions crucial for the survival and sustenance of their distinctive religious traditions.

The acceptance of community-specific rights brings us to the third feature of Indian secularism. Because it was born in a deeply multi-religious society, it is equally concerned with preventing both inter-religious and intra-religious domination. Unlike the two Western conceptions, which provided benefits to minorities only incidentally (Jews benefited in some European countries such as France, not because their special needs and demands were taken care of, but rather because of a change in the general climate of the society), in India, even community-specific political rights (political reservations for religious minorities) were almost granted and were withheld in the last instance only for contextual reasons.[1] In fact, it is arguable that a conceptual space is still available for them within the Indian Constitution.

Fourth, this conception does not erect a wall of separation between state and religion. There are boundaries, of course, but they are porous. This allows the state to intervene in religions, to help or hinder them without the impulse to control or destroy them. This involves multiple roles: granting aid to educational institutions of religious communities on a non-preferential basis and interfering in socio-religious institutions that deny equal dignity and status to members of their own religion or to those of others (for example, the ban on untouchability and the obligation to allow everyone, irrespective of their caste, to enter Hindu temples.) This interference could potentially include correcting gender inequalities on the basis of a more sensible understanding of equal concern and respect for all individuals and groups. In short, it interprets separation to mean not strict exclusion or strict neutrality, but rather what I call "principled distance," which is poles apart from one-sided exclusion, mutual exclusion, or strict neutrality (equidistance).

Fifth, it is not entirely averse to the public character of religions. Although the state does not identify with a particular religion or with religion more generally (there is no establishment of religion), there is official and therefore public recognition granted to religious communities. For example, religious minorities are granted a fundamental right in the constitution to set up and maintain their own educational institutions. This presupposes official recognition of minority religions.

Sixth, this model shows that, toward religion, we do not have to choose between active hostility and passive indifference, or between disrespectful hostility and respectful indifference. We can combine the two: have the necessary hostility as long as there is also active respect. The state may intervene to inhibit some practices, so long as it shows respect for other practices of the religious community and does so by publicly lending support to them. Thus, if Muslims qua minority are given official recognition and if any infringement on their right to run their educational institutions as they deem fit can be challenged and taken to the highest court, then, potentially, the state may in turn intervene in some practices which, though endorsed by orthodox Muslims, are deeply oppressive and degrading.

Seventh, by not fixing its commitment from the start exclusively to individual or community values or marking rigid boundaries between the public and private, India's constitutional secularism allows decisions on these matters to be taken either within the open dynamics of democratic politics or by contextual reasoning in the courts.

Eighth, the Indian model has opened up the possibility of multiple secularisms. It presupposes neither the presence of Christianity as part of its background conditions nor the specific historical trajectory of Western societies. It shows that a secularism, in every way as good if not better than other versions, can exist outside the West.

Finally, this commitment to multiple values and principled distance means that the state tries to balance different, ambiguous but equally important values. This makes its secular ideal more like a contextual, ethically sensitive, politically negotiated arrangement (which it really is), rather than a scientific doctrine conjured by ideologues and merely implemented by political agents.

A somewhat forced, formulaic articulation of Indian secularism goes something like this. The state must keep a principled distance from all public or private, individual-oriented or community-oriented religious institutions for the sake of the equally significant (and sometimes conflicting) values of peace, this-worldly goods, dignity, liberty, and equality (in all its complicated individualistic or non-individualistic versions). Indian secularism then is an ethically sensitive, negotiated settlement between diverse groups and divergent values. This model thus embodies what I call "contextual secularism." Allow me to elaborate on two features mentioned above: principled distance and contextual secularism.

PRINCIPLED DISTANCE

As seen above, for mainstream Western secularism, separation means mutual or one-sided exclusion. The idea of principled distance unpacks the metaphor of separation differently. It accepts a disconnection between state and religion at the level of ends and institutions, but does not make a fetish of it at the third level of public policy and law (this distinguishes it from all other models of secularism, moral and amoral, that disconnect state and religion at this third level). How else can it be in a society where religion frames some of its deepest interests? Recall that political secularism is an ethic whose concerns relating to religion are similar to theories that oppose unjust restrictions on freedom, morally indefensible inequalities, and intercommunal domination and exploitation. Yet a secularism based on principled distance is not committed to the mainstream Enlightenment idea of religion. It accepts that humans have an interest in relating to something beyond themselves including God and that this manifests itself as individual belief and feeling as well as social practice in the public domain. It also accepts that religion is a cumulative tradition, as well as a source of people's identities (Smith 1991). But it insists that even if it turned out that one religion was true and others false, this would not give adherents to the "true" doctrine or religion the right to force it down the throats of others who did not believe it. Nor does it give a ground for discrimination in the equal distribution of liberties and other valuable resources.

Similarly, a secularism based on principled distance accepts that religion may not have special public significance antecedently written into and defining the very character of the state or the nation, but it does not follow from this that it has no public significance at all. Sometimes, some versions of secularism assume precisely that: that religion has no public significance. As long as religion is publicly significant, a democratic state simply has to take it into account. Indeed, institutions of religion may influence individuals as long as they do so through the same process, and by access to the same resources, as any other institution and without undue advantage or unduly exploiting the fears and vulnerabilities that frequently accompany people in their experience of the religious.

But what precisely is principled distance? The policy of principled distance entails a flexible approach to the question of inclusion/exclusion of religion and the engagement/disengagement of the state, which at the level of law and policy depends on the context, nature, and current state of relevant religions. This engagement must be governed by principles undergirding a secular state, that is, principles that flow from a commitment to the values mentioned above. This means that religion may intervene in the affairs of the state if such intervention promotes freedom, equality, or any other value integral to secularism. For example, citizens may support a coercive law of the state grounded purely in a religious rationale if this law is compatible with freedom or equality. Equally, the state may engage with religion or disengage from it, engage positively or negatively, but it does so depending entirely on whether or not these values are promoted or undermined. A state that intervenes or refrains from interference on this basis keeps a principled distance from all religions. This is one constitutive idea of principled distance. This idea is different from strict neutrality, that is, the idea that the state may help or hinder all religions to an equal degree and in the same manner, that if it intervenes in one religion, it must also do so in others. Rather, it rests upon a distinction explicitly drawn by the American philosopher Ronald Dworkin (1978) between equal treatment and treating everyone as an equal.

The principle of equal treatment, in the relevant political sense, requires that the state treat all its citizens equally in the relevant respect, for example, in the distribution of a resource or opportunity. On the other hand, the principle of treating people as equals entails that every person or group is treated with equal concern and respect. This second principle may sometimes require equal treatment, say equal distribution of resources, but it may also occasionally dictate unequal treatment. Treating people or groups as equals is entirely consistent with differential treatment. This idea is the second ingredient in what I have called principled distance.

I said that principled distance allows for differential treatment. What kind of treatment do I have in mind? First, religious groups have sought exemptions from practices in which states intervene by promulgating a law to be applied neutrally to the rest of society. This demand for non-interference is made on the ground either that the law requires them to do things not permitted by their religion or prevents them from doing acts mandated by it. For example, Sikhs demand exemptions from mandatory helmet laws and from police dress codes to accommodate religiously required turbans. Elsewhere, Jews seek exemptions from Air Force regulations to accommodate their yarmulkes. Muslim women and girls demand that the state not interfere in their religiously required chador. Jews and Muslims seek exemption from Sunday closing laws on the ground that this is not required by their religion. Principled distance allows that a practice that is banned or regulated in one culture be permitted in the minority culture because of the distinctive status and meaning it has for its members.

For many republican or liberal theories, this is a problem because of their simple, somewhat absolutist morality that gives overwhelming importance to one value, particularly to equal treatment or equal liberty. Religious groups may demand that the state refrain from interference in their practices, but they may equally demand that the state interfere in such a way as to give them special assistance so that these groups are also able to secure what other groups are able to routinely get by virtue of their social dominance in the political community. The state may grant authority to religious officials to perform legally binding marriages, to have their own rules or methods of obtaining a divorce, their own rules about relations between ex-husbands and ex-wives, their way of defining a will, or their laws about postmortem allocation of property, arbitration of civil disputes, and even their method of establishing property rights. Principled distance allows the possibility of such policies on the grounds that it might be unfair to hold people accountable to an unfair law.

However, principled distance is not just a recipe for differential treatment in the form of special exemptions. It may even require state intervention in some religions more than in others, considering the historical and social conditions of all relevant religions. For the promotion of a particular value constitutive of secularism, some religion, relative to other religions, may require more interference from the state. For example, suppose that the value to be advanced is social equality. This requires in part undermining caste hierarchies. If this is the aim of the state, then it may be required of the state that it interferes in caste-ridden Hinduism much more than say Islam or Christianity. However, if a diversity-driven religious liberty is the value to be advanced by the state, then it may have to intervene in Christianity and Islam more than in Hinduism. If this is so, the state can neither strictly exclude considerations emanating from religion nor keep strict neutrality with respect to religion. It cannot antecedently decide that it will always refrain from interfering in religions or that it will interfere in each equally. Indeed, it may not relate to every religion in society in exactly the same way or intervene in each religion to the same degree or in the same manner. To want to do so would be plainly absurd. All it must ensure is that the relationship between the state and religions is guided by non-sectarian motives consistent with some values and principles. A state interfering in one religion more than in others does not automatically depart from secularism. Indian secularism rejects the assumption that "one size fits all."

CONTEXTUAL SECULARISM

Contextual secularism is contextual not only because it captures the idea that the precise form and content of secularism will vary from one context to another and from place to place, but also because it embodies a certain model of contextual moral reasoning (Taylor 1994; Parekh 2000; Carens 2000). It does this because of its character as a multi-value doctrine and by virtue of its commitment to principled distance. To accept that secularism is a multi-value doctrine is to acknowledge that its constitutive values do not always sit easily with one another. On the contrary, they are frequently in conflict. Some degree of internal discord and therefore a fair amount of instability is an integral part of contextual secularism. For this reason, it forever requires fresh interpretations, contextual judgments, and attempts at reconciliation and compromise. This contextual secularism recognizes that the conflict between individual rights and group rights or between claims of equality and liberty or between claims of liberty and the satisfaction of basic needs cannot always be adjudicated by recourse to some general and abstract principle. Rather, these conflicts can only be settled case by case and may require a fine balancing of competing claims. The eventual outcome may not be wholly satisfactory to either party, but still be reasonably satisfactory to both. Multi-value doctrines such as secularism encourage accommodation – not the giving up of one value for the sake of another but rather their reconciliation and possible harmonization, that is, to make each work without changing the basic content of apparently incompatible concepts and values.

This endeavor to make concepts, viewpoints, and values work simultaneously does not amount to a morally objectionable compromise. Nothing of importance is given up for the sake of a less significant thing, one without value or even with negative value. Rather, what is pursued is a mutually agreed middle way that combines elements from two or more equally valuable entities. The roots of such attempts at reconciliation and accommodation lie in a lack of dogmatism, in a willingness to experiment, to think at different levels and in separate spheres, and in a readiness to take decisions on a provisional basis. It captures a way of thinking characterized by the following dictum: "why look at things in terms of this or that, why not try to have both this and that" (Austin 1972). In this way of thinking, it is recognized that though we may currently be unable to secure the best of both values and therefore be forced to settle for a watered-down version of each, we must continue to have an abiding commitment to search for a way to transcend this second-best condition. It is frequently argued against

Indian secularism that it is contradictory because it tries to bring together individual and community rights, and that articles in the Indian Constitution that have a bearing on the secular nature of the Indian state are deeply conflictual and at best ambiguous.[2] This is to misrecognize a virtue as a vice. In my view, this attempt to bring together seemingly incompatible values is a great strength of Indian secularism.

Discerning students of Western secularism may now begin to find something familiar in this ideal. But then, Indian secularism has not dropped fully formed from the sky. It is not *sui generis*. It shares a history with the West. In part, it has learned from and built on it. Indian secularism may be seen as a route to retrieving the rich history of western secularism – forgotten, under emphasized, or frequently obscured by the formula of strict separation. If so, Western societies can find reflected in Indian secularism not only a compressed version of their own history but also a vision of their future.

THREE OBJECTIONS

Three objections might arise on reading this. First, it might be said: Look at the state of the subcontinent! Look at India! How deeply divided it remains! What about the violence against Muslims in Gujarat and against Christians in Orissa? How can success be claimed for the Indian version of secularism? I do not wish to underestimate the force of this objection. The secular ideal in India is in periodic crisis and is deeply contested. Besides, at the best of times, it generates as many problems as it solves.

But it should not be forgotten that a secular state was set up in India *despite* the massacre and displacement of millions of people on ethnoreligious grounds, and it has survived in a context in which ethnic nationalism remains dominant throughout the world. Moreover, it was set up to deal with the tensions continuously generated by deep religious diversity, not to offer "a final solution" by expulsion or liquidation of all but the dominant religious group. Regardless of the past, is it not fair to expect that European and North American states will not allow any attempt at "ethnic cleansing" on their soil today?

Practitioners of Indian secularism can learn from the institutional mechanism set up by European states to prevent inter-group violence: some facets of the institutional basis of Indian secularism can be strengthened by the example of Western states. To consolidate its minimally decent character, India can still learn from the contemporary West. Yet, as different religious cultures claim their place in societies across the world, it may be India's development of secularism that offers the most peaceful, freedom-sensitive, and democratic way forward. In any case, this account must not be read as an apologia for the Indian state but as a reasonable and sympathetic articulation of a conception that the Indian state frequently fails to realize in actuality. My discussion is meant to focus on the comparative value of this conception and its potential for the future, and not on how in fact it has fared in India. The fate of ideal conceptions with transcultural potential should not be decided purely on the basis of what happens to them in their place of origin.

Second, it might be objected that I do not focus on the best practices of Western states and emphasize the more vocal articulations of Western secular conceptions. But that precisely is my point. The dominant conception of Western secularism is derived from an idealized self-understanding of two of its versions rather than from the best practices of Western states, including the practices of the US and France. It is my view that this doctrinal conception (a) obstructs an understanding of alternative conceptions worked out on the ground by morally sensitive political agents; and (b) by influencing politicians and citizens alike, it frequently distorts the practice of many Western and non-Western states. Further, (c) it masks the many ways in which inter- or intra-religious domination persists in many Western societies. Moreover, it is this conception that has traveled to all parts of the world and is a continuing source of misunderstanding of the value of secular states. My objective is to displace these conceptions or at least put them in their place.

Third, the necessary link between secularism and Christianity is exaggerated, if not entirely mistaken. It is true that the institutional separation of church and state is an internal feature of Christianity and an integral part of Western secularisms. But as we have seen, this church-state disconnection is a necessary but not a sufficient condition for the development of secularism even in societies with church-based religions. It is clearly not a necessary condition for the development of all forms of secularism. Moreover, as I have argued, the mutual exclusion of religion and the state is not the defining feature of secularism. The idea of separation can be interpreted differently. Religious integrity, peace and toleration (interpreted broadly to mean "live and let live"), are not uniquely Christian values. Most non-Christian civilizations have given significant space to each. Therefore, none of them are exclusively Christian. It follows that, even though we find in Christian writings some of the clearest and most systematic articulation of this doctrine, even the Western conception of secularism is not exclusively Christian.

All right, one might say, secularism is not just a Christian doctrine, but is it not Western? The answer to this question is both yes and no. Up to a point, it is certainly a Western idea. More specifically, as a clearly articulated doctrine, it has distinct Western origins. Although elements that constitute secularism assume different cultural forms and are found in several civilizations, one cannot deny that the idea of the secular first achieved self-consciousness and was properly theorized in the West. One might then say that the early and middle history of secularism is almost entirely dominated by Western societies. However, the same cannot be said of its later history. Nationalism and democracy arrived in the West after the settlement of religious conflicts, in societies that had been made religiously homogenous, or had almost become so (with the exception of the Jews, of course who continued to face persistent persecution). The absence of deep religious diversity and conflict meant that issues of citizenship could be addressed almost entirely disregarding religious context; the important issue of community-specific rights to religious groups could be wholly ignored. This had a decisive bearing on the Western conception of secularism. However, for non-Western societies such as India, the case is different. Both national and democratic agendas in countries such as India had to face issues raised by deep religious difference and diversity. In India, nationalism had to choose between the religious and the secular. Similarly, the distribution of active citizenship rights could not be conceived or accomplished by ignoring religion. It had to be done either by actively disregarding religion (as in all political rights) or by developing a complex attitude to it, as in the case of cultural rights, where it had to balance claims of individual autonomy with those of community obligations, as well as claims of the necessity of keeping religion "private" despite its inescapable, often valuable presence in the public. By doing all this, Indian secularism never completely annulled particular religious identities.

In addressing these complex issues, the idea of the political secularism was taken further than had been evolved in the West. Mainstream theories or ideologies in modern, Western societies have take little notice of these features. Hence, they are struggling to deal with post-colonial religious diversity of their societies. The later history of secularism is more non-Western than Western.[3] To discover its own rich and complex structure, Western secularism can either look backward, to its own past, or else look sideways, at Indian secularism, which mirrors not only the past of secularism, but in a way, also its future. Doing so will certainly benefit the secularisms of many Western societies. For example, French secularism needs to look beyond its own conceptions of *laïcité* in order to take into account its own multicultural and multi-religious reality. It cannot continue to take refuge in claims of exceptionalism. A good hard look at Indian secularism could also change the self-understanding of other Western secularisms, including Canada's and perhaps even its neighbour's very individualist, libertarian secularism.

CONCLUSION

I hope to have demonstrated that there are at least two broad conceptions of secularism, one mainstream Western (the American and the French) and the other which provides an alternative and is embodied in the Indian model. Of these, the Indian conception has better ethical and moral potential to deal with deep religious diversity. I do not wish to suggest that this alternative model is found only in India. The Indian case is meant to show that such an alternative exists. It is not meant to resurrect a dichotomy between the West and the East. As I have mentioned, I am quite certain that this alternative version is embedded in the best practices of many states, including those Western states that are deeply enamored by mainstream conceptions of political secularism. My objective in this chapter is to draw attention to the frequent inability of ethical and political theorists to see the normative potential in the secular practices of these different states because they are obsessed with the normative value of mainstream conceptions. Western states need to improve the understanding of their own secular practices, just as Western secularism needs a better theoretical self-understanding. Rather than get stuck on models they developed at a particular time in their history, Western states would do well to more carefully examine the normative potential in their own political practices or to learn from the original Indian variant.

It follows that Canada and more specifically Quebec should reexamine its own well-honed practices of social and political accommodation rather than lean on the American or the French version. To clearly see what for instance might be wrong in Bill 94, Quebec may well look at the Indian version of secularism. Not of course to take it as a blue print, which would be absurd, but rather to see how it works (or fails to work). Furthermore, given its new diversity, Canada must devise a secularism that is less rooted in Christianity, less exclusively reliant on classical liberalism or republicanism and more openly sensitive to public and community-oriented religions.

NOTES

1 One of the most contentious issues in the Constituent Assembly was over separate electorates for Muslims. Not only would only Muslims contest from some constituencies (political reservations) but only Muslims would comprise the electorate that elects members of parliament from specific constituencies. The Muslim League opposed reservations based on joint electorates and demanded separate electorates instead. The Indian National Congress in turn opposed it. Congressmen agreed that if people were excluded from or discriminated against within the deliberative assembly solely on the ground that they belonged to a particular religion then the principle of equal citizenship (a core value of secularism) would be violated. But they argued that separate, not joint, electorates forced this exclusion and, by implication, breached the core principles of an inclusive polity and of secularism. After the partition of the sub-continent, the debate over a separate electorate was over. Muslims had received much more than that, it was argued, a separate country itself. But India could still have had a reservation of seats for Muslims to be elected by joint electorates. However, the context had become so different by then, that this demand was shelved by many Muslims themselves.

2 This charge is made by Stanley Tambiah (1998).

3 By implication, the history of secularism must include the history of other non-Western societies that have sought to install and maintain secular states.

REFERENCES

Ahmed, Ishtiaq. 1987. *The Concept of an Islamic State: An Analysis of the Ideological Controversy in Pakistan*. London: Frances Pinter.

Austin, Granville. 1972. *The Indian Constitution: Cornerstone of a Nation*. New Delhi: Oxford University Press.

Bader, Veit. 2007. *Secularism or Democracy? Associational Governance of Religious Diversity*. Amsterdam: Amsterdam University Press.

Barker, Christine R. 2004. "Church and State: Lessons from Germany?" *The Political Quarterly* 75 (2): 168–76.

Bhargava, Rajeev. 2004. "Inclusion and Exclusion in South Asia: The Role of Religion." Background paper for Human Development Report Office. United Nations Development Programme.

Bowen, John. 2007. *Why the French Don't Like Headscarves: Islam, the State and Public Space*. Princeton: Princeton University Press.

Buruma, Ian. 2006. *Murder in Amsterdam: The Death of Theo van Gogh and the Limits of Tolerance*. London: Penguin.

Carens, Joseph H. 2000. *Culture, Citizenship and Community: A Contextual Exploration of Justice as Evenhandedness*. Oxford: Oxford University Press.

Dworkin, Ronald. 1978. "Liberalism." In *Public and Private Morality*, edited by Stuart Hampshire, 113–43. Cambridge: Cambridge University Press.

Freedman, Jane. 2004. "Secularism as a Barrier to Integration? The French Dilemma." *International Migration* 42 (3): 5–27.

Hamburger, Philip. 2002. *Separation of Church and State*. Cambridge: Harvard University Press.

Juergensmeyer, Mark. 1994. *The New Cold War? Religious Nationalism Confronts the Secular State*. Berkeley: University of California Press.

Kepel, Giles. 1994. *The Revenge of God: The Resurgence of Islam, Christianity and Judaism in the Modern World*. Cambridge: Polity Press.

Klausen, Jytte. 2005. *The Islamic Challenge: Politics and Religion in Western Europe*. Oxford: Oxford University Press.

Levy, Leonard W. 1994. *The Establishment Clause: Religion and the First Amendment*. Chapel Hill: University of North Carolina Press.

Malik, Iftikhar Haider. 2002. *Religious Minorities in Pakistan*. London: Minority Rights Group International.

Modood, Tariq, Anna Triandafyllidou, and Ricard Zapata-Barrero, eds. 2006. *Multiculturalism, Muslims and Citizenship: A European Approach*. London: Routledge.

Mohsin, Amena. 1999. "National Security and the Minorities: The Bangladesh Case." In *Minority Identities and the Nation State*, edited by D. L. Sheth and Gurpreet Mahajan, 312–33. New Delhi: Oxford University Press.

Parekh, Bhikhu. 2000. *Rethinking Multiculturalism: Cultural Diversity and Political Theory*. London: MacMillan.

Ruthven, Malise. 2002. *A Fury for God: The Islamist Attack on America*. London: Granta.

Smith, Wilfred C. 1991. *The Meaning and End of Religion*. Minneapolis: Fortress.

Tambiah, Stanley. 1998. "The Crisis of Secularism in India." In *Secularism and Its Critics*, edited by Rajeev Bhargava, 445–453. Delhi: OUP.

Taylor, Charles. 1994. "Justice after Virtue." In *After MacIntyre*, edited by John Horton and Susan Mendus. Cambridge: Polity Press.

Turner, Brian S. 2001. "Cosmopolitan Virtue: On Religion in a Global Age." *European Journal of Social Theory* 4 (2): 131–52.

Westerlund, David. 1996. *Questioning the Secular State*. London: Hurst.

4

Secularism:
A Possible Gandhian Reconstruction

BINDU PURI

Secularism in the Indian avatar has largely been seen as having not Gandhian but Nehruvian origins. For Indian secularism emerged from a dialectics of modern science and the historical experience of religious conflict. Nehru's lack of personal religiosity supplemented such a dialectics between rational science and irrational, essentially conflict-ridden religious denominations, finding a resolution in the non-establishment clause. Yet it is interesting to note that Gandhi also appears in various ways in the mainstream social science discourse on secularism in India. Within that discourse, Gandhi's secularism is open to conflicting interpretations, for he is assimilated both as supportive of Indian secularism and as anti-secularist. For instance, Stanley J. Tambiah (1998, 420), writing on what he terms "The Gandhi-Nehru view on the Relation between Religion and State," says that, unlike Nehru, Gandhi had an "attachment to religion," and yet felt the need for "even-handed neutrality" on the part of the Indian state. Tambiah (ibid., 421) claims that, whatever his differences with Nehru, "Gandhi had as his unswerving purpose the winning of independence for India and the constitution of a united nation, and in a society where multiple religions were observed, this nation-making project entailed a separation of religion and state."

On this account, Gandhi had rational and non-religious arguments for advocating state secularism. His argument in *Hind Swaraj* seems to support such an interpretation: "India cannot cease to be one nation because people belonging to different religions live in it ... In reality there are as many religions as there are individuals; but those who are conscious of the spirit of nationality do not interfere with one another's religion. If they do, they are not fit to be considered one nation" (Gandhi 1968, 136). Paradoxically, however, for critics of Indian secularism such as T. N. Madan and Ashis Nandy, Gandhi serves as a religious resource for the anti-secularist argument. Nandy's assimilation of Gandhi begins by making a primary distinction within religion itself, between faith and ideology. Religion as faith is a way of life, "non-monolithic and operationally plural" (Nandy 1998, 322). Religion as ideology is religion as "a subnational, national, or cross-national identifier of populations contesting for or protecting non-religious, usually political or socio-economic interests" (ibid.). This is a contrast between the believer or man of faith's version of his religion, on the one hand, and the ideological versions produced by organized bodies such as the Sangh Parivar and the Muslim League, on the other. One may note in this context the lack of personal religiosity in the lives of ideologues like Vinayak Damodar Savarkar and Muhammad Ali Jinnah, who played foundational roles in such organizations. The point of Nandy's argument is that religion as ideology is the product of modernity and the associated grid of nationalism and statecraft. Once modernity is accepted, the only way to resist the distortion of religious faith by constructed ideologies is to offer secularism as a part of the same grid. Hence, secularism is as suspect as are religious ideologies of the Rashtriya Swayamsevak Sangh variety. All participate in the ideologies of progress and modernity.

For Nandy (1998, 343), the anti-secularist manifesto finds religious support in the position of M. K. Gandhi: "Gandhi, an arch anti-secularist if we use the proper scientific meaning of the word "secularist," claimed that his religion was his politics and his politics was his religion. He was not a cultural relativist and his rejection of the first principle of secularism – the separation of religion and politics – was not a political strategy meant to ensure his survival in a uniquely multi-ethnic society like India." The reference here is to Gandhi's arguments about the inseparability of religious and political spaces. For example, in Gandhi's statement in *The Harijan* paper on 10 February 1940: "Yes I still hold the view that I cannot conceive politics as divorced from religion ... Indeed religion should pervade every one of our actions" (quoted in Bose 1948, 256).

A similar assimilation of Gandhi to an anti-secularist agenda can be found in the work of T. N. Madan. According to him, secularism is a product of Protestant Christianity. It is impossible, impracticable, and impotent in the South Asian context, for South Asia's religious traditions are totalizing in character, with religion being constitutive of society and religious values being ranked above secular ones (Madan 1998, 302). In the course of his argument, Madan turns to Gandhi's statement about religion and politics, cited above, as evidence. Of statements made by Gandhi seemingly in support of secularism, Madan (1998, 305) says: "When he did advocate that 'religion and state should be separate,' he clarified that this was to limit the role of the state to 'secular welfare,' and to allow it no admittance into the religious life of the people ... Clearly the hierarchical relationship is irreversible."

None of the parties to this debate has attempted to reconcile the apparently conflicting Gandhian commitments to secularism and to its rejection. This reconciliation is both possible and necessary, given that Gandhi's work and writing show what Bilgrami (2006) describes as "integrity." Gandhi often appeared to derive both political and religious conclusions from a central core of moral beliefs. It is therefore reasonable to assume a certain consistency in Gandhi's thought. In this chapter, I will first attempt to reconcile the apparently conflicting statements by Gandhi appropriated by both sides of the debate of Indian secularism. I do this by reconstructing the Gandhian position on the proper relationship between the state and religion. In light of this reconstruction, I attempt, in the second part of the paper, to evaluate the relation between Gandhian secularism and the constitutional practice of secularism in India, asking whether these versions of secularism are consistent.

RECONSTRUCTING GANDHIAN SECULARISM

One can approach the attempt to reconstruct a Gandhian secularism by formulating a possible Gandhian answers to basic critical questions, such as: What, in Gandhi's view, ought to be the role of the personal vis-à-vis the religious community in sustaining the religious form of life? What should be the relationship between one religion and another, and one religious community and another? How must the modern state deal with religions and religious communities, given that the religious form of life is an authentic one? I will attempt to answer these questions, from a Gandhian perspective.

Regarding the role of the religious community in sustaining the religious form of life, a preliminary issue is how Gandhi understands religion itself. Using Nandy's distinction between religion as a form of life and as an ideology, it is obvious that Gandhi did not understand religious faith primarily as ideology. Religion as ideology can be understood as a set of cultural-linguistic conditions that are inalienable aspects of belonging to a religious community, and serve as constituents of the community's sense of self-identity. As identity markers, they also become the dominant part of the political agenda of that unique religious community to protect and preserve its identity. For Gandhi, religious faith is faith in a certain form of life, with the religious and non-religious aspects of such a form of life constructed into a system through the mediation of tradition and time. Most central to such a form of life, for Gandhi, is God, so that the primary relationship in religion is between the believer and his God.

One must, however, also take note of Gandhi's argument that religions in South Asia did not necessarily have a conception of God analogous to that of the Semitic religions. The Buddhist and the Jain metaphysics by which Gandhi was strongly influenced, for instance, did not conceive of God as a creator, sustainer, and destroyer of the world. Buddhism denied God and permanence entirely, believing only in moral progress toward the complete annihilation of the narrow personal self. Jainism included belief in *Tirthankaras*, or human souls achieving perfection through a progressive moral ascent and freedom from passions. That Gandhi was well acquainted with the religious metaphysics of this school is documented by his relationship with the Jain mystic Ravjibhai. Gandhi also reflected on Buddhism, speaking often on the Buddha's alleged denial of God, as he did in the weekly newspaper *Young India* on 24 November 1927: "I have heard it contended times without number ... that the Buddha did not believe in God. In my opinion such a belief contradicts the very central fact of the Buddha's teaching ... He undoubtedly rejected the notion that a being called God was actuated by malice, could repent of his actions ... He emphasized and re-declared the eternal and unalterable existence of the moral government of this universe. He unhesitatingly said that the law was God Himself" (quoted in Prabhu and Rao 1967, 96). With respect to the orthodox Hindu tradition, Gandhi was familiar with both *Advaita* and *Samkhya* metaphysics, neither of which seem to have endorsed the conception of a personal God. Gandhi referred to the former frequently, and familiarity with the latter is evidenced by his commentary on the Bhagavad-Gita.

It is in the philosophical context of such metaphysics that Gandhi constructed the conception of God so central to his understanding of religion. Gandhi identified God as Truth, an identification for which there is no precursor in any religious tradition with which he might have been acquainted. Gandhi seems to be arguing for an understanding of religion in terms of the progressive moral perfection of the devotee. He did not seek to secularize morality and make it independent of religion, but reconstructed religious faith itself, in line with certain parts of the Indian tradition, as a form of life primarily engaged with moral progress. Gandhi (quoted in Bose 1948) argues for this position extensively and in several places:

> To me God is truth and love, God is ethics and morality. (original quote in *Young India* 5 March 1925; Bose 1948, 3)

> I do not regard God as a person. Truth for me is God, and God's law and God are not different things or facts, in the sense that an earthly King and his law are different. Because God is an idea, law Himself. (original quote in *The Harijan* 23 March 1940; Bose 1948, 6)

> True Religion and True morality are inseparably bound up with each other. Religion is to morality what water is to the seed that is sown in the soil. (original quote in Gandhi's *Ethical Religion*; Bose 1948, 255)

From such statements, Gandhi's interpretation of any specific religion can be reconstructed as the articulation of a world view involving a set of linguistic-cultural conditions and a framework of texts, stories, myths, festivals, and idols that uniquely induct individuals into the primary human vocation of leading the moral life. The progress toward perfecting this vocation is religious salvation, variously defined in the Indian philosophical context as *moksha, kaivalya* and *nirvana*. It is important to emphasize that on this account religion necessarily involves a specific world view or set of conditions that make possible the devotee's primary engagement with morality.

Gandhi clearly understood the importance of religious identity and the sense of belonging to a religious community for the religious man. However, he understood the relationship that constituted such belonging differently from people like Savarkar and Jinnah. Significantly, Gandhi did not understand religions solely or primarily as ideologies, but as providing for the devotee's essential engagement with the human vocation of living the moral life. For Gandhi, the religious community and its constitutive factors were simply the enabling conditions for such a life. Hence, the devotee, for Gandhi, was certainly related to and most comfortable with his religious community and its constitutive factors – the temple, idol, and mosque. But this was a relationship between the moral agent and the religious community as constituted by the world view and set of symbols that expedited his living of the moral life. This position implies that (1) religion as a form of life for the man of faith is pervaded by a certain attachment and commitment to the religious community to which he belongs as the enabler of his living out the religious/moral form of life; and (2) if the community or the symbols become destructive of what they were constituted to enable – that is, the devotee's moral vocation – the devotee can reform that community or such symbols. It can even be argued that the devotee has, in that case, a moral duty to subject those aspects of the world view to examination and reform.[1]

For Gandhi there is an indissoluble bond between the religious community and the devotee due to the role played by the religious world view and the elements constituting the community's sense of self-identity in the devotee's life. To reconstruct Gandhi in such terms may seem a little difficult given that it may remind us of a context where the emphasis on the socio-cultural elements in religion have formed the substance of political strategies connected with religions as ideologies. However, such associations should not be taken to imply that socio-cultural conditions have no part in religion as faith. Simply through their relationship with time as the past, these non-religious elements become a part of the devotee's sense of self-identity. They enter the devotee's relation with the past through his act of remembering his ancestors and through his desire for continuity with them by participation in the same tradition. Many religions in their symbolic aspects recover the devotee's relation to the past through the memory of his own ancestors, via rituals propitiating those ancestors. These very rituals entrench the non-religious constituents of religion as felt constituents of self-identity, continuous through time, for the devotee. Gandhi, in *Young India* on 2 July 1926, thus speaks of this expression of a sort of solidarity with one's ancestors through following their set of cultural-symbolic rituals: "During our earthly existence there will always be these labels. I, therefore, prefer to retain the label of my forefathers so long as it does not cramp my growth and does not debar me from assimilating all that is good anywhere else" (quoted in Prabhu and Rao 1967, 92).

The other important insight here is the givenness or inevitability of the religious community, with its world view and attendant cultural-linguistic elements that, taken together, construct the devotee's sense of self-identity. This capital, as Gandhi puts it, is like a base in terms of which the devotee or believer lives out his moral life. The non-religious elements and the specific religious/moral beliefs that are constructive of the believer's sense of himself becomes so intimately linked that it is difficult to sieve them apart – hence Gandhi's belief that conversion would be destructive of a believer's sense of himself. At times, however, it might become necessary to distinguish the non-religious from the specifically religious/moral elements that make up sectarian religions. This is a conceptual possibility consistent with Gandhi's understanding of religion. Since religion is understood in this way, at any time when the non-religious elements disenable the living of the good life, the devotee must subject them to a re-examination.

It might now be possible to answer the question of how Gandhi understands the relationship between the devotee and the religious community in sustaining the religious form of life. Any answer will obviously have implications for the way in which secularism can be understood. Clearly, for Gandhi, both religious world view and the devotee's engagement with his moral vocation are inalienable aspects of religion as an institution. Yet the fact that the former exists as a given set of enabling conditions for the latter accords a certain priority to the individual's moral life vis-à-vis the religious community. Of the religious man's engagement with the moral life, Gandhi, it can be argued, believes in the autonomy of morals. There are two ways he might have construed the living of the good life within religion as world view and enabler of that life. He might have conceived of the world view as prior to the moral life, or he might have conceived of the moral life as prior to the religious world view. By "prior" here I mean not prior in time but independent of.

While Gandhi does not attempt to derive one from the other, he clearly seems to have argued for the priority of the individual moral life over the religious world view, in the sense that he understood morality as being independent of that world view and of the cultural-linguistic framework of institutionalized religion. Certainly, it is the religious world view provided by institutionalized religion that provides the conditions occasioning the devotee's induction into the moral life. Yet to be religious, for Gandhi, is to live the moral life rather than to share in the world view of a particular religious community. This is evident from Gandhi's (quoted in Bose 1948) arguments that an atheist can be a truly God-fearing man:

> I recall the name of Charles Bradlaugh who delighted to call Himself an atheist, but knowing as I do something of him, I would never regard him as an atheist. I would call him a God-fearing man, though, I know he would reject the claim ... I would automatically disarm his criticism by saying that Truth is God. (original quote in *Young India* 31 December 1931; Bose 1948, 4)

> As soon as we lose the moral basis we cease to be religious. There is no such thing as religion overriding morality. Man for instance cannot be

untruthful, cruel and incontinent and claim to have God on his side. (original quote in *Young India* 24 November 1921; Bose 1948, 255)

The question of the priority of the moral, or of the need for examination of the world view/ideology of particular religions, arises only in very specific contexts. By "world view/ideology," I reiterate that I mean the set of cultural-linguistic conditions, myths, rituals, language and so forth that constitute the non-religious beliefs of a particular religious community. In terms of Nandy's distinction, one can call such conditions the sub-national or national markers of a particular religious community. The context for the examination of such world views, associated with particular institutionalized religions, arises most frequently when there is confrontation with the religious other. This brings me to the second question: What in Gandhi's view ought to be the relationship between one religion and another, and between one religious community and another?

This question has special relevance for the Indian version of secularism, given India's situation as a multi-religious polity. The most common answer is in terms of being tolerant of, or having an equal respect for, all religions. However, it is important to consider the reasons given for such tolerance, or for respect for faiths other than one's own. We require here a preliminary answer to a related question, about the purpose of secularism. If we know the reasons for upholding secularism, we can determine why we should be tolerant or respectful toward religious world views different from our own. One answer, offered by Charles Taylor (1998), emphasizes the constitutive link between secularism and modern democracy, and equal citizenship. For him, democratic legitimacy presupposes a horizontal, direct-access society. Consequently, political secularism is a requirement of modern democracy. No matter our substantive conceptions of the good or our religious world views, we need to tolerate other ones because this is an inescapable requirement of the modern democratic state.

The "overlapping consensus view" made famous by Rawls (2005), on the other hand, recognizes that this common political ethic will not suffice by itself as a reason for secularism, or for being tolerant of the religious other. That is because the existing grounds for convergence may not be available to people with different moral and spiritual backgrounds. The people who agree on tolerance will have some deeper substantive understanding of the good in which their being tolerant is embedded. The aim is then to respect the diversity of all such views, while building agreement on the ethics about which there is an overlapping consensus. Here, the ground of convergence can be a set of politico-ethical principles and goods, but it is recognized that this ground requires support, and that there may be more than one set of reasons for accepting it.

How should we understand Gandhi's reasons for endorsing secularism in relation to these models? These reasons were rooted in a political ethics connected to Enlightenment values, such as democracy and the integrity and freedom of human beings. Gandhi (1968) says, in *Hind Swaraj*, that those who are conscious of the spirit of nationality cannot let religion be divisive. Yet he also had views on the nature of the relationship between different religious communities that went further than political secularism. For Gandhi, religion as a way of life (where that means living the good human life), requires being able to respect both the religious way of life and religious world view of the other. Gandhi (1963) often makes arguments suggesting that it is *irreligious* – and not only a political or moral mistake – to disrespect the religious other:

> Hindu-Muslim unity requires the mussalmans to tolerate not as a virtue of necessity, not as a policy, but as a part of their religion, the religion of others so long as they, the latter, believe it to be true. Even so it is expected that the Hindus extend the same tolerance as a matter of faith and religion to the religions of all others, no matter how repugnant they may appear to their (the Hindus) sense of religion. (40)

> To revile one another's faith, to make reckless statements, to utter untruth, to break the heads of innocent men, to desecrate temples or mosques, is a denial of God. (42)

These statements need to be interpreted in the context of Gandhi's understanding of religion. For Gandhi, as noted, religions are ways of living the good human life for the faithful. The non-religious elements that provide for the individual's induction into such a life are important, but it is the moral vocation of the faithful that accounts for the specifically religious beliefs of the institutionalized religions of the world. Thus, to lead the good human life is to be religious. As Gandhi writes in *The Harijan* on 25 May 1935, to follow truth and non-violence (often spoken of by Gandhi as love) is to be God-fearing, for truth is God (quoted in Prabhu and Rao 1967, 51.) And this path requires the location of the self in a context involving the other, from whose presence the exercise of virtue and the leading of the moral life gain their urgency. To break places of worship valued by others, therefore, to be violent to followers of other faiths – in other words, to be immoral in one's dealings with the religious other – is literally to deny God and hence to be irreligious.

At this point, Gandhi's position may seem to be circular. Gandhi claims that to follow the moral law is to be religious, a claim that rests on the distinction Gandhi himself draws between religion as faith and religion as world view. But what if other religious world views do not accept such a distinction? Or if followers of any one religion believe that other religious communities are constructed around a world view that does not enable the life of goodness?

Gandhi offers two arguments in this context. One involves the claim that it is incumbent on the religious man living in a multi-religious society to read sympathetically the scriptures of other faiths in order to develop an understanding of them. The second asserts that it is part of human goodness to assume the existence of the same goodness in others. In relation to the first claim, Gandhi argues that for any religious man living in a multi-religious society and seeking to follow his religion in the living out of a good human life, it will be essential to respond to the religious other. In order for such a response to be morally appropriate, some education about that other will be essential. Therefore: "I hold that it is the duty of every cultured man or woman to read sympathetically the scriptures of the world ... a friendly study of the world's religions is a sacred duty" (Gandhi 1963, 66).

Gandhi's argument clearly rules out the conceptual closure of one's own religion, which would transform institutional religion into nothing more than religion as world view or ideology. While ideology may remain alongside specifically religious moral beliefs, to negate the latter is to depart from the religious. Morality necessarily involves engagement with others, for one cannot be good, truthful, or non-violent, or indeed deepen one's understanding of moral concepts, as a solitary being. One might recall here Iris Murdoch's (2001) point that moral or value concepts are different from empirical concepts like "chair" in that our knowledge of them grows over time, and on account of our relations with others. In a society where those relevant others are religious others, relations with them structure the knowledge and practice of moral or value concepts. To enclose believers in a structure of belief is to rule out the deepening of the knowledge and understanding of value concepts within that structure. Hence, to be a true religious believer qua moral aspirant, one must interact with, and read sympathetically, religious scriptures other than one's own.

It could well be countered by a devotee that "other" religions do not offer the prospect for a deepening of the individual's understanding of

moral or value concepts. Such is the belief of those who claim that followers of other faiths are fundamentally mistaken. The second Gandhian
insight into the religious life rules out such a belief. Related to the first insight, it posits that in order to prevent the closure of our own religious system into ideology and nothing more, it is essential to sustain faith in other
systems and other human beings. In Kantian terms, one could perhaps reconstruct this Gandhian insight in the following manner. It is a postulate
entailed by the moral law as a law of practical reason that we believe in
the possibility of the moral life and the same law for all others who are
human like ourselves. To be rationally consistent, practical reason legis-
lates the universality of the moral law as a law of human reason. To make
the moral exception of ourselves the condition of our religious system as
moral beings is to enclose our system of beliefs and is essentially to negate
the possibility of leading the good human life. For Gandhi, the good
human life necessarily involves the other and equally necessarily involves
the belief that the other is good or can be good. Without this belief, there
is no conceptual possibility of seeking the truth in interactions with the
other. For Gandhi (1963, 33), truth is God and to rule out the possibility
of seeking truth in the religious other is to deny God in all such interactions: "We must trust each other always but in the last resort we must trust
ourselves and our God." Again, Gandhi wrote in *Young India* on 28 August
1924: "I am an iconoclast in the sense that I break down the subtle form
of idolatry in the shape of fanaticism that refuses to see any virtue in any
other form of worshipping the deity save one's own. This form of idolatry
is more deadly for being more fine and evasive than the tangible and gross
form of worship that identifies the Deity with a little bit of a stone or a
golden image" (quoted in Prabhu and Rao 1967, 104). For Gandhi, the
proper relationship between one religion and another is one of friendship
and fellowship, based, as friendship must be, in a mutual understanding
of each other.

I will now look briefly at the third question I posited in my approach
to reconstructing a Gandhian secularism, namely: How must the modern
state deal with religions and religious communities given that the religious form of life is an authentic form of life? Statements about the inseparability of politics and religion notwithstanding, Gandhi is clear that
the state and religion should be entirely separate, for two sorts of reasons.
The first are reasons deriving from the conception of the nation-state itself: for instance, the argument that the construction of the nation-state as
a contractual project requires that those who wish to participate in the
contract, and in the subsequent state, do not let religion be divisive. Fur-

thermore, the state is concerned with the regulation of the political, civic, and economic well-being of its citizens, not their moral and religious well-being.[2] The second sort of arguments regarding separation of state and religion in Gandhi's writings seems to be derived from the nature of religion. For instance, he argues that any religion that seeks state support for its sustenance is not a religion worth the name.[3] Gandhi was therefore not supportive of religious instruction in schools on the basis of state aid, or of temple reconstruction with state help.

But how can this position on secularism be reconciled with Gandhi's oft-quoted argument about the inseparability of politics and religion? As I have attempted to argue in my reconstruction of Gandhi's position, religion (for Gandhi) can be understood as the induction of the individual devotee into the moral life. In living the moral life, the religious devotee must engage with politics as setting the conditions for the possibility of such a life in society. In that context, the devotee's religion, qua living of the good human life, must involve his/her engagement with politics as a service of society. In this connection it is important to note that Gandhi himself distinguished between "true politics" and "power politics," and clarified that his contention regarding the inseparability of politics and religion was to be restricted to what he termed true politics. True politics is politics as service whereas power politics is the politics of seeking positions of power in the government, in political institutions and in political parties (Gandhi 1999, 371). Therefore the religious qua moral man's engagement with true politics does not compromise Gandhian statements about the absolute separation of state and denominational religions. Equally clearly, the devotee's religion in the form of world view or ideology, and as a political agenda/power politics, cannot have any relevance to the state. Gandhi clearly said that the state should have nothing to do with religion. He also said that morality politics and religion cannot be separated. However, Gandhi used the term politics, in this last statement, in the sense of true politics not politics of power. Therefore there is no opposition between the two sets of statements. Gandhi was not an anti-secularist, nor is it the case (as Nandy and Madan argue) that Gandhi rejected the separation of state and religion.

THE INDIAN STATE AND THE PRACTICE OF SECULARISM

Having attempted to reconcile the seemingly contradictory Gandhian statements appropriated by both sides of the debate on secularism, I move to the second part of my chapter, asking: Is it possible to describe the constitutional practice of secularism in India as Gandhian? Or can the secularism laid down in the constitution be made amenable to Gandhian commitments, even if the constitutional practice of secularism in India in the past decades has not been consistent with Gandhian principles?

While Gandhi was unequivocal on the need to separate the state and institutional religions, the practice of secularism in India does not reflect a total separation of the state and religion. On this issue, we need to examine Indian constitutionalism and the practice of secularism in the decades following independence. Quite clearly, the framework adopted by the constitution endorsed the non-establishment of religion without advocating the separation of state and religion. Distinguishing between the right to religious worship and the right to practice religion, the constitution of India allowed the state, in principle, to regulate religious life in the public domain.[4] Moreover, it is fair to say that the courts not only regulated religious practice but also interpreted religious belief. Perhaps practice and belief cannot be easily separated in the history of religions themselves.

Gurpreet Mahajan and Rajeev Bhargava have described Indian secularism as an alternative to mainstream Western secularism both in its idealized French and American models. Mahajan (1998, 300) claims that the fact that the Indian Constitution allowed the state in principle to interfere in religion "set it apart from other liberal politics of that time." Bhargava (Sikka and Beaman 92, this volume) argues that Western states would do well to learn from the "original Indian variant," the principled distance model of secularism, which has "better ethical and moral potential to deal with deep religious diversity." Such a model allows the state to interfere with inter-religious and intra-religious matters on the basis of values and principles to which it is committed. My purpose in this section is to examine this understanding of secular practice in India, with a view to evaluating its consistency with a reconstructed Gandhian position on secularism. To this end, I will examine Bhargava's understanding of Indian secularism, along with the chief arguments he advances in support of what he terms the "principled distance" model.

The idealized French conception of secularism views the state as separated from religion, but as retaining the power to interfere in religion. Religion, for its part, is divested of any power to interfere in matters of the state. Here separation means one-sided exclusion. By contrast, the idealized American self-understanding of secularism interprets separation to mean mutual exclusion. Neither the state nor religion is meant to interfere in the domains of the other. Such mutual separation is believed necessary for religious liberty and for the general liberties of individuals. This strict separation, it is argued, must take place at three distinct levels: ends, institutions and personnel, and law and public policy. The Congress has no power to legislate on any matters pertaining to religion.

The constitutional practice of secularism in India, by contrast, reflects the principled distance model, which Bhargava (Sikka and Beaman 85, this volume) describes in the following way: "The idea of principled distance unpacks the metaphor of separation differently. It accepts a disconnection between state and religion at the level of ends and institutions but does not make a fetish of it at the third level of policy and law." Bhargava makes two kinds of arguments in support of this model. First, he argues that it is an original Indian variant of secularism not based upon the post-Enlightenment view of religion, which implies that this version of secularism has arisen from Indian conditions and is not a derivative model dependent upon Western liberalism. The second sort of claim is normative. The principled distance model of secularism is said to be ethically superior to other available Western models of secularism. Bhargava states that there are two defining features of the Indian model that give it its normative superiority: principled distance and contextual secularism. I will consider whether principled distance can be interpreted as consistent with a Gandhian position on secularism. I will also ask whether the specific arguments made by Bhargava in support of that model are philosophically convincing or consistent with the Gandhian position I reconstructed in the first part of this chapter. The arguments offered for principled distance might influence not only the practice of secularism but also our conception of the idea of principled distance itself. Bhargava provides this definition:

> The policy of principled distance entails a flexible approach on the question of inclusion/exclusion of religion and the engagement/ disengagement of the state, which at the level of law and policy depends on the context, nature, or current state of relevant religions. This engagement must be governed by principles undergirding a secular state, that is, principles that flow from a commitment to the values mentioned above. This means that religion may intervene in the affairs of the state if such intervention promotes freedom, equality, or any other value integral to secularism ... Equally the state may engage with religion or disengage with it, engage positively or negatively, but it does so depending entirely on whether or not these values are promoted or undermined. A state that intervenes or refrains from interference on this basis keeps a principled distance from all religions. (Sikka and Beaman 85–6, this volume)

Bhargava supports this rejection of strict neutrality, entailed by principled distance, with a normative argument deriving from Dworkin's distinction between equal treatment and treating everyone as an equal (see Guest 2012, 147). The former requires that the state treat all its citizens equally in the relevant respect. The latter entails that every person or group is treated with equal respect and concern. This may sometimes require equal treatment, but it may sometimes require unequal treatment, because treating people or groups as equals is entirely consistent with differential treatment. Examples given by Bhargava include religious groups seeking exemptions from laws meant to apply neutrally to the rest of society, or the state intervening to grant special assistance to religious groups (for example, authority being granted to religious officials to perform legally binding marriages). Somewhat more problematically, he notes that for the promotion of a particular value constitutive of secularism, some religions may require more interference from the state relative to others. For example, the state may be required to interfere more in caste-ridden Hinduism to bring in social equality (Bhargava 2000).

The other constituent of the Indian model – what Bhargava calls its contextual character – defends this differential treatment by a normative argument of another kind. It is argued that this model of secularism embodies a form of contextual moral reasoning, due to its character as a multivalue doctrine. Since multiple values are always in conflict, they require fresh interpretations, contextual judgments, and attempts at reconciliation and compromise. For Bhargava, "Multi-value doctrines such as secularism encourage accommodation—not the giving up of one value for the sake of another but rather their reconciliation and possible harmonization, that is, to make each work without changing the basic content of apparently incompatible concepts and values" (Sikka and Beaman 88, this volume).

It might be possible to reconstruct the principled distance model of secularism in a Gandhian manner. However, both of the normative arguments used by Bhargava to establish the ethical superiority of this model are problematic. His first set of arguments, claiming that Indian secularism is substantially different from Western liberal versions, is difficult to accept in view of the role played by the courts on this issue in the decades following independence. It needs to be kept in mind here that Bhargava (Sikka and Beaman 76, this volume) speaks not about an idealized version of a principled distance model, but of "the best practices of non-Western states such as India." Does the practice of the principled distance model in India really articulate a view of religion that presents an alternative to the predominant Enlightenment understanding of religion? Bhargava claims that the Indian model does not share the Enlightenment view of religion. It accepts the fact that human beings have interests in relating to something beyond themselves, primarily to a God. This manifests as individual belief and also as social practice in the public domain. But one could argue that the constitutional practice of the principled distance model of Indian secularism, far from rejecting the Enlightenment view of religion, is more firmly entrenched in it than the idealized American model.

To begin, what is the Enlightenment view of religion? The post-Enlightenment world may be described as an age of skepticism and absence of faith, characterized by a commitment to humanist values and a particular epistemology. In pre-modern civilizations, man certainly occupied an important place, but the highest object of man's moral and spiritual attention was something other than himself. It might have been the spiritual reality permeating the world, the cosmic order, or God. For post-Enlightenment humanism, man in his ordinariness, as a biological creature with desires and emotions, is the only proper object of our moral attention. Moral endeavour must consist in the pursuit of the welfare of man understood in this sense. Accordingly, the values associated with this humanist stance are the value of human life, of human freedom, avoidance of pain, and the pursuit of pleasure. Another defining feature of modernity is its commitment to a Western epistemology dominated by natural science. Knowledge, within this epistemology, is supposed to be uncontaminated by human subjectivity and mediated by a disengaged human reason. Such reason reveals the disenchanted world denuded of spirituality and of any telos or proper end of human existence (Miri 2003, 118–19). That is why, after the Enlightenment, it has been difficult to establish religion and morality as playing a substantive role in the properly human qua rational life.

The principled distance model of secularism accepts that the state can interfere differentially in denominational religions in the interests of liberal humanist values such as human freedom, equality, human dignity, and the avoidance of pain. Thus, one could argue that this model is consistent with a post-Enlightenment understanding of the nature of religion. In that case, principled distance shares a history with liberalism. Furthermore, the practice of principled distance in India points toward a liberal and post-Enlightenment understanding of religion itself. Principled distance is then not an Indian variant of secularism, as Bhargava believes. In fact, it has been argued by Pratap Bhanu Mehta (2008) that the constitutional practice of secularism in India may be described as Hobbesian. The relevant point made by Mehta is that the normative idea that the state ought to be allowed in principle to interfere with religion has its source in Western liberalism. From the burdens of private judgment, Hobbes concluded that in setting up a state people give up the right to private judgment. Furthermore, the state is the final authority empowered to make judgments about when society is in peril. From this view, not only social peril but also putting the public purposes of the state in jeopardy can permit the state to curb the exercise of the right to private judgment. Hobbes argued that a sovereign could, in order to make contending religious doctrines congruent with the purposes of the state, acquire authority over the interpretation of religion.

Within contemporary liberalism, Rawls (2005, 61) has argued that some form of liberty of conscience or reasonable pluralism was produced due to the burdens of judgment: "Reasonable persons see the burdens of judgment set limits on what can be reasonably justified to others, and so endorse some forms of liberty of conscience or freedom of thought ... it is unreasonable to use political power to repress comprehensive doctrines that are not unreasonable." This position on liberty of conscience is not as different from Hobbes' view as may at first appear. Its presuppositions come from similar foundations in liberal philosophy. For reasonable pluralism can be taken to imply that religious persons are to have an attachment to their first-order beliefs coupled with a second-order belief in their insufficiency. The point is that, though liberalism claims to be able to accommodate various comprehensive doctrines, liberal values compete with other comprehensive doctrines in civil society. The tension produced leads to a watering down of comprehensive doctrines other than liberalism to a point where they are to be made compatible with liberalism and its central values. This is also true, according to Mehta, of the constitutional practice of secularism in India and the set of interpretative practices surrounding it.

In addition, the practice of principled distance in India by the courts seems to construe religion in line with a liberal and post-Enlightenment understanding of it. Recall Mehta's (2008, 313) claim that in India "constitutional practice has not only set the content of public purposes, it has also taken upon itself the task of interpreting religious doctrine." In light of the judgments of the Indian courts during the decades following independence, the Indian version of secularism can even be viewed as being more aggressively liberal than the American one. For in India the courts openly take on the task of reinterpreting religion in line with liberal values. At times, they even argue that the true meaning of the religion at issue, if properly understood, is completely consistent with liberal values of equality, human dignity, and liberty. Any incongruity that may arise is due to a wrong understanding of religion itself.[5]

Other factors cast doubt on Bhargava's assertion that Indian secularism rejects the Enlightenment understanding of religion in adopting a principled distance model. For instance, in the earliest cases on this subject, the courts rejected the assertion of religious practitioners as evidence and came up with what was called the "essential practices" test (Sen 2007, 24). They thereafter entrusted themselves with the task of differentiating essential from non-essential religious practices. The idea that this task properly belonged to the domain of law, as defined by the liberal democratic state and practiced by the Indian courts, seems to rest on the Enlightenment view of religion. In line with liberal values, it endorses the argument that religion, being less than rational, cannot serve to regulate itself and needs to be regulated by the state. Hence, the assertion about a religious practice made by a religious man cannot serve as evidence in this context, and the courts must replace it by bringing in the essential practices test, imposed on the religious community from outside that form of life. To use the distinction between "the mode of limitation and the mode of intervention" of "religious controls" by the state and legal system (Galanter 1998, 284), the Indian state is involved in a form of "internal re-interpretation of Hinduism" (ibid., 285–6).

This is quite in keeping with liberal humanist values and the presuppositions of modern epistemology about religion. I turn now to the normative arguments made on behalf of principled distance by Bhargava, beginning with his employment of the distinction between equal treatment and treating everyone as an equal. The latter entails differential treatment. However, the justification of differential treatment as normatively superior might lead not only to differential intervention on the basis of principles to which the state is committed, but to a differential intervention by the state in one religion over another. This could distort a particular religion by locating all reformist activity outside it, thereby incapacitating its internal life and vitality. Such treatment might end up (in practice) as being unjust and hence both normatively inferior and non-secular. Consequently, the arguments advanced in support of the normative superiority of principled distance need to be carefully examined.

Bhargava claims that the principled distance model of secularism is ethically superior to alternative Western models, as it permits differential treatment in the interest of treating everyone as an equal. Such differen-

tial intervention, as mentioned earlier, can involve external or internal regulation of religion, in the interest of principles to which the state is committed. Bhargava gives the example of permitting religious groups certain
exceptions from the common law. This is arguably an example of external
regulation, oriented toward measures vigorously debated within Western
models of secularism as well, where exceptions are often made for religious groups. An example is the case of Muslim women wearing head
scarves in Canada. There is insufficient basis to claim that only the principled distance model of Indian secularism permits the state to undertake
external regulation of religious communities in order to treat them (in
view of their special beliefs) as equal to other communities.

However, the Indian model also seems to permit the state to undertake
internal regulation of religious belief, as in the case of various interventions into Hinduism by the Indian courts. Here, it seems possible to make
a finer distinction between state interventions involving internal regulation of religious practice, and those involving regulation of belief. The
practice of the principled distance model of secularism through the Indian courts, however, makes no such fine distinction.

When the state intervenes in the form of internal regulation of religious
practice (for example by promulgating the temple entry acts in Hinduism), it is in keeping with Dworkin's principle of treating everyone as
equal. When the state intervenes by internally regulating religious belief,
however, it may sometimes depart from that principle. For it may then
treat a religious community as incapable of evaluating its own allegiance
to a set of religious beliefs. For instance, when it argues that a trust formed
to feed milk to cobras in a temple cannot count as a Hindu religious trust,
it discounts beliefs about the sacred nature of cobras. The court did exactly that in the case of *Shastri Yagnapurashdasji v. Muldas Bhundardas
Vaisya*, 1966 AIR 1119, [1966] SCR (3) 242 at 323. To evaluate a religious belief within the framework of modern science, pronouncing it not only
non-rational but also non-religious, is to pass the judgment that the religious community as irrational requires state regulation of its beliefs. On
this account, to be eligible for equal treatment by the state, the individual
or group must pass the test of being rational. As religion frequently fails
this test, its internal beliefs must be regulated by the state, even where
such beliefs do not conflict with any other value, principle or common
law to which the state is committed.

That such cases are equally expressive of principled distance makes it
difficult to sustain Bhargava's claim about the ethical superiority of the
principled distance model on the basis of Dworkin's distinction. I recog-

nize that this case and others could be seen as aberrations, and that in its idealized form principled distance would require interventions on the basis of normative principles. But this argument for equality of treatment through the normative superiority of principled intervention is not accompanied by a theoretical caveat about the possible principles or commitments on the basis of which principled distance might proceed so as to rule out these aberrations. The principles of principled distance are described only as "freedom, equality or any other value integral to secularism." This important theoretical gap permits discourses justifying interventions on the basis of other liberal principles. It can also allow justifications of differential treatment of religions based on their openness to such interventions. There has been serious criticism that the Indian nation-state used its agency for the religious reform of Hinduism and thereby violated the principal of separation of state and religion (Chatterjee 1998, 357).

Regarding Bhargava's second argument for the superiority of the Indian model, to argue that principled distance is based upon the recognition of multiple values (requiring fresh interpretations, contextual judgments and attempts at reconciliation) assumes that it may be possible for the state to reconcile conflicts of values in inter-religious space through intervention. But given a plurality of values, reconciling them will be difficult whether or not there is a constitutional framework that allows for differential interventions into religion. Indeed, reconciling diverse values such as the liberty of conscience with the demands of equality, rationality, and human dignity might not be possible at all. In Isaiah Berlin's (1998, 197) words: "Everything is what it is: liberty is liberty, not equality or fairness or justice or culture, or human happiness or a quiet conscience. If the liberty of myself or my class or nation depends on the misery of a number of human beings, the system which promotes this is immoral. But if I curtail or lose my freedom in order to lessen the shame of such inequality, and do not thereby materially increase the individual liberty of others, an absolute loss of liberty occurs." Contextual moral reasoning may not always lead to the reconciliation of conflicting values, and differential intervention by the state may lead to an absolute loss of religious liberty. This may happen predominantly in relation to a particular religion and so amount to a departure from secularism. The fact that it might happen ought to be noted, for to underscore the theoretical possibility is to become aware of practical possibilities at the same time.

My final question is whether this position is consistent with Gandhi's. Can there be Gandhian arguments for principled distance? As I noted earlier, the sort of arguments we accept for this position might substantially alter the conception and practice of principled distance itself. Gandhi insisted on the separation between state and religion. Yet he also said quite clearly that nation building requires a certain commitment to inter-religious harmony, respect for the law of the land and a decision not to let religion be divisive. These principles then might serve to construct Gandhian arguments for principled distance. Interestingly, Gandhi suggests that the state must not intervene in missionary efforts, even though he was himself very critical of conversion. Hence, if Gandhi believed that secularism could involve principled intervention by the state in the internal affairs of religions, he should have approved of legislation against conversion. On the face of it, however, Gandhi rejected such intervention. He wrote in *The Harijan* on 24 August 1947 (quoted in Bose 1948, 256): "The state should undoubtedly be secular. Everyone living in it should be entitled to profess his religion without let or hindrance, so long as the citizen obeyed the common law of the land. There should be no interference with missionary effort but no mission could enjoy the patronage of the state as it did during the foreign regime."

In the case of missionary effort, there can be two conflicting principles: the right to propagate religion and the right of the other person to religious freedom. Unless conversion involves threat, force, fraud or inducement, therefore, it might be difficult to justify the right of the state to intervene against missionary effort to propagate religion. Gandhi seemed to believe that this would be not only an ethical but a religious mistake. For to protect the believer qua believer legally from conversion, unless such threats were involved, would progressively take away the sense of agency from the religious believer as a religious man. It might then so emasculate his religious life that no religion worth the name would be left. Hence the danger of over-interpretation as a protective cover ought not to be forgotten. Consequently, Gandhi seems to have endorsed principled intervention only on the basis of clearly defined principles such as common law, social harmony, and secular welfare, to which citizens are committed by the act of entering the nation-state itself. A Gandhian position would then not lead to arguments supporting contextual moral reasoning where the court takes on a predominantly reinterpretative, and thereby reforming, role in religious belief.

It might still be possible to offer another Gandhian argument for principled distance. Perhaps the state could justifiably intervene in the religious world view of a community – its practices, rituals, texts, and festivals – on the basis of religious qua moral insights consistent with primary religious beliefs of that community. The state could then intervene to regulate internal religious practice or belief only if it could demonstrate that this practice or belief conflicted with moral principles to which that religious community either could have been committed to in the past, or could see itself committed to in the present. On this view, the *Satsangi* case would be consistent with Gandhian secularism while the cobra case would interpret principled distance too expansively.

A strong caveat in any Gandhian version of principled distance as a model of secularism has to be that the state must not intervene with any religion to the extent of undermining its relevance in the life process of the community and the believer. If one considers Gandhi's critique of modernity in *Hind Swaraj*, where a central theme is that modernity is an irreligious and immoral form of life, it becomes clear that Gandhi believed there is little space for religion in an Enlightenment framework. He argued that modernity (committed to humanism and modern epistemology) finds itself preoccupied with bodily welfare and has no space for an individual's spiritual or moral well-being. Therefore, it is likely that Gandhi would have wanted the courts (which he saw as symbols of modernity) to exercise great restraint in undertaking interventions into an individual's religious life.

In this context it is relevant that Gandhi drew a distinction between nation and state. In *Hind Swaraj*, he argued that, while India had been a nation from the time of the shankaracharyas (who established temples in all the corners of the land), those wanting to create an Indian state out of that nation ought not to let religion be divisive. He seemed to have endorsed the liberal contractual understanding of the state as an instrumental institution entered into by citizens purely for political and economic purposes. As part of that contract, citizens have to respect common law and live peacefully with persons of other religions. But Gandhi was clear that man could not surrender to the state his right to private judgment in the domains of religion and moral life, for these are not amenable to such an instrumental approach. The state is an institution with jurisdiction over empirical well-being. It has no jurisdiction over a man's religious life as long as the latter does not conflict with any other principle, political or moral, to which the religious man could be shown to be committed.

Hence, as a religious man, Gandhi insisted on retaining the right to private judgment in the matter of religion, other things remaining equal. In that case, the constitutional practice of Indian secularism in the years following independence may not be consistent with Gandhian secularism. Any version of principled distance acceptable to Gandhi would have to contain safeguards protecting the right of the believer to make private judgments in the religious domain. At the same time, arguments supporting principled distance such as those presented by Bhargava might be enriched by exploring alternative possibilities provided by Gandhi's thought. While existing arguments have taken cognizance of substantive notions of the good, their conception has seemed purely procedural. By contrast, Gandhian secularism, and possible Gandhian arguments in support of principled distance, can be characterized as seeking an internal route from religious belief to secularism. Hence, Gandhian secularism can be classified as a substantive and religious form of secularism.

NOTES

1 Consider, for instance, some of the arguments Gandhi made in *Young India* on 6 October 1921 in the context of his critique of conversion:

   I can no more describe my feeling for Hinduism any more than for my wife. She moves me as no other woman in the world can. Not that she has no faults. I dare say that she has many more than I see myself. But the feeling of an indissoluble bond is there. Even so I feel about Hinduism with all its faults and limitations … I am a reformer through and through. But my zeal never takes me to a rejection of any of the essential things in Hinduism. (quoted in Bose 1948, 261)

   I am both a supporter and opponent of image worship. When image worship degenerates into idolatry and becomes encrusted with false beliefs and doctrines it becomes necessary to combat it as a social evil. On the other hand, image worship in the sense of investing one's ideal with a concrete shape is inherent in man's nature, and even valuable as an aid to devotion. Thus we worship an image when we offer homage to a book which we regard as holy or sacred. (quoted in Prabhu and Rao 1967, 104)

2 For example, in *The Harijan*, 22 September 1946, Gandhi (quoted in Bose 1948, 257) explains: "If I was a dictator, religion and state would be separate. I swear by my religion. I will die for it. But it is my personal affair. The state has nothing to do with it … The state would look after your secular welfare, health, communications, foreign relations, currency and so on, but not your or my religion. That is everyone's personal concern."

3 Gandhi (quoted in Prabhu and Rao 1967, 70) explains in *The Harijan* on 23 March 1947, "We have suffered enough from state-aided religion and a state church. A society or a group, which depends partly or wholly on state aid for the existence of its religion, does not deserve, or, better still, does not have any religion worth the name."

4 Gurpreet Mahajan (2008, 300) writes, "The questions of religious belief and worship were more or less sheltered from state intervention, but the state could regulate religious practices in the interest of protecting public order, morality and health."

5 See for example the statement of the Supreme Court in the *Shastri Yagna-purashdasji v. Muldas Bhundardas Vaisya*, 1966 AIR 1119, [1966] SCR (3) 242 at 325, popularly known as the Satsang case: "The satsangis apprehension about the pollution of the temple is founded on superstition, ignorance and complete misunderstanding of the true teaching of Hinduism and the real significance of the tenets and philosophy taught by Swami Narayana himself."

REFERENCES

Berlin, Isaiah. 1998. "Two Concepts of Liberty." In *The Proper Study of Mankind*, edited by Henry Hardy, and Roger Hausheer. 191–242. London: Pimlico.

Bhargava, Rajeev. 1998. "What is Secularism For?" In *Secularism and Its Critics*, edited by Rajeev Bhargava, 486–543. New Delhi: Oxford University Press.

Bilgrami, Akeel. 2006. "Gandhi's Integrity: The Philosophy Behind Politics." In *Debating Gandhi: A Reader*, edited by A. Raghuram Raju, 248–68. Oxford: Oxford University Press.

Bose, Nirmal K. 1948. *Selections from Gandhi*. Ahmedabad: Navajivan Publishing House.

Chatterjee, Partha. 1998. "Secularism and Tolerance." In *Secularism and Its Critics*, edited by Rajeev Bhargava, 345–79. New Delhi: Oxford University Press.

Galanter, Marc. 1998. "Hinduism, Secularism, and the Indian Judiciary." In *Secularism and Its Critics*, edited by Rajeev Bhargava, 268–96. New Delhi: Oxford University Press.

Gandhi, Mahatma K. 1963. *The Way to Communal Harmony*, compiled and edited by U. R. Rao. Ahmedabad: Navajivan Publishing House.

– 1968. "Hind Swaraj." In *The Selected Works of Mahatma Gandhi, The Basic Works*, vol. 4, 83–207. Ahmedabad: Navajivan Trust.

– 1999. *Collected Works of Mahatma Gandhi*, vol. 77. New Delhi: Publications Division Government of India. Available at http://www.gandhiserve.org/e/cwmg/cwmg.htm.

Guest, Stephen. 2012. *Ronald Dworkin*. Stanford: Stanford University Press.

Madan, T. N. 1998. "Secularism in Its Place." In *Secularism and Its Critics*, edited by Rajeev Bhargava, 297–320. New Delhi: Oxford University Press.

Mahajan, Gurpreet. 2008. "Religion and the Indian Constitution: Questions of Separation and Equality." In *Politics and Ethics of the Indian Constitution*, edited by Rajeev Bhargava, 297–310. New Delhi: Oxford University Press.

Mehta, Pratap B. 2008. "Passion and Constraint: Courts and the Regulation of Religious Meaning." In *Politics and Ethics of the Indian Constitution*, edited by Rajeev Bhargava, 311–38. New Delhi: Oxford University Press.

Miri, Mrinal. 2003. *Identity and the Moral Life*. Oxford: Oxford University Press.

Murdoch, Iris. 2001. *The Sovereignty of Good*. New York: Routledge Classics.

Nandy, Ashis. 1998. "The Politics of Secularism.and the Recovery of Religious Tolerance." In *Secularism and Its Critics*, edited by Rajeev Bhargava, 321–44. New Delhi: Oxford University Press.

Prabhu, R. K., and U. R. Rao, eds. 1967. *The Mind of Mahatma Gandhi*. Ahmedabad: The Navajivan Trust.

Rawls, John. 2005. *Political Secularism*. New York: Columbia University Press.

Sen, Ronojoy. 2007. *Legalizing Religion: The Indian Supreme Court and Secularism*. Policy Studies 30. Washington: East-West Center.

Tambiah, Stanley J. 1998. "The Crisis of Secularism in India." In *Secularism and Its Critics*, edited by Rajeev Bhargava, 418–54. New Delhi: Oxford University Press.

Taylor, Charles. 1998. "Modes of Secularism." In *Secularism and Its Critics*, edited by Rajeev Bhargava, 31–53. New Delhi: Oxford University Press.

5

Lessons from the Management of Religious Diversity in Chinese Societies: A Diversity of Approaches to State Control

ANDRÉ LALIBERTÉ

As Canadian and Indian experts exchange views on the place of religion in their respective societies and compare the policies of multiculturalism and secularism of their respective governments to learn from each other, a discussion of Chinese approaches can be useful. It draws our attention to one key question raised in the introduction to this volume about the challenges for Canadian and Indian decision makers as they face vocal demands from some groups to limit the expression of religion in the public and political spheres. What happens when the state actively enforces such limitations? Followers of many political persuasions in Canada and India still look rather positively at the People's Republic of China (PRC)[1] as the way of the future with respect to the place of religion in contemporary society, and the popularity of views on atheism reinforces this perspective (Hitchens 2007). In this chapter, I propose a contrarian view: the PRC does not offer a model India and Canada could learn from, but it does shed light on the consequences of rigid limitation on the expression of religiosity in the public sphere. In fact, the Chinese Communist Party (CCP) is coming to that realization, and for many people who self-identify as Chinese outside the PRC, the issue of the place of religion in the public and political sphere resurfaces.

Setting aside the issue of religious freedom in the PRC, which remains hotly debated (Tong 2009; Brookings Institution 2008; Weller 2006), what can Canadian and Indian policy makers learn from the Chinese religious situation? This chapter argues that culture is not the main determinant of whether a society can be tolerant of religious diversity, and uses the apparently counterintuitive case of China to make the point. I will argue that there are many important similarities between the Indian and Chinese forms of religions, which suggests that in many ways thinking about the regulation of religion in India could benefit considerably from the experience of China in the *longue durée*. Namely, the religious reality of China shares with India an important characteristic: in both cases, the model of relations between religion and state based on Christianity's institutional features has serious limitations, as Daniel Overmyer (2009, 4–5) had demonstrated in the case of China, and W.C. Smith (Assad 2001) for India. As Vincent Goossaert and David Palmer (2010) argued, since the end of the nineteenth century, Chinese modernizers have sought to make a distinction between a model of religions, distinct from other institutions in society, with scriptures, an ecclesiastical organization, and specific places of worship, and a model of "superstitions." This project, which the CCP has pursued from the beginning of its existence, excludes from the religious sphere many rituals, practices, beliefs, and engagements that a considerable number of scholars consider religious phenomena, such as geomancy (*feng shui*), and divination (*ba gua*). As in India, religion is deeply embedded in the fabric of social, political, and legal spheres in China (Yang [1961]1994; Katz 2003), as well as in the tourism economy (Oakes and Sutton 2010), and medical science (Palmer 2005). Finally, the PRC also shares an important institutional characteristic with India that sets both countries apart from Canada: in both cases, the state grants formal recognition to distinct religious identities.[2] Although this chapter's focus on state recognition of specific identities does not do justice to the complexity of religious life in China today, it does have the merit of pointing to the perspective that the CCP leadership wants to promote.

That being said, I want to stress that while we cannot think of the PRC as an example of a liberal management of religious diversity that could suit India's approach, there were and there are cases of more pluralist and more tolerant approaches outside the PRC before the CCP gained control of China. In other words, although there exists a distinctive and unique Chinese cultural legacy of myths, symbols, and rituals shared by people in two polities, the PRC, in mainland China, and the Republic of China (ROC), in Taiwan,[3] as well as by over thirty million overseas Chinese, there is a diversity of practices in terms of management of religious diversity in space and time. This could compare with the variety of approaches adopted to manage diversity over history and across polities in the Western world, and in the Indic world. The West has examples of state-sponsored religious intolerance in the Inquisition and anti-Semitism in its not so ancient history, alongside opposite cases of tolerance such as the policy of multiculturalism in Canada. India has its emblematic figure of Mahatma Gandhi, but also its episodes of intolerance in the rise of fundamentalist and bigoted political parties that denounce others as not true Indians. But the Chinese world also has both: cases of political persecution of religion in the Taiping Rebellion and in the Cultural Revolution, alongside cases of tolerance such as the liberal approach adopted in Taiwan since the 1980s.

It is customary to consider the PRC as the antithesis of the liberal approach to religious freedom, and therefore to dismiss the relevance of China to discussions on religious freedom and policies of multiculturalism that are respectful of religious identities. However, I suggest this can be short sighted on empirical grounds. The discussion on the matter ignores the complexity and diversity of approaches adopted by the Chinese states over time. Discussions of China's approach to religion usually focus on the policy of the CCP since 1949 and in particular its excesses during the Cultural Revolution (1966–76). However, this approach overlooks the experience of the regime that preceded it, of the states where a majority of the population shares a Chinese heritage that exist outside of the CCP control, such as the ROC, and Singapore, as well as evolutions within the PRC society and government. Moreover, discussions about governments' approaches to religion overlook an important dimension of religious freedom: individual and communal religious tolerance. This has tremendous implication for the future of religious freedom in both India and the PRC.

My chapter will make two very contrasting observations. Although the government of the PRC implements one of the most rigid jurisdictions over religious affairs in the contemporary world, the evidence from a sociological survey in Chinese society before 1949, and outside of the PRC today, reveals that the attitudes of Chinese individuals on religion are among the most tolerant in the world. This suggests the possibility that Chinese approaches to religious diversity can be of interest to both Indian and Western societies, if we accept the premise that the current policy of the CCP in the PRC is not the only possible approach to the regulation of religion and the implementation of a policy of multiculturalism by a society with a Chinese cultural heritage. This chapter will flesh out the argument by first presenting the diversity of religions in the two most important contemporary societies directly influenced by Chinese culture: that is, mainland China and Taiwan.[4] Secondly, it will compare and contrast the approaches adopted by the governments of these two societies. I will conclude the chapter with remarks from recent field observations that demonstrate that the current governments in the PRC and the ROC are contemplating changes in their approach to the regulation of religion that move in the direction of greater inclusiveness. These changes could render

them, albeit to different degrees, susceptible to adopt multicultural policies that would take into account religious diversity.

MULTICULTURALISM AND RELIGIOUS DIVERSITY IN THE PRC AND THE ROC

The PRC and multiculturalism may not appear to go together, and yet,
beyond the superficial impressions that are left by media about the
homogeneous nature of Chinese culture, China (before 1949) has been
historically multicultural since its beginning, and especially so in the
realm of religion. In that sense, China shares a lot with India, with its deep
religious diversity. The paradox, of course, is that since the ancient monar-
chy some three thousand years ago, we can talk of one elemental form of
Chinese religion. This includes beliefs in ghosts and ancestors, an anthropocosmic view that posits the correspondence between elements, ideas
about predestination, and ritual practices that involve numerology, geomancy, and incense burning. In other words, there is a Chinese religiosity
that is recognized as distinctive from other traditions, such as Islam and
Christianity, the same way that there is a Hindu world view or tradition
that is seen as distinct from Islam and Christianity and the religions of
East Asia. Moreover, from the common pool of fundamental beliefs
among Chinese, a wide variety of practices have emerged, and in some
case evolved into institutional forms (Lopez 1996). Many different religious movements have grown, some merged with others into ever changing syncretism, or simply developed their own way into new religious
movements. Again, in this very fundamental aspect, China and India share
remarkable similarities.

In addition, as is the case for India, world religions like Islam, Christianity, and Judaism had all left a trace in China before the colonial era. It
is beyond the scope of this chapter to explore this wide variety. It will suffice, for the sake of argument, to note that there exists, still today, a significant variety of religious forms in China. We can approach this variety two
ways. We can look into the two different polities seen as the repositories
of Chinese culture today, the PRC and the ROC. If a comparison between
India and China makes sense because of each country's demographic
scale, their position as massive and continent-sized emerging economies,
the more relevant comparison to Taiwan is, arguably, a country like Canada. Both are liberal democracies living in the shadow of giants. In both
cases, settlers migrated to these territories and overwhelmed the Aboriginal populations. These settlers were coming from two of the cores of the

world economy, Western Europe in the case of Canada, and Ming China in the case of Taiwan. In sum, if we want to observe the variety of approaches to the management of religious diversity within the Chinese world, the PRC ought to be compared with India, the ROC with Canada. But before we consider this, it is important to stress the similarities in religious diversity between mainland China and Taiwan.

RELIGIOUS DIVERSITY AMONG THE HAN IN THE PRC

When we look at the religious diversity within China, we can observe two types of diversities of religious beliefs. The first one is a simple distinction between Han Chinese and non-Han. Most of the Han adhere to religious practices that share some fundamental basic characteristics, and in particular some myths about the shared origins of the Chinese people, which can be labeled altogether as "Chinese folk traditions." The ethnic minorities, on the other hand, do not recognize themselves as part of this ritual community.[5] This distinction mirrors in many ways that which we observe in India between the majority who identifies with Hinduism, and the others who are not Indo-Aryan or Dravidian language speakers.[6] The second type of diversity we can note on religious matters, and which will constitute the focus of the first part of this chapter, is the religious diversity within the Han Chinese population, and which we can compare with the diversity in the world of Indic traditions, that is, Hinduism, Sikhism, Jainism, etc. We can analyze this religious diversity in China in turn along five dimensions, four of which have to do with religious institutions themselves, and one with individual attitudes.

First, borrowing from Yang Ching-kun's ([1961] 1994) adaptation to the Chinese context of the distinction made by Joachim Wach (1944) between diffused and institutionalized religions, one can distinguish between different degrees of institutionalization. In this view, diffused religions are undifferentiated and intimately connected with different aspects of society, and institutionalized religions are distinct from other social institutions and are mutually exclusive. To be sure, different degrees of institutionalization are possible. Especially in the case of Buddhism, Taoism, and many other religions, such as Falun Gong and Yiguandao, which claim a special affiliation with Chinese traditions, some religions can be more or less institutionalized, and the less they are distinguished from diffused religion, the more difficult they are to identify. This is a very relevant approach to the sociological study of Chinese religion, and arguably the perspective that is the most suitable to comprehend Chinese religiosity in all its complexity. Even though Chinese sociologists are aware of this approach, they have yet to convince the authorities in the PRC to look at religion from this angle. This issue sets contemporary China apart from India, to the extent that it is unlikely under the present regime that China's diffused religions could openly evolve into institutional forms like Hinduism has, with the Sangh Parivar and others.

A second approach to the understanding of the variety of religions in China results from cross-fertilization between North American and Chinese sociologies of religion. This approach uses as a criterion to distinguish between different Chinese religions their respective degrees of proximity with the state. It derives from the American school of religious economy, which posits a constant "demand" for religion, but a widely changing "supply" of religions, depending on state control, evolutions within existing religions (Stark and Bainbridge 1987; Stark and Iannaccone 1994), and/or conditions of pluralism or monopoly within a given "religious market." Specifically it has inspired Chinese sociologists such as Yang Fenggang and Wei Dedong (2006) to look at China's religious market as a controlled economy. In their view, the state tightly regulates supply, and as a result, religious organizations will be associated with one of three different religious markets, according to their degree of proximity to the state. Religious institutions that are accepted by the state would be part of a "red market" of religions, which is limited to the five officially accepted religions of Buddhism, Taoism, Islam, protestant Christianity, and Catholicism. A "black market" of religion includes all the religions that have not received state recognition, that the state deems as criminal, and that fall within the categories of "heretic sect," "obscene cult," etc. This would include Falun Gong, but also a number of unrecognized and militant churches and syncretist religions. In between these two markets, argues Yang F. (2006), exists a vast "grey market" of religions that are not recognized, but are not criminalized either. In this approach, the grey market of religion can include the diffused religions as well as the institutionalized religions of the dichotomous approach to the study of religions mentioned previously. Yang F.'s (ibid.) approach is certainly germane to help us understand the evolution of religions and the complex relations between the state and religions, and may be fruitful to the examination of governments' policies toward religion. As it discusses state policies, this chapter will refer to the three markets of Yang F., but will also acknowledge the relevance of Yang C.'s ([1961] 1994) distinction between diffused and institutional religions. Looked at through this analytical lens, China stands in stark contrast to India, where the state does not control the "supply" of religion.

The above distinctions among the Han between diffused and institutional religions, or between the three markets of religions, however, do not render justice to a third aspect of Chinese religiosity, in which we can differentiate religions by varying degree of indigeneity. This criterion provides a distinction between Chinese indigenous religions and world religions originating from abroad. It is obviously controversial, both in China and India. On the one hand, most of the diffused religions mentioned above, as well as the institutionalized religions such as Taoism and Buddhism, belong to the first category. Even though Buddhism originates from India, most Chinese consider it as indigenized to the extent that it has its own scriptural tradition in Chinese characters, its own clergy, and its own schools of thought (Ch'en 1973, 1964).[7] After more than two millennia of development in China, adherents to that religion arguably constitute the largest Buddhist community on earth to such an extent that Chinese Buddhism could well represent the spiritual centre of the Great Vehicle school of that religion, if not of the religion itself. In other words, China can influence Buddhism, more than the other way around. This situation differs from that of other religions originating from abroad such as Islam and Christianity. The communities of the faithful in the Islamic world and in Christianity have enough influence and resources abroad to represent a challenge to the Chinese authorities. In the case of Islam, this is more complicated. Many ethnic Chinese, known as Hui, practise an indigenized form of Islam, but many other residents of China, who are not ethnic Chinese, abide by religious practices that have more in common with that of co-religionists in other Central Asian societies. It is also thought that, like Islam, the different branches of Christianity have also gone through a process of indigenization in the Han population. Still, the connections of these two religions abroad make them somewhat foreign in the eyes of the more nationalist leaders in China, as is the case with the most militant members of the Hindu nationalist movements.

Territoriality is a fourth aspect of religious diversity among the Han that bears mentioning. The religious cleavages within the Han people are not rigidly territorialized, at least not to an extent comparable to what is observed in western Europe or in the Balkans, where some of these differences have congealed into national identities. China did experience religious upheavals that were based in some regions and spread to other parts of China, seemingly representing the grievances of a region or a sub-ethnic group in the area populated by the Han. For example, the Taiping Tianguo (the Heavenly Kingdom of the Great Peace) grew out of a protest movement led by the aggrieved Hakka sub-ethnic group, and ruled for more than a decade a good part of south-central China. Once in power, the Taiping proclaimed the establishment of a new Christian revelation and persecuted traditional religions. Such movements may have represented the frustrations of groups among the Han, but their rapid spread outside of the regions they hailed from demonstrated the concordance between some aspects of these local religious movements and the fundamental beliefs of the more ancient Chinese religiosity. The eschatological hope for a Great Peace at the heart of the Taiping Rebellion reiterated an ancient theme, in which the rulers' loss of the "Mandate of Heaven" (Tianming) opened the way for a major upheaval, or "a Great Enterprise" (Dashi), to change the regime. That these themes have been present in movements associated loosely with Buddhism, such as the White Lotus (Ter Haar 1992), or associated with Taoism, such as the Yellow Turbans, suggests some common themes have been running across regions for a long time. It is significant, however, that none of these movements have established a durable presence in any region of the country. The territorial dimension of religion in China affects people at a much lower level, and at a smaller scale. In that respect, China differs from India, to the extent that we can find in the latter territories populated by a dominant religious community, including Sikhs in the Punjab and Muslims in Kashmir. However, as far as Hindu communities are concerned, the religious demography of Indian states mirrors that of Chinese provinces, with none of these second-tier administrative units identified with a denomination within Hinduism or a Chinese religion, respectively.

As we have seen above, most Chinese adhere to some fundamental beliefs, such as ancestor worship, and are familiar with some ritual practices, such as the burning of joss sticks. But beyond these similarities, there exist a number of variations from one community to another. Different communities, clans, and lineages worship specific ancestors, alongside their respect for some deities that are the object of a widespread devotion throughout the country, such as the Stove God or the Jade Emperor. Although David Faure's (2006) study of the ritual revolution during the mid-Ming dynasty in Guangdong and Shanxi provinces shows some fundamental themes in the provinces' religious practices, he also documents many significant local differences resulting from the different periods in which various provinces and regions were incorporated into the empire. Adam Chau's (2006) ethnography in the Shanbei region and Kenneth Dean's (1998) observations in Fujian point out that even today there are different local traditions with dissimilar pantheons and foundational myths. This diversity among localities within the Han population is obvious when one considers the figures of the local pantheons, which represent local notables, generals, and other worthies,[8] who have been promoted as gods as a result of their loyalty to the rulers. Villages have their local saints and founders, who are worshipped in communal temples. Some of them have acquired a greater stature, perhaps reflecting the position of their locality in the economy of the empire at a given time. But in most cases, the cults of these heroes testify to the resilience of local memories. It is not a surprise then that these cults were among the first targets of the CCP, as it tried to establish the foundations of a centralized state (Perry 2002). And the CCP was not alone in that endeavour. Before it, the Nationalist Party of China (Kuomintang or KMT), equally committed to its modernist ideal, tried to root out these local popular religions (Duara 1991), which it saw as obstacles to its political program. In this respect, the experience of China contrasts with India, where since 1947, the state has not sought to intervene in such a way vis-à-vis Hinduism.

Finally, a fifth dimension of China's religious diversity needs to be taken into account, although this one relates to individual attitudes. This dimension has to do with different degrees of religiosity. This refers to levels of devotion, or intensity, ranging from the indifferent to the devout. The former may include those students who go to a Buddhist temple once a year before the exam period, hoping for the best, and who never return if they believe that their propitiatory act was unsuccessful. The latter may include a variety of devout, from the pietistic believer who practises at home to those who are active in lay associations and spread the Dharma or preach the Gospel. This issue of religiosity brings to attention the question of skepticism, indifference, and atheism or irreligiosity, probably existing in most societies, but particularly salient in China because of its specific historical trajectory, which for more than half a century has included the active promotion of atheism by the state. An analysis of multiculturalism and its possible transmission to China is perhaps conceivable in relation to ethnolinguistic identities, but with respect to religion, it was unthinkable until recently because authorities assumed that the only possible position on religion deserving of state promotion was the belief in its ineluctable withering away. Again, in this respect China differs widely from India, where religion is considered an important component of its public sphere.

We cannot conclude this discussion without looking at an important aspect of the Chinese people's contemporary self-understanding of their religious traditions, which helps explain the difficulty in thinking through a multicultural policy: the ambiguous status of Confucianism. In the world of Chinese religions today in the PRC, this tradition is not recognized as one of the five religions, but rather as a philosophy, a school of thought, or a tradition. This conception, while compatible with a certain idea of tradition as developed by the founders of Confucianism, who saw in the teaching of Master Kong a school of thought (*jia*) rather than a religion (*jiao*), has often generated controversies. To start with, many Confucians in Taiwan and elsewhere see things differently and see a spiritual and religious dimension to Confucianism (Yao 2000, 190–230; Tu 1996). The refusal to consider Confucianism as a religion, however, could serve the CCP cadres well, as they start to re-evaluate this tradition as a source of ethical values compatible with socialism (Liu 2000). Since party cadres cannot adhere to any religion, the promotion of Confucianism as a national philosophy or as a moral system skirts the intractable dilemma of reconciling the adherence to ethical values inspired by religious belief and the explicit rule that aspirant party members cannot join any religious organization if they want to enter the CCP. This kind of creative ambiguity with respect to a religion that cannot say its name has been tried before in the PRC. However, it has led to disastrous results and personal tragedy for those in the CCP, the public administration, and the military, who believed that they could remain party members and continue seeking healing through participation at a series of breathing exercises, unaware that for some they had crossed a line that made them religious believers. In 2000, CCP leaders were horrified to find out that many members of the Party were also adherents of Falun Gong. Among the latter, many more were even more shocked to realize that what they deemed a healthy exercise was suddenly deemed by the authorities an evil cult (Ownby 2008; Palmer 2005). This authoritarian approach of the state in the PRC sets it apart from India.[9]

DIVERSITY WITHIN RELIGIONS AMONG THE HAN IN THE PRC

The discussion so far has approached diversity among the Han, but it has presented rather crude schemes to distinguish between different forms of religiosity. The discussion above has presented a dichotomous scheme to differentiate among religions, as in the difference between diffused and institutional religions, or as in the cleavage between indigenous and so-called religions from abroad. It has presented a tripartite division between the three religious markets of religion. It has also alluded to the territorial and regional dimension of religious diversity. Finally, it has also pointed out the individual attitudes with respect to degrees of religiosity, ranging from atheism to devout belief. But these ways of looking at religious plurality do not tell us much about the difference within the five recognized religions, which can be even more significant. At this point the distinction made by Rajeev Bhargava (2013) between diversity between religions, which was discussed in the previous section, and diversity within religions, becomes useful.

Buddhism, for example, knows many cleavages, along several dimensions. The religion is divided between three traditions: Mahayana, Theravada, and Tibetan, or esoteric. The most important of the three, numerically speaking, is the Mahayana tradition, which has been split historically into eight different schools. Although only the Buddhist Association of China (*Zhongguo fojiao xiehui*) can represent Buddhists in the PRC, this religion has traditionally avoided any centralized organization. During the imperial era and at the beginning of the republican period, abbots could derive their authority from important political patronage, the value of their scholarship, their lineage with other temples or eminent monks, or their own entrepreneurship (Welch 1967, 1968). Evidence from the ROC and the provinces of Hebei and Anhui suggests that this tradition has been revitalized (Yang 2006; Yang and Wei 2006). As a result, there is a variety of networks, some of which have endured for centuries, and which transcend regional boundaries. In contrast with the kinship temples of the folk religions, which connect people within a community at the village or township level (Tsai 2002), Buddhists can rely on a series of nationwide networks, along with one national association. As a result of religious entrepreneurship from monks or lay people, links are also developing between Hong Kong and Taiwan Buddhist organizations, a trend that only increases diversity within the Buddhist community. Thanks to these connections, Buddhists get involved in philanthropic activities, thereby reviving a tradition that dates from the Ming dynasty, seven centuries ago (Liang 1997).

Taoists find themselves in a situation that parallels Chinese Buddhism. Their affairs are conducted by the Taoist Association of China (*Zhongguo daojiao xiehui*), even though historically this religious tradition did not have a centralized leadership nor an undisputed canonical scripture. The Association manages the activities of temples (*gongguan*) and monasteries (*daoyuan*), tries to uniformize the ritual, and strives to place the clergy (*daoshi*) under a unified leadership. After the interruption of its activities during the Cultural Revolution, the Association has been busy since the 1980s trying to restore temples destroyed by the Red Guards or taken over and occupied by other organizations (Lai 2003, 415). The Association is trying to take charge of the *daoshi*'s ordination revival and it seeks to ensure the transmission of the main schools' teachings. The tradition continues to endure thanks to the activities of the *sanju daoshi*, members of the lay clergy who live in monasteries and can get married (Dean 2003). But the diversity of forms taken by local Taoist associations reveals that the boundaries between what represents an authentic Taoist institution and what represents popular religion can be difficult to identify with any accuracy. Goossaert (2000) suggests looking at the Taoist clergy as the institutionalized expression of popular religion.

Islam is the religion of seven different Turkic-speaking national minorities, mostly in Xinjiang (Becquelin 2004), but it is also a religion practised by millions of Chinese. This religion has been in China long enough to be considered a national religion, at least as much as Buddhism. Chinese Muslims are known collectively as the Hui. This identification makes them the only group of religious believers among Han Chinese that are also designated as an ethnic group because of their religion. This has nothing to do with the exclusivist nature of Islam, because Christianity, which is equally exclusivist, is not considered an ethnic group in China. The identity markers differentiating the Hui from other Chinese are not clear, and as Dru Gladney (2003) has indicated, the Hui represent a very diversified group of people. They speak a variety of languages, adopt different dress codes, have adopted a variety of diets, and even their religious practice changes according to their location (Gladney 2003). The Hui can differ among themselves according to their lesser or greater degree of conformity to orthodox practice, or their greater or lesser degree of faith.

Chinese Catholics have also established a presence in China for centuries, and Protestants have been present since the nineteenth century. Catholic and Protestant clergy, as well as lay people, operate officially under the supervision of three nationwide organizations: the National Committee for the Christian Three-Self Patriotic Movement of Protestant Churches in China (*Zhongguo jidujiao sanzi aiguo yundong weiyuanhui*), the China Christian Council (*Zhongguo jidujiao xiehui*) for Protestants, and the Chinese Catholic Patriotic Association (*Zhongguo tianzhujiao aiguohui*) for Catholics. However, alongside these formal institutions, greater numbers join alternative organizations, which they judge more authentic in their theology or their forms of worship (Kindopp and Hamrin 2004). Some of these Protestant "house churches" have developed theological innovations that depart from the official canon imposed by the "three self-ers" association. Some of these churches, such as the "Eastern

Lightning" (*dongfang shandian*) and the "Three Degrees Servants" (*sanban puren*) have been involved in sectarian violence (Kahn 2004), and have adopted apocalyptic theologies similar to those of non-Christian sectarian movements (Kurlantzick 2004; Cheng 2003). The Catholics who decide to worship in "underground churches" do not intend to create new theologies, but mostly want to assert their loyalty to the Pope, whom they believe should supersede the Chinese Catholic Patriotic Association's leadership (Madsen 2003).

The experience of adherents to the sectarian religious movements is more difficult to analyze than that of Catholics or Protestants. Data is almost impossible to obtain for the adherents to sects such as Yiguandao, not to mention the Falun Gong, who live in the PRC and practice clandestinely. Some of these movements claim a lineage with dissident sects within the Buddhist or Taoist traditions that go back centuries, others represent an amalgam of more than one tradition that blend in new ways the three components of the folk religions of Confucianism, Taoism, or Buddhism. These new movements can also include the incorporation of Islam, Christianity, or other beliefs in their theologies. Although many of these movements are recent, some of them, such as the Doctrine of Reason (*lijiao*), the School of Celestial Wisdom (*tiandejiao*), or the School of the Heavenly Emperor (*xuanhuanjiao*), were founded a century ago. Historians and social scientists have argued that such movements have never ceased to exist in the PRC (Perry 2002). Furthermore, their social composition and their goals have varied since 1949 (ibid., 285–6). During the first years of the new regime, they supported the landed gentry and resisted the state's efforts to extend its authority. During the 1980s, after the process of decollectivization was underway, they continued to defend the interests of kinship groups, but this time their targets were not the state, but rival clans (ibid., 294).

RELIGIOUS DIVERSITY IN TAIWAN

The situation of religious diversity in Taiwan does not differ radically from that of China in many respects, but it would be wrong to conclude that Taiwan is only a variant of Chinese culture. Taiwan's religions share with China the following characteristics: a difference between the traditions of non-Chinese Aboriginal people and those of the Han population; among the latter, a similar dichotomy between diffused and institutional religions, a difference between native Chinese and non-Chinese religions, and a certain variety, on a reduced scale, of local practices. However, in two respects, Taiwan differs significantly from China, especially since 1987 when the island embarked on its trajectory of democratization. Firstly, there is a single market of religion because no religion is forbidden. While some religions are still recognized by the government, this is not at the expense of other religions because there are no cases of anti-religious persecutions. In other words, there is no reason to speak of a "black market" of religion, and therefore to speak of a "red market" of recognized religions and a "gray market." Secondly, even though Taiwan's population includes many people who are atheists, agnostics, or indifferent to religious matters, there is no policy that encourages unbelief, and there is no policy that forces people to adopt a religion.

In Taiwan, about half the population is registered in one of the twenty-six religions that are recognized. As in mainland China, Buddhism and Taoism have the greater number of adherents, and the overwhelming majority of the population also worship according to the rites of folk religions, which are not registered. Buddhism represents the most dynamic religious tradition on the island: it is present in the media, has an important role in the provision of a variety of social services, and Buddhist scholarship has been developed by eminent monks, such as the late Sheng Yan, and lay Buddhist scholars, such as Jiang Canteng (Chandler 2004; Huang and Weller 1998). As in China, it is difficult to distinguish between Taoist associations and groups that identify themselves as belonging to the world of folk religions. Protestants and Catholics, as in China, represent a very small minority of the island's population, and are especially influential among Aboriginal people. Despite these small numbers – less than 2 per cent of the population of Taiwan are Protestant Christians – the influence of their churches has been important because prominent politicians have themselves been Methodists or Presbyterians. Finally, a wide variety of sectarian movements have prospered and developed on the island, and up to 10 per cent of religious believers in Taiwan have joined the largest of them, the Yiguandao (Jordan and Overmyer 1986). As the next section elaborates, the PRC and the ROC approach these dimensions of diversity through mechanisms that are very different.

THE MANAGEMENT OF RELIGIOUS DIVERSITY
IN THE PRC AND THE ROC

How the governments of the PRC and the ROC respond to their religious diversity and approach the questions of multiculturalism and the inclusion of religion in a multicultural policy differs in many important respects. Mainland China and Taiwan differ markedly, and substantive similarities between Taiwan, on the one hand, and Canada and India, on the other, abound. The PRC stands apart: it has an official policy of recognizing cultural diversity – even though we do not know it as multiculturalism – which includes both the recognition of ethnolinguistic groups, and the recognition of religious diversity. Local governments often conflate the two policies, with offices dealing both with ethnic and religious affairs at the provincial, prefectural, and district levels. They premise these policies on the themes of maintaining harmony between different groups and the maintenance of separate and distinctive identities. In that context, the emergence of new identities is precluded, and the recognition of new religions is a highly charged political matter. In Taiwan, a similar logic prevailed during the period of martial law, between 1947 and 1987. However, since the beginning of the process of democratization, the island has experienced significant changes in its management of cultural diversity. Although there is no official policy of multiculturalism, the policy of recognizing ethnolinguistic minorities has been much more open and flexible, and the policy of recognition of religion has been increasingly liberal. The recognition of ethnic identities includes the recognition of minorities, such as the Hakkas, within the Han population. In religious matters, the authorities have deferred to the demands of religious actors themselves in granting recognition. Both polities, the PRC and the ROC, claim to uphold a Chinese way of managing religious affairs. Before we look at these claims, it is important to know what were the Chinese practices of regulating religious affairs before these two states were established.

REGULATION OF RELIGION IN ANCIENT CHINA

Any claim that the PRC or the ROC implements a Chinese way of governing religious affairs must first clarify which China it is referring to. During its long history, that part of the world has experienced a wide variety of regimes, long periods of political divisions, and long periods of unity as part of larger empires that were multicultural, if not always tolerant of differences, and has even been governed by non-Chinese rulers. The approach of these different polities to religion was diverse. During the formative period of Chinese culture, which corresponds to the period of ancient Greece, the Chinese monarchs of the Shang dynasty were seen as divine rulers (Schwartz 1985). The elementary forms of the religions known today, such as ancestor worship, belief in geomancy, etc., emerged during that period. In the last centuries of the following dynasty, the Zhou, China experienced a period of political division but also a great period of intellectual ferment, with the development of the new schools of what would later be known as Confucianism and Taoism, among others. With the Han dynasty, rulers were not seen anymore as divine, but simply as intermediates between heaven and earth. Their role was not very different from that of their contemporaries in Rome, where the emperor was both supreme commander and *pontifex maximus*. That is, as head of state, the emperor was made responsible for the performance of rites ensuring prosperity to all. In periods of uncertainty, many saw natural disasters as omens that the emperor had lost the Mandate of Heaven and that a new ruler must replace him. This reading of dynastic cycles, with periods of ascendancy, glory, and fall, represented an anthropocosmic view of the world that would hold sway until the Qing dynasty, but with considerable variations over time.

For example, after the fall of the Han, China experienced a period of division and fell under the control of Northern people. Most of the new rulers rejected the religious belief systems that prevailed under the Han, with the belief that they were corrupt. The new rulers preferred to adopt Buddhism, a new religion that was not yet embraced by many Chinese, because of its remote origins in India a few centuries before. As a result of this adoption of Buddhism by Northern dynasties' rulers, once China experienced a new period of unity under the Sui and the Tang, Buddhism emerged as the de facto state religion, its prosperous clergy wealthy, influential, and present all over the empire. This influence, however, would be detrimental to the religion's future, once the Taoist clergy and the Confucian gentry reacted to the imposition of Buddhism as the only religion of the empire under the Empress Wu Zetian, and supported a brief but lethal persecution of the religion. This case of state suppression of one of the three main traditions of China, however, was short lived and exceptional. By the Song dynasty, the relationship between the emperor and the clergy of the different institutionalized religions can be described as a concordat, in which the state authority and religious institutions had reached a state of peaceful coexistence, the Central Government looking after their welfare, and the organized religions lending legitimacy to the secular authority (Goossaert 2000).

Under the Mongol Yuan dynasty and Manchu rule under the Qing dynasty, the empire's religious tolerance extended to Muslim and Christians, because the vast territorial expanses of these empires included a great number of subjects who belonged to these religious communities. This

policy of peaceful coexistence between the state and different religious institutions, however, did not preclude the outbreak of some serious instances of religious intolerance by the state. The government was willing
to persecute religions that it saw as a threat to its authority, as Philip Kuhn
(1990) has documented in his study of the harsh Qing state response to
the "soul-stealer," a public campaign in the empire that targeted people
suspected by many of witchcraft and sorcery, a collective scare that was
groundless. The Qing dynasty, after first welcoming Catholic missionaries,
became wary of the political influence of the religion and forbade prose-
lytizing before finally declaring it a dangerous sect. In the waning years of
the dynasty, as we have seen before, religious intolerance was the hallmark
of the contender to the Qing rulers, the Taiping.

During the Republican era, the weakness of the state made it difficult
to speak of a cohesive policy toward religion. The KMT tried to impose an
assertive form of *laïcité*, similar to policies implemented in Turkey and
Mexico at the time. KMT leaders were zealous modernists and believed that
popular religions represented feudal superstitions to be eradicated. In a
way, they pursued parts of the Taiping agenda against popular religions,
and if some of their harshest policies were eventually abandoned because
of pressure from the more conservative elements of the KMT, their actions
had provided a blueprint for the more radical policies of the CCP later on,
and for milder versions of these policies once the KMT went into exile in
Taiwan. In one crucial respect, however, the KMT differed from the CCP
from the beginning: it was more accepting of Christianity and encouraged its growth in China.

THE REGULATION OF RELIGIOUS DIVERSITY
IN THE PRC

The PRC policy toward religion is a policy of limited recognition to just
five religions, and of denial of recognition to the religions that do not fit
within the existing five. This policy of recognition granted to just five religions, moreover, distinguishes between two different forms of Christianity, Protestant Christianity and Catholicism, as two different official
religions, but does not extend the same degree of recognition to the two
main branches of Islam, Sunni and Shi'a, nor to the three different forms
of Buddhism. This policy also denies any recognition to two other categories of religions: the practices of popular religions, at worst dismissed as
"feudal superstitions" (*fengjian mixin*), and at best seen as part of the traditional folklore. It harasses congregational religious organizations that

fall within the category of heretical cults or "obscene religions" (*xiejiao*). According to available statistics from the state, the total number of people who believe in one of the five organized religions represent at most about a fifth of China's population. Official figures claim that up to eight hundred million Chinese are atheists. The same sources say that Buddhists and Taoists each number about one hundred million, and counted twenty-five million Muslims, barely five million Catholics and around fifteen million Protestants. To complete the picture, the state security bureau claimed that around five million Chinese were adherents of Falun Gong. Adding up these figures still leaves close to two hundred million Chinese unaccounted for. The important thing to keep in mind is that these numbers are contested and even sociologists in China don't rely on them. Evangelical organizations headquartered outside China make fantastic claims about a hundred million Christian Chinese, and Li Hongzhi, the leader of Falun Gong, made the same claim for his group. The numbers of people who worship occasionally according to the rites of popular religions are unaccounted for, and they would probably represent the largest group of religious believers, if one was to extrapolate from the situation in Taiwan.

We can understand the recognition of Buddhism, Taoism, Islam, Protestantism, and Catholicism as official religions since the first decades of the socialist regime in the PRC as part of the CCP United Front work strategy, rather than as a genuine policy of multiculturalism that seeks to promote diversity for its own sake.[10] In this policy, recognition of the five religions serves to present a good image of China as a tolerant society to other countries where Buddhists, Muslims, and Christians live. It also serves to demonstrate the CCP's support for the religions of the national minorities. This includes Tibetans, Mongols, and a few others who have traditionally adhered to Buddhism – although in a form that differs from the Mahayana Buddhist practice of the Han. It also includes Uygurs, Kazakhs, and others who share with the Hui their Muslim identity, and many small national minorities who have converted to Christianity (Covell 2001). We can plausibly attribute the recognition of Taoism, which is not an international religion – or in Chinese official taxonomy, a world religion – like the four other religions, to a need to serve the United Front work policy vis-à-vis overseas Chinese. This argument, however, is not entirely persuasive because the Chinese government does not recognize popular religions, such as Confucianism – which governments in South Korea and Taiwan recognize as a religion – and other institutional religions, such as Yiguandao, even though many overseas Chinese identify with them.

This policy of recognition for some religions, and denial for others, however, is not entirely static. The CCP has clearly moved away from the anti-religious stance of the Cultural Revolution, and officials since Jiang Zemin hold to the line that religion and socialism can be mutually compatible. Even the attitude toward popular religions is changing. They are increasingly tolerated by local governments (Eng and Lin 2002), even though they present the CCP with some dilemmas. As we have seen before, by incorporating Buddhism, Taoism, and Confucianism together in the popular tradition of the *sanjiao*, they have ipso facto accorded to Confucianism a religious dimension. The religious dimension of Confucianism, obviously on display in the folk religions, thus represents a thorny problem for those cadres who wish to assert that Confucianism is a humanistic philosophy entirely compatible with scientific socialism (Liu 2000).

The ban on sects and new religious movements follows a different logic. The recent literature on the ban against Falun Gong suggests that the CCP fears the emergence of trends that it cannot control (Ostergaard 2004; Keith and Lin 2003; Ching 2001). Falun Gong appeared a particularly troubling phenomenon because it was urban, recruited among members of the party, and seemed to have developed a sophisticated governance structure (Tong 2002). CCP leaders seem to believe that Falun Gong represents a more serious threat than any other sectarian movement: its resilience, its linkages with the outside world, the willingness of its members to endure hardship and persecution, this all reminded many cadres of the Taiping. Yet, besides the demand that they be free to worship, adherents to that organization did not have obvious political objectives. The opposition of sectarian movements did not need to be militant to be seen as a challenge: sometimes, these movements were seen as a form of resistance by the simple fact of their resilience (Feuchtwang 2000), or they were believed to represent a barely disguised form of protest, through their activities in the open (Thornton 2002). In sum, the CCP feared that by recognizing the Falun Gong, they would open the door to demands from other religious organizations for legal status, thereby making obsolete the current system of supervision for the currently recognized five religions. Available evidence from the Public Security Bureau (*Gong'an bu*) reveals that the CCP has indeed failed to prevent the emergence of sectarian religious movements since the launch of economic reforms in 1978: reports from that governmental organization revealed that thousands of "heretic sects" continued to proliferate well into 2000 (Li and Fu 2002). It is impossible to tell now if the Chinese government is in control of the various sects, but its ability and its will to impose a clampdown on Falun

Gong is not in doubt (Tong 2009). The campaign is ongoing, and even though a few lone voices express their disagreement, no one has managed in any significant way to successfully change this policy within China.

The proliferation of "underground churches" and "house churches" also worries the regime, but not to the same extent as the sects. The Catholic Church and the Protestant denominations have external linkages, and for that reason, can represent an asset for the regime as much as a possible threat. Like Islam, Christianity can serve as a conduit for the PRC diplomacy, as it seeks to expand relations with Africa and Latin America, and other Asian countries, such as South Korea and the Philippines, where live an important proportion of Christians. It is not clear how much Chinese churches may be tempted to play that role, or whether they are willing to act like their co-religionists in Taiwan and South Korea, who have used their powerful connections abroad to advocate progress on political and social rights in their respective polities. Many Chinese Christians are aware of the contribution of Churches in the transition away from socialism in Eastern and Central Europe, and many CCP cadres fear similar developments in China (Kindopp and Hamrin 2004).

Taoists represent less of a concern because they do not have many external links. The only concern of the CCP relates to the inability of officials to distinguish between the Taoist rituals performed by *sanju daoshi* and those that are performed by religious specialists of the unrecognized folk religions in the same temples, and that are judged superstitious by authorities (Lai 2003, 423). The cadres responsible for the supervision of Daoism are unable to supervise the *sanju daoshi* because the transmission of the rituals occurs at home, away from governmental supervision. Buddhist organizations within the Han population represent perhaps the least problematic religious trend, despite their international connection with Japanese, Korean, and overseas Chinese co-religionists. The state has seized on the tourism potential of Buddhist monasteries and has rewarded the cooperative and quietist behaviour of Buddhist associations by facilitating or investing directly in the restoration of temples. In sum, even though the Chinese government is fine-tuning its policy of control over religion, it is not yet embarking on the path of implementing a genuinely liberal policy of recognition. Can that be attributed to the nature of Chinese culture itself? Can one say that Chinese traditional religion – and Confucianism – possesses features that predispose it to authoritarianism, the same way that the diversity of Hinduism made it more likely that India would adopt a more tolerant approach? Hardly, if one looks at Taiwan, the other Chinese polity that the current government in Beijing claims is an integral part of China.

THE POLITICS OF RECOGNITION FOR RELIGIOUS
ORGANIZATIONS IN TAIWAN

The first four decades of the KMT rule in Taiwan were difficult for religious associations. After the ROC asserted its sovereignty over Taiwan at the end of the Second World War, the ruling party was concerned with eradicating the remnants of Japanese colonial influence on the island, defeating communist infiltration, and clamping down on a Taiwan-based movement for autonomy. These priorities affected the regime's policy toward religions until the beginning of the process of democratization became irreversible (Katz 2003). To meet its objective of control and supervision, the KMT imposed a corporatist form of supervision that bore remarkable similarities to the CCP-sponsored system of national religious associations that were granted by the state a monopoly of representation for the adherents of their respective religion. The institutions of the ROC, however, recognized more religions than the CCP and the PRC institutions did. Along with Buddhism, Taoism, Islam, Protestantism, and Catholicism, the KMT also recognized some new religious movements, such as the Doctrine of Order (Lijiao) and the Religion of the Celestial Worthy (Tiandejiao). Arguably, this was made possible because the leaders of these two movements were close to the KMT. The fact that the KMT attitude toward syncretism and other new religious movements was far less moderate supports that argument. Other movements without connection to the ruling party did not fare that well. For example, the KMT looked at the Way of Unity as seditious and subjected its leadership to harassment, and granted it recognition only in 1987 (Ho 1996). During the early stages of economic growth, the authorities also looked down on the rituals of the local folk religions, which they considered wasteful, but they never went as far as the CCP in trying to eradicate them (Ahern 1981).

The issue of Chinese nationalism – in opposition to Japan in the immediate aftermath of the Second World War and in opposition to the Taiwanese *bendiren* independence activists – represented a major factor behind the religious policy of the KMT. For example, the authorities clamped down hard on a religious association originating from Japan, the Soka Gakkai, because of suspicions over the loyalty of its adherents to Japan instead of China (Ho 1996).[11] It would seem that this action was not targeting Japanese religions specifically because the Ministry of the Interior had granted recognition since 1973 to another Japan-based religion, Tenrikyo. The problem of Taiwanese nationalism gave the KMT more concern, because it received support from the Presbyterian Church in Taiwan, a *bendiren* association that maintained a network of support in Canada and the United States. Because the KMT was anxious to cultivate good relations with the United States, on whose economic, political, and military support it relied, the ruling party tried to develop good relations with churches and avoided antagonizing them. Conversely, aware of this relatively ambiguous status, some churches felt emboldened to speak out on human rights, and spearheaded the movement for democratization (Baker 1997). Yet, this initiative could not go too far: the leadership of the Presbyterian Church, by supporting Taiwan's right for self-determination, was subjected to persecution in the 1970s and 1980s (Cohen 1988).

During the first decades of KMT rule in Taiwan, the other major concern was the fear of CCP espionage and destabilization. In that tense context, Buddhist monks who were hoping to seek refuge in Taiwan and avoid persecution from the CCP often had to hurriedly escape mainland China and could not come to Taiwan with proper identification. As a result, many were suspected of subversive activities by the KMT security forces and were harassed well into the 1950s (Jiang 1996). The KMT, however, gradually changed its attitude in the 1960s when its leadership realized that the regime could benefit from increasingly well-organized and popular lay organizations such as the Tzu Chi Foundation. Such organizations had set up charities, indirectly helping the state by relieving it from some of its duties and providing some social services in remote areas of the country (Wang 1999, 1991).

The situation of all religious institutions improved considerably during the transition toward democracy. In 1992, President Lee approved the passing of a law on civil organizations that put an end to the corporatist structure of representation that had prevailed until then. Religious institutions did not need to register to a single recognized association to operate legally. Lay organizations and clerical or monastic organizations increased in number as a result of this evolution. This increase in the number of religious associations, and the laxity of authorities, presented opportunities to individuals who presented themselves as spiritual masters and managed as a result to amass from individuals considerable sums of money. The established religious associations, concerned that these cases of manipulation and fraud could affect their reputation, pressed the authorities to pass legislation to preventing such behaviour. The authorities were reluctant and preferred instead to increase the number of officially recognized religions, which grew from eleven in 1992 to twenty-six in

2006. In 2000, a consultative committee on religious affairs (*zongjiao shiwu zixun weiyuanhui*) comprising academics and people from the religious milieu was convened to help the Ministry of the Interior draft a law on religious organizations (*zongjiao tuanti fa*). One year later, the same ministry granted people who did not want to enlist in the armed forces the right to perform civic duties, provided that they could produce a certificate confirming that they belonged to a genuine religious organization. Overall, the attitude of the Taiwanese government has been radically different from that of the Chinese government with respect to religion: an inclination for a laissez-faire attitude has been preferred to an interventionist approach. As a result, religious actors in Taiwan have been supportive of the political regime, and have seldom intervened in the political process. With the noticeable exception of the Presbyterian Church, which came out in favour of the rights of Taiwanese to self-determination, none of the Buddhist and Taoist organizations, Christian churches, or the other recognized religious organizations have faced a crisis over their collective identity of the kind that could spill over into the political process.

Since the lift of martial law, the gap between the two sides of the Strait has widened as far as relations between the state and religion are concerned. The Taiwanese authorities, responding to pressures from civil society as well as from religious institutions, have consolidated the legal protections that the latter already enjoyed. The situation of the ROC, in many ways, mirrors Canada's, where the state supports freedom of conscience, but does not proclaim a specific commitment to secularism the way India does. Pending a demonstration that they have a membership, a source of revenue, and their own organization, religious associations can register as independent religions or as affiliates of one of the twenty-eight religions already registered to the Bureau for Religions, a unit within the Civil Affairs Department of the Ministry of the Interior.

CONCLUSION

We can now return to the initial query raised at the beginning of this chapter: To what extent is a given culture more or less germane to the design of institutions respectful of diversity and to substantive policies of multiculturalism? The example of China, whose culture is different in so many ways from both Canada's and India's, clearly demonstrates that political context is more significant than culture. This chapter has argued that two very different approaches have been implemented toward the

management of religious affairs in societies that are unquestionably regarded as the embodiment of Chinese culture. For many years, the two
different political systems of the PRC and the ROC had both an authoritarian and interventionist policy on religious affairs. However, while the
mainland Chinese authorities continue to implement control over religion, successive Taiwanese governments have decisively moved away from
that approach as democracy consolidated. These differences resulted from
choices that gradually led to divergent trajectories: on the one hand, the
path dependency of the 1949 revolution in the PRC, which kept the CCP
and its social engineering above the constitution, and, on the other hand,
the growing importance of the rule of law in the ROC, which supersedes
the role of political parties.

The management of religious affairs by the CCP, which stresses uniformity of religious practice and orthodoxy within the five established religions, contributes much to the widespread perception outside of China
that the state is biased against the recognition of diversity. In the ROC, the
KMT, the previously ruling party, had enforced a system of regulation that
was remarkably similar to that of the PRC until 1987, when martial law
was lifted. A different geopolitical context and the emergence of a democratic movement in the island have led to a new and different dynamic
leading to the recognition of religious diversity. That trend is now consolidated after more than two decades of development. A crucial element of
that process was the interaction between Taiwanese scholars and their
peers in Japan, North America, and Western Europe. Unbiased approaches to the study of religion in different disciplines, such as sociology,
ethnology, political science, and history have helped create a better appreciation of the religious diversity of Taiwan and the means to recognize this
within a democratic context.

We may need to add one promising and encouraging note to the above
observations. Although the current Chinese government does not show
signs of changing its policies, the epistemic communities of Chinese experts who know religion in their country, in all its diversity, are making
huge strides in our knowledge of that aspect of contemporary Chinese society. They continue to establish research centres on religion, create programs for the sociological study of religion in universities, organize
workshops to inform decision makers, and increasingly interact with their
colleagues abroad to exchange views. This allows these experts to develop
a more sophisticated theoretical apparatus for understanding their country's situation and to adapt the conceptual tools of other countries to the

context of China, and their colleagues abroad get a more nuanced understanding of China's complex situation. Employees from the State Administration of Religious Affairs attend conferences organized by sociologists of religion and get a better grasp of the situation they have to attend to. Although this may not amount to much transformation on the ground now, this development of the scientific study of religion is a very positive sign: it is via such kinds of interactions that politicians in Taiwan were gradually convinced to adopt more tolerant policies.

To sum up, the Chinese situation underscores that culture is not the primary determinant of a state's ability to develop a policy of multiculturalism that is supportive of religious diversity. This finding has implications that affect India as an exporter of norms for the recognition and the support of religious diversity. The argument that the Indian civilization and Indic religions have specific characteristics making the implementation of India's policies and institutions irrelevant to other regions becomes more difficult to sustain.

NOTES

1   I use "China" to mean the territory governed by a succession of dynasties and two successive regimes, the Republic of China (ROC), from 1911 to 1949, and the PRC, after 1949. The jurisdiction of the ROC since 1949 is limited to Taiwan.

2   For India, see Madan 1998, and for China, see Yang 2006.

3   Taiwan is known officially as the ROC. I use both interchangeably.

4   Japan, Vietnam, and Korea have to a degree been influenced by Chinese culture, but less so than Taiwan because of linguistic differences. Hong Kong, Singapore, and Macau are societies where majorities speak Chinese languages, but they have smaller population than Taiwan. Moreover, Hong Kong and Macau are not sovereign states.

5   Some minorities have adopted the practices of Han Chinese religions. But the most important of the minorities, such as the Uygur, Tibetans, and Mongols have religious beliefs that differ from those of the Chinese.

6   This comparison, I acknowledge, is not perfect: we do not consider the people who are not native speakers of the Indo-Aryan languages nor the Dravidian ethnolinguistic groups as national minorities, even if their status can sometimes be compared to that of marginalized people such as the Tibetans and Mongols in China.

7   Some cultural nationalists, however, consider Buddhism as a foreign religion.

Their position is not very different from that of Hindu nationalists who argue that Islam, after more than a millennium of presence in the subcontinent, is an alien religion.

8 They could be judges, merchants, or meritorious individuals whose virtues were encouraged.

9 Although the Indian state has used force to quell insurgencies in the Punjab and Kashmir based on religious grievances, it did not contest the legitimacy of the religious identity of its opponents.

10 The decade of the Cultural Revolution was an exception.

11 The KMT sees Taiwan as part of China.

REFERENCES

Ahern, Emily M. 1981. "The Thai Ti Kong Festival." In *The Anthropology of Tai-wanese Society*, edited by Emily Ahern, and Hill Gates, 397–425. Stanford: Stanford University Press.

Asad, Talal. 2001. "On Re-reading a Modern Classic: W.C. Smith's 'The Meaning and End of Religion." *History of Religions* 40(3): 205–22.

Baker, Don. 1997. "World Religions and National States: Competing Claims in East Asia." In *Transnational Religion and Failed States*, edited by Susanne Hoeber Rudolph, and James P. Piscatori, 144–72. Boulder: Westview Press.

Becquelin, Nicolas. 2004. "Staged Development in Xinjiang." *The China Quarterly* 178: 358–78.

Bhargava, Rajeev. 2013. "Can Secularism be Rehabilitated?" In *The Secular State and Religious Diversity*, edited by Bruce Berman, Rajeev Bhargava, and André Laliberté, 69–93. Vancouver: University of British Columbia.

Brookings Institution. 2008. "Religion in China: Perspectives from Chinese Religious Leaders and Officials." Washington, September 11. http://www.brookings.edu/~/media/events/2008/9/11%20china%20religion/20080911_china_religion.pdf.

Chandler, Stuart. 2004. *Establishing a Pure Land on Earth: The Foguang Buddhist Perspective on Modernization and Globalization*. Honolulu: University of Hawai'i Press.

Chau, Adam Y. 2006. *Miraculous Response: Doing Popular Religion in Contemporary China*. Stanford: Stanford University Press.

Ch'en, Kenneth K. S. 1964. *Buddhism in China: A Historical Survey.* Princeton: Princeton University Press.

– 1973. *The Chinese Transformation of Buddhism in China*. Princeton: Princeton University Press.

Cheng, May M. C. 2003. "House Church Movement and Religious Freedom in China." *China: An International Journal* 1(1): 16–45.

Ching, Julia. 2001. "The Falun Gong: Religious and Political Implication." *The American Asian Review* 29(4): 1–18.

Cohen, Marc J. 1988. *Taiwan at the Crossroads: Human Rights, Political Developments and Social Change in the Beautiful Island.* Washington: Asia Resource Center.

Covell, Ralph R. 2001. "Christianity and China's Minority Nationalities – Faith and Unbelief." In *China and Christianity: Burdened Past, Hopeful Future*, edited by Stephen Uhalley Jr., and Xiaoxin Wu, 271–82. Armonk and London: M. E. Sharpe.

Dean, Kenneth. 1998. *Lord of Three in One: The Spread of a Cult in Southeast China.* Princeton: Princeton University Press.

– 2003. "Local Communal Religion in Contemporary Southeast China." *The China Quarterly* 174: 338–58.

Duara, Prasenjit. 1991. "Knowledge and Power in the Discourse of Modernity: The Campaigns against Popular Religion in Early Twentieth-Century China." *Journal of Asian Studies* 50 (1): 67–83.

Eng, Irene, and Yi-Min Lin. 2002. "Religious Festivities, Communal Rivalry, and Restructuring of Authority in Rural Chaozhou, Southeast China." *The Journal of Asian Studies* 61 (4): 1259–85.

Faure, David. 2006. "La solution lignagère : la révolution rituelle du XVIe siècle et l'État impérial chinois." *Annales. Histoire, Sciences Sociales* 61(6): 1291–316.

Feuchtwang, Stephan. 2000. "Religion as Resistance." In *Chinese Society: Change, Conflict and Resistance*, edited by Elizabeth J. Perry, and Mark Selden, 161–77. London: Routledge.

Gladney, Dru. 2003. "Islam in China: Accommodation or Separatism?" *The China Quarterly* 174: 451–67.

Goossaert, Vincent. 2000. *Dans les temples de la Chine : Histoire des cultes, vie des communautés.* Paris: Albin Michel: Science des religions.

Goossaert, Vincent, and David Palmer. 2010. *The Religious Question in Modern China.* Chicago: University of Chicago Press.

Hitchens, Christopher. 2007. *God is Not Great: How Religion Poisons Everything.* New York: Twelve/Hachette Book Group USA.

Ho Fang-jiau [He Fengjiao] 何鳳嬌. 1996. "台灣省警務檔案彙編:民意宗教篇." [Documentary Collection of Taiwan's Police Administration: Folklore and Religion]. 新店, Taipei County: Academia Historica.

Huang Chien-yu, Julia, and Robert P. Weller. 1998. "Merit and Mothering: Women and Social Welfare in Taiwanese Buddhism." *The Journal of Asian Studies* 57 (2): 379–96.

Jiang Canteng 江燦騰. 1996. 台灣佛教百年史之研究, 1895–1995 [Research on a Century of Buddhism in Taiwan, 1895 –1995]. Taipei: Nantian 南天.

Jordan, David K., and Daniel L. Overmyer. 1986. *The Flying Phoenix: Aspects of Chinese Sectarianism in Taiwan*. Taipei: Caves.

Kahn, Joseph. 2004. "Violence Taints Religion's Solace for China's Poor." *New York Times*, November 24.

Katz, Paul R. 2003. "Identity Politics and the Study of Popular Religion in Postwar Taiwan." In *Religion and the Formation of Taiwanese Identities*, edited Paul R. Katz and Murray A. Rubinstein, 157–80. New York: Palgrave Macmillan.

Keith, Ronald C., and Lin Zhiqiu. 2003. "The 'Falun gong Problem': Politics and the Struggle for the Rule of Law in China." *The China Quarterly* 175: 623–42.

Kindopp, Jason, and Carol Lee Hamrin, eds. 2004. *God and Caesar in China: Policy Implications of Church-State Relations in China*. Washington: Brookings Institution Press.

Kuhn, Philip A. 1990. *Soulstealers: The Chinese Sorcery Scare of 1768*. Cambridge: Harvard University Press.

Kurlantzick, Joshua. 2004. "Chinese Christians Are a Force, But What Kind?" *Washington Post*, November 28, B04.

Lai Chi-tim. 2003. "Daoism in China Today." *China Quarterly* 174: 413–27.

Li Shixiong, and Fu Xiqiu. 2002. *Religion and National Security in China: Secret Documents from China's Security Sector.* (document printed in January 2003).

Liang Qizi 梁其姿. 1997.施善與文化明清的慈善組織 [Almsgiving and Culture: Welfare Institutions During the Ming-Qing]. Taipei: Lianjing 聯經.

Liu Xiaoxin. 2000. "监论儒学与东亚地区经济社会的发展" [An Examination on Confucianism and the Social and Economic Development of East Asia] 江西社会科学 *Jiangxi Social Science* 12: 85–8.

Lopez, Donald Jr., ed. 1996. *Religions of China in Practice*. Princeton: Princeton University Press.

Madan, T. N. 1998. "Secularism in Its Place." In *Secularism and Its Critics*, edited by Rajeev Bhargava, 297–320. Delhi: Oxford University Press.

Madsen, Richard. 2003. "Catholic Revival During the Reform Era." *The China Quarterly* 174: 469–87.

Oakes, Tim, and Donald Sutton, eds. 2010. *Faiths on Display: Religion, Tourism, and the Chinese State*. New York: Rowman and Littlefield.

Ostergaard, Clemens. 2004. "Governance and the Political Challenge of Falun Gong." In *Governance in China*, edited by Jude Howell, 207–25. New York: Rowman and Littlefield.

Overmyer, Daniel L. 2009. *Local Religion in North China in the Twentieth Century: The Structure and Organization of Community Rituals and Beliefs*. Leiden: Brill.

Ownby, David. 2008. *Falun Gong and the Future of China*. New York: Oxford University Press.

Palmer, David. 2005. *La fièvre du qigong: guérison, religion et politique en Chine, 1949-1999*. Paris: Éditions de l'école des hautes études en sciences sociale.

Perry, Elizabeth J. 2002. *Challenging the Mandate of Heaven: Social Protest and State Power in China*, 275–308. Armonk: M.E. Sharpe.

Schwartz, Benjamin. 1985. *World of Thought in Ancient China*. Cambridge: Harvard University Press.

Stark, Rodney, and Laurence R. Iannaccone. 1994. "A Supply-Side Reinterpretation of the 'Secularization' of Europe." *Journal for the Scientific Study of Religion* 33(3): 230–252.

Stark, Rodney, and William Sims Bainbridge. 1987. *A Theory of Religion*. New York: Peter Lang

Ter Haar, Barend J. 1992. *The White Lotus Teachings in Chinese Religious History*. Honolulu: University of Hawai'i Press.

Thornton, Patricia M. 2002. "Framing Dissent in Contemporary China: Irony, Ambiguity and Metonymy." *China Quarterly* 171: 661–81.

Tong, James. 2002. "An Organizational Analysis of the Falun Gong: Structure, Communications, Financing." *The China Quarterly* 171: 636–60.

– 2009. *Revenge of the Forbidden City: The Suppression of the Falun Gong in China, 1999–2005*. New York: Oxford University Press.

Tsai, Lily L. 2002. "Cadres, Temple and Lineage Institutions, and Governance in Rural China." *The China Journal* 48: 1–27.

Tu, Wei-ming, ed. 1996. *Confucian Traditions in East Asian Modernity: Moral Education and Economic Culture in Japan and the Four Mini-Dragons.* Cambridge: Harvard University Press.

Wach, Joachim. 1944. *Sociology of Religion*. Chicago: University of Chicago Press.

Wang Shunmin王順民. 1999.宗教福利 [Religious Welfare]. Taipei:亞太 Tushu.

– 1991. "宗教福利思想與福利服務之探究–以慈濟功德會,台灣基督長老會為例 [Religious Thought on Welfare and the Provision of Welfare: An Enquiry Using the Buddhist Compassion Relief Tzu Chi Foundation and the Presbyterian Church as Examples]." Taichung: Tunghai 東海University.

Welch, Holmes. 1967. *The Practice of Chinese Buddhism, 1900-1950*. Harvard East Asian Studies; no. 26. Cambridge: Harvard University Press.

– 1968. *The Buddhist Revival in China*. Harvard East Asian Series, 33. Cambridge: Harvard University Press.

Weller, Paul. 2006. "'Human Rights,' 'Religion,' and the 'Secular': Variants Configurations of Religion(s), State(s) and Society(ies)." *Religion and Human Rights* 1(1): 17–39.

Yang Ching-Kun. (1961) 1994. *Religion in Chinese Society: A Study of Contemporary Social Functions of Religion and some of their Historical Factors.* Berkeley: University of California Press. Reprint, Taipei: SMC Publishing.

Yang Fenggang. 2006. "The Red, Black, and Gray Markets of Religion in China." *The Sociological Quarterly* 47: 93–122.

Yang Fenggang, and Wei Dedong. 2006. "The Bailin Buddhist Temple: Thriving Under Communism." In *State, Market, and Religions in Chinese Societies*, edited by Yang Fenggang and Joseph B. Tamney, 63–86. Boston: Brill.

Yao Xinzhong. 2000. *An Introduction to Confucianism.* Cambridge: Cambridge University Press.

PART TWO

Multiculturalism and Religion

6

Justice, Diversity, and Dialogue: Rawlsian Multiculturalism

ASHWANI PEETUSH

In this chapter, I argue that John Rawls' later work presents one of the most fruitful liberal frameworks from which to approach global cultural diversity. In his *Law of Peoples* (1999), the normative architecture Rawls provides is much more open to an intercultural/religious dialogue with various non-Western communities, such as the First Nations, than are other liberal approaches. Surprisingly, this has gone unnoticed in the literature on multiculturalism. At the same time, Rawls' framework is not problem free. Here, I am concerned with Rawls' conception of overlapping consensus as political, rather than comprehensive; or the idea that dialogue and discussion concerning issues of justice must necessarily, as a matter of principle, exclude philosophical or religious reasons. I argue that this constraint will only add to the unfair exclusion of legitimate concerns. Such problems are compounded in a colonial context where the voices of non-Western communities have been excluded and their self-understandings consistently denigrated for centuries. In the context of a globally diverse world, and in light of a history of Western colonialism, justice and fairness require that others be able to articulate their concerns according to their own self-understandings and as they see fit, even if we do not agree with these.

RAWLS, LIBERAL, AND DECENT SOCIETIES

Discussions of liberal multiculturalism tend to focus on Will Kymlicka's view, even though this view is riddled with serious difficulties. One of the key respects in which Rawls' approach differs from Kymlicka's is that it does not require the development of individual autonomy (as defined and prioritized by the liberal) as a pre-requirement to be a member in good standing with the international community, or what Rawls calls the "Society of Peoples." Rather, one might say, Rawls' liberalism is grounded more on the value of toleration. Indeed, Kymlicka brands Rawls' view as such, and attacks him for moving from a comprehensive liberalism premised on the foundational value of individual autonomy (again, as defined by the liberal perspective) to a political conception (see Kymlicka 1995, 154–63). Kymlicka (2001, 53, 59–60, 208–9; 1995, 80–4, 87–9, 75, 101; 1989, 162–7, 177, 197, 253) attempts to convince fellow liberals that cultural membership is important because it provides the social conditions without which individual autonomy could not develop. This is ironic as one of the groups with which he himself is most concerned, the First Nations, desire collective rights so that they may pursue, in their public and governmental institutions, shared conceptions of the good life, thereby limiting an individual's autonomy. This does not appear to present an obstacle to Kymlicka; he makes no distinction in kind between non-liberal and anti-liberal cultures and argues that liberality is a matter of degree, with Aboriginals on the march of historical progress toward an individualistic secular culture (Kymlicka 1995, 235, 171, 94; 1989, 180). To say the least, First Nations peoples do not see it this way (see Peetush 2003 for a detailed analysis of Kymlicka's position).

The Rawlsian view of the relationship between liberal and non-liberal peoples is dramatically different from that of liberals like Kymlicka, whose position is grounded in the value of autonomy. Rawls argues, first of all, that we ought, as a matter of principle, to distinguish between cultures and nations that are non-liberal and those that are simply anti-liberal or outlaw states. Rawls argues that non-liberal peoples should be recognized and accepted as what he calls "decent" societies; that is, legitimate partners in an equal relationship with liberal peoples. Moreover, Rawls (1999, 59–60) argues that to "tolerate" non-liberal peoples means "not only to refrain from exercising political sanctions ... to tolerate also means to recognize these non-liberal societies as equal participating members in good standing of the Society of Peoples." In addition, Rawls (1999, 61) remarks that "if liberal peoples require that all societies be liberal and subject those that are not to politically enforced sanctions, then decent non-liberal peoples ... will be denied a due measure of respect by liberal peoples" and that this "argues for preserving significant room for the idea of a people's self-determination."

On the other hand, Rawls' (1999, 62) respect for non-liberal societies is on occasion muted by some of his other comments, such as, for example:

"when offered due respect by liberal peoples, [a non-liberal society] may be more likely, over time, to recognize the advantages of liberal institutions and take steps toward becoming liberal on its own." This sounds closer to what Kymlicka has in mind for non-liberal peoples. But there is nothing in Rawlsian multiculturalism that theoretically requires such a view. This is in contrast to Kymlicka, the theoretical architecture of whose view hinges on developing liberal institutions as a prerequisite for being granted collective rights.

What does it mean for peoples to be considered decent? For Rawls, this judgment has a few basic conditions. Decent societies must not have aggressive aims; they must secure for their members "urgent" or fundamental human rights; in the least, they must allow members consultation in political decisions and allow members a meaningful role in political decisions; they must allow for dissent and provide official channels in which dissent is heard; and they must allow emigration (see Rawls 1999, 37, 61, 65–7, 74–5). Rawls' (1999, 65) set of urgent or human rights include: "the right to life (to the means of subsistence and security); to liberty (to freedom from slavery, serfdom, and forced occupation, and to a sufficient measure of liberty of conscience to ensure freedom of religion and thought); to property (personal property); and to formal equality as expressed by the natural rules of justice (that is that similar cases be treated similarly)." From the perspective of a liberal democratic schedule of rights, this list seems rather limited. But Rawls thinks that it is a mistake to conflate the extensive list of liberal democratic rights with the minimal conditions a society needs to meet in order for it to be considered decent. Along these lines, societies based around more substantive or comprehensive views of the good, or non-secular nations (e.g., various Aboriginal communities, Islamic peoples), are to be considered decent as long as they can protect their members from various abuses and harms.

Of course, in such a society freedom of conscience would not be as extensive as in a liberal society, since one particular view of the good or a particular religion may dominate public policy. But, as long as such a society could protect members who did not share the dominant view from threat or persecution, it would be deemed a decent society.

In a similar vein, Graham Walker (1997) contends that liberalism and constitutionalism do not historically or conceptually coincide. Historically, Walker argues, constitutionalism came first and seeks as its object to fetter political power. Indeed, as long as a society has norms and institutions constitutionally enshrined that can protect its members from the arbitrary abuse of political power, there is no reason why such a society should not be seen as an acceptable form of social order. James Tully (1995), Charles Taylor (1995, 1999), and Bhikhu Parekh (2000) share a broadly analogous approach in this regard.

This is in stark contrast to theorists such as Jack Donnelly (1999), Inoue Tatsuo (1999), the late Brian Barry (2001), and Kymlicka, who assumes that to be an acceptable or legitimate form of social organization, to be considered "decent," one needs not only to agree on certain basic ethical norms, but to adopt liberalism as a whole. This includes adopting the primacy of individual autonomy as conceptualized within liberal theory, and the language and philosophy of individual rights, along with its concomitant philosophical assumptions, for example, the division between church and state, the private and public sphere, and its various legal forms and institutions.

I think this is unreasonable. That a society does not have a division between church and state, does not instantiate ethical norms in terms of individual rights, or is based on substantive ideals or religious values does not mean that it does not have moral or ethical standards against various abuses, such as rape, murder, torture, slavery, or genocide. It does not mean that it does not have positive duties to help and protect the vulnerable and the weak, that it does not respect life, or prize the values of compassion, care, fairness, and trust. Ethical conduct was not invented by Western liberal societies. Of course, how such cross-cultural values are defined, prioritized, and balanced is a matter of cultural context, but that is to be expected. How else could it be? Even if we have a socio-biological story of why it is that human beings as a species share various kinds of norms, such norms always interact with stories and narratives about purpose and meaning, or frameworks of significance as Clifford Geertz (1973) points out. This is a part of what it means to be human. In the context of globalization, transnational corporations, and certain shared features of modern life that represent common threats, we need to work out together what exactly such cross-cultural values are and the range of legitimate variance we are willing to accommodate. In addition to ensuring equality among various peoples, this is why cross-cultural dialogue becomes critical.

HUMAN RIGHTS AND OVERLAPPING CONSENSUS

Building consensus on practical norms, while not being concerned about various peoples' justifications for doing so, seems like a good strategy in a globally divergent context. This is certainly a useful approach because sometimes our philosophical and spiritual reasons, or horizons of significance and meaning, in relation to ethical norms can be so disparate, and even antagonistic, that discussion seems pointless. Indeed, discussions in this area can be counter-productive. They are often enmeshed in the context of power relationships between historically, socially, and economically divergent groups; dominant parties exert an enormous force on what is to count as the good, the reasonable, and the rational. So, why not agree to disagree when it comes to fundamentals, and discuss things that we can all relate to, like security, bodily integrity, freedom from hunger, access to education, and basic health care? These matter to all of us, and in a way that does not require that we discuss issues of meaning and purpose. There is much to be said for this approach, yet at the same time, I find myself uncomfortable with it.

One of the key reasons for my discomfort is that even basic goods, things that we can indeed all relate to (for example, the right to life, security of person, freedom from torture) are perhaps sometimes themselves the subject of disagreement, even though there may be overlapping similarities. Such differences are often a result of our deeper conceptions of the good, and lead to divergences when we attempt to specify, in practice, various norms and how they should be defined and balanced. This is evident in various non-Western challenges to human rights articles as not cross-culturally applicable (see Peetush 2008 for discussion). We need to ask here: How does Rawls propose to separate the purely practical and political from the comprehensive? The distinction rests on the idea that the former is more limited in terms of scope and applies only to the basic economic, social, and political structure of a society. In contrast, a comprehensive doctrine applies to and includes wider-reaching subjects that deal with, for instance, "what is of value in human life, and ideals of personal character" (Rawls 1993, 13). Accepting "political liberalism," according to Rawls, "does not presuppose accepting any particular comprehensive, religious, philosophical, or moral doctrine" (ibid., 175).

This is where I am not entirely convinced: the very idea that a conception of justice should only apply to the economic, social, and political domain of a society, and that this can and ought to be distinguished from the "non-political" domain, is itself a comprehensive doctrine integral to Western liberal secular society and not found in many other traditions of thought. This view certainly has wide-ranging implications for issues of value in human life. For example, as various spokespersons of Aboriginal communities in Canada argue, this is a culturally embedded view that privileges liberal secular modes of social organization (see Peetush 2009). Specifically, the very notions of what one considers limited or political, and extensive or comprehensive, are themselves intricately embedded in substantive philosophical views: in other words, there is no "political" as opposed to "comprehensive."

According to Rawls (1993, 18–19), the normative "political" conception of person conceives the latter as having two moral powers: the capacity for a sense of justice and the capacity for a conception of the good. This clearly excludes, for example, other sentient beings. But how is this not a "comprehensive" view – even in the domestic context? From whose perspective does it, as Rawls says, "involve no particular metaphysical doctrine about the nature of persons?" (29). This is certainly not so, for example, from various Aboriginal, Buddhist, or Hindu perspectives where the basic unit of moral and political consideration may also encompass other sentient beings. From such other various perspectives, a restriction of this notion to include only human beings itself constitutes a comprehensive and deeply metaphysical doctrine.

So, while it is true that we may all agree that security, bodily integrity, freedom from hunger are important to all of us – we have an overlapping consensus here – our understanding of these notions may differ in important ways that do not overlap, and that involve deeper philosophical or religious values to which we subscribe. There is no use pretending that we are on neutral political ground while everyone else is not, especially in a highly globalized and interconnected world.

In this context, it is not possible to avoid discussions of value. For example, one would have to explain, in opposition to Aboriginal peoples or Buddhists, why animals or the environment are not included. How does one avoid getting into deep philosophical terrain here? Moreover, who gets to determine whether one's views are metaphysical or not? From whose perspective are they so? Sometimes tension between Western and non-Western nations results when basic concepts are not in accord. This can certainly be the case in conflicts between Aboriginal and non-Aboriginal societies; for example, on issues concerning self, agency, property, secularism. This is why it is important to lay these out clearly on the table.

But on Rawls' view, such discussions are, in principle, barred from the public domain by his conception of public reason. Particular "comprehensive" philosophical doctrines, religious or non-religious, should not in principle enter into discussions concerning basic issues of justice, either at a domestic or an international level. The content of public reason must be constrained by a purely "political" conception of justice. I recognize that the content of such reason will differ at the domestic and global levels. In terms of discussions held by the United Nations (un), dialogue concerning human rights articles must be constrained by international public reason, but even here, as in the domestic case, the content of public reason must be given in non-metaphysical, non-religious and non-philosophical terms (see Rawls 1999, 18, 55, 68, 123). Rawls later revises this account to allow parties to introduce philosophical doctrines into political discussion, but only if they give public reasons to support whatever such views are introduced. But this proviso does not alter the ideal, which is still that comprehensive doctrines should be kept to the "non-public" realm (e.g., in universities or in homes). If these do enter discussions concerning basic issues of justice, then parties had better be prepared to justify themselves by the use of public reasons appropriately constrained by a political conception of justice (see Rawls 1999, 37, 54–7, 134, 140–6, 175; 1993, l–lvii, 220, 223–8, 245–6).

Within such constraints, how is it possible for the relationship between various divergent communities to fully develop on the basis of equality, where all have the freedom fully to articulate their reasons and justifications according to their various self-understandings? This is a matter not only of fostering and furthering mutual understanding; it is a struggle for equality, respect, and acceptance of cultural differences and the legitimacy of such differences. That is especially important in a historical context where the self-understandings of formerly colonized peoples, such as those of the indigenous peoples of Canada, are not only repeatedly excluded, but denigrated. Indeed, the history of colonialism is replete with not only the illegal acquisition of territory, but the uncritical and illegitimate universalization of a narrow and specific perspective to all of humankind. Various self-understandings, ideas, and ways of life are uncritically presumed to be universal, objective, and neutral, and non-Western communities are simply required (or forced) to assimilate. Cultural difference is constructed as deviance and the self-understandings, beliefs, values, practices, and forms of social organization of non-Western nations are considered to be inferior and in need of civilization and progress. This kind of discourse is still alive and hinders intercultural dialogue and mutual cooperation. Voices are often excluded and marginalized.

Thus, the distinction between the political and comprehensive is more than just overdrawn; it can be misleading in a manner that silences those that have views divergent from our own. It is far too easy and tempting for dominant groups simply to label others' views as involving comprehensive or religious doctrines, and therefore as having no place in public discourse. This is something of concern, given the unequal historical power relationship between Euro-Western and non-Western nations.

Let me draw on Rawls' own example of one's attitude toward animals and the environment, as it shows just the sort of concerns I have about equality and the illegitimate exclusion of voices. In discussing "non-public" reasons for being concerned with animals and the environment, Rawls (1993, 245–6) actually refers to a view that is similar to that of Aboriginal peoples: "suppose our attitude toward the world is one of natural religion" and we think that "human beings should bear a certain stewardship toward nature." Rawls (ibid., 227–30) asserts that, apart from the fact that such an attitude rests in the non-public realm, "the status of the natural world and our proper relation to it is not a constitutional essential or a basic issue of justice."

But again, from whose perspective is this so? For Aboriginal communities, this is certainly a basic matter of justice that cannot be relegated to the domain of "non-public" reason where it should not enter into political discussion. Members of various Aboriginal nations argue that their relationship to the earth constitutes the cornerstone of their various cultural self-understandings. Such a relationship is integral to notions of self and agency. For example, in her paper "Iyani: It Goes This Way" (1980), Paula Gunn Allen (191) explains:

We are the land. To the best of my understanding, that is the fundamental idea embodied in Native American life and cultures ... More than remembered, the earth is the mind of the people as we are the mind of the earth. The land is not really the place (separate from ourselves) where we act out the drama of our isolate destinies. It is not a means of survival, a setting for our affairs, a resource on which we draw in order to keep our own act functioning. It is not the ever-present "Other" which supplies us with a sense of "I." It is rather a part of our being, dynamic, significant, real. It is ourselves, in as real a sense as such notion as "ego," "libido" or social network, in a sense more real than any conceptualization or abstraction about the nature of human being can ever be. The land is not an image in our eyes but rather it is as truly an integral aspect of our being as we are of its being ... Nor is this relationship one of mere "affinity" for the earth. It is not a matter of being "close to nature." The relation is more one of identity, in the mathematical sense, than of affinity. The Earth is, in a very real sense, the same as ourself (or selves).

The crucial importance of land to self and identity is widely shared amongst many Aboriginal peoples. For example, James Sakj Youngblood

Henderson (1995, 217) (Chickasaw and Cheyenne) in Saskatoon explains that land is the "ecological space that creates our consciousness, not an ideological construct or a fungible resource." And, land defines and has "always" defined Aboriginal "identity, their spiritual ecology, their reality" (ibid., 293). Elder Alex Skead (quoted in *Royal Commission on Aboriginal Peoples* 1995, 435) in Winnipeg (Ojibway) similarly remarks that "this is my body when you see this mother earth." Oren Lyons (1980, 173) (Onondaga and Iroquois Confederacy) in New York describes the relationship between self and land as so critical that it is conceived as the re-- lationship between mother and child. Justice Mary Ellen Turpel (1989–90, 29) (Cree) argues that moral agency in Aboriginal communities is derived from their spiritual relationship and responsibility for "Mother Earth."

Such sentiments are echoed countless times across various Aboriginal tribes in Canada; as illustrated, for example, by the hundreds of interviews taken by the Government of Canada for the Royal Commission on Aboriginal Peoples (RCAP) (1996). RCAP (1996, 430) commissioners argued that disputes will never be wholly resolved unless dialogue and negotiations are "guided by one of the fundamental insights from our hearings: that is, to aboriginal peoples, land is not just a commodity; it is an inextricable part of aboriginal identity, deeply rooted in moral and spiritual values."

Of course, I am not claiming all Aboriginal peoples share the same traditional views of the land, which are closed, homogenous, and unchanging. Nevertheless, I contend there exist certain distinct and pervasive resemblances among specific ideas that continue to flourish in many of these communities. Land as an intimate aspect of one's being is one of these.

After hundreds of years of subjugation and resistance, Aboriginal peoples continue to struggle for the power to determine the lives of their communities. A key conflict between Aboriginal peoples and Canada is not simply about demanding the return of land; it is deeper than this. They seek self-definition; they seek to be able to promote and live by their various distinct understandings. As importantly, they demand that such self-understandings be recognized by the Crown with respect and be seen as legitimate differences regarding living and being in the world. This is why the Delgamuukw decision of 1997 was critical. For the first time in Canadian history, Aboriginal oral traditions were recognized and given some weight in relation to non-Aboriginal traditions.

The importance of this insight has been recognized by the UN as a matter of international justice; for example, in the recently passed Declaration on the Rights of Indigenous Peoples (United Nations General Assembly,

2007). The Declaration makes no qualms about respecting substantive indigenous doctrines. It states that "respect for indigenous knowledge, cultures and traditional practices contributes to sustainable and equitable development and proper management of the environment" (ibid., 2). It goes on to argue that self-determination for Aboriginal peoples means that they "have the collective and individual right to develop their distinct identities and characteristics ... Have a right to maintain their distinctive spiritual and material relationship with the lands, territories, waters, and coastal seas and other resources which they have traditionally owned" (2007, 4).

But on Rawls' account of public reason, one would have to argue that such views have no place in a discussion of human rights or self-determination. They are not a legitimate matter for the discussion of public policy surrounding essentials of justice. These are, to use Rawls' own words, attitudes of natural religion, involving deep philosophical questions of value (1993, 245–6). According to Rawls, all we can say is that, in the international context (and perhaps in the case of internal formerly colonized peoples), non-liberal peoples ought to be allowed to live according to their various substantive doctrines as long as they ensure for their members urgent human rights, are not aggressive, and have some form of political accountability. This goes a long way toward the cultural recognition of non-liberal communities, but such a consensus is potentially too fragile for a number of reasons.

First, it has the danger of unjustly excluding potentially legitimate concerns because supposedly substantive and comprehensive issues are not matters for the political domain. These issues are relegated to the private realm and the margins of political debate. At the same time, it privileges liberal conceptions (e.g., of self, agency, property) because these are held to be "political" and non-substantive. This is conceptually problematic, as so-called "liberal political values" are as comprehensive and philosophical as any other perspective. One cannot assume that Western liberal principles of social and political organization are somehow natural and shared by all other cultures. These are themselves the particular manifestation of a particular collective imagination of how human beings and society ought to work. As such, in contact with other cultures, I do not see how one can avoid discussing deep and substantive views in the public and political domain, especially when basic concepts may not be shared. This problem is only exacerbated in the colonial context.

Rawls' distinction between the comprehensive and political is therefore a throwback to the idea of liberal neutrality, even though he attempts to distance himself from this idea. But liberalism is not neutral, and indeed, should not remain neutral when it comes to discussing important issues such as human rights.

Rawls' later revised proviso – that Aboriginal peoples, when bringing up their philosophical doctrines, should provide "public reasons" shared by dominant Western parties – also does not help in furthering mutual understanding. Understanding and appreciating the importance of these issues in such a diverse context requires being open to reasons that may not be public or that Western communities may simply not share. Of course, this is not to say that others need to agree with or adopt these doctrines.

Second, the Rawlsian overlapping consensus is rather close to a modus vivendi (in other words, a delicate balance of making sure we have as many guns as they do). The problem is that differences in substantive views will lead to continual differences in practice. As Charles Taylor argues, and Jacques Maritain before him, such divergences usually manifest when we attempt to clarify with others the exact nature and prioritization of basic ethical standards/human rights articles around which we need to build consensus. They will manifest in our accounts of what we are willing to live with as an acceptable range of interpretation regarding the specification and application of such articles. This is something Maritain argued in 1948 (VII–VIII):

> Where the difficulties and arguments begin is the determination of the scale of values governing the exercise and concrete integration of these various rights. Here we are no longer dealing with the mere enumeration of Human Rights, but with the principle of dynamic unification whereby they are brought into play, with the tone, scale, with the specific key in which different kinds of music are played on the same keyboard, music which in the event is in tune with, or harmful to, human dignity.

In the global context of attempting to build consensus on basic ethical norms or human rights, it seems to be that the way to decide on a range of acceptable interpretations is through a thorough discussion of such differences, which will invariably implicate discussion of deeper philosophical doctrines. How else are we to understand why they do or do not agree? How else are we to judge whether their justifications are not simply self-interested distortions, constructed by those who are in power for the sake of power? Dialogue is the key here, but it cannot proceed in the way it needs to without access to comprehensive and deeply philosophical doctrines.

FUSION OF HORIZONS

Discussion of various comprehensive doctrines seems especially salient in the context of colonialism, where the charge is that the self-understandings, ideas, and works of non-Western peoples, like the First Nations, have been denigrated for centuries. As previously mentioned, the demand for cultural recognition is not always just a demand that others acknowledge the pursuit of cultural identity-in-general as a legitimate goal, or that shared ends be allowed as legitimate considerations in public policy. Oppressed communities further request that we recognize and respect aspects of their particular traditions, that these are seen to be of equal value. In the context of Aboriginal Canadians, the demand is not simply that they be provided with economic protections, for instance. It is also that their modes of existence be recognized and respected as worthwhile ways of living in the world, a sense that colonialism attempted to destroy. The demand for recognition in this stronger form is crucial to a dialogue between Western and non-Western groups. Decolonization is in part about this struggle for respect.

As Charles Taylor argues, however, an acknowledgment of worth, if it is to be sincere, has to be based on study and understanding. It cannot just be made out of hand, without any knowledge of the particulars in question. This requires a theoretical framework in which such substantive issues can be fully articulated and conceived to be legitimate matters for public and political dialogue.

Let me emphasize that this does not necessarily require that one agree with, convert to, or develop a personal preference for the particular views or practices or works in question. One can acknowledge and appreciate the worth of many things without doing so. On the other hand, at the outset, we may not have the theoretical resources to make any such judgments of value. As Taylor (1995, 252) explains, "for a culture sufficiently different, the very understanding of what it means to be of worth will be strange and unfamiliar to us." The standards or "horizons" by which we decide what is meaningful and significant, or of worth, may be too disparate. This does not imply that different cultures are therefore imprisoned within their own cultural boundaries, or that we do not already share some cross-cultural horizons of meaning or worth. But that is why intercultural dialogue is critical. In the most fruitful cases, exchange results in the expansion, transformation, or fusion of our standards of meaning, significance, and worth.

Taylor illustrates this with the example of a raga, an Indian form of classical musical composition that has no fixed notes apart from a wide melodic and complex rhythmic structure in which the musician must improvise. "To approach, say a raga with the presumptions of value implicit in the well-tempered clavier would be forever to miss the point." Appreciation occurs here when there is an expansion or a "fusion of horizons," to use Gadamar's (1995, 252) idea, or when our standards of value expand, transform, or fuse. Although we may have hitherto taken certain standards as "given" in our judgments (for example, that musical pieces have fixed compositions), our judgments now become situated as one possibility alongside the differing standards of the unfamiliar culture. So when we do arrive at an appraisal of worth, it will be through a viewpoint that we could not have had before dialogue, exchange, and study. In this sense, intercultural dialogue alters and changes us as much as it does the other; it is transformative. We learn more not only about others but ourselves in such a process. In this way, dialogue can also help us to become aware of critical exclusions.

The idea of a fusion of horizons, or at least a partial fusion, leaves open the possibility that our conceptions of human rights may be transformed through cross-cultural discussion and dialogue with members of other communities. Through cultural exchange, our horizons of meaning or significance may expand, transform, or fuse – even if partially. For example, in the interaction with Aboriginal or Buddhist or Hindu and Jain communities, one learns that their conception of the self encompasses a much wider space to include animals. Thus, respect for "persons" or "human" life and integrity will also include respect for animals. This awareness can affect the range of what one had hitherto considered a legitimate notion of the person, and consequently, taken to be the basic unit of moral and political consideration. In turn, one's emphasis on certain values, of course, affects others' self-understandings.

The view that one should always be open to learning from other peoples, that perhaps they too might have something insightful to offer, does not mean that Western liberals need now to abandon their concern with fundamental norms. It is not one step away from allowing torture and slavery, as Jeremy Waldron (1992) or Brian Barry (2001) might have us believe. Rather, the legitimacy of variances in fundamental norms needs to be arrived at through cross-cultural dialogue and mutual understanding, on all sides. Many times, accommodation will not be possible and toleration or a modus vivendi will present the only viable solutions. This does not, however, count against adopting an attitude of openness toward one another as an ideal to which we should aspire. Convergence on human rights requires just such an attitude, which the colonial context has made difficult.

CONCLUSION

I believe that the normative architecture of a Rawlsian framework for global relations provides the most fruitful liberal pathway for Western nations to approach issues of cultural and religious diversity. It allows for the development of a just and equitable relationship between Western and non-Western cultures, as it conceptualizes these others on equal standing in a Society of Peoples, with no theoretical requirement that they must convert to liberal values. However, Rawls' insistence that the political be extracted from the comprehensive, philosophical, or religious, and that the latter be barred from political dialogue on issues of justice carries the danger of uncritically and unfairly excluding legitimate concerns and voices. The proposed separation is neither possible nor desirable. In the wake of an interconnected and decolonizing world, political unity cannot come from uniformity or the suppression of differences – history is replete with such disastrous attempts. It can only be achieved through a creative self-transformation that emerges from a dialogue with our interdependent others.

REFERENCES

Barry, Brian M. 2001. *Culture and Equality: An Egalitarian Critique of Multiculturalism*. Cambridge: Harvard University Press.

Donnelly, Jack. 1999. "Human Rights and Asian Values: A Defense of 'Western' Universalism." In *The East Asian Challenge For Human Rights*, edited by Joanne R. Bauer, and Daniel A. Bell, 60–87. New York: Cambridge University Press.

Geertz, Clifford. 1973. *The Interpretation of Cultures*. New York: Basic Books-Harper Collins.

Gunn Allen, Paula. 1980. "Iyani: It Goes This Way." In *The Remembered Earth: An Anthology of Contemporary American Indian Literature*, edited by Geary Hobson, 191–3. Albuquerque: University of New Mexico Press.

Henderson, James S. Y. 1995. "Mi'kmaw Tenure in Atlantic Canada." *Dalhousie Law Journal* 18(2): 196–294.

Maritain, Jacques. 1948. "Introduction." In *Human Rights: Comments and Interpretations; a symposium*, edited by UNESCO, 1–9. Accessed May 18 2010. http://unesdoc.unesco.org/images/0015/001550/155042eb.pdf.

Kymlicka, Will. 1989. *Liberalism, Community and Culture*. Oxford: Clarendon Press.

– 1995. *Multicultural Citizenship: A Liberal Theory of Minority Rights*. Oxford: Clarendon Press.

– 1998. *Finding Our Way: Rethinking Ethnocultural Relations in Canada*. Toronto: Oxford University Press.

– 2001. *Politics in the Vernacular: Nationalism, Multiculturalism, and Citizenship*. New York: Oxford University Press.

Lyons, Oren. 1980. "An Iroquois Perspective." In *American Indian Environments: Ecological Issues in Native American History*, edited by Christopher Vecsey and Robert W. Venables, 171–4. Syracuse: Syracuse University Press.

Parekh, Bhikhu. 2000. *Rethinking Multiculturalism: Cultural Diversity and Political Theory*. Cambridge: Harvard University Press.

Peetush, Ashwani K. 2003. "Kymlicka, Multiculturalism, and Non-Western Nations." *Public Affairs Quarterly* 17(4): 291–318.

– 2008. "Global Ethics, Human Rights, and Non-Western Values." *The Global Studies Journal* 1(2): 63–9.

– 2009. "Indigenizing Human Rights: First Nations, Self-Determination, and Cultural Identity." In *Indigenous Identity and Activism*, edited by Priti Singh, 190–204. New Delhi: Shipra Press.

Rawls, John. 1993. *Political Liberalism*. New York: Columbia University Press.

– 1999. *The Law Of Peoples: With The Idea of Public Reason Revisited*. Cambridge: Harvard University Press.

Royal Commission on Aboriginal Peoples. 1996. *Restructuring the Relationship*. Vol. 2, part one. Ottawa: The Government of Canada.

Taylor, Charles. 1995. "The Politics of Recognition." In *Philosophical Arguments*, 225–56. Cambridge: Harvard University Press.

– 1999. "Conditions of an Unforced Consensus on Human Rights." In *The East Asian Challenge for Human Rights*, edited by Joanne R. Bauer, and Daniel A. Bell, 124–44. New York: Cambridge University Press.

Tatsuo, Inoue. 1999. "Liberal Democracy and Asian Orientalism." In *The East Asian Challenge For Human Rights*, edited by Joanne R. Bauer, and Daniel A. Bell, 27–59. New York: Cambridge University Press.

Tully, James. 1995. *Strange Multiplicity: Constitutionalism in an Age of Diversity*. Cambridge: Cambridge University Press.

Turpel, Mary Ellen. 1989–1990. "Aboriginal Peoples and the Canadian Charter: Interpretive Monopolies, Cultural Differences." *Canadian Human Rights Yearbook* 6: 3–45.

United Nations General Assembly, 61st session. 2007. "United Nations Declaration on the Rights of Indigenous Peoples" (A/RES/61/295), 13 September. http://www.un.org/esa/socdev/unpfii/documents/DRIPS_en.pdf.

Jeremy Waldron. 1992. "Minority Cultures and the Cosmopolitan Alternative." *University of Michigan Journal of Law Reform* 25 (751–93).

Walker, Graham. 1997. "The Idea of Nonliberal Constitutionalism." In *Ethnicity and Group Rights*, edited by Ian Shapiro, and Will Kymlicka, 154–84. New York: New York University Press.

7

The Normativity of Inclusion and Exclusion: Should Multiculturalism Encompass Religious Identities?

GORDON DAVIS

Some aspects of how multiculturalism can or should relate to religious identities have not yet been widely discussed in contemporary political theory, but we can already anticipate what one of the greatest sources of resistance will be, from both theorists and policymakers, especially to the idea of public support for cultural activities that are either religious in nature or are specifically connected to a religion or religious group. As in other areas, an argument we can expect to loom large is a "slippery slope" argument. Used as an argument against extending multiculturalism to religion, the argument would be that offering public support to a few respected and valued religious groups would require – on pain of incurring charges of discrimination – offering public support to more and more groups, until eventually some will come to light as endorsing views or practices that are widely and rightly[1] considered to be deeply problematic, either morally or socially. If defenders of this extended multiculturalism were to counter that such lines can never be clearly drawn, they might thereby inadvertently concede what they would rather not concede: the slipperiness of this slope. Indeed, the argument that challenges them here can be construed as saying precisely that the difficulty of drawing lines makes it dangerous to try, resulting in an all or nothing choice (i.e., public support for all, or for no religious groups). Since support for all may be both unrealistic and morally unacceptable, the argument goes, there should be support for none.

The moral concern I shall highlight here focuses on what I shall call "exclusionary soteriology," which characterizes beliefs and doctrines that deny the possibility of salvation for those outside a certain religious community or affiliation. Though moral qualms about such doctrines are common, we might have more than mere qualms in cases where the exclusionary doctrines are explicit, inflammatory, and regularly communicated to the members of a community or tradition. Whether a particular religious community qualifies for support from a broadened policy of multiculturalism, however, will depend less on the content of its doctrines than on its ability to mobilize political support (speaking here de facto, and perhaps politically and/or legally de jure but not morally de jure, and assuming the context of a modern democratic society). And most modern societies contain religious communities that both have that ability and feature some form of exclusionary soteriology. Some forms may be relatively harmless; but since these communities will be impossible to exclude from multicultural program support, it may become impossible to exclude others with even more exclusionary views. These views may conflict with the values of inclusion and mutual respect, which some would consider to be the normative basis of multiculturalism itself. At any rate, that is the slippery slope that might open up when multicultural program support is offered to some relatively mainstream religious traditions.

However, slippery slope arguments can be deceptive. Even when the premise of indefinite expansion of scope is granted (so that there is a slope, or trend, to consider), we often overlook the possibility that support for all possible cases may be ethically defensible or even ethically required. For instance, even when feelings about some cultural practices being "morally unacceptable" are widely shared, we should be careful to subject such "moral" attitudes to higher-order ethical or normative assessment. Sometimes slipping on a slippery slope leads in the right direction, even when a tolerance for intolerance is where a slope is headed (consider, e.g., tolerance for civil disobedience among environmental activists). Also, we should not despair too quickly over finding places to draw lines between supportable and unsupportable cultural activities, whether religiously rooted or not. Sometimes there are places, on an otherwise slippery slope, where society can stand firm and stop itself sliding further.

Although I will be raising considerations here that may seem to offer fodder to those wishing to use slippery slope arguments against multiculturalism, I do not intend in advance to rule out these other types of response to those considerations. Indeed, looking at the multi-religious landscapes of Canada and India provides an interesting contrast of slopes that may lead to dangers and slopes that may not. Considering the incidence of so-called "communal violence" in India, it may come as a surprise to some that the particular dangers I have in mind may be greater in Canada than in India. That is, the fear of a "slippery slope" may be more justified in the Canadian context, or so I will argue. In any case, a broader conclusion one might draw is that certain policies of multiculturalism are better suited to some countries than others, even when comparing countries with similar degrees and kinds of cultural and religious diversity (and a fortiori when comparing countries with dissimilar degrees and kinds of diversity).

This contrast could vindicate at least the theoretical possibility of a morally defensible policy of religion-encompassing multiculturalism – no more than "theoretical" for a country like Canada, perhaps, if I am right about the dangers that exist there; but perhaps more than merely theoretical for some other societies. However, in practice, our moral concern with mutual respect in society requires attention to familiar sources of distrust and prejudice, and one of these, in the religious sphere, is exclusionary soteriology. Rather than applying broad brushstrokes to develop general objections along the lines of "slippery slope" arguments, I will be considering this specific aspect of some religious associations, which – in some societies – may make the risk of a slippery slope acute.

RELIGIOUS COMMUNITIES AND RELIGIOUS ASSOCIATIONS: SOME PRELIMINARY DISTINCTIONS

Before considering how we might characterize different forms and levels of religious grouping, I will begin with some preliminary remarks about varieties of multiculturalism, as they relate to cultures that are centred on a religion. Multiculturalism, even in its normative forms, need not be characterized in terms of rights; but I will simplify the first phase of my discussion by using the language of rights.[2] In particular, I shall begin by contrasting negative rights and positive rights, in relation to cultures rather than individuals – such that the negative rights that interest us serve to protect a culture against certain kinds of interference or oppression, whereas positive rights are claims made by and for communities to certain goods or resources or forms of assistance.

It is generally understood that the distinction between negative and positive rights is neither sharp nor exhaustive. There do, however, seem to be some clear paradigm cases of each, and this is also true in relation to the claims of religious communities to the protection or promotion of their culture. In the case of rights claims made on the basis of one or another form of multiculturalism, there are for example the negative rights that a community can claim when resisting a publicly mandated and standardized educational curriculum, and at the opposite end of this spectrum, there are positive rights that a community can claim, such as claims to public funding for organizing conferences or even religious festivals that feature some degree of public outreach.[3]

While political theory in the last fifteen years has seen a marked rise in the number of defenders of a civic role for religion(s) in modern liberal society, most have represented an American perspective (see Quinn 1997; Wolterstorff 1997; Tomasi 2001; Weithman 2002), and some a British perspective (see Fergusson 2004; Modood 2006). This has resulted in some fairly uncontroversial suggestions, focused essentially on the negative rights that are secured by religious toleration (and some other themes noted below). The context of debate over multiculturalism in Canada, on the other hand, is bound to generate more provocative claims, because Canada's laws and policies on multiculturalism permit forms of positive public support that are virtually unheard of in both the US and the UK (Kymlicka 1995; 1998). Any political philosopher wishing to speak to the Canadian context, and wishing to extend these writers' sympathetic view of the status of religion in civic and cultural life, will have to consider the possibility of public funding being directed toward religious groups that may eventually qualify as beneficiaries of multiculturalism program support.

Many of the politically interesting claims of champions of multiculturalism do fall in between or outside of the categories of negative and positive rights – for instance, claims in relation to immigration policy or to measures intended to counter employment discrimination (Modood 2006). I will, however, focus on the sorts of positive rights claims just mentioned, not only in order to address the Canadian context, but also in order to raise challenging questions about the ethical limits of cherished political norms. Unlike many liberals and libertarians, I see no a priori reason to exclude the possibility of public funding for culturally enriching events or programs – privately organized but in some way publicly projected – some of which may be rooted in a religious tradition. Yet not all such activities are bound to garner, or, more to the point, bound to deserve public support in the form of funding or governmental assistance. What considerations are normatively, and in particular ethically, relevant to drawing such contentious distinctions?

One simple proposal would be that any religious community should be able to qualify for such support, but religious *organizations* should not. However, it may be that many religious organizations are benign while some religious communities are not. And in any case, a community – not to mention a "religion" – may be too decentralized to be in a position to seek such support, unlike organizations or associations. We may be required, in fact, to focus on religious associations (a term I shall define presently), and to try to draw some distinctions among them. If one were to try to compare religions or religious traditions themselves, we would be at a loss to know how to appropriately characterize them. It is a familiar fact that the myriad differences between what are commonly referred to as "world religions" threaten even the very concept of "religion." Nevertheless it is important to remind ourselves that any politically useful description of a religious group cannot be assumed to apply to a religion as a whole.

In relation to intersections of religion and culture, I shall consider a religious *association* to be a group in which members are either registered or at least affiliated by virtue of regular contact for the purposes of rituals, sacraments, or organizational activities. Many church groups are loosely referred to as associations; but sometimes an entire branch of a religious tradition is centred around or even defined by something that is effectively an association. An example may be Roman Catholicism, the authorities of which do not use the term "association," but by my usage, it qualifies as an association. (It may be significant that lapsed Catholics who call themselves Catholic by virtue of family background – and perhaps even with childhood rituals such as "confirmation" in mind – rarely call themselves *Roman* Catholic. Merely having been "registered" by a parent, so to speak, is seen as insufficient for membership). Even if association membership may be too narrow for the purposes of defining Roman Catholicism, it seems at least *centred around* an institution that functions as an association.

By contrast, neither Christianity as a whole nor Judaism nor any other broad religious grouping could be called an association. These broad groupings might be thought of, among other things, as umbrella categories encompassing both communities and associations. The status of a religious group as a *community*, meanwhile, will of course depend on geographical context. In Canadian cities, the Christian population is too diffuse to qualify as a community; but it is often possible to speak of a Jewish community even though it may span a range of institutional branches, each of which might constitute a distinct association. Each religious tradition manifests a different pattern of overlapping cultural and institutional traditions in different countries, but I take it that a rough and ready distinction between communities and associations can serve certain purposes in political theory.

Another point to keep in mind here is that while we might expect general advocacy for multicultural program funding to be *voiced* mainly by associations but *intended* for education about and celebration of religious communities, a religious association that makes a particular claim to funding – in the event of such funding becoming available – may be inclined to use any subsidy to support the association as much as the community. There will be exceptions to this pattern, of course, but even the possibility is one that policymakers should be mindful of.

Finally, we can consider the doctrinal dimension of religious associations. The role of doctrines, not to mention their content, varies greatly across different religious traditions. For Westerners this becomes most vividly apparent when traditions such as Buddhism and Hinduism are compared to the Abrahamic faiths of the Western world, whose doctrines are sometimes codified in a relatively condensed form. Even this statement requires qualification since it ranges over such broad groupings, but the situation becomes more definite when we turn to religious *associations*. Whatever tradition is in question, a subsidy to support a program or event that is organized by a religious association provides support and recognition to a group that may be partly defined in terms of common adherence to certain doctrines. Such support to other types of cultural community will rarely have such an effect, that is, will rarely promote or entrench any definite beliefs or forms of belief. But this now raises a more substantive question: While these policies can have repercussions for the survival of certain doctrines and doctrinal beliefs, do such beliefs have any significant civic repercussions themselves?

EXCLUSIONARY SOTERIOLOGY IN CONTEMPORARY SOCIETY AND THE ROUSSEAUIAN RESPONSE

One thing that is distinctive about religious associations, whether beyond or only within the association, is their expression of doctrines, which have a strong tendency to frame the beliefs and values of members, if not also those citizens who find themselves participating in publicly supported events organized by those associations.[4] In any given case, these doctrines will range across many areas of thought and practice. It is worth bearing in mind at the outset, once we distinguish different sorts of doctrines and their potential for intercultural repercussions, that we should guard against an overreliance on normative concepts that concern only the *indirect* practical implications of the spread of certain doctrines, concepts such as "dangerous," "destabilizing," or even "divisive." I have already used the term "danger," but there is a risk in being too loose with this term. If these concepts provide the tests we use for assessing the moral or legal status of certain doctrines, then we will only notice some of the extrinsic features of those doctrines (insofar as many of the social ramifications of doctrinal advocacy are extrinsic to the thoughts and ideas at the heart of the doctrines themselves). So, for example, we risk taking too narrow a view if we consider only an association's social engagements on issues like abortion or the environment rather than their doctrines concerning divinity and divine intercession in society and politics; eschatology and messianism; the relations between science, reason, and faith; and interfaith relations. The main reason for looking at these latter areas may not be the same as the reason for considering their views on the status of the unborn or on certain kinds of science and technology; that is, it may not be a matter of considering how their votes and advocacy will affect public affairs (or affect things of vital concern to themselves, such as their own health care), but rather a matter of considering what these doctrines express about their attitudes to fellow citizens who are not fellow believers.

The above topics were listed randomly for the sake of illustration, but I did not mention one topic that gets surprisingly little attention in contemporary discussions of multiculturalism and mutual respect: soteriology, the domain of views and methods concerning salvation, including doctrines about eternal rewards and punishments in the afterlife.[5] What, if anything, does it say about democratic liberal citizenship that fellow citizens can, and frequently do, regard each other as headed for eternal separation from God? – i.e. that many citizens regard many or most others as condemned to an eternally inferior spiritual status? What social challenges and moral dilemmas arise from the fact that such mutual contempt is often entrenched along sectarian lines, rather than arising out of intracommunity personal differences? Interestingly, a passage from Rousseau's *Social Contract* (1973) shows not only that he took this problem more seriously than we now tend to, but that he nearly equated the problem of interreligious intolerance in general with this problem of what I will call "exclusionary soteriology." In the penultimate chapter of *Du Contrat Social* (Pt. IV, ch. 8), we find a disconcerting combination of liberalism and apparent illiberalism:

Those who distinguish civil from theological intolerance are, to my mind, mistaken. The two forms are inseparable. It is impossible to live at peace with those we regard as damned; to love them would be to hate God who punishes them: we positively must either reclaim or torment them. Wherever theological intolerance is admitted, it must inevitably have some civil effect ... Now that there is and can be no longer an exclusive national religion, tolerance should be given to all religions that tolerate others, so long as their dogmas contain nothing contrary to the duties of citizenship. But whoever dares to say: "Outside the Church is no salvation," ought to be driven from the State. (Rousseau 1973, 308)[6]

I will not attempt to analyze this entire passage, but we can note at least that Rousseau includes beliefs about the damnation of others (by virtue of religious membership alone) among the "dogmas" that are contrary to the duties of citizenship. It is necessary, though, to distinguish exclusionary soteriological doctrines (considered in the abstract) from exclusionary soteriological attitudes. Some branches of Christianity, for example, may have codified doctrines of this nature, but it is a further question whether such doctrines are reflected in the actual attitudes of contemporary members of the branch. Rousseau's use of the term "*dogme*/dogma" obscures this distinction. A reformulation of his concern might emphasize the role of attitudes as the elements of exclusionary soteriology that can undermine the mutual civic respect that is a "duty of citizenship." However, like beliefs, attitudes can be latent, and their problematic aspect can surface as a result of a religious association's members acknowledging their commitment to some feature of the belief system which itself endorses exclusionary soteriology. It may even simply be a matter of acknowledging a scripture as sacred, where the member knows that the scripture affirms a form of soteriology that excludes non-members outright.

From a certain point of view, it seems very puzzling that widespread belief in the eternally inferior spiritual status of others has rarely torn societies apart (at least not since 1648,[7] in the West). One could imagine an extraterrestrial visitor being utterly astonished by this feature of modern society. This thought prompts us to look beneath the surface, to look past the contingencies of modern social and economic development, and to ask: what civic values might be threatened by such attitudes if those attitudes were to become more widespread or more intense? This question encompasses two more specific questions: (1) how might political stability and civic spirit be indirectly affected by the spread of such attitudes (if at all)? and (2) how might civic values be directly challenged or violated by the attitudes themselves (if at all)?

A host of contemporary biases often conspire to keep our attention focused on the first question – both normative biases, such as those of political liberalism, and methodological biases, such as those that favour empirical groundings in political theory. (Note that the first question is, with appropriate specification, open to empirical investigation.) The second question may require an ethical perspective, but it is an illusion that political liberalism – or any other normative theory – might do without such a perspective, so despite the qualms of both empirically-minded sociologists and neutrality-oriented political liberals, some genuine ethical reflection is called for here.

Before broaching the direct ethical wrongs that may be involved in beliefs about the culturally determined spiritual status of others,[8] let us pause to consider the complexity of social patterns that relate to the first question, that is, the question of how exclusionary soteriological attitudes might eventually result in certain social or political problems, for example, discrimination, tension, or violence. (This may seem to be the question Rousseau has in mind, but I take it that the passage above does not settle whether he is mainly worried about indirect effects on social relations or the direct undermining of civic spirit and civic values; we can gather in any case that he worried about both.)[9] Both history and everyday experience show that people find it relatively easy to compartmentalize religious beliefs and attitudes of this kind, and carry on many social interactions while more or less oblivious to aspects of their own beliefs; at the very least, such attitudes can exacerbate tendencies toward violence in the context of certain unresolved political issues. This may be the case when violent actions are directed against doctors who perform abortions, as inhibitions against violence may be weakened when opponents of abortion rights think of those doctors as beyond spiritual redemption. But, if we are to be *de rigueur* here, we should leave these conjectures for empirical research to judge, so I will not press these considerations further.

These reflections concern indirect practical repercussions, but the second question above concerns direct normative implications. That second question need not only concern moral or ethical rights and wrongs. In fact, broaching "direct" normative concerns immediately raises issues about how the parameters of our discussion may be affected by our orientation with respect to so-called comprehensive and political liberalisms. This is because some forms of political liberalism would have us hold off *any* judgments about the ethical rights and wrongs of the doxastic and attitudinal roots of respect and contempt (e.g., Rawls 1994).

For those who are open either to a form of comprehensive liberalism or to any other political philosophy that allows itself to judge (at least some) policies according to robust moral norms, we can briefly note some moral concerns before moving on to address political liberalism. Interestingly, Rousseau chose to stress the extent of the problem (of what I am calling exclusionary soteriology) by taking up the standpoint of one who believes *others* are damned – albeit through no fault of their own, other than continued group membership. Moral intuitions can also be focused by taking the point of view of those who are being relegated, in this way, to an eternally inferior status;[10] and obviously Rousseau wishes us ultimately to consider those on the receiving end of these attitudes. However, these moral intuitions are not always so strong when seen in light of what is at stake socially and politically. That is, whatever moral indignation we might feel when others make explicit their belief that we are spiritually beyond redemption, or even deserve eternal damnation, it is an indignation that fades with our general awareness that although such beliefs are common, they rarely affect the everyday trust and esteem that bind us together in society. What might sharpen moral intuitions, though, would be to consider how we feel about those who believe our children – taking "our" with whatever scope one wishes – deserve eternal damnation (again, through no fault of their own).[11] It seems ethically wrong to believe this, regardless of whether the belief is ever openly expressed.

As well as noting that even a near-universal sharing of this intuition would not automatically justify an (all-things-considered) ethical conclusion, we will want to keep in mind that there may be broadly ethical reasons for abstaining from political or legal responses to this ethical problem. But let us go even further, for the sake of argument, and concede the political liberal's starker separation of ethics and politics. As Blain Neufeld and I (Davis and Neufeld 2007) argue in an article on Rawlsian political liberalism, this view has its own distinctive conception of mutual respect as a civic duty, which is less demanding in terms of what it implies about reforming personal attitudes in society. We argue that many writers have overestimated the spillover that would result from inculcating that form of mutual respect in schools (a spillover that is often alleged to result in the necessity of exercises in robust forms of critique directed at cultural and religious traditions, i.e., in the classroom). However, even if we are right about that, this leaves open the question of whether, in the public sphere generally, certain kinds of attitudes would threaten even the modest form of mutual respect that political liberalism requires. Rawlsian political liberalism would limit the scope for policy moves targeting intolerant but deeply held attitudes that do *not* undermine basic standards of mutual regard (i.e., a general regard for one another as citizens entitled to explanations that operate according to the norms of public reason).

Whenever those basic standards are threatened, however, public policy can scrutinize and address the sources of the threats.

If we turn to consider how religious associations may encourage beliefs or attitudes that threaten those standards of mutual respect, we would of course have to proceed on a case by case basis. To reiterate, we cannot generalize about any religion; nor can we generalize about how any religious tradition tends to subdivide into certain kinds of religious associations. But a general point emerges here, even without our having to spell out what the "norms of public reason" should be, or what other aspects of political liberal civic respect come into play. Any conception of these features of mutual respect will refer to what we must see other citizens as entitled to, merely by virtue of being citizens. But beliefs and attitudes that are based on an exclusionary soteriology may prevent believers from acknowledging that (certain) citizens are entitled to anything at all. Those beliefs and attitudes, and the teachings and doctrines that foster them, would thereby threaten even a minimal form of mutual respect.

These very general remarks do not amount to a defence of Rousseau, and I am not speaking from any particular liberal perspective. However, with various elements of liberalism deeply entrenched in almost every modern society (if not also the sort of civic republicanism that puts the greatest emphasis on mutual civic respect), there is a significant conditional conclusion one may draw: if one's society is to uphold elements of *either* ethical liberalism or political liberalism, there will be normative limits to what kinds of religious associations society can afford to nurture.

It is important here to speak in terms of what society can afford to nurture, instead of what society can afford to tolerate. The danger – or even the inherent vice – of deeply exclusionary attitudes does not necessarily justify curbing the basic freedoms of association and religion that enable some people to hold these attitudes (notwithstanding Rousseau's more restrictive conclusion). Even though the "danger" is not merely a practical concern, we can think of it as comparable to practical dangers, in that we may simply want to minimize the damage – in this case, by making such associations ineligible for multiculturalism program support.

No doubt there are many who would argue that there are more pressing concerns with respect to issues where multiculturalism and religion intersect – for example, the treatment of women in religious communities or in religious associations (Okin 1999). Even if such concerns are more pressing in some ways, it is at least of theoretical interest that such dangers are of a different kind, being largely intracultural rather than intercultural. Exclusionary soteriology and other aspects of religious belief raise unique issues regarding intercultural understanding and mutual civic respect.

SOME IMPLICATIONS FOR CANADA AND INDIA

It might be thought that the positive rights incorporated into the versions of multiculturalism discussed above are more at home in Canada than in India. This could be for historical or economic reasons, but it could also be due to the perception that the dividing lines of religion and culture are less stark in Canada than in at least some parts of India. However, when it comes to religion as an aspect of culture, there is some reason to question this assumption, at least once we begin to see exclusionary soteriology as a potentially problematic feature of some religious associations. That is, Canadians may have some reason to be more wary of including religious identity within the scope of multiculturalism programs.

While Canada features a diverse range of religious faiths and communities, India features an arguably even greater diversity. No single paragraph could do justice to this diversity. Nonetheless, one might try to describe the situation in India (after listing important groups such as Jains, Zoroastrians and others, who each account for less than 1 per cent of the population) as comprising Hindus, Sikhs, and a modest but growing number of Buddhists, as well as Muslims and Christians, whose religions are more familiar in the West.

Compared to all these other groups, it could be argued that Christian associations have a greater tendency to encourage exclusionary soteriological attitudes (even if often indirectly, and with many notable exceptions).[12] Considering that Canada's largest religious groups are Christian, and considering that religious life in Canada may be more association-centred than it is in India, Canada is arguably less ready for a multiculturalism that encompasses religion, if the considerations above are both ethically and politically important.[13] It might help to illustrate this by comparing some even more clear-cut cases, within India and – for the moment – within the United States. On the one hand, many Hindu communities in India, as well as many mixed Hindu, Muslim, and "tribal" communities, make use of a variety of temples and local traditions simultaneously, rather than structuring themselves around associations as I have defined them; and, in those cases where certain scriptures can be singled out as being of particular importance, exclusionary soteriology is often absent.[14] On the other hand, the strength of fundamentalist Christian communities in the United States (where "fundamentalism" is taken to involve, *inter alia*, literalist interpretations of scripture) is well-known; and it is well-known that their beliefs about salvation are often exclusionary. Now, religious associations along these lines may be less common in Canada, but it is safe to say that, at least outside major urban centres, Canadian religious life is more akin to this facet of American religious culture than it is to the Indian model described above. In light of history and geography, this is rather obvious – so that even without precise details for comparative purposes, one might conjecture that the sphere of religion in Canada would be, in some respects, less well-suited to multiculturalism program support than in India.

Some would point to controversies surrounding charter school options in education as evidence of these dangers, and also as evidence of the cultural similarities between much of the United States and much of Canada. Without attempting a full analysis of doctrinal patterns and relations among various Christian movements and denominations, we can at least acknowledge that there is a partial but significant overlap among creationists, evangelicals, and fundamentalists. Some creationists fall outside the latter two groupings, and some evangelicals may not qualify as fundamentalists; accordingly, exclusionary soteriology is likely to progress from weaker to stronger forms, in this order. As I just noted, this whole spectrum may be more attenuated in Canada than in the United States, and yet educators in Canada have often worried about the impact of these groups, especially when there has been discussion of systemic reforms involving school choice policies.[15] One reform along these lines has involved the introduction of publicly funded charter schools. While this is common in the United States, where many states have looked to the constitutional separation of church and state to contain religious influences in charter schools (with varying degrees of success), the lack of such an official separation in Canada arouses more acute worries about the – albeit less widespread – tendency to support charter schools as a way of funding schools that will accommodate the priorities of the above groups.[16] This may help to explain why only one province in Canada has introduced publicly funded charter schools.[17] In any case, despite political differences between the United States and Canada, and many cultural differences, a similar incidence of religious affiliation in at least some regions of Canada has been the source of these concerns about schooling, which themselves go to the heart of the concerns outlined in the previous section.

An objection to these reservations about the prospect of religion-encompassing multiculturalism in Canada could come from historians, sociologists, or Christians themselves – to the effect that we should recognize that in recent times, in practice, Christians have been more tolerant of one another than has been the case with many other religious traditions, and that as a result, multiculturalism funding for religious groups in Canada would – according to this objection – generate less social tension than it would in a country like India. However, one wonders whether a Canada mired in economic stagnation would remain as indifferent to shadowy doctrinal differences as Indians may become in the midst of economic prosperity.[18] That is, relations between religious groups in Canada may be more precarious than they look at present, and such relations in India less so.

To some extent this objection is, moreover, cancelled out by another one. This other objection would point out that *both* religious communities and religious associations – and Christian ones in particular – have evolved so as to play down the overall importance of ancient scriptures. Some might go so far as to call the whole set of problems outlined in the previous section a red herring. But the premise of this objection may just reinforce the point I made there. Some Christian groups do minimize their reliance on ancient scripture; and some groups do this simply by virtue of their cultural traditions, rather than via policy or discussion or reform. These groups might justifiably qualify, then, for full privileges within multiculturalism programs; the dilemmas arise meanwhile with respect to those associations that make their faith in the sacred status of scriptures very clear (along with other hard cases, such as, perhaps, Roman Catholicism, where ancient scripture is heavily filtered via frameworks such as the catechism). Perhaps, in addition to favourable social and economic conditions, a reduced reliance on the words of scripture has enabled Christian groups in the West to be on better terms than was the case a few centuries ago. But this just confirms the dangers inherent in (some) scriptures, and these are dangers that are unlikely to disappear completely.

Another objection to my argument, which might equally have been acknowledged in the previous section, concerns the nature of an association's beliefs about the "eternally inferior spiritual status" of others. This phrase may tend to obscure the fact that, even in most exclusionary religions, eternal inferiority is not a *fait accompli*; on the contrary, in this life, all people may be regarded – by such religions – as having the capacity for salvation. This acknowledgement may be considered sufficient to secure the sort of mutual respect discussed earlier. Moreover, some religions comprise cultural groups that retain a collective historical memory of their forebears' conversion, and their adherents may thus harbour an important kind of fellow feeling with those not yet converted. The reason I mention this here is that it may be argued that Christianity – particularly in Canada – is indeed like this, while perhaps some of the main religions in India are not.

There are two serious flaws in this objection, however. Firstly, if the adherents of a religion – in India, for example – do not tend to compare outsiders to their own forebears, this is hardly a problem if the religion is not soteriologically exclusionary in the first place. Secondly, the sort of mutual respect that is made possible by this soteriological openness seems too fragile to mitigate the kinds of concerns outlined in the previous section. For example, a readiness to respect those who do not *yet* subscribe to one's own religion may result in a kind of respect that persists for as long as these others show an interest in religion of some kind or other; but this favourable attitude could easily evaporate in cases where outsiders show an increasing commitment to secularism, agnosticism, or atheism. Unfortunately, it seems that we may have no choice but to somehow acknowledge the differences between religious identities that permit genuine respect for such outsiders and those that do not.

It is very tempting to conclude that this can of worms is best left unopened. Such a conclusion could take one of two forms. On the one hand, there is the option of simply refraining from offering any kind of public support to religious associations in general. This option has the advantage of guaranteeing a form of non-discrimination, or at least – the more ethically dubious advantage – of reinforcing an impression of non-discrimination. On the other hand, any society that already offers such support, but to only *some* religious associations, may develop a culture of public denial, that is, denial that those associations promote any kind of exclusionary ideology; or, if it so happens that the sanctioned associations are non-exclusionary, policymakers and constitutional experts could be looked to for non-partisan approaches to explaining the status quo. One might wonder whether a culture of public denial would not also be an option in the case of a maximally non-discriminatory openness to public support for all lawful religious associations – as if the "can of worms" that appears set to be opened would in fact stay safely closed. But that prospect seems entirely unrealistic. While it may be relatively easy for a society to maintain a cordially mute status quo, it is much more difficult to suppress public reactions to unfamiliar forms of exclusionary religion (as some recent European experiences with alleged "cults" might be taken to illustrate).

But we should remain on guard against a premature recoil from an apparently slippery slope (from treating some religious associations as eligible for public support to feeling obliged to treat all as eligible). In any case, even if proponents of multiculturalism favour a tactical retreat from the specific area of public support for activities organized by religious associations, that need not undermine interest in the idea in principle. However, if multiculturalism does retreat from the sphere of such positive rights, and concentrates merely on mutual tolerance and non-discrimination, one wonders what the difference would ultimately be, between that form of multiculturalism and more traditional forms of political liberalism.

NOTES

1 I have no particular examples in mind of religious groups that are "rightly" considered problematic. When any particular example is offered, we should not be impressed merely by the addition of such a normative phrase to an expression of mistrust or skepticism. Without some normative qualifier, however, to speak only of what is "widely" considered problematic would itself be problematic, for familiar and obvious reasons: there is widespread prejudice against certain religious groups, sometimes so widespread as to encompass large majorities in democratic societies, with prejudices sometimes directed against religious groups that are benign or even exemplary in ways that go unappreciated.

2 I am also simplifying by considering multiculturalism as a policy guide, rather than as a justificatory foundation for any or all aspects of social and political reform (e.g., in the way that Isaiah Berlin's (1969) value-pluralism can be construed as a justification for institutional arrangements that may be intended to promote overall value, even if those institutions are themselves most effective when not guided by any conception of value-pluralism). Many political philosophers are skeptical about "justificatory foundations," but even if their skepticism is misplaced, multiculturalism in particular is hard to formulate as a justificatory foundation.

3 It may be worth noting that what Kymlicka (1995) calls the "external protections" sought by some cultural communities can involve both negative and positive cultural rights – the latter possibly including a right to assistance in developing institutions that can be the site of some degree of autonomous decision making.

4 While it is also true that non-religious cultural identities can condition beliefs and values, this is often – if not generally – less marked than in cases involving membership in a religious association. Particular comparisons may suggest the reverse, e.g., if one were to compare a non-denominational soci-

ety of Swiss expatriates and a Zen community (highlighting, in this case, on the one hand, the self-conscious work ethic that diverse Swiss citizens often share, and on the other, the agnostic doxology of many Zen communities). Without being in a position to provide a full-scale survey here, I can only note that such cases are outliers, especially those, on the religious side, such as Zen; very few religious communities (let alone associations) are similarly agnostic in moral and metaphysical matters.

5 In the rest of the chapter, I will generally not draw fine distinctions between soteriologies and theories of the afterlife; but for the record, soteriology almost always has implications for conceptions of the afterlife, but the reverse is not so generally true, especially as regards exclusionary soteriologies – e.g., some cyclical theories of reincarnation may not exclude anyone from salvation, or may even treat salvation independently. When I use a phrase like "eternal separation from God," I refer merely to an example of an alleged state of non-salvation, one that is familiar in Western religions, not meaning to imply that either monotheistic beliefs or beliefs about hell are presuppositions of any exclusionary soteriology. Though "soteriology" is sometimes defined in terms of Christian concepts, I take it that almost every religion includes at least an implicit soteriology in a broader sense, i.e., some conception of spiritual welfare and how one may come to have it. (And of course, not every soteriology is exclusionary – as e.g., in some branches of Hinduism and Buddhism.) In some religions, communal welfare may be more important than individual spiritual welfare; but some of these pose even more acute problems with respect to exclusionary attitudes than the ones I mainly discuss here.

6 "Ceux qui distinguent l'intolérance civile et l'intolérance théologique se trompent, à mon avis. Ces deux intolérances sont inséparables. Il est impossible de vivre en paix avec des gens qu'on croit damnés; les aimer serait haïr Dieu qui les punit : il faut absolument qu'on les ramène ou qu'on les tourmente. Partout où l'intolérance théologique est admise, il est impossible qu'elle n'ait pas quelque effet civil … Maintenant qu'il n'y a plus et qu'il ne peut plus y avoir de Religion nationale exclusive, on doit tolérer toutes celles qui tolèrent les autres, autant que leurs dogmes n'ont rien de contraire aux devoirs du Citoyen. Mais quiconque ose dire, hors de l'Eglise point de Salut, doit être chassé de l'Etat" (Rousseau 2001, 179).

7 That is, since the end of the Thirty Years War in Europe, the most devastating war of all those that took place between Catholics and Protestants.

8 The most problematic beliefs are not beliefs about individuals who bring damnation upon themselves through vice (after all, there could be civic analogues of this in the context of crime and punishment); rather, the most

problematic cases are those where the identification of the "damned" is via mere cultural affiliation.

9 When Rousseau (1973, 308) says, "tolerance should be given to all religions that tolerate others, so long as their dogmas contain nothing contrary to the duties of citizenship," he does not just mean "insofar as their dogmas do not impede the performance of civic duties"; he also means "insofar as their dogmas do not express ideas that, as such, run counter to the values bound up with civic duty" – or else it would be hard to explain his own conception of a "civil religion" (which is also articulated in this chapter of *Du Contrat Social*).

10 Actually, we could either consult raw moral intuitions, or consider the threat to mutual respect and self-respect in terms of a moral principle such as Kant's "formula of humanity," which emphasizes respect for all people qua rational beings. But nothing I say here depends on acceptance of such a general (and contestable) principle.

11 Some religious groups with an exclusionary soteriology might deflect this point by stressing that children will not be truly "judged" until they have grown old enough to decide where they stand in regard to their faith; however, there is the familiar question of what will become of a child who dies before that day comes, and some belief systems do not make room for such a child to overcome the alleged disadvantages resulting from their belonging to a group judged to be beyond redemption.

12 The indirectness, again, may result from an association's position on the authoritative status of a scripture (or in the case of Catholicism, papal encyclicals or the catechism), such that members endorse this position on scripture and meanwhile scripture endorses exclusionary soteriology – rather than members directly endorsing the latter.

13 It must be stressed here that this would imply a limit to the *positive* rights promoted by some versions of multiculturalism. I have not defended the idea of limiting traditional negative rights, such as those to freedom of association and freedom of religion. There is indeed a complex and difficult problem about whether and when threats to basic standards of mutual respect justify restrictions on both (which Rousseau thought were justified, in both cases); but for present purposes, I have focused only on positive support via multiculturalism programs.

14 It might be tempting to regard texts such as the *Bhagavad Gita* as expressing a non-exclusionary soteriology (along with many, if not all, of the Upanishads and Puranas), while seeing texts such as Manu's "Law Code" (*Dharmasastra*) as exclusionary; but the latter is less exclusionary than it might appear, since it assumes that all those who are currently remote from spiritual liberation, including those excluded due to birth or race, will grow closer

over many cycles of rebirth (Olivelle 2005). Nonetheless, it is an interesting question whether such doctrinal details significantly mitigate the tendencies to social divisiveness that such texts help to entrench.

15 E.g., Kuehn (1995); cf. Smith and Meier (1995), and the concerns noted in relevant Ontario court decisions, discussed in Dickinson and Dolmage (1996).

16 Kuehn (1995); cf. Weinberg (2007), for a discussion of the situation in the United States.

17 Namely, the province of Alberta (see Ritchie (2010, 3 ff)).

18 That is to say, as Indians may come to be in a situation of economic prosperity that may one day become the norm in India. Meanwhile, the role of doctrinal differences in communal conflict in India may be difficult to disentangle from non-doctrinal differences; but admittedly, a case can be made that the latter have been primary, at least in the most destructive conflicts. Other tensions, such as those between anti-Hindu Dalits and Hindus, relate to both kinds of differences. (The fact that a non-doctrinal impetus initially led some Dalits to oppose Hinduism does not necessarily diminish the importance of newly adopted non-Hindu doctrines – such as Ambedkar-inspired Buddhist doctrines – in escalating tensions. The issue at hand, though, is whether these tensions may subside in the event of an economic prosperity that encompasses Dalits as well as other disadvantaged groups).

REFERENCES

Berlin, Isaiah. 1969. *Four Essays on Liberty*. Oxford: Oxford University Press.
Davis, Gordon, and Blain Neufeld. 2007. "Political Liberalism, Civic Education and Educational Choice." *Social Theory and Practice* 33(1): 47–74.
Dickinson, Greg M., and W. Rod Dolmage. 1996. "Education, Religion, and the Courts in Ontario." *Canadian Journal of Education* 21 (4): 363–83.
Fergusson, David. 2004. *Church, State and Civil Society*. Cambridge: Cambridge University Press.
Kuehn, Larry. 1995. *Ten Problems with Charter Schools*. Vancouver: British Columbia Teachers Federation.
Kymlicka, Will. 1995. *Multicultural Citizenship*. Oxford: Clarendon Press.
– 1998. *Finding Our Way: Rethinking Ethnocultural Relations in Canada*. Oxford: Oxford University Press.
Modood, Tariq. 2006. "British Muslims and the Politics of Multiculturalism." In *Multiculturalism, Muslims and Citizenship: A European Approach*, edited by Tariq Modood, Anna Triandafyllidou, and Ricard Zapata-Barrero, 37–56. London: Routledge.

Okin, Susan M. 1999. *Is Multiculturalism Bad for Women?* Princeton: Princeton University Press.

Olivelle, Patrick, ed., trans. 2005. *Manu's Code of Law: A Critical Edition and Translation of the Manava-Dharmasastra*. Oxford: Oxford University Press.

Quinn, Philip L. 1997. "Political Liberalisms and Their Exclusions of the Religious." In *Religion and Contemporary Liberalism*, edited by Paul J. Weithman, 138–61. Notre Dame: University of Notre Dame Press.

Rawls, John. 1994. *Political Liberalism*. New York: Columbia University Press.

Ritchie, Shawna. 2010. *Innovation in Action: An Examination of Charter Schools in Alberta*. Calgary: Canada West Foundation.

Rousseau, Jean-Jacques. 1973. *The Social Contract and Discourses*. Translated by G. D. H. Cole. London: J. M. Dent.

– 2001. *Du Contrat Social*. Edited by Bruno Bernardi. Paris: Flammarion.

Smith, Kevin B., and Kenneth J. Meier. 1995. *The Case against School Choice*. Armonk: M.E. Sharpe.

Tomasi, John. 2001. *Liberalism Beyond Justice: Citizens, Society and the Boundaries of Political Theory*. Princeton: Princeton University Press.

Weinberg, Lawrence D. 2007. *Religious Charter Schools: Legalities and Practicalities*. Charlotte: Information Age Publications.

Weithman, Paul. 2002. *Religion and the Obligations of Citizenship*. Cambridge: Cambridge University Press.

Wolterstorff, Nicholas. 1997. "Why We Should Reject What Liberalism Tells Us about Speaking and Acting in Public for Religious Reasons." In *Religion and Contemporary Liberalism*, edited by Paul J. Weithman, 162–81. Notre Dame: University of Notre Dame Press.

8

What Can Weberian Sociology Tell Us About Multiculturalism and Religion?

ELKE WINTER

The French sociologist Michel Wieviorka (2010) maintains that for the idea of multiculturalism to survive the hostile post-9/11 climate – marked by an ideology best characterized as that of a "clash of civilizations" (Huntington 1996) and a condemnation of the "M word" in media and politics (Vertovec and Wessendorf 2009) – the concept of multiculturalism is in need of profound reconstruction. In particular, Wieviorka identifies four dimensions where multiculturalism requires clarification. First, in order to overcome the opposition between an abstract universalism and the paradigm of communitarianism, it is necessary to attribute a clear meaning to the notion of "group rights." According to Wieviorka, the latter should be granted to individuals and not to the representatives of collective group identities. Second, multiculturalism as a principle should be conceptualized beyond the limits of "methodological nationalism" (Beck 2000) and attributed global relevance. Third, multiculturalism as a policy should be allowed the possibility of evolution by means of experimentation and evaluation. Fourth, the space of multiculturalism should be limited to cultural identities and questions. For Wieviorka (2010, 9; my translation), "the question of religion involves primarily another principle [than that implied in multiculturalism], namely the principle of secularism [*laïcité*]. [Furthermore, the question] of racial discrimination involves yet another struggle which is also specific," that is, also different from the cultural claims that are at stake within multiculturalism. It is this last dimension – the conceptual distinction between culture, "race," and religion and their respective sites of struggle and accommodation – that I want to address in this chapter. In other words, I am intrigued by the following question: Should multiculturalism be kept separate from the issue of religious identity?

Let me first introduce a short clarification. There are four ways in which the term multiculturalism is commonly understood. First, multiculturalism as a social fact or demographic reality relates to the amount and diversity of members from different cultural, "racial," national, and (usually) religious backgrounds in society. Second, multiculturalism as a demographic reality is often seen as involving a process of competition among members of different ethnocultural groups for economic and political resources, rights, and recognition. Third, multiculturalism as a state policy – as in Canada since 1971 – is often prompted by ethnic diversity and/or competition. It aims at the egalitarian integration of immigrants and ethnic minorities by recognizing and accommodating ethnocultural diversity within public institutions and by supporting minority organizations and the expression of "heritage cultures" for purposes of emancipation. Fourth, while multiculturalism policy certainly impacts social action and may promote specific values among citizens, it does not emerge out of nowhere. Rather, it is closely linked to – and sustained by – a philosophical ethos of multiculturalism that contains normative prescriptions for society building and national identity. It is the last two elements that are mostly at stake in Wieviorka's proposal to keep multiculturalism [read: as a normative principle and as a state policy] separate from the issue of religious identity. Nevertheless, as I will show below, the issue of economic and political competition in ethnically diverse societies cannot be fully removed from the picture.

Wieviorka is certainly right in reminding us about the specific historical and geographical context from which the issue of multiculturalism first emerged. He points to Canada where, in the late 1960s, cultural and linguistic claims made by Québécois nationalists inspired members of predominantly European "ethnic groups" (particularly Ukrainians, Germans, Poles, Finns, Dutch, and Jews) to voice a question that has preoccupied Canadians since: "If it is valuable for French Canadians to maintain their distinctive culture and identity, why is it not so for other groups?" (Palmer 1975, 516). In 1971, Prime Minister Pierre Trudeau addressed this question by implementing "multiculturalism within a bilingual framework" as an official state policy and "the very essence of Canadian identity" (House of Commons 1971, 8580). Though there are two official languages, there was to be no official culture and no ethnic group was to take precedence over any other (ibid., 8545).

In the first decade of multiculturalism policy, questions of "racial" inequality did not play a role. On the contrary, demands for rights and recognition concentrated on cultural and linguistic issues. The 1970s have often been called the "folk and dance" period of Canadian multiculturalism. This, however, changed drastically in the 1980s. While biologically grounded racism had become fundamentally discredited through the experience with Nazism and the Holocaust, Wieviorka reminds us that in the 1970s and 1980s, a new racism was on the rise, namely that of a cultural kind (Stolcke 1995), which cast immigrants, primarily those of non-European origin, not as biologically (read: intellectually) inferior but as culturally incapable of integrating into the white mainstream societies of Western nation-states.

Indeed, with the increased intake of immigrants from non-traditional north European sources, Canadian diversity became ethnically and "racially" more pronounced. This led to a rise in xenophobia and racism, as well as a temporary decrease of public support for multiculturalism.[1] By the late 1980s, "visible minorities"[2] displaced the original white ethnic groups as principal actors in the multiculturalism debates. Their demands however, were not for the sponsoring of cultural festivals and Saturday language schools, but for anti-racism and non-discrimination on the job market. While Wieviorka is correct in arguing that these demands are, analytically speaking, different from those for cultural/linguistic group rights, it remains an open question whether multiculturalism cannot be conceptualized in a way that addresses both of these concerns. In Canada at least, multiculturalism policy reacted to the changing demands and shifted its focus toward structural issues such as social participation and equity in the 1980s. Can this pragmatic adjustment be incorporated into a sociological understanding of multiculturalism's underlying premises?

In the 1980s and 1990s, much to the surprise of modernist thinkers, religion made its way back on the social and political scene. In most Western societies, fears arose that immigrant groups will invoke the ideology of multiculturalism to demand legal protection of illiberal practices such as forced marriages, female genital mutilation, and honour killings. Rightly or wrongly these practices are often associated with Islam. In recent years, Muslims have often been seen as culturally and religiously committed to illiberal practices, and as supporters of undemocratic political movements (Modood 2007). In Canada too, multiculturalism has not been spared from confrontations with religion. The debates surrounding Ontario's 2005 controversial ban to religious arbitration for family disputes (Schmitt and Winter 2009) and Quebec's reasonable accommodation crisis in 2007–2008 can serve as two cases in point.

To be sure, in neither of the aforementioned cases was it multiculturalism policy that was at stake. In Ontario, religious family arbitration was part of the general legal provisions, and not a group-specific right. In Quebec, reasonable accommodation involves at most interculturalism, but here too the cases at stake were not necessarily part of the official policy. Nevertheless, this did not prevent multiculturalism as a normative principle from being called into question in both cases, and this particularly with respect to its capacity to address issues of religious identity. This brings me back to the question asked above: Should multiculturalism be kept separate from the issue of religious identity? If multiculturalism was originally designed to address issues of inter-ethnic relations and inequality, what can we learn from classical sociological writings on these issues?

In this chapter, I want to address these questions by turning to one of the founding fathers of sociology Max Weber. Weber has often been heralded as one of the few "classics" whose writings can serve as a foundation for a sociology of ethnic relations and thus, by extension, for that of multiculturalism.

The following discussion is divided into five parts. I will first clarify the meaning of "identity" as I am using it here. I will then explain the ethnicization of social relations and show that "race," culture, language, and religion often serve similar functions within this process. Third, I propose that there is a difference in degree (but not of substance) between the ideal-types of majoritarian and minoritarian identities, and that the latter can help us to better understand minorities' requests for accommodation. Fourth, I will briefly distinguish between different types of minorities, such as national and ethnic groups. Fifth and more importantly for the purpose of my argument in this paper, I will draw upon the examples of "race" (phenotypical differences), language, and religion to show how these diverse markers of identity differ with respect to their impact on ethnic group formation. In the conclusion, I will return to Wieviorka's suggestion that multiculturalism be reserved for dealing with claims relating to cultural group rights, and that the latter be treated as being fundamentally different from those requesting "racial" equality and religious accommodation.

LOCATING THE ROLE OF IDENTITY
WITHIN SOCIAL RELATIONS

Writing in an era when the division of humanity into biologically different "races" was widely accepted and social inequalities were interpreted as the result of the gaps between individuals' "natural dispositions," Max Weber made a considerable intellectual effort to deconstruct these doctrines and to limit their ideological effect upon sociological research (Winter 2004, 31–56, 139–53). Here, I merely want to underline the now widely accepted insight that individuals who share certain observable material or ideal common traits (*Gemeinsamkeiten*) – such as those related to descent/"race," culture, religion, class, or special environment – do not automatically constitute a group. Weber's (1978, 42) rejection of any sort of objectivist approach to social group formation can be found on the very first pages of his book *Economy and Society*: "It is by no means true that the existence of common qualities, a common situation, or common modes of behaviour imply the existence of a communal social relationship. Thus, for instance, the possession of a common biological inheritance by virtue of which persons are classified as belonging to the same 'race,' naturally implies no sort of communal social relationship between them." For Weber, while there seem to exist some processes of ethnic attraction and ethnic repulsion, they are neither "mechanical" nor based on "instincts." On one hand, ethnic, religious, or cultural homogeneity does not always translate into social cohesion. On the other hand, even stark cultural, religious, or "racial" differences do not necessarily produce conflict. Similarly, the degree of seemingly objective "cultural distance" between the groups has little impact on the nature of social relationships. In sum, Weber does not deny the existence of profound physical and ethnoreligious differences between human beings, but he argues that these differences only become significant once they are attributed subjective meaning. This brings me to the second point that I want to make in this section, namely a clarification related to the notion of identity.

For Weber, persons who are categorized as belonging to a specific "race," ethnicity, sex/gender, etc., may individually internalize stigmata, feel resentment, and may even react in a similar way against oppression and still not share a collective identity. To give a contemporary example, women wearing a veil in Western societies do not necessarily express a sense of collective belonging. Rather, they may choose this practice for a variety of reasons on an individual basis. For example, wearing a veil may be motivated by personal religious or cultural reasons or as an individual political or identificational reaction to the surrounding social environment (see, e.g., Alvi, Hoodfar, and McDonough 2003). In neither case should the veil be interpreted as an expression of shared Muslim identity. Rather, for Weber, it is only when mental representations of commonality (*Gemeinsamkeit*) lead to the mutual orientation of social action that a process of group formation begins. The following quote from *Economy and Society* demonstrates this:

> By restrictions on social intercourse and on marriage persons may find themselves in … a situation of isolation from the environment which imposes these distinctions. But even if they all react to this situation in the same way, this does not constitute a communal relationship. The latter does not even exist if they have a common "feeling" about this situation and its consequences. It is only when this feeling leads to a mutual orientation of their behaviour to each other that a social relationship arises between them rather than of each [of them] to the environment. Furthermore, it is only [in] so far as this relationship involves feelings of belonging together that it is a "communal" relationship. (Weber 1978, 42)

In order to become conducive to the establishment of social relationships, ethnic communalities must be subjectively recognized as such and informed with meaning. The emergence of a "feeling of commonality" (*Gemeinsamkeitsgefühl*) – the mental representation of a collective "we" through the encounter with (real or imagined) third persons (Weber 1978, 43) – is mandatory for the mutual orientation of individuals' actions toward each other, and thus for the formation of a social relation. Defined in this way, "identity" – or better, the relational, contextual, and temporarily limited "identification" with commonality (shared situation, common interests, common ideas/values, common memories, common future, etc.) – is intrinsically political.

Identity is political not merely because once it arises, it can be mobilized, negotiated, represented, reinvented, distorted, etc., but foremost because without "identity" – without the emergence of a mental representation, a more or less irrational "feeling" of commonality – meaningfully oriented collective action would simply not be possible. In other words, while shared identity does not necessarily lead to collective action, it is the only way for the latter to emerge. For Weber, collective identity is a means of empowerment. It allows individuals to realize their will even against resistance by associating themselves with other individuals.

THE ETHNICIZATION OF SOCIAL RELATIONS

For Weber (1978, 395) the "seemingly uniform phenomenon ... of 'ethnically' determined social action" actually refers to a wide range of factors that include "the influence of common language, religion and political action, past and present, upon the formation of customs; the extent to which such factors create attraction and repulsion [as well as] the belief in affinity and disaffinity of blood; the consequences of this belief for social action" (ibid., 394). Given the amorphous character of these factors, Weber (ibid., 395) suggests that ultimately "the collective term 'ethnic' would [have to] be abandoned, for it is unsuitable for really rigorous [sociological] analysis." He nevertheless proposes a widely cited definition of ethnic groups as "those human groups that entertain a subjective belief in their common descent because of similarities of physical type or of customs or both, or because of memories of colonization and migration" (ibid., 389). He not only insists that "this belief must be important for the propagation of group formation" (ibid.), but also locates the production of this type of subjective belief within a context of conflict and unequal power relations.

These unequal power relations, their motives and consequences with respect to ethnic or religious group formations are best described with the term of social closure.[3] Formally, the closure of social relations can be motivated irrationally (i.e., for traditional or affective motives), involving, for example, the belief in the superiority of the group's customs and religion, or a distrust vis-à-vis the unknown Other. The closure of social relations can also involve the rational (in terms of value or means-ends)[4] attempt by social actors to secure collective interests – which can be material (such as employment opportunities, resources, customers, etc.) or ideal (the appropriation or restriction of social honour, the will to uphold the quality of religious practices or the "purity" of the "race").[5] In practice, social closure is most likely to occur when a social relation provides the participating individuals with opportunities for the satisfaction of spiritual *and* material interests. Furthermore, social closure tends to be based on both irrational and rational factors.

Using instrumentally rational motives for the purpose of ideal-type construction, Weber argues that individuals have an interest to act collectively in order to curb competition for access to social and economic opportunities. He describes the process of economically motivated group closure in the following way:

Usually one group of competitors takes some externally identifiable characteristic of another group of (actual or potential) competitors – race, language, religion, local or social origin, descent, residence, etc. – as a pretext for attempting their exclusion. It does not matter which characteristic is chosen in the individual case: whatever suggests itself most easily is seized upon. Such community action [*Gemeinschaftshandeln*] may provoke reaction on the part of those against whom it is directed. (Weber 1978, 342; my translation)

This quotation contains a series of important insights for the study of inter-ethnic group relations, which will be discussed in more detail further below. Let me here briefly summarize these insights. The quote above situates the process of attaching meaning to the various dimensions that are often summarized under the heading of ethnicity – "'race,' language, religion, local or social origin, descent, residence" – in a social relation of conflict and exclusion/marginalization. It shows that the boundaries between "us" and "them" are chosen relatively arbitrarily within unequal power relations. It also shows that for the purpose of exclusion, individuals do not discriminate between ethnocultural, ethnoracial, and ethnoreligious signifiers. On the contrary, Weber underlines that "whatever [characteristic] suggests itself most easily is seized upon." This interpretation would therefore suggest that multiculturalism as a modest remedy of collectively operating exclusion/marginalization cannot be restricted to "cultural claims" as suggested by Wieviorka. Rather, it must also be able to address racism and religious discrimination.

Furthermore, the quote above indicates that the differences are attributed to those excluded/marginalized. Weber's statement furthermore indicates that the closure of the dominant group is achieved through collective action ("community action") and that it may provoke the counter-reaction by those excluded. Expanding Weber's interpretation of groups as constituted within social relationships, we can define a group that successfully effectuates social closure as a "majority." Categories that become "excluded" in this process are "minorities" (Wirth 1945, 347). While not necessarily constituted as "groups" through the process of exclusion, they may react to the closure of the dominant group by developing a shared identity and by attempting to pursue their own group closure.

In the quotation above, Weber underlines individuals' material motivations for the closure of social relationships. However, he is widely known for not neglecting the non-material "ideal" motivations for social action.

Indeed, for Weber, the will, on the part of individuals, to monopolize social honor also leads to situations of social closure and the formation of groups as described by his concept of status groups (*Stände*), which will be discussed in the following section.

MAJORITARIAN VERSUS MINORITARIAN IDENTITY

Social stratification based on majority/minority relations differs from the vision of a "purely economically determined 'class situation'" (Weber 1978, 932), insofar as it involves social interaction between status groups (*Stände*). Status groups are defined by the attribution of "a specific, positive or negative, social estimation of *honour*" (1978, 932; emphasis in original), which is not monopolized merely by individuals, but rather operates collectively, that is, it generates unequal treatment not of individuals but of groups.[6] This is precisely the type of social stratification that multiculturalism as a normative approach aims to address: it remedies collective discrimination based on ethnocultural, ethnoracial, and ethnoreligious discrimination while operating within a liberal and capitalist framework, where (for good or for bad) social status based on individual merit remains fairly unchallenged.

While stratification based on majority/minority relations – or in Weber's terminology, status – is generally merely conventional, "the road to legal privilege, positive or negative, is easily traveled as soon as a certain stratification of the social order has in fact been 'lived in' and has achieved stability by virtue of a stable distribution of economic power" (Weber 1978, 933). Furthermore, social status in society is often – though not necessarily – based upon the group's material situation: "[Material] possession has not always a social value [*ständisch*], but it is often the case" (ibid., 934; translation altered). In return, the superior social or religious status of one group can also foster this group's appropriation of economic advantages, as it produces a situation of unequal access to legal rights, economic power, and social resources such as education and communication.

Where the underlying differences between status groups are held to be "ethnic," Weber anticipates a social stratification similar to that of Indian "castes," that is, a social order that is guaranteed not merely by conventions and laws, but also by a particular belief system (1978, 933; Weber speaks of "religious sanctions"). Based on his studies of the caste system, Weber argues that minority categories tend to accept and internalize ideologies that justify their subordination. He thereby provides us with insights about a phenomenon that recent scholarship has theorized as ideal-types of differential majoritarian and minoritarian identities.

Weber locates the origins of the caste system in the conquest of the dark-skinned Dravidians by the light-skinned Aryans, and the exclusion of the former from all occupations associated with a superior status and social honour.[7] He argues that although most probably predate conquest, the karma doctrine was subsequently transformed into a powerful religious tool that was accepted by the members of all social strata and thus sanctioned the "cultural division of labour" (Hechter 1976) and the superior status of the Brahmans (Weber 1978, 468–518; cf. Schmuhl 1991). Weber (1978, 934) observes that the "sense of dignity" (identity) that characterizes positively privileged status groups is "related to their 'being' which does not transcend itself, that is, it is related to their 'beauty and excellence.'" Members of the majority category in society "live for the present and by exploiting their great past" (ibid.). By contrast, the identity of the negatively privileged strata "must be nurtured by the belief in a providential mission and a belief in a specific honour before God" (ibid.). In sum, their hopes must concentrate on a better life after death.

It can be argued that these tendential majority/minority dispositions can be associated with the premises of modern Enlightenment-influenced culture (which stipulates life as a supreme value) and the diverse forms of counter-Enlightenment that it provokes (Taylor 2001). As Weber (1978) observes, in the process of social closure the dominant group (majority) identifies others' "differences" and not its own "commonalities." Given the inherent heterogeneity of all collectivities, it is much easier to define others in a necessarily arbitrary and reductionist way than to account for the multiple facets and internal differences of one's own group. Majority group members therefore remain "individuals": they are neither determined nor even marked by "race," sex/gender, culture, ethnicity – or, in Guillaumin's (1972) terms, "nature." At most, they are characterized by "civilization." Indeed, the cultural specificity of the dominant group is masked, as it is conceived as incarnating the social norm. It is, therefore, represented in universal terms.

By contrast, "difference" (from an unmarked referent) and the social "marks" that signify the boundary between "us" and "them" are imposed onto the minority. A negatively privileged or "minoritarian" status therefore limits and circumscribes the volatility of minority groups' collective identities and the horizon of possible shapes that the latter may take. As contemporary scholarship in ethnicity maintains, members of minority categories tend to interiorize the essentialist view that the majority imputes to them, so that "the self-construction of ethnic and national groups as homogeneous and timeless entities results from the fact that they were originally perceived as static by others" (Juteau 1996, 57). The ideal-typical minoritarian identity also leads to the perpetuation of social inequality, the intensification of closed boundaries, and the rise of fundamentalism. Members of ethnoreligious and racialized categories have a tendency to view it as "normal" not to be fully included in society. Women resort to a biologist discourse to justify inferior pay at the workplace or to explain a missing spirit of "brother"-hood among themselves. Ethnic minorities interiorize essentialist "ethnic" self-conceptions and use them for the purpose of identity politics and for imposing traditional, orthodox interpretations of culture and religion upon all members of the group. It is widely acknowledged that women are often at the receiving end of this type of traditionalist reification of group identities (Stasiulis and Yuval-Davis 1995).

EMERGING ETHNIC BOUNDARIES: EXTERNAL POWER RELATIONS

The Canadian sociologist Danielle Juteau (1996) theorizes ethnic groups as being constructed through internal and external power relations. The two sides of the ethnic boundary are analytically distinct but empirically intertwined, as the external dimension of the boundary impacts on the internal one.

The external dimension of the boundary is produced through confrontation with (real or imagined) other groups within the process of social closure described by Weber earlier in this chapter. It is within this unequal relation of power that the social marks delimiting the identity of minority categories are chosen and invested with meaning. These marks are later mistaken as being the cause – and not the consequence – of the relationship between the dominant group and the minority. Weber (1978, 388) observes that there are predominantly two types of domination that are at the cause of emerging ethnic boundaries: migration or (peaceful or warlike) expansion such as colonization or conquest.

The difference between these processes of domination has been further theorized in contemporary scholarship. National minorities are often described as previously self-governing peoples who – through colonization, conquest, or treaties of federation – have become incorporated into states in which they do not constitute the majority. They are territorially concentrated and usually characterized by a great degree of institutional completeness (Breton 1964). In fact, ethnic commonalities seem to be strongest when they are (re)produced through institutions like family, schooling, and charities, as well as through the religious, economic, and political organization of collective life. The members of immigration-derived ethnic groups, by contrast, are said to have become members of society "individually" through more or less "voluntary" immigration (Kymlicka 1995, 96). They are geographically dispersed and often lack the capacity to create fully functional social, political, and economic institutions of their own.

These sociological differences create demands for different kinds of pluralist accommodations. National minorities, typically, ask for rights that enable them to pursue their own cultural values, religious beliefs, language, and lifestyle. They want to create or maintain separate societal institutions. By contrast, members of ethnic groups are said to strive for more integration into the dominant society. Integration is not synonymous with assimilation. Members of ethnic groups also ask for group-specific accommodation and the right to express their cultural particularity. However, they seldom demand the right to form "parallel societies."[8] It is those two types of minorities that are at stake in policies addressing multiculturalism, secularism, and some sorts of multinational arrangements in India and Canada. Other forms of domination producing the "external" dimension of the ethnic boundary are, for example, slavery or "sexage," that is, the appropriation of women (Guillaumin 1972).

Any external group boundary is constantly redefined from within. According to Juteau (1996), the internal dimension of the group boundary consists of pre-existing histories, forged memories, economic situations, and non-material elements of culture. It is the outcome of social relations, group formations, and negotiated representations of the world. The elements that become staged as "typical" group characteristics are extracted out of discursive conflicts. Below, I will further scrutinize the role of the internal dimension of the ethnic boundary.

MOBILIZING ETHNIC BOUNDARIES FROM WITHIN: "RACE," LANGUAGE, AND RELIGION

While the relationship in which groups are constituted (i.e., migration, colonialism, slavery, etc.) is pivotal for defining group identities, it also matters what can be mobilized from within: elements of culture and history, religious beliefs, population size, social, political, and economic structures, etc. What marks ethnic boundaries are rarely empty signifiers.

Criteria that are chosen to draw and redefine ethnic boundaries often involve elements that have been produced and invested with meaning (by the minority) long before the establishment of the new relationship: language, religion, food are only some examples. These are pre-existing elements and histories that the excluding/marginalizing majority may not be aware of. These internal characteristics are constantly (re)constructed and informed with meaning from within the minority group. According to Juteau (1996), these elements characterize the internal dimension of the ethnic boundary. They can be mobilized during the process of "ethnic communalizations," or the construction of ethnic boundaries from within.

The insight that the internal dimension of the ethnic boundary matters – the "cultural content" as Nagel (1994) puts it – brings us to a final objective of this paper, which is tracing the difference between diverse ethnic markers, such as "race," language, and religion. As we have seen above, for Weber (1978), diverse externally identifiable characteristics such "race," language, religion, local or social origin, descent, residence serve almost equally well as pretexts for the purpose of exclusion. However, he notices qualitative differences with respect to certain elements that can be used to constitute group identities from within. In fact, Weber differentiates between two types of characteristics that, with respect to their impact on ethnic group formation, can be situated at opposing poles.

First, Weber (1978, 392) observes that "racial qualities are effective only as limiting factors [in terms of group 'repulsion']; they are not positively group-forming." Indeed, skin colour is only meaningful within a relation of exclusion. It gained a particular meaning within colonialism and slavery. On the one hand, in the case of racialized groups (and women!), where the marks are inscribed on the body, the reification of "racial" differences such as skin colour is relatively easy and permanent, that is, the mark does not vanish from the body despite all potential attempts at assimilation. On the other hand, the individuals upon whom the mark is imposed have few things in common other than sharing the experience of racism and subordination. In other words, the mark constituted by skin colour does not have a sense of its own outside the relationship of unequal power relation.[9] As such, the absence of meaningful material and non-material communality within the internal boundary can be detrimental for the empowerment of individuals categorized as minorities.

Second, Weber argues that what generally enhances communal relations is some sort of shared culture. In particular, a common language, religion, and the "ritual regulation of life" provide group members with a "cultural key" to the subjective meaning of others' actions (Weber, 1978, 387). He emphasizes the importance of the "intelligibility of the behaviour of others [as] the most fundamental presupposition of group formation" (1978, 238; translation altered). In fact, language and religion, for example, have a specific sense for the group even without the external dimension of power. As "an open and unstable process of the negotiation of meaning" (Wimmer 2002, 26), shared cultural characteristics including language and religion assure that potential conflict can be maintained within a relatively stable and circumscribed "horizon" within which individuals can argue in order to make claims or establish their world-views as legitimate perspectives (Wimmer 2002, 35). As such, language and religion are highly efficient resources not only for the production of shared identities but also for that of a minority's distinctive lifestyle(s) and institutions. Higher degrees of institutional completeness, in turn (as noted in the section above), allow for an easier reproduction of group identities.

These reproductions gain even more importance if we agree that ethnic and religious communalizations involve histories: they are constituted within past and intergenerational social relations, and the histories they (re)produce are histories of social relations informed with power. These histories, the lived ones and the narrated ones, have material and symbolic effects, shape ideas and interests, and explain why and who "we" are as much as they produce "us" (Hall 1996). It should therefore not come as a surprise that, historically, racialized groups have been most vocal in making claims for anti-discrimination and equal rights as individuals, whereas linguistic and religious minorities often have a stronger sense of – but also need for – community and, therefore request group rights and separate institutions as a means of empowerment and cultural (linguistic and religious) reproduction.

CONCLUSION

What can the return to Weberian sociology teach us about the relationship between multiculturalism and the accommodation of religious identities? First of all, it becomes clear that Weber situates the emergence of all types of group identities – whether they are primarily "racial," ethnocultural, linguistic, or religious – within the context of unequal social relations. As we have seen in the section entitled "The Ethnicization of Social Relations," the ethnicization of social relations is a direct outcome of (attempted) social closure. Social closure, in turn, is the process at stake in any type of nation-state formation. It is the basis upon which our societies are built. Historically, as contemporary scholarship convincingly demonstrates, the closure of Western nation-states operated along assumed "racial" (Goldberg 2002), linguistic (Anderson 1991), cultural, and religious (Baumann 1999) lines. It is in this context that unmarked national majorities emerge and that categories of "racial," linguistic, cultural, and religious "difference" are imposed on those who become minorities in the process. In other words, nationalist social closure creates a "status group" defined by a specific lifestyle and a social estimation of honour, which – as argued in the "Majoritarian versus Minoritarian Identity" section of the chapter – is not monopolized merely by individuals, but rather operates collectively, thus generating unequal treatment not of individuals but of collective social categories (turning eventually into groups, as I will argue below).

Multiculturalism is thus best thought of as a modest remedy for the effects of nationalist exclusion, which always favours some groups (and their cultures, religions, phenotypical features, and views of society) over others. Encouraging the expression of ethnic diversity within the public space, it provides for the "allocation of symbolic resources" (Breton 1984) and allows members of ethnocultural/-racial/-religious minorities to identify with the nation and to redefine it from within. In other words, since nationalist social closure operates on a number of ethnocultural levels, including "race" and religion, multiculturalism as a normative principle should not discard some markers of difference in favour of others. Contrary to Wieviorka's suggestion to rid multiculturalism of the task of dealing with claims for anti-racism and religious accommodation, I maintain that multiculturalism should be conceptualized as an overarching principle that addresses the multiple forms of discrimination that are associated with nationalist closure. Religious discrimination is one of them.

The Weberian perspective favoured in this chapter does not deny the existence of different phenotypical characteristics ("races"), cultures, languages, religions, etc. However, it does not view them as producing clashes of values or of civilizations. Rather, it proposes that the elements which become invested with meaning are selected and reinforced within unequal social relationships. Naturalized and reproduced over generations, the categories of "difference" that obtain their social significance within the process of social closure obtain an "ethnic" qualification by being associated with the vague and highly subjective belief of shared descent. While the emergence of shared collective identity – of both the majority and the minority/ies – is quintessential for the process of group closure, Weber cautions that the notion of "ethnically determined social action" actually refers to the impact of (real or believed) common language, religion, nationality, "race," and cultural customs upon the motivation for collective action.

Here, by contrast, he observes a fundamental difference between "ethnic" and "racial" markers for the potential of minority group formation: carrying very little meaning (other than that of collective discrimination), phenotypical features such as those associated with "race" do not prove to be a strong motivation for group formation outside of the context of collective discrimination (which, obviously, can have severe consequences). In other words, according to Weber, in the first instance, phenotypical characteristics only tend to work in the negative, that is, as "markers" for the discrimination of others. They only acquire meaning for the positive formation of a collective "we" in the context of collectively experienced discrimination where *then* (but not previously) skin colour, hair texture, bodily or facial features are used to identify members of "us." The African American slogan "black is beautiful" is probably the most widely known example of this phenomenon. By contrast, shared language and religion inhibit a positive potential for group formation in the first instance, that is, whether or not a situation of collective discrimination is experienced: invested heavily with meaning other than that produced through a relationship of domination, these particular ethnic markers are in themselves catalysts for the process of group formation. They offer a large variety of elements – such as material and non-material elements of culture, narratives, literature, communication, religious symbols, food, wear, customs, and law – that can be drawn upon by minorities to produce their own group closure and to (re)articulate what defines them.

If we add to this the totalitarian claim that is inherent to many religions – one can speak a second language but is usually not allowed to practice a second religion – it becomes obvious why claims for religious accommodation challenge the relatively shallow, inoffensive expression of individual-based "first level diversity" – as Charles Taylor (1993) puts it – promoted by liberal multiculturalism. Indeed, after banning Québécois and Aboriginal peoples' claims for very specific group rights to a different realm – that of national minorities' second level "deep diversity," to use the language of Kymlicka (1995) and Taylor (1993) – official versions of Canadian multiculturalism have increasingly downplayed the notion of group identities and rights. While this seems to have rendered multiculturalism policy more acceptable in the eyes of some observers, it also undermines the principle of multiculturalism as a modest remedy for collectively operating inequalities produced through nationalist group closure. In sum, banning religious group identities per se out of our conceptualization of multiculturalism as a normative principle and policy overestimates the existence of a truly secular state. Rather, this chapter has argued that we should view the principle itself as being produced through conflict and struggle between the national majority and members of minority groups. Since nationalist exclusion also operated along religious lines, multiculturalism as a principle requires that we listen to both religious majorities and minorities and propose creative solutions on the policy level.

NOTES

1 Public support for multiculturalism dipped only temporarily in the early 1990s during and after the "Quebec crisis" that almost tore the country apart in 1995; it rose again in the second half of the 1990s and even reached historic heights in the early 2000s (Winter 2011).

2 The category of "visible minorities" is an ambiguous construct. The criteria of "visibility" refers sometimes to skin colour (e.g., Blacks), sometimes to cultural belonging and/or religion (e.g., Arabs and South Asians), and sometimes to the nationality of origin (e.g., Chinese).

3 For Weber, social relationships are always open/closed in various degrees. The act of closure is rarely total. On the contrary, the smallest degree of closure merely refers to the definitions of a collectivity's objectives. This implies an identification of insiders without the group being entirely closed to potential newcomers.

4 Weber (1978, 24–5) suggests four ideal-types of meaningful social action: value-rational, means-end rational, affectual (emotional), and traditional. While affectual and traditional are fairly self-explanatory, the two forms of rationality may require some explanation: value-rational social action is oriented toward higher ends or values; means-end rational social action designates instrumental or utilitarian actions that mostly aim at the maximisation of (material or ideal) gains.

5 According to Weber (1978, 46), the principle motives for social closure are: "(a) the maintenance of quality [of the real or imagined characteristics of the group], which is often combined with the interest in prestige and the consequent opportunities to enjoy honour, and even profit ..., (b) the contraction of advantages in relations to consumption needs ..., (c) the growing scarcity of opportunities for acquisition." Weber concludes: "Usually motive (a) is combined with (b) or (c)."

6 Furthermore, "status groups" are communities whose members share a certain lifestyle and "habitus."

7 Romila Thapar (1980) cautions that Weber's studies on the Indian caste system rely on ideologically biased sources, that Weber overestimates the impact of religion, and that he accepts the racially distinct character of upper and lower castes. While Thapar is certainly right on the first and second point, I hold her for mistaken on the last. Weber is particularly interested in the creation of a status system through social (here particularly: religious) causes.

8 Ethnic associations are usually assumed to do both: promote the community's cultural life, language, and values, *and* facilitate the social, economic, and political integration of immigrants and their descendants into mainstream institutions.

9 E.g., slavery, colonialism, and other forms of racial subordination.

REFERENCES

Alvi, Sajida S., Homa Hoodfar, and Sheila McDonough, eds. 2003. *The Muslim Veil in North America: Issues and Debates*. Toronto: Women's Press.

Anderson, Benedict. 1991. *Imagined Communities: Reflections on the Origin and Spread of Nationalism*, 2nd ed. London: Verso.

Baumann, Gerd. 1999. *The Multicultural Riddle: Rethinking National, Ethnic, and Religious Identities*. New York: Routledge.

Beck, Ulrich. 2000. *What Is Globalization?* Cambridge: Polity Press.

Breton, Raymond. 1964. "Institutional Completeness of Ethnic Communities and Personal Relations of Immigrants." *American Journal of Sociology* 70 (2): 193–205.

– 1984. "The Production and Allocation of Symbolic Resources: An Analysis of the Linguistic and Ethnocultural Fields in Canada." *Canadian Review of Sociology and Anthropology* 21 (2): 123–44.

Goldberg, David Theo. 2002. "Racial States." In *A Companion to Racial and Ethnic Studies*, edited by David Theo Goldberg, and John Solomos, 233–58. Malden: Blackwell.

Guillaumin, Colette. 1972. *L'idéologie raciste: genèse et langage actuel*. La Haye: Mouton & Co.

Hall, Stuart. 1996. "Introduction: Who Needs 'Identity'?" In *Questions of Cultural Identity*, edited by Stuart Hall, and Paul du Gay, 1–17. London: Sage.

Hechter, Michael. 1976. "Ethnicity and Industrialization: On the Proliferation of the Cultural Division of Labour." *Ethnicity* 3: 214–24.

House of Commons. 1971. *Debates*. Ottawa: Queen's Printer, 8 October.

Huntington, Samuel P. 1996. *The Clash of Civilizations and the Remaking of World Order*. New York: Simon & Schuster.

Juteau, Danielle. 1996. "Theorizing Ethnicity and Ethnic Communalisations at the Margins: From Quebec to the World System." *Nations and Nationalism* 2 (1): 45–66.

Kymlicka, Will. 1995. *Multicultural Citizenship: A Liberal Theory of Minority Rights*. Oxford: Clarendon Press.

Modood, Tariq. 2007. *Multiculturalism: A Civic Idea*. Cambridge: Polity Press.

Nagel, Joane. 1994. "Constructing Ethnicity: Creating and Recreating Ethnic Identity and Culture." *Social Problems* 41 (1): 152–276.

Palmer, Howard. 1975. "Mosaic versus Melting Pot? Immigration and Ethnicity in Canada and the United States." *International Journal* 31 (6): 488–528.

Schmitt, Irina, and Elke Winter. 2009. "Current Debates on Citizenship and Belonging: Multiculturalism, Gender and Sexuality." In *Canada in Grainau. Le Canada à Grainau. A Multidisciplinary Survey of Canadian Studies after 30 Years. Tour d'horizon multidisciplinaire d'Études canadiennes, 30 ans après*, edited by Klaud-Dieter Ertler, and Hartmut Lutz, 129–53. Wien: Peter Lang.

Schmuhl, Hans-Walter. 1991. "Max Weber und das Rassenproblem." In *Was ist Gesellschaftsgeschichte? Positionen, Themen, Analysen (Festschrift für Hans-Ulrich Wehler)*, edited by Heraugegeben von Manfred Hettling, Claudia Huerkamp, Paul Nolte, and Hans-Walter Schmuhl, 331–41. Munich: C.H. Beck.

Stasiulis, Daiva, and Nira Yuval-Davis, eds. 1995. *Unsettling Settler Societies: Articulations of Gender, Race, Ethnicity and Class*. London: Sage.

Stolcke, Verena. 1995. "Talking Culture: New Boundaries, New Rhetorics of Exclusion in Europe." *Current Anthropology* 36: 1–24.

Taylor, Charles. 1993. *Reconciling the Solitudes: Essays on Canadian Federalism and Nationalism*. Montreal: McGill-Queen's University Press.

– 2001. "The Immanent Counter-Enlightenment." In *Canadian Political Philosophy: Contemporary Reflections*, edited by Ronald Beiner, and Wayne Norman, 386–400. Oxford: Oxford University Press.

Thapar, Romila. 1980. "Durkheim and Weber on Theories of Society and Race Relating to Pre-colonial India." In *Sociological Theories: Race and Colonialism*, edited by UNESCO, 93–116. Poole: Sydenhams Printers.

Vertovec, Steven, and Susanne Wessendorf, eds. 2009. *The Multiculturalism Backlash: European Discourses, Policies and Practices*. London: Routledge.

Weber, Max. 1978. *Economy and Society. An Outline of Interpretive Sociology*. 2 vols. Berkeley, Los Angeles: University of California Press.

Wieviorka, Michel. 2010. "Le multiculturalisme: un concept à reconstruire." Paper presented at *Le multiculturalisme a-t-il un avenir?*, Sorbonne-Paris 1, February 26–27, 1–10. http://www.raison-publique.fr/Le-multiculturalisme-un-concept-a.html.

Wimmer, Andreas. 2002. *Nationalist Exclusion and Ethnic Conflict: Shadows of Modernity*. Cambridge: Cambridge University Press.

Winter, Elke. 2004. *Max Weber et les relations ethniques. Du refus du biologisme racial à l'État multinational*. Quebec: Presses de l'Université Laval.

– 2011. *We, Others, and Them: Pluralism and National Identity in Diverse Societies*. Toronto: University of Toronto Press.

Wirth, Louis. 1945. "The Problem of Minority Groups." In *The Science of Man in the World Crisis*, edited by Ralph Linton, 347–72. New York: Columbia Press.

PART THREE

Religious Majorities

9

The Ayodhya Dispute:
Law's Imagination and the Functions of
the Status Quo

DEEPAK MEHTA

As a shorthand index of the Babri Masjid-Ram Janmabhumi impasse, the Ayodhya dispute is notoriously difficult to pin down. It is at once a contest over property, historical and archaeological interpretation, cultural tradition, and the place of Muslims in India. From the point of view of legal material, the dispute, at a minimum, points to a government bound by fixed rules applicable to all, but the connotative qualities of the court cases are more expansive, covering the history of late colonial north India and putting into crisis the guarantee of constitutional secularism in postcolonial India. Strictly speaking, the dispute in law is modern but its genealogy is more complicated, troubling the boundary between myth and history.[1] While the impasse is not to be confused with the specific content of law, the Ayodhya dispute, as iterated in law courts, displaces the deadlock and frames it in specific ways. In this chapter I provide one reading of the frame. Focusing on the legal and administrative literature by which the dispute acquires a life in law, I argue that the law is conditioned by the restoration of the status quo, not by ideas of justice, reparation, and rehabilitation.

My concern in this chapter is neither to propose that the status quo establishes a legal standard, nor that it is part of a legal doctrine. As I understand it, the official record is set against the moment of violence – threat to security, secularism, communal amity. Instead, this moment is dealt with through the observations and operations of law, characterized by marking, prioritization, and making invisible. None of these operations is solved forever, merely postponed. The postponement of violence is achieved through the status quo, and in this lies its relevance. The status quo has an almost life-giving quality, which is affirmed in a gesture of withdrawal from violence. The withdrawal turns into a creative principle because the judgments try so hard to avoid and conceal the violence that lies at the heart of the dispute.

In which way, then, is the status quo implicated in the judgments? Through the status quo the Ayodhya dispute enters into the official public domain and colours the administrative and legal literature. Since its initial elaboration in 1885, the term points to a crust of temporal change, in the absence of which the dispute cannot be recognized. Each of the contending parties – and there are at least four – evokes the status quo to establish the legitimacy of its claims. In this sense, the status quo is open to occupation from all sides so much so that specific legal and administrative strategies would no longer be possible without it. It is almost as if the legal institutions (law courts, commissions of inquiry, administrative agencies of the government) dealing with the dispute build conventions and transactions by which the status quo becomes the mobilizing power. In this way, the status quo is a kind of "circulating reference" in Latour's (1999, 24) usage. What is marked in this circulation is a continuous transportation of time in which the various events that make up the dispute enter into the lexicon of legal interdiction.[2] In effect, that status quo bridges law with the politico-religious.[3] That is to say the status quo brings together various strands of the political and the religious, while at the same time distinguishing one from the other. Strictly speaking, the function of the status quo is not to deliver the law, but to posit a space in which the enunciation of law is evaluated by administrative agencies and modes of governance.

The questions that this chapter asks are both empirical and normative: from what does the status quo emerge and which choices does it bring into being? What are the limits within which change is possible? Normatively, what motors the imagination of the status quo and what forms its power? In addressing these questions I will show that the status quo comprises the temporality of the dispute. This temporality may be portrayed as a present, made up of competing and antagonistic social groups. The social that is insinuated in this present is institutionalized through courts of law and various state agencies. Such institutionalization details and adjudicates claims made by Hindus and Muslims to religious property, conceived of either as temple or mosque. Religious property is a label under which various phenomena are arranged: it brings together political agitation and modes of worship; it is also marked by rational procedures of delimitation and accountability. I use the term religious property in two senses: it signals continuously changing processes that establish threshold conditions for political and religious events; it submits to a form of judicial power that solicits and sometimes incites the cooperation of governmental procedures. In the dispute, these two senses show that religious property is a process, not a product – it is both a field of action and a basis of action, both actual and potential, both qualitative and quantitative. One may argue that the dispute produces the property as much as occupies it. It does this by deploying the term status quo.

The chapter is divided into two sections, one that describes the functions of the status quo, and the second, its imagination. To describe the functions I provide a timeline of the dispute. My purpose is not to mark the chronology of the impasse. It is to show how claims to the disputed spot – temple and mosque – become part of legal conventions. The second section examines two reports – one produced by the Central Government and the other a contempt of court case that comes up for hearing in the Supreme Court of India – to argue that the Ayodhya dispute imagines a form of power where the religious lies at the heart of the political. Here, the social imaginary, expressed in technologies of government, reveals relations of power by which we can chart how the legitimacy of procedure is forged in times of conflict.

THE TIME OF THE STATUS QUO

Ayodhya, situated in the district of Faizabad in the state of Uttar Pradesh in north India, is regarded as the birthplace of the Hindu deity Ram.[4] Some accounts (specifically the court-mandated Archaeological Survey of India excavations of 2003) suggest that in the twelfth century a temple dedicated to Ram Lala (infant god Ram) stood at the site, marking his birthplace.[5] A European traveler, Joseph Tieffenthaler, who visited the site between 1766 and 1771, noted the existence of a platform (in later accounts called the *Ram Chabutra*) that marked the birthplace on the site of the Babri mosque (Ayodhya Matter, 249). We may assume that the platform came into existence before the visit of Tieffenthaler but after the construction of the mosque.

The dispute has moved around 1500 square yards of land – in the words of the Allahabad High Court judgment of 2010, a "small piece of land where angels fear to tread" (ibid., 4). Hindu opinion is divided on the exact status of the birthplace, as is the Muslim with regard to claims of ownership of the land around the Babri Masjid (hereafter BM). In the administrative records one kind of Hindu opinion argues that a temple was destroyed to build a mosque in 1528, while the Nirmohi Akhara claims that there was never a mosque at the birthplace and that the sect has been its sole custodian since the time of Ram.[6] Mir Baqi Isfahani, a Shia general in the army of the Mughal emperor Babur, constructed the mosque in 1528. British administrative records show that the dispute began around 1853, when armed Hindu ascetics occupied the birthplace. This was followed by a Muslim offensive, leading to a compromise.[7] Accordingly, a railing divided the site into an inner and outer courtyard. The Hindus were allowed to pray in the outer courtyard and Muslims in the inner. Sunni Muslims claimed that the mosque was *waqf* property and the Sunni waqf board its sole legatee.[8] This claim was challenged by the Shia waqf board, who argued that since Mir Baqi was a Shia the mosque belonged to the Shia waqf board. In March 1946 the mosque was declared a Sunni mosque.

The summary of legal findings can be traced to 27 January 1885, when Raghubar Das, the priest (*mahant*) of the Ram Chabutra, filed a civil suit against the Secretary of State for India in Council in the office of the sub-judge of Faizabad (Noorani 2003, 1:175–7). The suit was filed following the attempt of Hindu ascetics to forcibly extend the boundary of the outer courtyard and occupy a Muslim cemetery. The suit was contested by the *mutawalli* (Muslim keeper of the BM), who claimed that the entire land belonged to the mosque. The mahant's suit, discussed later, is important since it brought the Ayodhya dispute within the scope of the law courts, where the term status quo was used for the first time. In positioning this term as a way of addressing the suit of the mahant, the courts charted the movement from impasse to dispute. As a result, the courts formally divided the disputed property into a Hindu and Muslim section.

The division of property was further reinforced by the local and district administration of Ayodhya/Faizabad from 1934 to 1947. In April 1934 the Bairagi Sadhus, led by the Nirmohi Akhara, occupied the BM, severely damaging it (Singh 1991, 31). The occupation occurred during a communal riot, following the slaughter of a cow, in a village near Ayodhya. In retaliation, the local administration levied fines on the local population and used the money for rebuilding the mosque. In April 1947, following consistent appeals by the commissioner of Faizabad asking for the status of the land around the BM, the city magistrate of Faizabad provided a handwritten order, saying that the *chabutra* could not be converted into a permanent structure. Equally, the Muslims were prohibited from rebuilding the broken wall on the south gate of the mosque that adjoined the cemetery. The status quo of 1885, as elaborated by the district administration from 1934–47, insisted on the earlier division of property but also upheld the legal sanctity of the dispute and distinguished law from other social discourses or institutions.

In independent India the dispute can be dated to December 1949. Through the month of December communal passions in Ayodhya had been stoked, following rumors that a solution to the dispute was imminent. On the night of 22–23 December 1949 the icons of Ram Lala Virajman appeared in the middle of the floor space under the central dome of the mosque and soon after thousands of devotees gathered for worship. Ramchandra Das of the Nirmohi Akhara claimed that he had personally installed the icons, following a vision.[9] Prior to the appearance of the icons, various letters were exchanged between government officials regarding the status of the land around the BM. In July 1949 the deputy secretary of the United Provinces (UP) asked the city magistrate of Faizabad whether the BM was on *nazul* municipal land and for the status of construction near the BM.[10] The reply was that a mosque and temple stood side by side, but that the land was *nazul*. Three days after the installation of the icons the district magistrate of Faizabad, in a letter to the chief secretary of UP, argued that Hindus be given permission to erect a "decent and vishal (large) temple."[11] On 5 January 1950 the state took possession of the mosque under section 145 CRPC, and Hindus, not Muslims, were allowed their worship. Following this, the additional city magistrate of Faizabad and Ayodhya appointed a Hindu receiver to take care of the property in dispute till the court was able to determine the right to ownership.

The status quo elaborated here rested on institutional creativity. What was retained from the 1885 judgment was the division of property into a Hindu and Muslim section, but what was new was the appearance of deities in the central dome of the mosque and the recognition in law and administration of their installation. Later it would be argued that the deity and the spot of its installation were juristic personalities. The installation of icons was the first step in establishing that the legal person has no necessary correspondence to social, psychological, or biological individuality. That the legal personality of the deity would be taken as an attribute of real individuals and administrative doctrines would reinforce those expectations.[12] After 1949 the Muslims were not allowed to offer prayers in the BM and in appointing a Hindu receiver to oversee the property in dispute the district administration allowed, at least implicitly, Hindus their mode of worship. The enclosure where the deities were placed was fenced off and worshippers could offer *darshan* only from outside the fence.

From the 1950s till the mid-1980s the Ayodhya dispute languished in local and district courts and there does not seem to have been a significant change in its nature. On 25 January 1986 an application was moved in the Court of Munsif Sadar, Faizabad for opening the locks to the BM.[13] Since the file of the suit was in the high court, the Munsif fixed a date keeping in view the judicial history of the dispute. Against this order, the applicant, Umesh Chandra Pandey, filed an appeal before the district judge of Faizabad, praying for the removal of the locks from the fenced off portion. The appeal did not include interested Muslim parties or the waqf board to the dispute. The district judge fixed 31 January 1986 for the disposal of the suit.[14] Without hearing applications for inclusion, the district judge directed the district magistrate of Faizabad to open the locks of the BM on 1 February 1986. Within half an hour of the pronouncement the locks of the BM were broken.

In passing this order the district judge said that a solution to the dispute would not create problems of law and order. More urgently, he pleaded with interested Muslim parties to recognize the legal personality of the deity and to allow Hindu worshippers access to the inner courtyard of the mosque. One may argue that the presumption of the court was based on norms of worship as practiced by Vaishnavite Hindus and that these were taken to be encrypted experiences. Yet, if we focus on the mosque-temple complex, we find a peculiar lacuna in the judgment. Rather than being saturated with social and religious meanings, the complex was constituted by an institutional technique that secured and delimited it as essentially Hindu. In other words, the question that animated the order for opening the locks was, what values reflected the present status of the disputed area? This question called attention to the rules and institutions that maintained the security of rights to worship. It was as if only secular civil law backed by administrative authority could materialize the temple, and yet the order of the judge appeared as an article of belief. In explaining his order Justice Pandey (1996, 215) said that "when the order was passed a Black Monkey was sitting for the whole day on the roof of the Court room ... Strangely the said Monkey did not touch any of the offerings and left the place when the final order was passed at 4:40 p.m. ... I just saluted him treating him to be some Divine Power."

The opening of the locks to the inner courtyard of the BM corresponded with the emergence of Hindu political parties, led by the Bharatiya Janata Party (BJP), on a national scale. The rhetoric of the Hindu right took Rama's birthplace as an eternal focus of Hindu devotion and nationalist revival, evoking in the process a Manichean historical vision of ancient harmony, Muslim iconoclasm, and brave indigenous resistance. The year 1989 seems to have been crucial in the career of the Ayodhya dispute, signaling the interest of the state in acquiring the property associated with the BM complex. In that year, the Vishva Hindu Parishad (VHP), a member organization of the Hindu political right, decided to consecrate bricks that would be used in the construction of a Ram temple in Ayodhya. Its architect was to be the grandson of the one who designed the temple at Somnath. The VHP formed committees in cities and villages of more than 2000 inhabitants to make bricks for the temple. On 7 November 1989, the Allahabad High Court declined to pass an injunction against blessing the bricks and their transport into Ayodhya, but directed that the status quo be maintained over the disputed site.[15] It is estimated that by 1990 300,000 bricks had streamed into Ayodhya (Bakker 1991). In October 1990 about seven hundred Hindu religious workers stormed the mosque, damaging three domes and planting saffron flags on them. In an attempt to maintain the status quo, the police fired upon the riotous crowd. Five workers lost their lives and three were grievously injured.

To prevent this kind of violence, the state government in UP had in 1989 applied for temporary injunction asking to maintain the status quo over the property. The high court at Allahabad upheld the injunction of the state. As far as the state government was concerned this was the first step in acquiring the entire BM complex. The acquisition of land was consolidated in October 1991, when the state government in UP acquired 2.77 acres, including the graveyard and outer portion of the BM.[16] The ostensive motive was to provide facilities for pilgrims and for developing tourism. The order of the high court was challenged by a number of writ petitions. Of these, Mohd Hashim's writ of 1986 (Writ Petition 3540 M/B of 1991) was the most important. This petition argued that since the notified land around the BM was waqf property, the state could not pass orders dealing with land acquisition. Further, the exercise of power by the state was "colourable" – the real purpose was to destroy the BM and transfer the land to some organization to construct a temple. The court agreed with the defence's argument that waqf property could be acquired, but that the exercise of power had to be bona fide.[17] For this reason, while the state could acquire the notified land, its possession would be subject to further orders of the court, and the acquired land could not be transferred or alienated.[18]

On 20 March 1992, the government of UP executed a lease deed with the Shri Ramjanmabhumi Trust, by which the acquired land would be developed as a park by the trust, "using its own resources" (Noorani 2002). The judgment overturning the notification for acquisition was pronounced on 11 December 1992, five days after the BM had been demolished. A month after the demolition (7 January 1993), the Central Government issued an

ordinance acquiring certain areas in Ayodhya. The ordinance was later replaced by an act.[19] Simultaneously the president of India made a reference
to the Supreme Court for giving its opinion on whether a temple existed
at the site of the BM.[20] The Central Government also abated all suits pending in the high court regarding the adjudication of the title of the BM. In
February 1993 the government of India produced its *White Paper on Ayodhya* that mapped the dispute in the language of governmentality. The
presidential reference was returned while Section 4(3) of the Ayodhya
Acquisition Act (providing for abatement of suits) was repealed and declared unconstitutional. The suits were referred back to the high court for
being decided in accordance with the law. The three-judge bench of the
Allahabad High Court in Lucknow recommenced proceedings in January
1995 and a verdict, or what passed off as one, was delivered on 30 September 2010.

The status quo, in relation to the acquisition of land, rested on making
anew the BM complex. Here, the status quo was concerned with the production of the complex as a site of worship itself lodged in "feedback"
loops of circulating reference. This gave the status quo a mobile character.
Starting from 1949, we can isolate at least six links in this loop, each in the
nature of an event: (1) installation of deities (1949), (2) opening the locks
to the temple (1986), (3) building the temple and the nation (1989 onwards), (4) land acquisition by the state government (1991), (5) religious
tourism (1992), and (6) reversion of the BM complex to the state after the
BM was demolished and recommencing the original suits in the Allahabad
High Court (1993 onwards).

In this circulation legal and state institutions became links in an ongoing process of remaking the complex in which the meaning of the complex was hostage to the performance of each chain or event. Put simply,
each event was inscribed as the status quo through legal and administrative discourse. One may argue that the links outlined above continue to
be in motion and there is no reason to assume an end to this kind of
process – the shifting contents of the loop are what the law and its basic
technologies of reports, files, archiving and retrieval make possible. In
terms of the dispute, these links fed back into the process of adjudication
and occasional legislation. In answer to the question of what the law did
or made, one could reply that it crystallized religious property at a given
point of time. And it achieved this through the status quo. The importance of circulating reference was precisely this: the loop was constitutive
of the space that I have been calling religious property. Whatever the form
of this loop at a given link, it always harked back to the same enigma – of

a break that instituted and established relations and an exercise of power that required periodic and repeated contest. Alongside the making of religious property as space, the loop also highlighted a notion of time, but not as a continuous historical narrative. The time that this loop marked was not the distance covered from 1885 to contemporary legal pronouncements. The time that I allude to is a kind of moment where the past bled into, even recreated itself in, the present. Let me briefly develop how the status quo expressed this notion of time.

It could be argued that the status quo marked time as "epochality" in the way that Blumenberg (1985) used the term in his understanding of modernity in the West. Epochality, for him, established a kind of self-reflexivity that was mediated by an awareness of the historical present and identified with it. This present was differentiated as a separate, new period, with the important assumption that the duration of this history was unitary. The status quo that I deal with was also epochal in the sense that it established new grounds of imagining the temple/mosque complex. However, the forms of temporality were not unitary. Fragmentary, partial histories, claimed by groups of Hindus and Muslims, unfolded in different ways from different points and these found their resonance in the court and administrative literature. In spite of overlaps, there was no single, unbroken line that described the duration of the status quo – it had more than one possible past, and there was no single, normative framework of intentionality toward the past that could properly be observed or remembered. Every moment, or event, in the circulating reference was an opportunity to re-appropriate, drop, and grant new meaning to parts of the past. Every event was an opportunity to draw new lines of continuity between past and present, and alongside it, lines of crucial difference dividing before and after.

IMAGINATION AND THE STATUS QUO

Thus far, I have put the argument schematically – the status quo coupled property to modes of worship. Both property and worship were marked by contests, within and across groups of Hindus and Muslims. The law, as it dealt with this contest, moved in two ways: it maintained the property, dividing the complex into Hindu and Muslim sections. Here the law acknowledged, if not followed, the claims of different groups of Hindus. In a second move, the law was marked by institutional creativity, seen most starkly in the ability of courts to incarnate the temple. But there was and has been a third actor in this dispute – the state as it intervened in controlling the property. We find that the BM complex was acquired both by the state government (to develop religious tourism) and the Central Government (after the demolition).

If the function of the status quo was to crystallize claims to religious property, as I have argued in the preceding section, could we also mark out the imagination of the status quo through such procedures?[21] In this section, I argue that such procedures imagined religious property and the status quo in a specific way – as the place of power. The distinctive characteristic of this place was, and one may argue still is, that it brought together modes of worship and political agitation, but in a way that this conjunction always demanded an address by the law and statecraft. With this address, conflict – between Hindus and Muslims and within each group – became institutional, and the field of competition between protagonists made claims to the exercise of public right to be legislated through the courts. The problem was that such rights rested on the unity of the religious and the political. To counter the religious basis of political power the courts and the Central Government evoked the status quo. Let me elaborate on how this term acquired an almost ontological character.

In its initial elaboration in 1885, the term was the name for a provisional nexus that held social and legal actors together in a kind of emergent bond.[22] The juridical form of this bond rested not so much on the accumulation of facts as on the relevant point of law. I had mentioned that in 1885 Raghubar Das had petitioned the courts for permission to construct a temple over the birthplace. The plea provided precise dimensions of the territory claimed by the mahant: "North 17 feet, east 21 feet, south 17 feet, west 21 feet" (Noorani 2003, 1:175–81). The mahant claimed that the "chabutra was in his possession but he experienced great hardship on account of excessive heat in summer and excessive cold in winter and rain in rainy season" (ibid.). The plea was rejected in the court of the sub-judge of Faizabad, with Judge Pandit Hari Kishan Singh arguing of an imminent threat to public law and order: "If a temple is constructed on the Chabutra at such a place then there will be sound of bells of the temple … and if permission is given to Hindus for constructing temple then one day or the other a criminal case will be started and thousands of people will be killed." Raghubar Das moved to the Faizabad District Court (Civil Appeal No. 27, 9.1. [1886]) praying in vain for the dismissal of the judgment of the lower court. After visiting the disputed spot, Judge Colonel Chamier (ibid.) admitted, "it is most unfortunate that a Masjid should have been built on the land especially held sacred by the Hindus. But as that occurred

356 years ago, it is too late now to remedy the grievance. All that can be done is to maintain the parties in status quo."[23] On 25 May 1886, the plaintiff moved the highest court in the province, but the judicial commissioner of Oudh, W. Young, upheld the judgment of the district court. The judgment stated that the "Hindus want to create a new temple or marble baldacchino over the supposed holy spot in Ajodhya, said to be the birthplace of Shri Ram Chander ... [The Hindus] have for a series of years been persistently trying to ... erect buildings on two spots in the enclosure: (1) Sita ki Rasoi, (2) Ram Chander ki Janam Bhumi" (ibid.). Henceforth, the Babri complex would be divided into two: the first made up of the mosque proper and the second of two spots in the enclosure, where Hindus were allowed their worship. The status quo elaborated here imputed to both Hindus and Muslims a precisely evaluated position, arrived at in accordance with the decision of law. It was, to use Buchanan's (2004) terms, based on a "balance sheet" metaphor.[24] The terms, Hindu and Muslim would of course refer to differential resources invested in specific modes of worship and the link of the latter to collective activity. More important, the judgments of 1885 called attention to the problems of evaluation, specifically, how could modes of worship and the corresponding claims to property be evaluated? The judgment of the judicial commissioner parceled out the land and in the process pointed to the rules and institutions by which delimitation could occur. These rules were vital elements of the balance sheet itself. That is to say, the plea of the mahant depended upon the institution of law and the courts. Only by making claims to these institutions could his plea acquire value. The problem was that this value rested on the security of ownership. For this reason, the legal structure that determined security became a feature of the status quo itself. For this reason, too, to describe the status quo only in terms of a balance sheet is misleading since the plea of the mahant could not be separated from the institutional structure that heard and generated his plea. What is clear is that the idea of security was vitally linked to the status quo.

The idea of security was made available through what Latour (1986) calls "material inscriptions." In the 1885–86 judgments these inscriptions provided an emergent form of governmental procedure that would set the tone for future litigation. The judgments enclosed the referential chains of the dispute by recording them through specific technical instruments. The judges visited the disputed site; the site itself was delimited by techniques of numeration and calculation; routines were established for the timing and spacing of prayer. The judges asked for and obtained surveys and architectural maps of the site, drawing up rules and guidelines for regulating entry into the complex. While through such mundane tools the dispute acquired a life in law, the imagination that girded such procedures emerged from unruly moments of violence. In this way, the imaginary was constitutive of the meaning of the dispute.

In what follows, I will detail two cases and show that the documents associated with them functioned as emergent modes of shaping a specific set of responses.[25] I look at the government's *White Paper on Ayodhya* and a contempt petition heard by the Supreme Court.[26]

In its overview of the Ayodhya dispute, the government's *White Paper on Ayodhya* provided a chronology of the destruction. Starting from 1949 (the "placing of the idols in the disputed structure") till 1992 ("in effect, therefore, from December, 1949 till December 6, 1992 the structure had not been used as a mosque") this document amplified finality (*White Paper on Ayodhya*, 5–8). When the actual process of demolition ruptured this finality, the *White Paper on Ayodhya* attempted to domesticate the violence by placing it both within clock time and a representational template of the communal riot:

9:30 am	Union Home Secretary (HS [Home Special]) telephoned the Director General, Indo-Tibetan Border Police … in Faizabad to keep the CPMF [Central Para Military Forces] ready and to respond immediately to any request for assistance.
11:30 am	Everything was reported to be peaceful. Gathering of about 50,000–60,000 kar sevaks was being addressed by top leaders of VHP and BJP.
12 noon	Information was received in the Home Ministry through Intelligence Bureau … that about 150 kar sevaks had stormed the disputed complex. The State Police and the Provincial Armed Constabulary did not check them though senior officers were present close to the structure.
12:10 pm	HS [Home Secretary] tried to speak to Chief Secretary, Government of Uttar Pradesh who was not available. He spoke to Director General of Police, Uttar Pradesh, and urged him to make use of Central forces located near Ayodhya.

From 12:10 till late afternoon, the *White Paper on Ayodhya* mentioned the various measures taken to get the central forces and various officials of

law near the Babri mosque and the inaction of the UP police force in
containing damage to the mosque.

> 3:30–4:30 pm   HS was informed that communal incidents had started
> occurring in Ayodhya, and spoke to DGP [Director
> General of Police], UP and told him that the situation
> was fast deteriorating and not only Central forces had
> been unable to move but there was serious apprehen-
> sion of communal riots ... HS also spoke to Chief of
> Army Staff requesting him that in case of communal
> situation deteriorating in other parts of the country,
> assistance of Army authorities may be provided. (*White
> Paper on Ayodhya*, 5–8)

The *White Paper on Ayodhya* thus recognized that the stability of rules and
representations that characterized governmental discourse was constantly
challenged by the fury of riots. Clock time threaded together with terms
such as "disputed structure" and "communal incidents," read the demolition as a problem of law and order. In so doing, the *White Paper on Ayodhya* established the primacy of state practices based on governmental
rationality. This rationality, in turn, highlighted three characteristics: the
site, or disputes over the title to property; the treatment of the uncertain,
or the emergency and the proposed form of normalization, framed
through a recursive law; and the technology of managing populations by
which relief could be provided to those affected by the demolition. The
last need not concern us here.[27] Within this scheme, security was characterized less by the use of force and violence, than by an implicit logic that
allowed a constitutive power (of the government) to re-inscribe the status
quo. This normative character of governmental power rested on a calcu-
lus of possibilities where the ambition was not to expunge communal violence from the body politic, but to find a point of support by which the
rule of law and the laws of rule could be maintained.[28]

The emphasis of the *White Paper on Ayodhya* on the failure of policing
highlighted how rules were not followed and how, in the process, the utility of governance was attenuated. At least implicitly, this utility rested on
a calculation of how many police personnel were needed, the size of the
territory, the number of kar sevaks. Policing, thus, was directed to the activity of the kar sevaks to the extent that their actions threatened security.[29] In this link – between the police and the kar sevaks – the sovereignty
of the state was allied to forms of governmentality and rested on the self-

production of law. Nowhere was this relationship made clearer than in the concluding paragraphs of the overview of the *White Paper on Ayodhya* (11): "What happened on December 6, 1992, was not a failure of the system as a whole, nor of the wisdom inherent in India's Constitution ... It was, the Supreme Court observed on that day, 'a great pity that a Constitutionally elected Government could not discharge its duties in a matter of this sensitivity and magnitude.' Commitments to the Court and Constitution, pledges to Parliament and people, were simply cast aside." If the *White Paper on Ayodhya* evoked the demolition as transgressive of the law and the constitution it also staked a claim for the primacy of governmental procedure in establishing order. This order would be achieved by re-emphasizing the status quo. The imagination that informed the status quo of the *Paper* rested on a view of violence as agent of Hindu revival, as external to the Indian Constitution, and as conspiratorially determined. This reading galvanized, in turn, a utopian vision of the constitution. In effect, the social imaginary combined in itself two contradictory tendencies – an abstract social order and Hindu revival.

A second characteristic of the status quo was its elaboration in concert with a kind of evidence that was available for study and comparison. In this task, the status quo broke with social context but was referenced by citational practices of legal convention. In such references the status quo acquired the capacity of translatability and transportation and appeared to be unanchored from its immediate environment. In this transportation, the status quo was imagined as an artifact, contributing evidence in the interpretation of experience, as well as a catalogue arranged in an organized, meaningful relationship with judicial evidence, most obviously with spoken testimony, but also with non-verbal acts.

In discussing this imagination I focus on a Supreme Court judgment of Chief Justice Venktachaliah and Justice G. N. Ray, regarding the contempt petition, decided on 24 October 1994, in which the chief minister of UP at the time of the demolition, Kalyan Singh, was found guilty of contempt. The judgment is instructive since it exemplified the character of the status quo: a technical substrate and the rule of experts, citational practices, and altered contexts. In the process, the judgment distinguished between the rule of law and the authority of government officials. In terms of the former, law emerged as a system that reflected an abstract idea of equality with its own internal dynamic based on a self-generating technicality. The authority of high officials challenged the hermeneutical insularity of law by arguing that the exercise of authority was the only antidote to the violence of the mob. This distinction, between law and authority, would eventually be played out in the emergency promulgations.

The contempt of court judgment was preceded by a public interest litigation in the Supreme Court, with Justices G. N. Ray and Ranganath Misra on the bench,[30] challenging the Land Acquisition Act, 1894, by which the state government of UP had acquired 2.77 acres of land around the BM for the development of tourism.[31]

The contempt proceedings reflected on the 2.77 acres of land in Ayodhya acquired by the state government through a notification of 7 October 1991, under Section 4 of the Land Acquisition Act, 1894. The acquisition was earlier challenged in the high court and the Supreme Court and the present proceedings adverted to those orders. The high court had restrained the parties from raising construction on the land unless the court granted permission. The present petition claimed that these orders had been deliberately flouted by the state of Uttar Pradesh. "By order dated 5th August, 1992, this Court while recording the finding that the alleged demolitions did not strictly fall within the interdiction of the order of this Court dated 15th November, 1991, however, found that there were certain constructional activity undertaken on the land which prima-facie violated the orders of this Court" (*Aslam, Mohd. alias Bhure v. the Union of India* at para 3).

In his defence, the lawyer for Kalyan Singh asked for time to "traverse" the charges. In his response he did not dispute that construction had indeed been carried out on the acquired land in July 1992. The state government and its authorities had carried out such works. What was pleaded was that the land in question, "by a long religious tradition in Ayodhya," (ibid., at para 7), attracted a large number of pilgrims, particularly in the month of July, which coincides with the period of *chaturmas*, where a large number of ascetics congregate to celebrate *sarvadev anusthan*. These ascetics had constructed a cement concrete platform and their number was so large that any coercive preventive action may have triggered a riot and endangered the safety of the disputed structure.

As far as the undertaking of the chief minister to the National Integration Council was concerned, the defence argued that this undertaking was in the nature of a personal promise and did not in any way impugn the office of the government. In response, the court held that in a "Government of laws and not of men the Executive Branch of the Government bears a grave responsibility for upholding and obeying judicial orders" (ibid., at para 8). Referring to a judgment of the Supreme Court of the

United States[32] the judgment noted that a violent resistance to the law could not be made a legal reason for its suspension, and that the rule of law meant that all were subject to the ordinary law of the land. Furthermore, law was the only integrating factor in a pluralist society. On the issue of whether construction near the BM violated the court's orders, the judgment referred to the chief engineer's report, which said that concrete foundation had been laid in three layers, and brick walls, of cement and sandmortar and up to 1.56 meters in height, had been built. The engineer said that this construction was the first step toward building the "Singh Dwar" of the proposed "Ram Mandir." The court also referred to the report of a committee that it had constituted to examine the extent of construction in the BM complex.[33] The committee reported that "the magnitude of the work is such that it could not have been carried out without the use of construction equipments such as water-tankers, cement concrete mixers, concrete vibrators, earth moving equipment etc" (ibid., at para 11.) Accordingly, the court did not hesitate to find that there was "massive work undertaken and executed on the land in violation of the Court's orders" (ibid., at para 12).

On the matter of whether a congregation of ascetics and not the state government, had undertaken construction activity, the court found that the state government did little to prevent construction material from reaching the BM complex. "The presumption is that the Government intended not to take such preventive steps" (ibid., at para 13). Finally, on the issue of the chief minister's undertaking, the court found that Kalyan Singh was in contempt, both in his personal and official capacity. This position was established by referring to two cases, the first drawn from England and the second from the state of Bihar.[34]

The object of this judgment was at once the disputed site and the personal and official responsibility of Kalyan Singh. This site of course had foundations with precise coordinates, authorized by expert opinion, and within the scope of law. If illegal, as in the present case, the offender was to be disciplined by recourse to a norm drawn equally from the opinion of experts and a self-referential legal world. In the process, the judgment highlighted an image of law as an autonomous zone in relation to the executive. It reserved its right of disciplining errant members of the government. But more than that, the punishment that it recommended was not so much about innocence or guilt, as it was performative – an expression of judicial power itself. At the heart of this performance was the view that only law could make the state and that the state, in turn, was the basis of understanding the law, not religion or custom.

At the most general level, the judgment tried to account for the acquisition of land and the demolition within a set of rules, institutions, conventions, and practices that could be identified and defined. In so doing the judgment considered acquisition to be exogenous to its decision. Here, the decision reached by the judges was not to re-state the *status quo ante*, so much as to break from land acquisition and illegal construction on it. In so doing, the decision constituted the status quo as the ability of the court to arrive at a decision not by institutionalizing the social, but by underscoring the technical nature of evidence. The status quo here was imagined as a specific way of seeing and diagnosing the dispute. In the process, the authority of the courts over the executive was asserted, as was the ability of technical means to intervene in social processes. And yet this imagination rested on a peculiar enigma: did the status quo involve the security of its inhabitants, or of state order? To the extent that the status quo elaborated by the decision rested on the efficacy in performing functions demanded for survival, it may be argued that the judgment achieved its task. But to the extent that the decision eliminated any role for the state as reformer, the status quo that it expressed was based on a holding pattern.

CONCLUSION

I have mentioned that the documents were interdictory in the sense of establishing separation and shared meaning. We can isolate at least four different kinds of interdictory responses. In the first interdiction of 1886 the appeal of the mahant was turned down in favour of maintaining the status quo. Here the dispute entered into legal language with the Muslims being the silent third party. In April 1947 the city magistrate of Ayodhya reiterated the status quo and disallowed construction over the chabutra. The second kind of interdiction referred to the internal disputes among Muslims (Shia and Sunni) and Hindus (Nirmohi Akhara against the Hindu receiver of the temple, claims of the Sakshi Gopal temple), with the courts again valuing the importance of the status quo. The dispute became irrevocably three-sided – Hindus, Muslims, and the judicial and executive bodies of the government. The third kind of interdiction occurred in 1949 with the placing of the Ram deity in the BM. The maintenance of the status quo, promulgated by the Civil Court of Faizabad, referred now to the right to worship of Hindus, a right solidified in 1986, when the locks to the temple were opened. The final interdiction referred to the aborted attempt to preserve the state government's move to acquire land around the BM for the development of tourism.

In these interdictions the boundaries of the status quo became mobile according to a straightforward litany of complaints. On the surface, the status quo seems to have been a kind of bad faith: the courts and the administration firmly believed what they knew not to be true. It is as if the status quo was a notation that was strictly symbolic, which in the understanding of ordinary language pointed merely to venal, political interests. This indeed has been the gist of much of the writing on the BM. The argument can be summarized in two moves: bad faith enables the transformation of the BM into a temple; when accompanied with visceral resentment and political dogma, bad faith becomes a rule unto itself.

I think the status quo is doing something more than bad faith. It demarcates the legal world. That is to say, the constitutional structure that determines security was a feature of the status quo. One may argue that the status quo emerged from a multiplicity of choices made independently by groups acting separately and in relation to other groups. This demarcation was the condition of any meaningful articulation. From the point of view of Hindu litigants, the status quo kept alive that which might otherwise have been killed by the weight of authority or necessity – it expanded the space in which the right to worship trumped administrative procedure. The position of Muslim litigants in demanding the status quo was one that considered the right to worship in terms of administrative rationality – a decision that rested on historical time was the necessary corrective to Hindu claims. In either case, legal opinion was privileged. At the heart of this legal world, the status quo recognized, if not constituted, interests represented by terms such as Hindu and Muslim and linked these vitally to material benefit. These interests were shaped through disputes over property (mosque and temple) and its links with sectarian identity. Governed by legal language, the term described a particular multiplicity that was self-referential, but when faced with the destruction of the mosque, the status quo lost its bearing. Instead, we pass into a language of blame (as in the *White Paper on Ayodhya*) and later the carte blanche authority of the courts. When read together with legal discourse, the demolition lay in excess of legal language and governmental procedure (seen both in the *White Paper on Ayodhya* and the contempt petition) and their capacity to represent. Here, the demolition was a force that ruptured the status quo by blowing a hole in procedure and discourse and thereby destroying the claims of both the courts and the government to express the totality of the Ayodhya dispute. From the point of view of government, the demolition thus required a decision in the form of a proposition that testified to its truth. The proclamation of emergency was one such proposition.

NOTES

1 In civil jurisdiction, four basic suits deal with the Ayodhya dispute. The first
   suit was filed in 1885 by Mahant Raghubar Das asking for permission to
   build a temple on the land adjoining the Babri mosque. The second suit,
   filed on 16 January 1950 by a Hindu Mahasabha member Gopal Singh
   Visharad and paramhans Ramchandra Das, claimed their right to worship at
   the birthplace without hindrance. This right was being denied because of
   Section 145 CrPC, according to which devotees could only practice *darshan*
   from behind a railing. The third suit was filed on 17 December 1959 by the
   Nirmohi Akhara against the court receiver and the UP government seeking
   delivery of the property itself. It claimed that the Akhara was the sole religious order charged with maintaining and managing the birthplace. The
   fourth suit, filed by the Sunni Waqf Board (no.12 of 18 December 1961
   against Gopal Singh Visharad and others) sought a decree that the disputed
   structure was a mosque to be handed over to the Board. The four suits (regular suit no. 2 of 1950, 25 of 1950, 26 of 1959, and 12 of 1961) were consolidated with the suit of the Sunni Waqf Board being treated as the leading
   one. The final suit was filed in 1989 by the next friends of the deity on behalf of Ram Lala Virajman, claiming that both the deity and birthplace were
   juristic personalities, capable of holding land in their own name, of suing
   and being sued.

2 I follow Alain Supiot's (2007) view of interdiction as capturing something
   that is said and of something said between. Interdiction thus implies both a
   separation and a link that make shared meaning possible. Through interdiction the Ayodhya dispute becomes an index by which particular collectives
   become entangled with each other.

3 The politico-religious does not have the means to resolve the dispute since it
   evokes a multiplicity of reference points that can only relate to each other se-
   lectively. Instead, in responding to the dispute, the status quo indicates a flux
   that is not so much the expression of a doubt as it is an opening up to the
   possibilities of substitutability. Perhaps the status quo confounds the boundary between reference and supplement (see Derrida 1976, 141–56).

4 Ayodhya is a town of holy pilgrimage for Vaishnavite Hindus. In post-colonial India the name also references a state of emergency. As the name of an
   emergency, Ayodhya signals both violence between Hindus and Muslims
   and the necessity of government action in containing it. The emergency represents the force of the state at its purest – the necessary condition if both
   law and the state are to survive. But the moment of emergency also signals a
   crisis in law and statecraft. The proclamation of emergency is thus double-

edged: it is a constitutive act of will, connecting law and violent force; it accounts for troubling events and imagines them to emphasize their unpredictability. I deal with this elsewhere.

5 See the Allahabad's high court order on excavation (5 March 2003, in OOS No.4 of 1989, *Sunni Central Waqf Board and Others v. Gopal Singh Visharad and Others* in Noorani 2003, 1:135–9). For a full discussion and critique of the ASI account see Mandal and Ratnagar (2007).

6 In Ayodhya there are seven cloisters or *akharas* of the monastic orders. All the orders worship Vishnu, whose avatar is Ram. The worshippers are known as Bairagis. Each order is presided over by a mahant or priest. The seven orders are Nirbani, Nirmohi, Digambari, Khakhi, Mahanirbani, Santokhi, and Niralambhi. See Hans Bakker (1986, 1991) for the rise of Hindu religious orders in Ayodhya and the violence around the Hanumangarhi temple complex.

7 Not much is known of the exact nature of this compromise. The Gazetteers mention that Hindus and Muslims were together allowed their prayer.

8 This claim was made in 1938, after the constitution of the waqf boards in 1913. Waqf means the "permanent dedication by a person professing Islam, of any movable or immovable property for any purpose recognized by the Muslim law as pious, religious or charitable" (Waqf Act 1995. See Mansfield 2001). Waqf also means any person making such dedication. The act of 1995, which repealed the Waqf Act, 1954, and the Mussalman Waqf (Validating) Act, 1913, deals with the administration of waqf throughout India, except the state of Jammu and Kashmir. Each waqf (pl. *awqaf*) has a Muslim *waqif* (trustee) and each mosque, a *mutawalli* (keeper). The *mutawalli*, unlike the Hindu mahant, has no propriety interest in the property and cannot derive financial gain from it. The waqf boards are made up of survey commissioners and their assistants, whose function is to categorise the waqf into Shia or Sunni properties, calculate the income of the properties and assign taxable rates.

9 Peter van der Veer (1996, 156) reports the mahant's claim.

10 See Noorani (2003, 1: 205–7). *Nazul* land is under the control of public authority (in this case the state government of UP) that maintains the land for the express purpose of developing it in accordance with well-established precedence. In the case of the BM, the land adjoining the mosque proper was to be maintained in accordance with the waqf boards.

11 The district magistrate, one K. K. K. Nayar, ICS (Indian Civil Service), believed that the icons could not be removed ("a step of administrative bankruptcy and tyranny") as that would lead to immense suffering, but also that the restoration of the status quo that existed before the installation "could not be allowed to become a fetish with a corban of gory shambles" (Noorani

2003, 1: 215–8). Instead, the structure needed to be policed on a permanent basis. He then quoted the constant slogans raised by crowds near his house: "Nayar anyaya karna chor do, Nayar bhagwan ka phatak khol do" (Nayar refrain from being unjust, Nayar open the doors of the lord). In 1950, Nayar, his wife, and office staff would contest the UP assembly elections, supported by Hindu organizations.

12 Both Davis (1997) and Derrett (1999) show that for Hindus religious images are animate beings, but that they are also subject to political and economic motivations. Animated icons may also be seen as magical beings and "idols."

13 *Umesh Chandra Pandey v. State of Uttar Pradesh* (1986, Civil Appeal No. 66/198).

14 On coming to know of this fixation, two Muslims, Hashim Ansari and Farooq Ahmad, plaintiffs in regular suit no. 12 of 1961 moved applications for impleadment in the appeal of Pandey. Two days after the opening of the locks, Mohd. Hashim filed a writ petition in the Allahabad High Court, challenging the order of 1 February (Noorani 2003, 1:270).

15 See Akhtar (1997, 95–103) for the reproduction of the Allahabad High Court (Lucknow Bench) order, asking for a clarification under Section 145 of the Civil Procedure Code.

16 The 1991 acquisition had a background. Approximately 55.67 acres of land, well beyond the BM, were acquired on 20 and 23 January 1989 and on 27 September 1989 for building Ram Katha Park. The aim of this acquisition, as expressed in the order, was to use the park to "create experience of the cultural aspects emerging from the great epic Ramayana ... The park should be integrated with the overall development of Ayodhya ... in order to have wider appeal and to uphold secular ideas, the emphasis should lie on the philosophic and on the unique aspects of Rama's life, rather than on the ritualistic aspect." See UP State Government notification numbers 3814/41-33/86, 7 October 1991 and 3838/41-33/86, 10 October 1991.

17 The Ismail Farooqi judgment, (Transferred case of 1993, 1 SCC 642, decided on 24 October 1994) heard in the Supreme Court would provide variations to this argument. The judgment is the subject of a separate paper.

18 A second writ (3579 of 1991) was filed on behalf of the Sakshi Gopal temple, with the deity being the first petitioner and the mahant the second. The writ sought an injunction against the acquisition. Situated on Plot 160 of the BM complex, the temple was to be acquired by the notification. The petitioner argued that acquisition was contrary to the Places of Worship (Special Provisions) Act, 1991, by which the religious character of a place of worship existing on 15 August 1947 would continue to be the same as it existed on that day. Since the temple was in existence on that day, its religious character could not be converted. The defence pointed to Section 5 of the act, which provides that the act will

not apply to the Ramjanmabhumi-Babri Masjid dispute. Since the Sakshi Gopal Temple was included in the area of "place" and not of "place of worship," the act would not be applicable to this area. The court agreed with this argument and refused to vacate the order for acquisition but with the following caveats: the deity installed in the temple would be preserved; no permanent structure could be constructed; the land could not be transferred or alienated; possession would be subject to further orders of the court (see Noorani 2003, 1: 340–4 and The Places of Worship (Special Provisions) Act, 1991).

19 Acquisition of Certain Area at Ayodhya Ordinance, No. 8 of 1993, was replaced by The Acquisition of Certain Area at Ayodhya Act, No. 33 of 1993, 3 April 1993. This act now covers 71.36 acres of land.

20 The presidential reference is known as the Ismail Faruqui case.

21 As identified by Castoriadis (1987), the social imaginary was the creative force in the making of the social. The 2002 special issue of *Public Culture* accepts the analytic purchase of the term social imaginary, but also provides a somewhat more nuanced reading than Castoriadis' Eurocentric and optimistic account of autonomy and creation. Instead, the authors aim to ground the social imaginary in the ethnographic. The term becomes part of the social itself. I follow this line to show that the institutional sites that inhabit the social imaginary evoke a relation between legal authority and sacral power. Nowhere is this clearer than in documenting the rationality of governmental and legal procedure.

22 This bond had potent effects on a variety of social practices, ranging from the regulation of marriages, inheritances, and caste-based community relations. In the process new legal precedents replaced the flexibility and contingency of local usages. Analyses of South Asian legal studies outline the standardization of personal law (Derrett 1999), the tension between rule of law and customary modes of arbitration, both Hindu and Muslim (Cohn 1996; Metcalf 1994), and the privatizing of Hindu and Muslim laws (Fisch 1983). See also Birla (2009).

23 Interested parties in the dispute use this oft-quoted paragraph variously. The first sentence is used by the Hindu right as vindication of their claims of Muslim iconoclasm, while the second sentence is used by members of the All India Babri Masjid Action Committee to argue for the status quo as it existed before the demolition. The third sentence is the argument of the courts and the administration.

24 The phrase is from Buchanan (2004). I find this metaphor useful since it directs our attention to the problem of evaluation.

25 Riles (2006) discusses the relation between ethnographic response and documents.

26 *Mohd. Aslam alias Bhure v. the Union of India* No. 97 of 1992 in writ petition Nos. 977 and 972 of 1991 (in MANU/SC/0111/1995).

27 As is evident, my argument is derived from Foucault's (2007) views of governmentality, especially in *Security, Territory, Population*.

28 The phrase, a rule of law as a law of rules, is from Hussain (2003, 16) quoting Antonin Scalia. Overshadowing agents and action, the rule of law imagines a spectral landscape, characterized by its implacable insularity. For this reason its inversion also generates meaning. In their edited volume, Corbridge et al. (2005), consider how people, located in a variety of institutions and networks in rural India, see the state. In the process, they aim to provide a corrective to the technologies of visuality deployed by the state to survey its populations. The absence of a discussion of the state in relation to legal institutions is telling. Any consideration of this view must take into account how the state both sees and writes itself. In large part, this visuality and writing are linked to the assumed insularity of government and the recursive features of governmental procedure.

29 Beginning in 1990 till the demolition, Ayodhya had turned into a military fortress and defences of barbed wire were laced around the fenced spot of the mosque. In 1990, 28,000 personnel of the Provincial Armed Constabulary had been stationed in Ayodhya alone (Liberhan Report 240).

30 *Naveed Yar Khan v. State of Uttar Pradesh and Others*, Writ petition (Civil) No. 1000 of 1991, and *Mohd. Aslam alias Bhure and Others v. the Union of India and Others*, in 1991 INDLAW SC 366.

31 In its order, the Supreme Court quoted the promises the chief minister of UP, Kalyan Singh, made before the national integration council in November 1991. The chief minister had said that until an amicable resolution to the dispute was found, the state government would be responsible for protecting the disputed sites and fully implementing the orders of the court in regard to the land acquisition proceedings. The Supreme Court refused to intervene further. Instead, the writ petitions were transferred to the Lucknow bench of the Allahabad High Court (see *Mohd. Aslam alias Bhure v. Union of India*).

32 William Cooper, Member of the Board of Directors of the *Little Rock v. John Aaron* 358 US 1.

33 The committee was made up of the registrar of the Supreme Court, and two professors, one from the Indian Institue of Technology, Delhi and the other from the School of Planning and Architecture, Delhi.

34 The case from England was *M. v. Home Office*, 1994 (1) AC 377 and the one from Bihar was *State of Bihar v. Rani Sonabati Kumari*, (MANU/SC/002/1960). In the first case, the term "Crown" was divided into the monarch and the executive, with the latter indicating the supremacy of the parliament over the monarch as well as the judiciary. The monarch bowed to the executive, while the power of the executive over the judiciary could only be exercised through statute. While judges could not enforce the law against the Crown as

monarch (since the monarch can do no wrong), they could enforce the law against the Crown as executive and against individuals who represent the Crown. As far as the personal element was concerned, the judgment held that the minister may or may not have been personally guilty of contempt. But this position would be the equivalent of that which needed to exist for the court to give relief to the minister in proceedings for judicial review. The Bihar case was evoked to impose a fine on the chief minister, the fine being analogous to sequestering the corporate property of the person in contempt. Accordingly, the chief minister was sentenced to pay a fine of INR 2,000.

REFERENCES

Akhtar, Mohammad J. 1997. *Babri Masjid: A Tale Untold*. New Delhi: Genuine Publications and Media Ltd.

Bakker, Hans. 1986. *Ayodhya*. Groningen: E. Forsten.

– 1991. "Ayodhya: A Hindu Jerusalem." *Numen* 38 (1): 80–109.

Birla, Ritu. 2009. *Stages of Capital: Law, Culture and Market Governance in Late Colonial India*. Durham: Duke University Press.

Blumenberg, Hans. 1985. *The Legitimacy of the Modern Age*. Translated by Robert M. Wallace. Cambridge: MIT Press.

Buchanan, James M. 2004. "The Status of the Status Quo." *Constitutional Political Economy* 15(2): 133–44.

Castoriadis, Cornelius. 1987. *The Imaginary Institution of Society*. Cambridge: Polity Press.

Cohn, Bernard S. 1996. *Colonialism and Its Forms of Knowledge: The British in India*. Princeton: Princeton University Press.

Corbridge, Stuart, Glyn Williams, Manoj Srivstava, and René Véron, eds. 2005. *Seeing the State: Governance and Governmentality in India*. Cambridge: Cambridge University Press.

Davis, Richard R. 1997. *Lives of Indian Images*. Princeton: Princeton University Press.

Derrett, J. Duncan. 1999. *Religion, Law and the State in India*. Delhi: Oxford University Press.

Derrida, Jacques. 1976. *Of Grammatology*. Translated by Gayatri Chakravorty Spivak. Baltimore: Johns Hopkins University Press.

Fisch, Jorg. 1983. *Cheap Lives and Dear Limbs: The British Transformation of the Bengal Criminal Law*. Weisbaden: F. Steiner.

Foucault, Michel. 2007. *Security, Territory, Population: Lectures at the Collège de France, 1977–78*. Translated by Graham Burchell. Edited by Michel Senellart. New York: Palgrave Macmillan.

Hussain, Nasser. 2003. *The Jurisprudence of Emergency: Colonialism and the Rule of Law*. Ann Arbor: University of Michigan Press.

Latour, Bruno. 1986. "Visualisation and Cognition: Drawing Things Together." *Knowledge and Society: Studies in the Sociology of Culture and Present* 6: 1–40.

– 1999. *Pandora's Hope: Essays in the Reality of Science Studies*. Cambridge: Harvard University Press.

Lee, Benjamin, and Dilip Parameshwar Gaonkar, eds. 2002. "New Imaginaries." Special issue, *Public Culture* 14 (36).

Mandal, Dhaneshwar, and Shereen Ratnagar. 2007. *Ayodhya: Archaeology After Excavation*. New Delhi: Tulika Books.

Mansfield, John H. 2001. "Religious and Charitable Endowments and a Uniform Civil Code." In *Religious and Personal Law in Secular India*, edited by Gerald J. Larson, 70–103. New Delhi: Social Science Press.

Metcalf, Thomas R. 1994. *Ideologies of the Raj*. Cambridge: Cambridge University Press.

Noorani, Abdul G. 2002. "Ayodhya: The text of the lease deed." *Frontline* (19) 9: April 27–May 10. http://www.hindu.com/fline/fl1909/19090500.htm.

– ed. 2003. *The Babri Masjid Question, 1528–2004: A Matter of National Honor*. 2 vols. New Delhi: Tulika Books.

Pandey, K. M. 1996. *Voice of Conscience*. Lucknow: Din Dayal Upadhyay Prakashan.

Riles, Annelise, ed. 2006: *Documents: Artifacts of Modern Knowledge*. Ann Arbor: University of Michigan Press.

Supiot, Alain. 2007. *Homo Juridicus: On the Anthropological Function of the Law*. New York: Verso.

Van der Veer, Peter. 1996. *Religious Nationalism: Hindus and Muslims in India*. Delhi: Oxford University Press.

OFFICIAL DOCUMENTS AND REPORTS

Aslam, Mohd. alias Bhure v. the Union of India. 1994. Writ Petition Nos. 977 and 972 of 1991. In MANU/SC/0111/1995.

Ayodhya Matter: Ram Janam Bhoomi Babri Masjid Disputes. Special Full Bench Judgment Allahabad High Court, Lucknow Bench. 3 vols.

Gazetteer of India. 1991. "The Places of Worship (Special Provisions) Act, 1991 (Act No. 42 of 1991)." 23.8.1991. Part II, S.2, Ext.:4 (No.26). Government of India. 18 September 1991.

10

Laws of General Application:
The Retreat from Multiculturalism and
Its Implications for Religious Freedom

LORI G. BEAMAN

In Canada, as in other Western "receiving" nations, there is increased discussion about the value of multiculturalism and its role in a diverse Canada. While the language of diversity has been primarily associated with multiculturalism, pluralism has been conceptually linked to minority existence within majoritarian culture. Recently, the discourse of pluralism has enjoyed a resurgence in popularity especially in institutional settings. Pluralism is being positioned as being in greater harmony with "Canadian values," which are imagined as representative of a cohesive whole with which citizens (or those who would like to be citizens) comply and agree.

Law is one social institution within which some of this shift can be observed. The Supreme Court of Canada has consistently noted the "multicultural nature" of Canada and has elaborated on Canadian values, naming multiculturalism as one of them, during its adjudication of religious freedom cases. The decisions of the Supreme Court are one important barometer of the ways in which religious freedom and multiculturalism are playing out in the public sphere. In the past two years, however, there has been a marked change in the court's tone. This paper explores the shifting discourse of the Supreme Court of Canada related to multiculturalism in the context of religious freedom cases. Drawing on three important decisions on religious freedom, this paper examines the Court's values discourse, the ways in which it talks about multiculturalism and pluralism, and the manner in which religious freedom is defined and delimited in the context of these debates.

MULTICULTURALISM

In their edited collection, *The Multiculturalism Backlash*, Vertovec and Wessendorf (2010) explore the idea that there is a withdrawal from multiculturalism as public policy in Europe. The editors and many of the authors argue that state policies and practices around multiculturalism are not so much retracting or shrinking as they are undergoing a metamorphosis that can largely be understood as being focused on the management of diversity. Thus, they argue, the dirty "M" word has been replaced to a certain extent by the "D" word. It is, therefore, at least from the perspective of Vertovec and Wessendorf, the language rather than the actual implementation or support for multiculturalism that has changed.

One of the challenges of assessing the success, failure, implementation, or even presence of multiculturalism is its very definition. Elke Winter's chapter in this volume explicates these problems more fully than I can here, but briefly, multiculturalism can refer to demographic reality, ideology, government program, and so on. A statement such as "we live in a multicultural nation" can be interpreted solely as a demographic description, or it could also be understood as an ideological accomplishment. Further, multiculturalism and both its demographic as well as programmatic aspects must also be understood in differentiated spheres. Thus, for example, as I watch parents walk their children to the school in my neighbourhood I reflect on how "multicultural" the school is based on the appearance of the parents and the children. However, in the east coast community where I live in the summers, the school is almost completely monocultural. Spatially, then, multiculturalism as a demographic reality differs between places. It also differs as an ideological or programmatic accomplishment from sphere to sphere. Amongst the student body at a university, for example, it may be more readily embraced as a desirable goal (or even an accomplished goal) than it may be amongst other groups.[1] With this caution in mind, I will consider multiculturalism in the Canadian context and more specifically, its presence in religious freedom cases from the Supreme Court of Canada.

Canadian multiculturalism has been viewed by some as one of Canada's most important contributions to global discourse on diversity and its management. Will Kymlicka (see 2005, 1995) is perhaps its best known ambassador internationally. His work has continued to describe both the uniqueness of Canadian multiculturalism while at the same time suggesting it as a valuable export and tool of liberal democracies. Like Vertovec and Wessendorf (he has also made a contribution to their edited volume) he maintains that multiculturalism continues to be a viable programme and is a necessary protector of diversity. Nationally, multiculturalism is supported at the level of policy, public opinion (see Adams 2008), legislatively by the Multiculturalism Act, and constitutionally by s. 27 of the *Canadian Charter of Rights and Freedoms*, which states, "This *Charter* shall be interpreted in a manner consistent with the preservation and enhancement of the multicultural heritage of Canadians." There is arguably a local as well as a political-legal accommodation, to use the words of Kymlicka, Vertovec, et al., of immigrant practices, most often around religion.

Multiculturalism is not without its critics. For instance, Markell (2003, 173) notes that multicultural recognition, even when there are gains, leaves those who benefit subject "to the perpetually needy and often suspicious gaze of the state and its normative citizens, dependent on their continued good will, and vulnerable to sudden swings in the national mood that can provoke transformations in the organization of social and political privilege." Others, such as Day (2000), Kernerman (2005), and Bannerji (2001) highlight the ongoing colonial agenda embedded in multicultural policies. Feminist scholars too have generated some important criticisms of multiculturalism in relation to its failure to protect women within minority cultures. While these criticisms demand serious consideration and response, they do not necessitate a jettisoning of multiculturalism completely. The *Charter* requirement that the multicultural heritage of Canada be maintained and indeed enhanced, together with the (until recently) political commitment to that ideal, coupled with relatively high popular support for it, can encourage and support courts to take a broader view of the type of society we live in and how society might change to more fully accomplish justice and fairness.

DIVERSITY AND PLURALISM

Although diversity and pluralism are sometimes used interchangeably, they are often saying quite different things. It is therefore important to pay attention to the context in which one or the other is used. In the European context, diversity has to some measure come to replace the idea of multiculturalism, lending a more acceptable framework to discussions about difference and its management. Although this may simply be the project of multiculturalism being carried out under another name, the turn toward interculturalism (Foblets and Kulakowski 2010) suggests that the shift is more complex than simply changing words. In the Canadian context diversity and multiculturalism have been used in concert with one another, with diversity often being used to describe the nature of society (we live in a diverse Canada) and multiculturalism often being used to describe a project or ideology that accompanies diversity. Together, both have highlighted difference as something to be valued rather than eliminated. The focus on difference has not been without its critics, who argue that an emphasis on difference can still privilege a particular group as the majoritarian group from which every other is different. Kernerman, Day, and Bannerji have all raised the problems of recognizing "difference" and "diversity."

Pluralism as a concept has attracted a great deal of debate. The central critique of pluralism as it was traditionally understood was its failure to critique core organizing structures that govern the multiplicity of practices, beliefs, and so on that diversity brings. This critique is important to keep in mind as we hear public officials particularly making comments like "we live in a plural society." These comments seem to be made in contexts that would suggest precisely that critical debate is not to be brought to bear on social institutions.

Some, like William Connolly, have sought to reshape the idea of pluralism by imbuing it with the very critical edge that it is charged with missing. According to Schoolman and Campbell in their introduction to *The New Pluralism* (2008, 5), an edited volume primarily dedicated to a discussion of Connolly's work on pluralism, "Connolly corrects the picture by showing how the larger societal context is biased in favour of certain types of groups and against others." The lesson to be learned, it would seem, is that the nuance of pluralism must be carefully attended to. This caution is offered from outside of political theory as well.

Sociologist James Beckford's (2003) commentary on pluralism sets out the multiple meanings this concept can have in various social contexts. Beckford argues that the notion of pluralism in the context of religion and society contains three separate ideas: first, that societies differ in the extent of their religious diversity; second, that the degree of acceptance of recognition in the public sphere is variable, and third, that support for the moral or political value of widening the public acceptance of religions is also variable. It is the third aspect of pluralism that is specifically normative, and Beckford (2003, 81) reads it as a positive statement about the desirability of a "diversity of religious outlooks and collectivities" that is "within limits, beneficial." Beckford notes the complexity of this formulation of pluralism, especially when there are power differentials.

Current public use of the term pluralism would seem to incorporate both a somewhat superficial positive read of religious diversity at the same time as it preserves the power differentials between religious groups. We can link this to what Kymlicka (2010), referring to Alibhai-Brown (2000), calls 3S multiculturalism – saris, samosas, and steel drums. The normative stance that approves of pluralism also includes an implicit, and sometimes explicit, understanding of limits. The general lesson to be learned from Beckford's work is that diversity and pluralism are sometimes used interchangeably, that they are sometimes used in normative and sometimes in descriptive ways, and that it is important to pay attention to how they are being used. Paying attention to how "pluralism" is used can tell us something about how various actors'imagine social order. Often partnered with discussions of pluralism are discussions of values, which frame, bind, or limit the boundaries of pluralism. The value statements made in the endorsement of pluralism or diversity structure the ways in which religious minorities are heard in the public sphere generally and in law specifically.

VALUES

Like many Western democracies, Canada has begun to engage in a peculiar promotional campaign that is focused on constructing and reconstructing an identity based on a cohesive set of national values. At the political level this has included, for example, the recent renaming of the Canadian Armed Forces,[2] as well as the introduction of a private members' bill promoting the use of the Canadian flag,[3] and a modification of the citizenship and immigration guidelines to include specific mention of female genital mutilation and honour killings as being contrary to Canadian values (*Discover Canada* 2010).[4] This values-based strategy is founded on a number of assumptions, including that it is possible to identify uniquely "Canadian" values; that there is agreement on these values; and that social cohesion both exists and is dependent on the values identified.

Values talk has never been completely absent from political rhetoric or social discourse. Indeed, in the legal context, the notion of "*Charter* values" has developed in decisions that do not explicitly rely on the *Charter of Rights and Freedoms* but where courts wish to invoke the general principles of the *Charter*.[5] What seems to be a bit different about the present tendencies in values talk is that, while values have often been used to protect minority groups in the past, in the current context they are being deployed against or in opposition to minorities. In other words, there has been a directional shift, from an inclusive, even accomodationist, attitude owed to minority groups to one that is exclusivist: "this is who we are, and if you want to belong, these are our values." An assumption underlying much of the present values discourse is that minority groups are by definition outside of "our" values.

The use of values rhetoric is not necessarily unidirectional. Minority groups themselves use values talk to engage in public discourse. In their research on the veil controversy in Europe, Leila Hadj-Abdou and Linda Woodhead (2011) have observed that those engaged in debates about the presence of the veil in public space have, on both sides, used values rhetoric to support their positions. Thus the value of "freedom" for example, can be used both by a woman who wishes to wear a head covering (I wish to exercise my freedom to choose) as well as those who wish to ban head coverings from public space (women who wear the veil are not free). However, although values talk can be used by minority groups to make claims for "freedom" or equality, it is also important to consider the social and political framework within which those claims are made. What I mean by this is that minority arguments may not have the same purchase as those of majorities. In Quebec, for example, arguments against the imposition of legislation that would force women to expose their faces if they wish to receive public services have been met with little public support, despite the fact that the legislation is framed as being oppressive to women by forcing them to dress (or undress) in a particular way.[6]

A second relevant observation from the research Hadj-Abdou and Woodhead carried out is that it is important to focus on values talk outside of political regimes, ideologies, and discourses. At first glance, law might not seem to give access to the extra-political realm, but in fact embedded in legal decisions are presentations of self and values deployed by the parties to actions which become matters of public record. Further, courts use values talk in rendering decisions, sometimes in differing and even contradictory ways.

THREE IMPORTANT MOMENTS

The discussions below focus on three cases that have at their core the notion of religious freedom. Conceptually, the idea of religious freedom is situated in law, but practically it is located in the everyday lives of citizens. When cases come before the courts these two worlds meet, bringing into view the ways in which state practices intersect and sometimes clash with citizen practices (and beliefs). The line is not so neat between state and citizen, as state policies often reflect the religious beliefs and practices of the majority. Not surprisingly, more often than not, it is religious minorities who find themselves before the courts.

In Canada, religious freedom is protected under section 2(a) of the *Charter of Rights and Freedoms*. The equality provisions of the *Charter* also protect against discrimination on a number of bases, including religion. Canada also has a pre-*Charter* history of religious freedom through case law which focused predominantly on religious groups like Jehovah's Witnesses and other minority Christian groups. With the advent of the *Charter*, however, religious freedom became more explicitly entangled with broader "*Charter* values," including equality, multiculturalism, and diversity. In its interpretation of religious freedom the Supreme Court of Canada has taken an approach that has not imposed "internal limits" on the idea of religious freedom, choosing instead to use the balancing clause of the *Charter*, s. 1, to place limits on religious practice.

During the past decade the Supreme Court has moved to an expansive understanding of religious freedom, emphasizing a subjective approach while at the same time acknowledging the group-based nature of much religious practice. This is not the same thing as acknowledging "group rights," but rather is a recognition of the complexity of religious practice as both an individual experience as well as a group phenomenon. The discussion below traces some of these developments through the last three Supreme Court of Canada cases on religious freedom, focusing on the shift in tone from an expansive approach that celebrates multiculturalism and diversity to an approach that narrowly construes religious diversity as something to be managed and controlled by the state with the help of the court.

While the discussion below highlights the legal trajectory of religious freedom in recent years, it is important to remember that these cases are situated in broader historical moments that are key to understanding the subtle yet significant shift in tone in the approach of the Supreme Court. Immigration has brought increased visibility to religious diversity, especially from outside of the traditional mainstream Christian majority. Public attention to religious extremism as well as a climate of securitization has also led to a change in context. Neoliberalism has influenced the ways in which risk is understood, shifting the discourse from one of harm to a more overt cost-benefit analysis. A fear of the religious Other, especially the Muslim Other, has also shaped the social and legal framework within which religious freedom claims are made and negotiated.

Moment #1: Syndicat North Crest v. Amselem (2004)

In this case the claimant was an Orthodox Jew who lived in a condominium building in Montreal. Under the terms of the bylaws in the declaration of co-ownership, decorations, alterations, and constructions on the balconies were prohibited. During the festival of Sukkot the claimant wished to build a sukkah on his balcony, a structure resembling a tent that was prohibited by co-ownership bylaws. Although there was some evidence that a communal sukkah would fulfill the requirements of his religion, the claimant's interpretation was that he should build his own sukkah on his balcony. The Supreme Court agreed, holding that aesthetic concerns should not outweigh religious freedom.

Amselem represented an important turn in post-*Charter* (1982) case law on religious freedom for three reasons: (1) it solidified the formal requirement for an inquiry into sincerity of belief in religious freedom claims; (2) it explicitly recognized the importance of the religious subject in determining the importance and validity of religious beliefs/practices; and (3) it included a specific consideration of the definition of religion and acknowledged the relationship between the individual beliefs/ practices and a "nexus" to religion. The case is an important affirmation of a broad interpretation of religion and an acknowledgement by the courts that religious freedom is important. The case seemed to return to the very broad expansive approach taken by Justice Dickson in early post-*Charter* jurisprudence in *R. v. Big M Drug Mart Ltd.* In striking down Sunday closing law, Justice Dickson held that minority religious groups and individuals should not be forced to act contrary to their beliefs or consciences, and the effect of Sunday closing laws was to do exactly that. The court subsequently moved away from this expansive approach, but *Amselem* signalled a return of the court's willingness to bring together a broader *Charter* sensibility that ultimately, as noted by Justice Dickson in *Big M*, was linked to notions of justice and fairness not specifically situated in law.

In *Amselem* the court acknowledges multiculturalism as foundational. In its description of multiculturalism and the duties attached thereto it is clear that the court is not simply talking about a descriptive fact, but a program of sorts that involves tolerance, democracy, and rights. Religious freedom in the case is thus situated within this multicultural fact and program:

In a multiethnic and multicultural country such as ours, which accentuates and advertises its modern record of respecting cultural diversity and human rights and of promoting tolerance of religious and ethnic minorities – and is in many ways an example thereof for other societies –, the argument of the respondent that nominal, minimally intruded-upon aesthetic interests should outweigh the exercise of the appellants' religious freedom is unacceptable. Indeed, mutual tolerance is one of the cornerstones of all democratic societies. Living in a community that attempts to maximize human rights invariably requires openness to and recognition of the rights of others. (*Syndicat North Crest v. Amselem* at para 87)

In *Amselem* the notions of diversity and multiculturalism offer a protective shield to the claimant, situating him in a society that recognizes religious freedom as an important right in a matrix of respect, tolerance, and democracy. In this narrative of Canadian society, human rights are to be maximized and society is characterized by diversity and tolerance. Although *Amselem* does not involve a direct conflict with the state, the court clearly imagines the state as involved in ensuring that the diverse, multicultural character of the nation is preserved. The court, in this imagined space, is the protector of human rights and of a free and democratic society.

In linking with the themes introduced at the beginning – multiculturalism, diversity, and values – the court constructs a narrative that situates religious freedom in a diverse Canada that does not privilege a majority culture, and that values diversity, which is in turn protected through a program of multiculturalism. As an exporter of this particular model of state and citizenship, Canada is called upon to demonstrate the highest standards of human rights protection, rejecting trivial concerns (such as aesthetic preference) that would interfere with the exercise of (in this instance) religious freedom. These themes are picked up again when the court is called upon to decide its next religious freedom case.

Moment #2: Multani v. Commission scolaire Marguerite-Bourgeoys (2006)

While *Amselem* was a substantively important case, *Multani* became a politically important case that sparked a debate that continues to this day. In *Multani* a Sikh schoolboy wore his kirpan to school in compliance with an agreement entered into between his parents and school authorities. The conditions agreed upon were quite onerous, and included the kirpan being contained in a sheath that was to be out of view and sewn shut. Despite the agreement of the parties, the school commission objected, and the case made its way to the Supreme Court of Canada. The Supreme Court supported Mr Multani's wearing of the kirpan under the religious freedom provisions of the Quebec Human Rights Act.

In *Multani*, as in *Amselem*, the court endorses the "promotion" of multiculturalism and diversity and sees them not just as descriptors but as values to be protected. The court slides between rights and values language in its assessment, and while it names security as a "value," it comes down on the side of freedom and equality after assessing the risks to be minimal.

> An absolute prohibition would stifle the promotion of values such as multiculturalism, diversity, and the development of an educational culture respectful of the rights of others. This court has on numerous occasions reiterated the importance of these values. (*Multani* at para. 78)

> A total prohibition against wearing a kirpan to school undermines the value of this religious symbol and sends students the message that some religious practices do not merit the same protection as others. On the other hand, accommodating Gurbaj Singh and allowing him to wear his kirpan under certain conditions demonstrates the importance that our society attaches to protecting freedom of religion and to showing respect for its minorities. The deleterious effects of a total prohibition thus outweigh its salutary effects. (at para 79)

> In making its determinations, the school board must take all fundamental values into consideration, including not only security, but also freedom of religion and the right to equality. The prohibition on the wearing of a kirpan cannot be imposed without considering conditions that would interfere less with freedom of religion. (at para 99)

Embedded in the *Multani* decision is an underlying commitment to substantive equality for religious minorities. The court weaves the equality ethic of the *Charter* through its analysis. Multiculturalism and diversity are "values," not demographic descriptors. Rather than identifying a singular "value path" to national identity or social cohesion, the court recognizes that there are sometimes competing or conflicting values, each legitimate, that must be weighed and assessed in such situations. It imagines its role as the arbiter of these tensions and protector of minorities.

As alluded to above, the *Multani* decision was highly controversial and is largely recognized as having had the effect of sparking the formation of the Bouchard-Taylor (2008) Commission, which examined what have become known as the reasonable accommodation debates in Quebec. Although the commission was based in Quebec, the language of reasonable accommodation has permeated public discourse across Canada. The idea that there is "too much" accommodation of religious minorities has in part informed the renewed interest in "Canadian values," the downplaying if not outright rejection of multiculturalism, and a renewed nationalism.

Moment #3: Alberta v. Hutterian Brethren of Wilson Colony (2009)

Known most famously as "the driver's licence case," this decision represents a radical turn from the Supreme Court's open and expansive approach to religious freedom. The case involves a group of approximately 250 Hutterites who believe that having their pictures taken contravenes their religious beliefs. This belief brought them head-to-head with an Alberta provincial statute, which requires individuals' photographs to appear on their driver's licences. The Hutterites have always been exempt from the photograph requirement. They live a lifestyle that is rural, communal, and agriculturally based, and depend on their driver's licences to do related business in surrounding communities. The court held that the requirement to have their pictures taken is not unreasonable, and that, if they wish to refrain from having their pictures taken they can find other ways to do their business, such as to hire someone to drive them. The court emphasized security and law of general application in its decision.

Because religion touches so many facets of daily life, and because a host of different religions with different rites and practices co-exist in our society, it is inevitable that some religious practices will come into conflict with laws and regulatory systems of general application. As recognized by the European Court of Human Rights in *Kokkinakis v. Greece*, judgment of 25 May 1993, Series A No. 260-A, cited by my colleague Abella J., this pluralistic context also includes "atheists, agnostics, sceptics and the unconcerned" (para. 31). Their interests are equally protected by s. 2(a): *R. v. Big M Drug Mart Ltd.*, [1985] 1 S.C.R. 295, at 347. In judging the seriousness of the limit in a particular case, the perspective of the religious or conscientious claimant is important. However, this perspective must be considered in the context of a multicultural, multi-religious society where the duty of state authorities to legislate for the general good inevitably produces conflicts with individual beliefs. The bare assertion by a claimant that a particular limit curtails his or her religious practice does not, without more, establish the seriousness of the limit for purposes of the proportionality analysis. Indeed to end the inquiry with such an assertion would cast an impossibly high burden of justification on the state (*Alberta v. Hutterian Brethren of Wilson Colony* at para 90).

The approach of the court in this case is dramatically different from that in both *Amselem* and *Multani* and has important implications for the protection of religious minorities. In shifting from a diversity to a pluralism model, the court draws on a European Court of Human Rights case (*Kokkinakis v. Greece*) to emphasize that religious groups are just one among many, including agnostics and atheists. This odd juxtaposition – atheists and religiously committed – in a religious freedom case sends a clear signal that religious minorities should not consider themselves to be unique (despite the explicit recognition of religious freedom in the *Charter* in both s. 2a and 15).

While *Amselem* and *Multani* see religion as a core part of identity, the *Hutterian Brethren* case reframes the religious claimant as having a perspective and "individual beliefs." The inextricable link between belief and practice is minimized, and a very protestant approach to religion is evidenced in the court. While this may seem inevitable given the subjective emphasis in *Amselem*, the court there maintained a requirement for a nexus with religion and clearly linked practice, belief, and identity. In *Hutterian Brethren* the individual becomes one of many individuals whose beliefs the state, and the court, must manage.

The court does not consider the possibility that the religious beliefs and practices that may come into conflict with laws of general application are more likely to be those of religious minorities. Significantly, the court introduces the idea of the "exception" in this case. This positions the religious minority as asking for a special favour and displaces the idea of equality with minority requests for accommodation. The emphasis shifts to the validity and importance of ensuring compliance with laws of general application and the general good. The court here imagines itself as the guardian of these state goals, rather than as the protector of minorities from the tyranny of the majority. This is in contrast to the position of the court in *R v. Big. M Drug Mart Ltd.* where Justice Dickinson writes (at para 96): "What may appear good and true to a majoritarian religious group, or to the state acting at their behest, may not, for religious reasons, be imposed upon citizens who take a contrary view. The *Charter* safeguards religious minorities from the threat of 'the tyranny of the majority.'" Finally, multiculturalism and the multi-religious society are not noted as values, desirable ends, or programs (nor are they recognized in the *Charter* itself). Instead, multiculturalism is a demographic reality that poses challenges for the state, which it must manage to maintain social cohesion and the general good.

CONCLUSIONS

This review of three recent Supreme Court decisions reveals a shift in tone from one that emphasizes diversity and multiculturalism as positive values as well as statements of demographic fact to one in which diversity and multiculturalism are portrayed as problems that states are called to manage.

Placed side by side, the decisions also illustrate the constructed nature not only of diversity and pluralism, but also of values and their hierarchicalization. In *Hutterian Brethren* the state's prioritization of security is transformed into a value that supersedes religious freedom. In *Multani*, security is named as a value, but religious freedom is given priority (after a brief assessment of harm). As Justice Abella's dissent highlights, 250 Hutterian Brethren without photographs on their drivers licences do not really pose a threat to security (at para 115).

In both *Amselem* and *Multani* the language of exemption or exception is absent, yet both could be framed as "exemption" cases. In contrast, exceptionalism advances a particular vision of normative/non-normative hierarchy that easily slips past any consideration of equality. It allows unfair or unjust power relations to remain unchanged and unchallenged. In other words, positioning the *Hutterian Brethren* as asking for an exception to the general rule frames them as (1) asking for special treatment not available to everybody; (2) glosses over the efficacy of the requirement for a photograph; and (3) side-steps the issue of alternative strategies for achieving the same results without harming the Hutterian Brethren. If religious minorities are positioned as asking for an exception, rather than as asking for equality, there is no opening to challenge the system itself. To frame religious minorities as seeking exemption or exception from laws of general application is a new turn of events at the Supreme Court level, and reflects, to some measure, a more general trend that sees multiculturalism as something that must be managed and kept under control rather than celebrated. Moreover, the precise point of the *Charter of Rights and Freedoms* is to recognize diversity and to provide legal protection, subject to reasonable limits (s. 1), to those whose practices, identities, structural disadvantage bring them face to face with majoritarian practices.

It is not clear whether the shifts I am suggesting are occurring are necessarily linked to a decline in multiculturalism. While Vertovec and Wessendorf's position that multiculturalism is unthreatened is perhaps too optimistic, so too is a conclusion that it is no longer a viable project. Moreover, a more sophisticated measure of multiculturalism is required than is presented here, one which would at the very least include an examination of institutional spheres, the presence or absence of multicultural demographics, as well as ideology and programs. In considering the question of whether multiculturalism is declining, it of course depends on what we mean when we talk about multiculturalism. If we mean a simple demographic description, then no, multiculturalism is not in decline. But if we mean something more, as is implied in the *Charter's* explicit instruction that "this *Charter* shall be interpreted in a manner consistent with the preservation and enhancement of the multicultural heritage of Canadians," then there is reason to believe, at least based on what we see in the case law, that multiculturalism may be under threat. The fact that the Supreme Court of Canada seems to have reimagined its role as one of support for the state in the creation and maintenance of laws of general application, rather than as a defender of the difference that can come with multiculturalism, should signal a potential shift that warrants more critical scholarly attention.

NOTES

I would like to acknowledge the role of the Religion and Diversity Project in the development of the ideas in this chapter as well as the ongoing financial support from my Canada Research Chair in the Contextualization of Religion in a Diverse Canada. I am also grateful to Marianne Abou-Hamad for her editorial assistance.

1 I thank Linda Woodhead for this comment on my discussion of multiculturalism and for her observation that the measurement of multicultural decline must be developed using more complex measures than are currently being employed by many researchers.

2 On 16 August 2011 Defence Minister Peter MacKay announced that after forty-three years the components of the Canadian Armed Forces would be renamed from Maritime Command, Air Command, and Land Forces Command to the Canadian Armed Forces: Royal Canadian Navy, Royal Canadian Air Force, and Canadian Army. MacKay said that "Our Conservative government believes that an important element of the Canadian military heritage

was lost when these three former services were required to relinquish their historic titles ... today, I am honoured to announce that the three elements of the Canadian Forces will have their historic names restored" (Fitzpatrick 2011a).

3 The proposed bill would make it against the law to prevent someone from displaying the Canadian flag, thus overriding, for example, contractually agreed upon condo regulations. Conservative MP John Carmichael, who proposed the legislation, stated that "Canadians have always assumed this right. However, we believe it is important to legally protect that right and we start with that today. All Canadians, no matter where they live, should be able to enjoy the privilege of expressing their love for our country by flying the Canadian flag" (Fitzpatrick 2011b).

4 The revamped citizenship guide reads, "In Canada, men and women are equal under the law. Canada's openness and generosity do not extend to barbaric cultural practices that tolerate spousal abuse, 'honour killings,' female genital mutilation, or other gender-based violence" (*Discover Canada*).

5 Justices Iacobucci and Bastarache make use of this language in *Trinity Western University v. British Columbia College of Teachers* at para 59 and 66.

6 In March 2010, the Quebec government introduced Bill 94 (*An Act to establish guidelines governing accommodation requests within the Administration and certain institutions*, 2010), which sets the standard of "un visage découvert" or an uncovered face when a person is either giving or receiving (section 6) provincial public services at (section 2(1)), schools (2(2); 2(5); 3(1)), childcare centres (section 3(3)), hospitals (section 2(2); 2(5)), and health and social service agencies (section 3(2)). The potential implications of this legislation were wide-ranging, and as my colleagues Pascale Fournier and Erica See (2012) have argued, significantly extended the notion of "public" in a way that forces *niqab*-wearing women from most aspects of social life. The proposed Bill 94 was never passed, but has been reconstituted in Quebec's newly proposed "Charter Affirming the Values of Secularism, State Religious Neutrality, and the Equality of Men and Women and the Framing of Accommodation Requests." (Charte affirmant les valeurs de laïcité et de neutralité religieuse de l'État ainsi que d'égalité entre les femmes et les hommes et encadrant les demandes d'accommodement).

REFERENCES

Adams, Michael. 2008. *Unlikely Utopia: The Surprising Triumph of Multiculturalism*. Toronto: Penguin.
Alibhai-Brown, Yasmin. 2000. *After Multiculturalism*. London: Foreign Policy Centre.

Bannerji, Himani, ed. 2001. *The Dark Side of the Nation: Essays on Multicultural-ism, Nationalism and Gender*. Toronto: Canadian Scholars' Press.

Beckford, James A. 2003. *Social Theory and Religion*. Cambridge: Cambridge University Press.

Bouchard, Gérard, and Charles Taylor. 2008. "Building the Future: A Time for Reconciliation." *Commission de Consultation sur les Pratiques d'Accommodement Reliées aux Différences Culturelles.*

Campbell, David, and Morton Schoolman. 2008. "Introduction: Pluralism 'Old' and 'New.'" In *The New Pluralism: William Connolly and the Contemporary Global Condition*, edited by David Campbell, and Morton Schoolman, 1–16. Durham: Duke University Press.

Day, Richard J. F. 2000. *Multiculturalism and the History of Canadian Diversity*. Toronto: University of Toronto Press.

Discover Canada: The Rights and Responsibilities of Canadian Citizenship. 2010. Government of Canada. Last modified April 27. www.cic.gc.ca/english/resources/publications/ discover/section-04.asp.

Fitzpatrick, Meagan. 2011a. "Peter MacKay hails 'royal' renaming of military." CBC *News*. August 16. http://www.cbc.ca/news/canada/toronto/story/2011/08/16/pol-military-renaming.html.

– 2011b. "Tory MP wants new law to protect the flag." CBC *News*. September 28. http://www.cbc.ca/news/politics/story/2011/09/28/pol-flag-law.html.

Foblets, Marie-Claire, and Christine Kulakowski. 2010. *Les Assises de l'Interculturalité*. Bruxelles: Ministère de l'Emploi et de l'Égalité des Chances.

Fournier, Pascale, and Erica See. 2012. "The 'Naked Face' Of Secular Exclusion: Bill 94 and The Privatization of Belief." *Windsor Yearbook of Access to Justice* 30 (1): 63–76.

Hadj-Abdou, Leila, and Linda Woodhead. 2011. "'Our Choice, Our Freedom, Our Right.' Muslim Women's Participation in the Controversy over Veiling: Austria and the UK Compared." In *Politics, Religion and Gender: Framing and Regulating the Veil*, edited by Sieglinde Rosenberger, and Birgit Sauer, 150–76. London: Routledge.

Kernerman, Gerald P. 2005. *Multicultural Nationalism: Civilizing Difference, Constituting Community*. Vancouver: University of British Colombia Press.

Kymlicka, Will. 1995. *Multicultural Citizenship: A Liberal Theory of Minority Rights*. Oxford: Oxford University Press.

– 2005. *Multicultural Odysseys: Navigating the New International Politics of Diversity*. Oxford: Oxford University Press.

– 2010. "The Rise and Fall of Multiculturalism? New Debates on Inclusion and Accommodation in Diverse Societies." In *The Multiculturalism Backlash: Euro-*

pean Discourses, Policies and Practices, edited by Steven Vertovec, and Susanne Wessendorf, 32–49. New York: Routledge.

Markell, Patchen. 2003. *Bound by Recognition*. Princeton: Princeton University Press.

Vertovec, Steven, and Susanne Wessendorf, eds. 2010. *The Multiculturalism Backlash*. New York: Routledge.

Legislation

Canadian Charter of Rights and Freedoms, R.S.C, 1985 Appendix II, No. 44 *see also* Part I (ss. 1 to 34) of the *Constitution Act, 1982*.

Cases

Alberta v. Hutterian Brethren of Wilson Colony, 2009 SCC 37.

Multani v. Commission scolaire Marguerite-Bourgeoys, 2006 SCC 6, [2006] 1 S.C.R. 256.

Kokkinakis v. Greece, (14307/88) [1993] ECHR 20 (25 May 1993).

R. v. Big M Drug Mart Ltd., [1985] 1 S.C.R. 295.

Syndicat Northcrest v. Amselem [2004] 2 S.C.R. 551 .

Trinity Western University v. British Columbia College of Teachers, 2001 SCC 31, [2001] 1 SCR 772.s

11

Theism and the Secular in Canada

SOLANGE LEFEBVRE

This chapter is about the conceptions and definitions of secularism and how their operationalization creates different possibilities for the expression of religion in the public sphere. Although the chapter does not explicitly discuss the case of India in comparison to Quebec and the rest of Canada, the questions outlined here are equally pertinent to India, a democracy that prides itself on its constitutional guarantee of religious freedom and its openness to religious minorities. The first section of the first part of the chapter will begin with a semantic and theoretical analysis of key concepts – secular, secularism, and *laïcité* as they appear in the Proulx Report, a report on religious education published in 1999, and in the report *Building the Future* ("Fonder l'avenir: le temps de la conciliation: rapport") (Bouchard and Taylor 2008). The second section will present a summary of the main positions taken by Gérard Bouchard and Charles Taylor, the co-chairmen of the commission on reasonable accommodation that took place in Quebec in 2007 and 2008, in their final report *Building the Future* (ibid.). The third section will briefly account for the development of the positions taken by these two authors in their own works, and raise questions about ways to address the issue of religion in the public arena. The conclusion will explore the different contexts found in a few countries and suggest a model for the Canadian context. I argue for a pluralist secular state open to some religious expression in the political arena.

In 1985, for the first time, the Supreme Court of Canada used Tocqueville's famous phrase: the "tyranny of the majority."[1] This concept has become central in our contemporary discussion about the relations between majority and minority groups in Canada. In what light should we examine the question of discrimination against minorities and individuals? In what context can discrimination be considered severe and in what other contexts can it be overcome? What kind of equality should we strive for? Since the 1980s, the impact of the *Canadian Charter of Rights and Freedoms* (along with new fears stirred by the events of 11 September 2001) has been the major force shaping debates about the politics of religion. Since then, even if there are still many ways in which religion is recognized (education, welfare systems, public ceremonies), in Western countries, with the exception of the United States, any reference to God in public life seems problematic. In pluralist societies, collective expressions of religion are often controversial in public life,[2] even if there are still many forms of recognition in schools, welfare systems, public ceremonies, and ethical debates. In light of the current situation in Quebec and the importance of conceptual frameworks such as "secular" and "*laïcité*" in relation to religion in the public sphere, in my conclusion I suggest that we encourage an approach to religion that is based on recognition.

DEBATES IN QUEBEC: FROM SECULARITY TO *LAÏCITÉ*

Secularity and laïcité *in Quebec*

The government of Quebec has been fairly proactive in coming up with strategies to deal with religious minorities. In the past fifteen years two major commissions were struck to come up with strategies to best integrate minorities. The first, formed in 1999, was called to reflect on the report produced by the *Groupe de travail sur la place de religion dans d'école*, dubbed the Proulx Report after the chair of the group, which sought to research the place of religion in schools. Eight years later, in 2007, the government formed the Consultation Commission on Accommodation Practices Related to Cultural Difference, called the Bouchard-Taylor Commission after its two co-chairs. In 2008, the Bouchard-Taylor Commission released a report entitled *Building the Future: A Time for Reconciliation*, with their findings. The analyses in this section are based on these reports and hundreds of briefs tabled at the two commissions.[3]

From a semantic analysis of this material, I observe two very simple but significant facts. In the debates on the secularization of schools in 1999, there was little overt hostility toward religions. A majority wanted to maintain parochial schools and with very few exceptions even the most strongly secularist contingent recognized the importance of religious culture, namely, teaching about world religions and spiritual trends. Only one brief – the one tabled by the *Fédération des femmes du Quebec* – was openly critical of religions and their treatment of women (Fédération 1999). It was in favour of teaching about religions from a cultural stand-point, a position based on human rights and equality. This brief mentions that its position is not "hostile" toward religion. However, it reminds read-ers that in the past the Catholic Church played a negative role in women's issues. Consequently, women, mothers, and teachers – women in general – are strongly linked to any action in favour of a secularization of educa-tion. It criticizes the inequalities still in place in religions, and informs readers that Christians from the community sector, or social Christians, are in line with their claims. The general tone of the discussion around the commission was quite calm; the most critical voices being in favour of the maintenance of an optional denominational course on religion in the public school system. But by 2007, things had changed radically. In the meantime, gender equality and religions had become the central concern for feminist groups and a great number of other groups and individuals. As in some European countries, the debates on the hijab and Islam brought to the forefront a number of questions relating to the nature of the bonds between public space, the state, and religion.

While discussions of religion are important for these documents, what is most noteworthy is the increase in the use of the concept of *laïcité* (Lefebvre 2008, 2012). How did *laïcité* become the term used in Quebec to shape the debates about religion? Paying attention to the semantic field can offer some important insights about the use of *laïcité* as opposed to secularism. A good number of scholarly works show that the concepts of secularity and *laïcité* come from very different backgrounds and ideolo-gies. Françoise Champion (1993) continues the comparative perspective of David Martin, and observes two very different patterns in the emanci-pation of European societies with respect to religion, that of laicization and that of secularization. There are "different types of idealistic logic" at work in countries with a dominant Catholic tradition as opposed to those with a dominant Protestant one. The difference is rooted in the language itself, since Catholic countries use concepts of "laicization," "laity," "*laicity*," which are practically unknown in Anglo-Saxon and Germanic countries that use words referring to the concept of secularization: "secular," "secu-larism," "secularity." Champion insists on the fundamental distinctions to which they refer. According to the logic of laicization, the Catholic Church often stands as a rival to the state. The dynamics of secularization prove to be very different, since the Protestant churches do not stand as ri-vals to the state, but as institutions within the state. They play very well-defined roles and to them secularization denotes a weakening of the meaning of these roles. In their final report, Bouchard and Taylor (2008) propose that a White Paper should be written on "secularism" (their translation of *laïcité*) in order to define Quebec's secular regime.

For several decades now, Quebec has been moving toward policies that respect freedom of belief and religion. The concept of *laïcité* came up from time to time in debates about religious education, but it was never the dominant concept in this discourse. *Laïcité* is, however, the defining concept of the 1999 Proulx Report. The Proulx Report recommends the laicization of the public school system but shies away from promoting the exclusion of religious education from schools, thus opting for a "*laïcité ouverte*" translated as "open, secular" schools in these terms:

> We ... came to the unanimous conclusion that the time has come to define the place of religion in our schools from a new perspective. This new perspective provides for open, secular schools that would draw on the common values of citizens and include the study of both religious and secular world views. It recognizes the spiritual dimension of individuals and allows schools to offer common spiritual and religious services if they wish to do so. It also provides that schools may, outside school hours and in keeping with their priorities, make facilities available to religious groups that wish to offer services to their members. (Proulx 1999, Foreword VII)

In relation to the different semantic cultural backgrounds for the concepts "secular" and "*laïcité*," it is useful to recall that there was some uncertainty about the translation of the term "*laïcité*." In the translation of the original French version of the Proulx Report, the concept of "secularism," later used by the Bouchard-Taylor Report to translate "*laïcité*," is absent. The authors of the Proulx Report translate "*laïcité ouverte*" as "open, secular" schools in their report, and sometimes translates *laïque* as "lay." Among the few studies that were conducted for the Proulx committee, two are in both languages (English and French) or translate English words. For instance, a study by Sonia Pratte (1998) translates "secular" or "secularism" as *sécularité, séculier*, as does the study by José Woehrling (1999). The only study in English translated by individuals hired by the government,[4] written by Smith and Foster, translates "secular" as the adjective *laïque* (Smith 1998). The noun or substantive *laïcité* is found once, to translate a subtitle, "The Denominational-Secular Continuum," as "Continuum confessionalité-*laïcité*" (Proulx 1999, VI). The term "secularism" is never used in English, since the authors make use of the term "secular." In the French version of the Proulx Report, it is interesting to see that they use the terms *laïcité* and *laïque*, but also maintain, here and there, the adjective *séculier*, sometimes putting the two together: *laïque* and *séculier*.

Regarding the concepts of "secularism" and "secularization," this semantic study of the Proulx Report, the studies requested by the committee, and the briefs tabled at the hearings following publication of the report show that the committee was guided by the distinction between secularization and *laïcité*, proposed by the historian Jean Baubérot (Baubérot 1994).[5] Baubérot characterizes the first process, secularization, as a sociocultural phenomenon associated with the decline of beliefs and practices, while applying the second process, *laïcité*, to the public sphere or that of the state. This distinction moves away from the Anglo-Saxon debates that prefer to discuss diverse forms of secularity or secularism, or diverse levels of secularization. The adjective "secular," which is sometimes used by the Proulx Commission, is used by the Bouchard-Taylor Commission to qualify approaches or world views: *visions séculières du monde*, for instance, which means non-religious views. The distinction made by Baubérot will come up again in the Bouchard-Taylor Report, but without any discussion, which means that they apply the concept of *laïcité* to the state and the public arena, and the concept of secular and secularization to the cultural and social sphere.

In 2006, the Committee on Culture, attached to the Directorate of the National Assembly of Quebec, a committee on religious heritage in Quebec, also used the concept of *laïcité*, this time explicitly referring to policies in France (Committee 2006). In its final report, the committee used the concept of *laïcité positive* to refer to some French policies that openly support the religious heritage of France whereby the state allots money for the maintenance of Catholic buildings. The concept is translated to "secularity" in English. From my point of view, the commission report contains one of the most precise texts on secularity produced so far, partly because it refers to the judicial field:

As a matter of fact, Quebec's legislation, and particularly its references to canon law, embodies a model of secularity that the Committee members endorse and feel should be maintained in a society mindful of its religious diversity. On this point, professor Ernest Caparros had this to say: "This canon law civilization is a very important legal model of collaborative or positive secularity, that is, a secularity that recognizes the religious phenomenon within civil society and stimulates its development. It is interesting to note that France is now closer to this type of secularity. It has moved away from the absolute secularity that sought to banish religion from civil society in the early days after the Revolution, and is now moving toward neutral secularity, also known as open or positive secularity." The Committee is of the opinion that any dialogue between religious and government authorities must be based on this model of secularity, in other words, on collaborative or "dialogue-friendly" secularity, and that the search for solutions to protect and enhance Quebec's religious heritage must take this model into account. (Committee 2006)[6]

Interestingly, at the end of the argument the commission insists on "collaborative secularity," which is another way to designate an "open secularism" or "*laïcité.*"

Very soon after the publication of the Bouchard-Taylor Report the consequences of the use of the concept of *laïcité ouverte* (open secularism) became apparent. Simply put, the opposition to this approach, comprising diverse people opposed to the recognition of religious expressions by minorities and, for some, any religious expression in the public arena, argued that Quebec needs a real *laïcité*, neither open nor positive. The opposing argument is made easy, in my view, by the weakness of the concept of *laïcité ouverte*. Indeed, if it needs to be "open" to be positive, the concept itself must present some problems. At its roots, the concept, as noted before by Champion, means that the Catholic Church stands as a rival to the state. In such circumstances, emancipation mobilizes political power to extricate individuals and society from the "hold" of the Church, with a background of conflicts between Catholicism and anti-clericalism. It formulates criticisms against Catholicism and against religion in general (Lefebvre 2008). In this regard, it is difficult to excerpt the concept from its conflictual background. There are still an important number of intellectuals and militants pleading for a strong and strict *laïcité* in France, without any openness. The term itself comes from the concept of "lay" people, who at some point in the history of the Church, opposed the clerics to gain power over spiritual matters.

In France, a *laïcité ouverte* or *positive* was promoted first by some youth and cultural Catholic organizations after the Second World War, in the area of leisure activities (Besse 2007). Some groups and individuals criticized this new openness, perceived as a "distortion" of *laïcité* or as a "false" *laïcité*. In my last section, I will come back to recent debates about secularity and *laïcité*, which show a new understanding of the cultural backgrounds of the words. But first, I examine the way Bouchard and Taylor elaborate their positions in the 2008 report.

The Underpinnings of the Bouchard-Taylor Report:
"laïcité ouverte"

As previously mentioned, the Bouchard-Taylor Commission received around 837 briefs reacting to a consultation document, and the co-chairs wrote their report after a process of consultation including public forums and public hearings. In the report concluding the process, Bouchard and Taylor discuss a number of principles that could underpin the open secularism they are endorsing. Key among these principles is the neutrality of the state, which is summed up thus: "The ideal proposed here is that of a pluralistic society that has reached an 'overlapping consensus' on basic political principles, this means a solid agreement among citizens on such principles, even if they are rooted in a broad variety of deeply felt reasons" (Proulx 1999, 134–5), notably those growing out of religious convictions. Though cited only once, this well-known principle borrowed from John Rawls (2005) in some ways constitutes a key idea in the vision of secularism recommended by this report. We shall later examine Taylor's reflection on this point. Concerning the way religion should be handled in such a regime, Bouchard and Taylor make recommendations on two contentious issues: religious symbols worn by civil servants and Quebec's religious heritage sites. In both cases their conclusions are artfully nuanced.

The Bouchard-Taylor Report recommends that civil servants be given the right to wear religious symbols, with two provisos. First, the religious symbol in question must not prove to be an excessive constraint in properly performing the task assigned. This would be the case, for example, if a female teacher were wearing a burka that completely covered her face and prevented her from communicating properly with her pupils. Second, the religious symbol must not contravene the neutrality of the state. Civil servants are subject to a "rule of discretion" and are obliged to embody the neutrality of the state. Judges, public prosecutors, police officers, and the president of the National Assembly should not put their religious affiliation on display. With this recommendation, the co-chairmen knowingly go against existing jurisprudence, as Canadian courts have already ruled that Sikh members of the Royal Canadian Mounted Police (RCMP) are allowed to wear their religious turbans instead of the regulatory hat, which is such a well-known Canadian symbol. Thus, in suggesting that certain civil servants should refrain from wearing their religious symbols, Bouchard and

Taylor defend a stricter vision of state neutrality by extending it to civil servants who assume important and sensitive positions in the name of the state. The section on Quebec's religious heritage contains the following sentences: "We must avoid maintaining practices that in point of fact identify the State with a religion, usually that of the majority, simply because they now seem to have only heritage value. The prayers recited at the beginning of municipal council meetings or the crucifix hanging above the president's chair in the National Assembly of Quebec come to mind" (Bouchard and Taylor 2008, 152). According to this principle of neutrality, certain privileges (parochial schooling) and institutional practices (theistic prayers opening municipal assemblies) no longer have a place. In this regard, the authors of the report partially endorse Canadian jurisprudence concerning general norms of religious origin – the most obvious case being the statutory Sunday holiday that, over the last decades, has been removed, at least partly, throughout Canada (*R. v. Big M Drug Mart Ltd*). Concerning symbols of religious heritage, the report distinguishes between those that play a regulatory role and those considered to be legacies of Quebec heritage. The cross on Mount Royal would be counted among the latter, whereas the crucifix in the National Assembly would be included among the former, it being the affirmation of the religion of the majority in a place set aside for the exercise of state power.

Over and above these particular recommendations, the co-chairmen endorse the concept of so-called *laïcité ouverte* (open secularism). This concept leaves room for individual expression of religion in public areas (except in certain specific cases), while being founded on a principle of equality, which in effect limits expressions of the majority religion, except when they take the form of religious heritage. There was little official reaction to the report apart from on the day the report was made public when the government voted unanimously to keep the crucifix on the wall of the National Assembly. This single reaction shows the gap between the government and the commission. To give an explanation of the co-chairs' positions, I will examine their genesis in the next section. Surprisingly, even after major hearings and hundreds of briefs, Bouchard and Taylor are quite in line with their initial positions.

Genesis of Bouchard's and Taylor's Positions

After a careful analysis of their respective writings, I can say without hesitation that the positions they take as commissioners are basically faithful to the ones they held previously, especially in the case of Bouchard (Lefebvre 2010), even if their reflection on the concrete situations related to reasonable accommodation is new. Their responses stick to perspectives defending, in the case of Bouchard, a nationalist model inclusive of differences, and, in Taylor's case, a model open to contemporary religious beliefs. However, despite their somewhat different perspectives, they are both rather secularist in their view of religion's role in the public sphere. Taylor, who has been defending a policy of cultural recognition for several years, is more restrictive when it comes to religion, at least in the context of Quebec. Yet, in the mindscape of contemporary philosophy, he is seen as one of the authors still daring to reflect on the ideas of transcendence, conversion, and God. While handling religion very concretely in the political sphere is not an issue to which he has given much thought, a single article entitled "Modes of Secularism," published in 1998, sums up his position on this topic very well (Taylor 1998).

"Modes of Secularism" traces the emergence of two strategies for the separation of church and state, dating from the beginnings of modernity. One strategy opposes the state's recognition of a single confession or religious tradition but does not exclude the common theistic or deistic space where numerous beliefs converge (strategy of the common space). This would be exemplified by the American case. The second strategy, initiated by Hobbes and Grotius, postulates the establishment of a political space and a totally independent ethic, relegating religion to the space of private life, but without entering into conflict with religion. This strategy could gain ground in the United States, even though the idea of "One nation under God" remains a powerful unifying force.

Religious diversity and particularly the presence of atheism put these two models in question. Atheists, being hostile to any trace of religious influence, want to push the model based on independence even further. But this is seen as unacceptable to many believers. Hence, Taylor says that we find ourselves literally in a *Kulturkampf* (culture war) over the "fundamentals" of our society. To counter this, he proposes a version of Rawls' idea of an "overlapping consensus," which aims to achieve a common agreement on a very restricted number of principles and dimensions. This requires scrapping both strategies, which date from the beginnings of modernity and are too closely related to Judeo-Christian norms and visions. As Taylor (1998, 33) puts it, "Secularism is not optional in the modern age." He develops the elements that could characterize an imagined community (Anderson 1991) and rally all its citizens. What is important to us is that Taylor admits there should be several forms of separation of church and state. He admits that the common space (rights for individuals and sometimes groups, democracy, common elements of identity) may sometimes include particularistic elements such as history, language, culture, and, in certain cases, religion. According to Rawls' vision, however, minimal national identity will not aspire to anything resembling a total convergence of religious and moral horizons. More broadly, in his other works Taylor discusses religious meaning as a real experience and something central to modernity. But one has the strong feeling that, when it comes to religion in the public sphere, he takes a position that resolutely favours a neutral, pluralist, and strictly egalitarian political space, which tends to endorse the belief that religious pluralism is a source of conflict. This position is also reflected in the report he co-signed with Bouchard.[7] I asked one of my students who participated in a debate with Taylor to question him about his "contradictory" position connecting recognition and secularism. Taylor responded that, because Quebec seemed particularly "Jacobean" to him, he didn't feel he could defend any recognition of religion other than strictly cultural or individual.

In comparison, what is Bouchard's stance on religion? The influence of Bouchard on the Bouchard-Taylor Report relates principally to two ideas, strongly rooted in his previous work. The first has to do with a national project open to diversity; the second concerns collective myths. Remember that the Bouchard-Taylor Report devotes several pages to defining political models, such as interculturalism and *laïcité ouverte* (open secularism), proposing that the government should draw up a legal text for the former and a white paper for the latter. For a number of years, Bouchard has been working on myths created by intellectuals to guide the nation. In his work with the commission, he no doubt felt beholden to this intellectual mission.

Thus, his favourite angle of analysis is the mobilizing myth of a society, seen as an essential condition of its dynamic project for the future. Far from being absent from our imaginative universe, national myths tend to recur (Bouchard 2003). In Quebec, there would have been a succession of powerful myths: the myth of the survival of French-Canadians, then the "unique and federative myth of the 1960s, and the myth of the Quiet Revolution," which Bouchard (2007, 151–2) calls the overarching myth. After these periods of mobilization, a fragmentation of the myth occurred, this fragmented mythical configuration being more habitual in the history of societies. Since the 1960s, Bouchard contends that several other myths have emerged, among which he enumerates interculturalism (of particular note), *laïcité*, Americanity, modernity, political sovereignty, Quebec-ness, Quebec's ascension in the business world, etc. – all of them "projective" myths (Bouchard 2007). What is the source of the myths? They stem from the work of intellectuals, from institutional power, and from social ritualization.

Note that, while the Bouchard-Taylor Report did stand by the idea that authoritative texts do have a role to play in defining national orientations; it discarded the notion of myth, which does indeed seem rather problematic. To my mind, even if it is true that some intellectuals can sometimes participate in the creation of a myth, the idea that intellectuals can easily formulate various myths *for* the nation does not seem very faithful to the foundational origins of myths, which are supposed to emerge spontaneously as expressions of collective experiences. What about present-day myths? From my observations, the myth of survival is undeniably very present in the French-Canadian imagination, along with the more recent myth of the "Quebec model." It is true that this more recent myth is one to which our commission could claim again, around the "reasonable accommodation" public discussion, as a model for other societies. As Bouchard asked previously, are interculturalism and *laïcité* influential myths in contemporary Quebec society? The answer is not yet known. But certainly, they were in the mind of Bouchard who strongly promoted the two notions in the final report. In brief, it is interesting to see how Bouchard and Taylor's handling of fundamental issues in the report was coherent with their previous reflections.

A PROBLEMATIC OF THE SECULAR IN THE PUBLIC ARENA

In this conclusion, I discuss the concepts of secular and *laïcité* as well as their proper meaning, and I argue for a pluralist secular state open to some religious expressions in the political arena. In my first point, I come back to the debate around religious education. The *Groupe de travail sur la place de religion à l'école*, dubbed the Proulx Report after the chair of the group, chose a "*laïcité ouverte*," meaning that religious culture could be taught in the public school system as a specific discipline. In reality, the approach chosen in Quebec is more in line with the non-denominational British approach, which would be secular and not *laïque*. Second, I will argue in favour of keeping a few discrete expressions of religiosity in the public arena, arguing against the Bouchard-Taylor Commission on the particular matter that limits collective expressions of religion strictly to religious heritage.

Where does this leave us then, with respect to the concepts of *laïcité* and secularism? What is the framework that can work in Quebec? It is impor-

tant that any analyses of the results of the Bouchard-Taylor Report in relation to religion in the public sphere account for the fact that there is strong
evidence that the co-chairs' theoretical positions are woven into the report
and thus the public hearings submissions are filtered through these lenses.

Revisiting the Secular/Laïque

The French sociologist Jean-Paul Willaime is both a colleague and some-
time opponent of Baubérot (Willaime 2008). While proposing a more cooperative form of *laïcité* based on compromise – regardless of whether
Christianity or other religions are the historical majority – he recognizes
that the concept of *laïcité* itself poses a problem on the international
scene. It is quite revealing that despite the efforts of the network around
Baubérot, so far the European Union has refused to translate the concept
of *laïcité* into English (as "laicity" instead of "secular"). More interestingly,
Willaime and Béraud's recent comparative study on religious education
contains a chapter examining divergences and convergences in different
European models where they distinguish between two non-confessional
approaches, one being secular (*séculière*) and the other *laïque*:

> In the last analysis, there would seem to be two versions of the non-
> confessional approach to religions in schools—one that could be
> called *séculière* and the other, *laïque*. The first, which is gathering
> strength in the United Kingdom, takes a perfectly profane but com-
> prehensive approach to religions, using resources from the human sci-
> ences but considering religion an ordinary dimension of human
> experience that must be understood with empathy ... The second ap-
> proach, which is developing in France, favors approaching religion
> through its works, its cultural traces and refuses to recognize the reli-
> gious fact and its self-consistency more specifically by means of a par-
> ticular discipline. (Béraud and Willaime 2009)

Briefly, in France, the public school system acknowledges "religious fact"
(the necessary distance from religion), if mediated through specific disciplines like history and literature. In Quebec, as is the case in England and
other countries, "religion" is taught as such; there is a "religious education," not only religious culture in some other disciplinary contexts.
Would this distinction be of service to Quebec? In relation to education,
the answer is "yes." It is clear that, though the contexts differ, Quebec's approach is closer to that of the United Kingdom. Béraud and Willaime's

distinction has the advantage of showing that, in the so-called non-confessional field, "*laïcité*" is only one path among others.[8]

This example concerns only one aspect of collective life, education, but it is interesting that the pattern adopted by Quebec, regarding religious education, shows more proximity to England than to France. However, the use of the concept of *laïcité* has already brought about important consequences, notably it gives ammunition to those who are contesting the teaching of religious culture as a particular discipline. When using the concept of *laïcité*, in a Francophone province like Quebec, France and its debates are never far away. They exercise a powerful influence through writings, intellectual networks, and so on.

I would add that the British context is also more open to the majority religion as a cultural matrix, even if the country is quite secularized. Thus such an approach has the advantage of both recognizing the religious heritage of the context as well as opening the possibility of equality for those who do not share that heritage.

Religious Expressions in the Public Arena

A second consideration merits some attention. I would like to briefly discuss theistic expressions in Canada. God is mentioned in the Constitution, in oaths, in some mottos, in prayers at the House of Commons, and in many municipal assemblies in different provinces. For example, in *Allen v. Renfrew* prayer in a municipal assembly was considered. The facts are as follows:

> The Renfrew County Council commences its monthly meetings with a prayer. This practice has been followed as long as anyone can remember and likely since the Council was established in 1861. The prayer recited was the Lord's Prayer until November 2000 when a new non-secular prayer was adopted in its place. The applicant Robert Allen is a resident of Renfrew County who does not believe in God or in participation in prayers. He seeks a declaration that the respondent Council's practice of opening meetings with a prayer is a violation of his *Charter* right to freedom of conscience and religion, together with an injunction restraining this practice and damages for mental distress. (*Allen v. Renfrew (Corp. of the County)*)

In 1999, a decision of the Superior Court of Appeal for Ontario had stated that the prayer, then the Lord's Prayer, was not acceptable (*Freitag v.*

Penetanguishene (Town)), and that to read scriptures from the bible was to "impose Christian observances on non-Christians and religious observances on non-believers." The prayer recited at the Renfrew Council was the following: "Almighty God, we give thanks for the great blessings which have been bestowed on Canada and its citizens, including the gifts of freedom, opportunity, and peace that we enjoy. Guide us in our deliberations as [County Councillors], and strengthen us in our awareness of our duties and responsibilities. Grant us wisdom, knowledge, and understanding to preserve the blessings of this country for the benefit of all and to make good laws and wise decisions. Amen" (*Allen v. Renfrew (Corp. of the County)* at para 3). This particular prayer, inspired by the one pronounced at the House of Commons,[9] was adopted in 2000, to replace the Lord's prayer, hoping to include a maximum of believers. But an expert in religious studies, Dr. Antonia R. Gualtieri, said to the court that the prayer offered a theistic framework and could not be maintained, because it was "no longer considered sufficiently generic and comprehensive to serve as a definition of religion because it excludes groups whose supreme authority is a moral law which does not involve the worship of an objectively existing divine being ... Any activity which claimed to be non-sectarian in the sense of encompassing all religions (i.e. symbolically mediated world-and-value-views) in a pluralist society would have to accommodate the Humanist phenomenon" (at para 13). In spite of this objection, the court ruled that the prayer was acceptable. The Superior Court admits the religious meaning of the prayer:

> On my reading of this prayer it can be characterized as an effort to impose a moral tone on the proceedings and to promote certain values, in particular good governance. The prayer identifies the gifts of "freedom, opportunity, and peace" that we enjoy in Canada and asks for "wisdom, knowledge, and understanding" to preserve the blessings of this country. In my opinion there is no specifically theological message in this, Christian or otherwise. However, the prayer does begin with phrase "All mighty God, we give thanks for the great blessings which have been bestowed on Canada and its citizens ..." and the prayer clearly reflects the belief that God is the source of these blessings and that the requested wisdom, knowledge, and understanding derives from God. In this limited respect there is a religious message. (at para 18)

But even more interestingly:

> In a pluralistic society religious, moral or cultural values put forward
> in a public governmental context cannot always be expected to meet
> with universal acceptance. This is to be contrasted with the use of a
> specifically Christian prayer, such as the Lord's Prayer or readings
> from the bible, when non-Christians are involved (i.e. as in *Freitag* and
> *Zylberberg*). In my view, it would be incongruous and contrary to the
> intent of the *Charter* to hold that the practice of offering a prayer to
> God per se, is a violation of the religious freedom of non-believers.
> This conclusion derives considerable support from the fact that the
> preamble to the *Charter* itself specifically refers to the supremacy of
> God. (at para 19)

In sharp contrast, in Quebec the human rights tribunal has ruled more
clearly in favour of banning all prayers, in the name of the neutrality of
the state (*Simoneau v. Tremblay*). Even if the jurisdiction of this particular
tribunal does not concern the state but instead individual discriminations, it chooses to establish its main argument on state neutrality, as it did
more recently for a similar case (*Simoneau v. Tremblay*). The province's
Court of Appeal overturned this 2011 decision of the rights tribunal and
decided that the prayer, as well as a few religious symbols, could stay
(*Saguenay (Ville de) v. Mouvement laïque québécois*). At the moment of the
publication of this chapter, we can anticipate that the Supreme Court of
Canada will likely field an appeal of this court ruling within a few years.

CONCLUSION

In his comparative work on global religions, Peter Beyer argues that the
power of religions in diverse countries depends a lot on their control of
religious freedom and school education. In Canada, he remarks that even
if there is no official religion, the implicit model of an "acceptable" religion is Christian. One consequence is that "the courts tend to have doubts
about the status of religions that do not so fit" (Beyer 2006, 295). Lori G.
Beaman (2008) argues that Canada is dominated by Christian hegemony.
Does this mean that there can be no recognition of religious minorities?
In this regard, I do agree Canada needs to push its understanding of religious freedom further. But when it comes to religious expressions in the
public arena, how can we address the challenge of equality?

On this matter, I would agree with the Ontario judge saying that "In a pluralistic society religious, moral or cultural values put forward in a public governmental context cannot always be expected to meet with universal acceptance" (see above). If equality means that in all circumstances, a government has to take all religions and beliefs into account, there cannot be religions and beliefs taken into account. The opponents to the program on religious culture in Quebec are precisely playing this card. They argue that a course on world religions and some secular convictions cannot honour all the beliefs of the pupils in a class, and they ask that the course be abolished because it infringes on religious freedom and equality. They could be right, if we maintain a strict comprehension of equality, meaning that we have to explicitly represent all possible beliefs and religions in a course. There is a way to transmit a sense of respect for all beliefs in their variety, without having to explain all their contents in detail.

In this regard and on the same grounds, keeping some religious expressions in the political arena could be possible. The question is the following: does any common religious reference of the majority violate minority rights? Some Ontarian courts concluded that it did not, when it was adapted in a proper and inclusive way, as did the Quebec Court of Appeal. I think any country needs to balance historical religious expressions and the recognition of minorities and individuals' rights. In these religious expressions, at least in Canada, there is a "moral tone," a statement on values and their fundamental "otherness" source, as the Ontarian judges observe, though civic society could choose to abolish or change these traditions over time.

Incidentally, the latest decision of the European court around the crucifix in Italy is also of interest. In 2009, the court stated that the presence of a crucifix in a classroom was discriminatory toward parents and their children with non-Christian convictions, provoking a huge reaction in civil and political European circles (*Lautsi v. Italy*). In 2011, the court reversed its decision, mentioning that the presence of a symbol of the religious majority does not suffice to characterize a process of indoctrination by the state (*Lautsi and Others v. Italy*).

In Europe, some countries are seeking a balance between majority rights and minority rights. For instance, despite its official church, England is known as a champion of diversity, at least in education. Many minority groups support the state church to show their respect to the country's history, to show respect for the historic majority's rights. There is also the hope that the existence of a religious establishment or recognized religious majority (even in the face of the factual decline of that majority) will maintain a space for religion in the public sphere and ward off strong secularism. In France, supposedly *laïque*, there is a strong support for historical religions in many ways (Catholicism, Protestantism, Judaism), but a strong anti-cult suspicion, which is visible in some public policies. To conclude this chapter, I ask whether Quebec or Canada adopt a strong secularist view of public life.

After examining Bouchard's and Taylor's positions, and the discussion around the concepts of secular and *laïcité*, two main positions present themselves. First, Rawls' vision of the overlapping consensus, extended to religions in the public arena, which amounts to no religion in the public sphere except in the very strict historical sense (also Bouchard's and Taylor's position). Second, a country keeping some religious traditions in the public arena, while at the same time creating a favourable environment for religious pluralism. I would favour the second approach for Quebec and the rest of Canada, allowing civic society to keep and adapt some religious traditions, without seeking to indoctrinate individuals, as part of its historical and symbolic horizons. How to pluralistically share this horizon could be negotiated through time. For some years, many thinkers have been discussing religious pluralism and the state without paying attention to discrete practices like prayers, oaths, mottos, and other national symbols. The courts are reminding us that they are still at play, and should be part of our discussions.

NOTES

1 *R. v. Big M Drug Mart Ltd*, [1985] 1 R.C.S. 295.
2 See J. D. May 2003.
3 Thanks to sshrc, which funded my research project entitled *La sécularisation, la laïcité et les identités religieuses dans le contexte québécois* (2008–2011). Co-investigator Lori G. Beaman and I are currently examining how the commissions respond to religion. There are 254 briefs for the commission on religious education, reacting to the Proulx Report, supported by six research reports. The Bouchard-Taylor Commission received around 837 briefs reacting to a consultation document, and the co-chairs wrote their report after the process of consultation.
4 In the French translation of the report, it is mentioned that "La version française de ce rapport a été rédigée par les Services linguistiques du ministère de l'Éducation du Québec."
5 The distinction was first quoted by Micheline Milot, a member of the Task

Force on the Place of Religion in Schools in Quebec that produced the Proulx Report, in an issue of the journal *Théologiques* on *laïcité* that I edited in 1998 (Lefebvre 1998).

6 (Committee June 2006, 11). The Committee quotes Ernest Caparros, in a brief presented on January 26, 2005 (no. 109), p. 8.

7 During a workshop organized by Sonia Sikka, in which the proceedings of the report were elaborated, I was delighted to meet the editor of the book in which Taylor wrote his paper on secularism, Professor Bhargava, who confirmed my comprehension of Taylor's position. But even more interestingly, Professor Bhargava explained that the Indian context had a huge influence on Taylor's stance.

8 One should note that some French thinkers, including Baubérot, do not like the concept of *laïcité ouverte*, which suggests that French *laïcité* is "closed" (Baubérot 2008).

9 "Since 1877, writes the Superior Court, Parliament has commenced its proceedings with a prayer read by the Speaker before the doors of the House were opened to the public … In 1994, the sectarian prayer which had historically been used was replaced with the following non-sectarian prayer, which is read in English and French before the doors are opened to the public: *'Almighty God: We give thanks for the great blessings which have been bestowed on Canada and its citizens, including the gifts of freedom, opportunity and peace that we enjoy. We pray for our Sovereign, Queen Elizabeth, and the Governor General. Guide us in our deliberations as Members of Parliament, and strengthen us in our awareness of our duties and responsibilities as Members. Grant us wisdom, knowledge, and understanding to preserve the blessings of this country for the benefit of all and to make good laws and wise decisions. Amen. We will now have a moment of silence for private reflection and meditation. Amen.'"* (*Freitag v. Penetanguishene (Town)*) at para 45). Except for the mention of Queen Elizabeth and the General Governor, the prayer at Renfrew County Council is the same.

REFERENCES

Anderson, Benedict. 1991. *Imagined Communities*. 2nd ed. London: Verso.
Baubérot, Jean, dir. 1994. *Religions et laïcité dans l'Europe des douze*. Paris: Syros.
Baubérot, Jean. 2008. *Une laïcité interculturelle: le Québec, avenir de la France?* La Tour d'Aigues: Aube.
Beaman, Lori G. 2008. *Defining Harm: Religious Freedom and the Limits of the Law*. Vancouver: UBC Press.

Béraud, Céline, and Jean-Paul Willaime, ed. 2009. *Les jeunes, l'école et la religion.* Paris: Bayard.

Besse, Laurent. 2007. "Une 'laïcité ouverte.' Les maisons de jeunes et de la culture (de la Libération au milieu des années 1980)." In *Politiques de la laïcité au XXè siècle*, edited by P. Weil. Paris: PUF.

Beyer, Peter. 2006. *Religions in Global Society.* London: Routledge.

Bouchard, Gérard. 2003. *Raison et contradiction : le mythe au secours de la pensée.* Quebec: Éditions Nota bene.

– 2007. "Crise de la culture ou transition? Pour une nouvelle alliance du discours et de l'action." In *La culture québécoise est-elle en crise?*, edited by Marc-Henry Soulet, 61–94. Montreal: Boréal.

Bouchard, Gérard, and Charles Taylor. 2008. "Fonder l'avenir: le temps de la conciliation: rapport." Quebec: Commission de consultation sur les pratiques d'accommodement reliées aux différences culturelles.

Champion, Françoise. 1993. "Les rapports église-État dans les pays européens de tradition protestante et de tradition catholique: essai d'analyse." *Social Compass* 40 (4): 589–609.

The Committee on Culture. 2006. "Believing in Quebec's Religious Heritage." Proceedings initiated by the committee on culture. Quebec: Committee Secretariat Directorate of the National Assembly of Quebec.

Fédération des femmes du Québec. 1999. "La déconfessionnalisation du système scolaire. Un enjeu majeur pour les groupes de femmes." In Mémoire présenté à la Commission de l'Éducation: MELS, Gouvernement du Québec.

Lefebvre, Solange, ed. 1998. "Un autre regard sur la laïcité." *Théologiques* 6 (1): 3–7.

– 2008. "Between Law and Public Opinion." In *Diversity and Religion in Canada*, edited by Lori G. Beaman, and Peter Beyer, 175–98. Leiden: Brill.

– 2010. "Commission Bouchard-Taylor. Genèse d'une réflexion sur la laïcité." In *Les enjeux du pluralisme; l'actualité du modèle québécois*, edited by Jean-François Plamondon, and Anne D. Vaucher, 213–29. Bologna: Centro interuniersitario di studi quebecchesi. Édizioni Pendragon.

– 2012. "L'approche québécoise, entre laïcité et sécularité." In *Le programme d'éthique et culture religieuse : De l'exigeante conciliation entre le soi, l'autre et le nous*, edited by Mireille Estivalèzes, and Solange Lefebvre, 85–107. Quebec: Presses de l'Université Laval.

May, J. D. 2003. "God in Public: The Religions in Pluralist Societies." *Bijdragen: International Journal in Philosophy and Theology* 64: 249–64.

Pratte, Sonia. 1998. "La place de la religion dans les écoles publiques des provinces anglo-canadiennes." Rapport de recherche. Étude no 4. Quebec:

Ministère de l'Éducation, Groupe de travail sur la place de la religion à l'école.

Proulx, Jean-Pierre, and Task Force on the Place of Religion in Schools in Quebec. 1999. "Religion in Secular Schools: A New Perspective for Quebec." Quebec: Ministère de l'Éducation, Gouvernement du Québec.

Rawls, John. 2005. *Political Liberalism*. 3rd ed. New York: Columbia University Press.

Smith, William J., and William F. Foster. 1998. "Rétablir l'équilibre entre les droits et les valeurs: La place de la religion dans les écoles du Québec [Balancing Rights and Values: The Place of Religion in Quebec Schools]." Étude 5. Translated by S. l. d. m. d. l. é. d. Quebec. Montreal: Ministère de l'Éducation, Quebec, Groupe de travail sur la place de la religion à l'école.

Taylor, Charles. 1998. "Modes of Secularism." In *Secularism and Its Critics*, edited by Rajeev Bhargava. Delhi: Oxford University Press.

Willaime, Jean-Paul. 2008. *Le retour du religieux dans la sphère publique. Vers une laïcité de reconnaissance et de dialogue*. Lyon: Éditions Olivétan.

Woehrling, José. 1999. "Groupe de travail sur la place de la religion à l'école." Étude sur le rapport entre les droits fondamentaux de la personne et les droits des parents en matière d'éducation religieuse [Format PDF 6 26 Mo ; 163 p]. Ministère de l'éducation, Gouvernement du Québec. Available from http://collections.banq.qc.ca/ark:/52327/41783.

Cases

Allen v. Renfrew (Corp. of the County), 2004 CanLII 13978 (ON S.C.)

Freitag v. Penetanguishene (Town), 1999 CanLII 3786 (ON C.A.)

Lautsi v. Italy. 2009. ECHR. No. 30814/06.

Lautsi and Others v. Italy. 2011. ECHR. No. 30814/06.

R. v. Big M Drug Mart Ltd, *[1985]* 1 R.C.S. 295.

Saguenay (Ville de) c. Mouvement laïque québécois 2013 QCCA 936

Simoneau c. Tremblay, *2011* QCTDP 1.

PART FOUR

Problems of Recognition

12

The Limits of Multiculturalism in Contemporary India[1]

SHAIL MAYARAM

Canada is widely regarded as the birthplace of multiculturalism, but India has had an unstated, unofficial, unproclaimed multiculturalism since the inception of the Republic in 1950. Although the Indian Constitution, to begin with, used neither the terms multicultural nor secular, it endorsed the idea of equality among groups, which is at the core of multiculturalism. As Mahajan (2002) points out, however, there has been little attempt to theorize India's multicultural democracy. In contrast, there has been extensive discussion of secularism (Bhargava 1988, 2007a, 2007b; Sikka and Beaman, this volume; Raghuramaraju 1998). India's multiculturalism, which is embedded in the constitution itself, extends recognition through cultural and politico-economic rights to various groups. It recognizes regional, religious, and linguistic difference.

This chapter foregrounds the limits of Indian multiculturalism and political secularism drawing on constellations of events in two regions of India, namely, the northern state of Jammu and Kashmir and the other largely "tribal" populated region of central India said to be affected by the so-called Maoist insurgency. In both cases a civilizational fabric built over three millennia has been tragically eroded in the last two decades.

The cultural region of Kashmir has been a complex landscape where Kashmir Saivism, Buddhism, and Islam including Sufic theologies encountered and mutually transformed each other over centuries. There were also strong caste hierarchies and markers of ethnic difference that manifested in moments of violence. Nonetheless, practices of co-living were developed in a vernacularity, which also coloured early Kashmiri nationalism. A combination of state overuse of coercion, civil societal militancy, and the play of numerous political leaders driven exclusively by self-interest has severely undermined the old civilizational multiculturalism. The development of a new multiculturalism embedded in democracy and secularism has hence been severely impaired.

In Central India the forest communities were detribalized by the legal-institutional apparatus even as they were recognized as "scheduled tribes" having lost their ownership and traditional access to the forest. This is a region variously described as a "red corridor" and "war zone" being under the influence of Maoist cadres but clearly marks the democratic, developmental, and distributive failure of the Republic. In this heartland of the Indian subcontinent the juridico-legal privileging of "world religions" has undermined acknowledgement of Adivasi universes of belief and practice that anchor complex agro-pastoral forest ecologies. In effect, civilizational deep diversity comprising cultural fluidity, multiple religious belonging, and enclaved cosmologies has not been adequately recognized by the Indian state. Hence, the cycle of escalating violence, by actors linked to state and non-state.

I raise then two sets of questions. The first concerns the limits of Indian multiculturalism and secularism suggested by the tension between statist multiculturalism/secularism and civilizational/lived multiculturalism. A second set of questions follows from the first but is discussed only tangentially in this chapter and concerns multicultural theory and the quest for more meaningful categories. Given the privileging of the state in multicultural theory, the term interculturalism has been suggested as an alternative, drawing upon the Quebec model adopted in the wake of 9/11 (Bharucha 1999).[2] An alternative understanding of cosmopolitanism rescued from the historically oppressive idea of civilizational (read European) cosmopolitanism might be a preferred alternative since it foregrounds the mundane acts of living together (Mayaram 2010). Both the conceptual and historical discussion of cosmopolitanism, however, must spell out its antithesis, that is, the other of cosmopolitanism.

There is also a deeper problem, which is that the multiculturalism/secularism embedded in the Constitution continues with the colonial privileging of "world religions." Thus, Hinduism, Islam, Christianity, Jainism, Buddhism, and Sikhism figure in the statist understanding of "religion," but what have been completely ignored are the religio-cultural imaginaries of mobile peoples that we classify as pastoral and tribal. It is largely their cosmological approaches to land, nature, and divinity that have protected eco-zones of forests and the subcontinent's rich biodiversity. Their inadequate recognition as "scheduled tribes" and the onslaught of the state on mobile peoples including hunter-gatherers, transhumant pastoralists and nomads for nearly two hundred years and greatly intensified in the last two decades has culminated in what is called the Maoist problem in contemporary India. Ancient world views and ways of being are being threatened with extinction. The following section uses art and literature to make an incision into the contemporary crisis as well as to indicate the sensibility of loss and pain, which is usually effaced by the language of social science.

KASHMIR ART AND LITERATURE AS WITNESS TO PLACES "FALLING OFF THE MAP"

Nilima Sheikh's exhibition "Drawing trails: work on paper 2008–9" is a stunning portrayal of facets of state violence expressed in seventeen superb paintings, mostly tempura on sanganer handmade paper.[3] The exhibition catalogue is a remarkable supplement put together by a Baroda-based scholar and human rights activist Deeptha Achar, who has been part of the civil liberties team involved in the documentation of the growing violence in Gujarat. Nilima Sheikh's paintings map sites of violence metaphored by Kashmir and the troubled and traumatized shapes of memory. The exhibition raises many questions. What has been the nature of state violence? What does it mean to return, to rehabilitate, and to restore? Is a return at all possible? What are the limits of the rehabilitation and restoration undertaken by the state? What are the non-state sources of violence? Is there any possibility of healing the torn fabric of inter-communal life?

This body of work is really at the conjuncture of painting, poetry, and prose; the actual and the historical, a backdrop for a fantasized terrain in which events and processes unfold involving the brutalization of community. The artist draws upon the well-known Kashmiri poet, Agha Shahid Ali (1997) and his collections titled *Firdaus* and *Country without a Post Office, Poems 1991–95*. One painting is evocatively titled "No two yards: he rowed me into the sunset" and another uses an excerpt from his poem "Not all, only a few return" and is called "Just a few return from dust disguised as roses." Another painting draws upon Salman Rushdie's *Shalimar the Clown* (2005), inscribing lines from his novel evoking an all too familiar terror-scape of how entire places "fall off the map," as it were:

What happened that day in Pachigam need not be set down here in full detail because brutality is brutality and excess is excess and that's all there is to it. There are things that must be looked at indirectly because they would blind you if you looked them in the face, like the fire of the sun. So to repeat: there was no Pachigam any more. Pachigam was destroyed. Imagine it for yourself.

Second attempt: The village of Pachigam still existed on maps of Kashmir, but that day it ceased to exist anywhere else, except in memory.

Third and final attempt: The beautiful village of Pachigam still exists. The village is nothing more, nothing less than a memory.

In another painting of the series Sheikh uses the assassinated Kashmiri leader Abdul Ghani Lone's photographs and details a spot of blood on the street and an inset of people carrying home a corpse ("I follow him through blood on the floor"). In another section of the same painting a woman mourns, her hands passively folded across her lap as though realizing the futility of it all. A closed door signifying waiting? A painted portrait of a woman watching as a man digs a grave – the chilling everyday of violence and the violence of the everyday.

One of the seventeen paintings relates to Kashmir's multicultural past. The text refers to the great fourteenth-century Sufi, Nund Rishi's Kashmiri verse about a Hindu Brahmin (pandit) girl. Bhawan as she was called was believed to spend all the money she earned from fetching and carrying water for a village on feeding her birds even as she herself starved: "Bhawan / The dumb girl in a small village / Who quenched the thirst of the thirsty / Flew in the high heavens with her pet birds / Bestow on me my Lord the same praise."[4]

The Saiva woman mystic, Lalleshwari (also called Lal Ded or Lalla), born in a Brahmin family is said to have breastfed Nuruddin and thereby transmitted esoteric knowledge to him. She is also described as Nuruddin's first follower (Sikand 2003). Lalla had been married to a Brahmin priest but fled her home to become a naked, wandering ascetic preaching against caste and the oneness of God and humanity. What the verse intimates is also the close relationship between Sufic and Brahmanical ascetic traditions, hence also the naming of Kashmir Sufis as the "Rishi" order. The Brahmanical, one needs to remember, was also in conversation with Buddhist philosophical heritage.

Nilima Sheikh's moving paintings tell the story of the violent underside of the state, which has worldwide parallels. Art highlights human vulnerability, powerlessness, helplessness, and the yawning gap between death and life. Literature can on occasion provide the aesthetic surface with historical depth. This is the case with Rushdie's *Shalimar the Clown* (2005). In Rushdie's narrative, Shalimar comes to the US and kills the Jewish father of Kashmira, born of Max and Shalimar's wife, Boonyi. Shalimar's name is resonant of the great Mughal garden in Kashmir meaning "abode of joy," but he is also described as "the clown" having played that role in *bhand* (folk theatre) performances at his village, Pachigam. Rushdie writes evocatively of Shalimar whose hair was a mountain stream. "There were narcissi from the banks of rushing rivers and peonies from the high meadows growing on his chest, poking out through his open collar" (Rushdie 2005, 11). "Flowers grew out of the sidewalk at his feet and his hands and clothes were red with blood" (ibid., 23). The end takes place at the beginning of the novel and the rest of the story describes Pachigam before it "fell off the map."

Pachigam is the locus of what has been called Kashmiriyat (Kashmiriness for Rushdie), before the "time of demons" began (Rushdie 2005, 89). Kashmiriness inhered in the friendship between Pamposh, the Hindu pandit's wife and Firdaus Noman, the Muslim headman's wife. Despite the cultural and ritual distance of Hindus and Mulims, Pamposh is able to penetrate Firdaus' hard exterior and reveals to Firdaus her passionate side and feelings that their society is a hundred years behind. Both are simultaneously pregnant.

The eclecticism of Kashmiri Islam is marked in Shalimar's father, Abdullah Noman's belief that after death the souls of their family members entered the local birds and flew around the village singing the same songs. Abdullah plays the part of the Hindu god Ram, in the *bhand* theatre performance.[5] Kashmiri Muslims venerate saints and even worship at shrines, and the village is known for the hospitality of the *wazwaan*, the Banquet of 36 courses. The pandits eat meat and Boonyi's father states, "'Here in Kashmir, our stories sit happily side by side on the same double bill, we eat from the same dishes, we laugh at the same jokes. We will joyfully celebrate the reign of the good king Zain-ul-abidin, and as for our Muslim brothers and sisters, no problem! They all like to see Sita rescued from the demon-king, and besides, there will be fireworks" (Rushdie 2005, 71).

The unusual event in the village is Shalimar's falling in love with the (Hindu) pandit's daughter Boonyi/Bhoomi. Intermarriage is proscribed on both sides, following caste norms. But Abdullah Noman speaks of Kashmiriness and Pachigaminess and the panchayat or village council finally agrees to the marriage of the two lovers, Shalimar and Boonyi. Issues of cultural difference continue to arise. For Muslims the idea of treating newlyweds as Shiva and Parvati is idolatry; for Hindus there are prohibitions on interdining. Eventually two kitchens are decided on and the musicians are ordered to alternate between Hindu and Sufi songs.

Around 1960 the rapacity of the Indian army intensifies, which seems to be an army of occupation and the number of deaths escalates. People hate it and forget about the earlier invasion of the *kabalis* (the tribal warriors who help carve Azad Kashmir supported by the Pakistani army, which is part of contemporary Pakistan). The liberation movement begins. The army colonel thinks of Kashmir for Kashmiris as a moronic idea! There is the new presence of iron mullahs although they were not very popular with the secular nationalist liberation front wallahs. Amanullah Khan and Maqbool Bhat form an armed group called the Jammu Kashmir National Liberation Front that begins raids against the Indian army. With war breaking out between India and Pakistan, higher levels of suspicion fall on Abdullah Noman. Abdullah and Firdaus speak of their disillusion, for up to now Kashmiriness has been compatible with an association with India. Pandit Pyarelal Kaul questions the anti-communalist principles of Kashmiriyat and begins to get literature pointing out the forced conversions, iconoclasm, and persecution by Kashmir's Muslim rulers. "The crimes of the fourteenth century needed to be avenged in the twentieth" (Rushdie 2005, 239).

As the news of the hijacking is announced in the village by the evening news bulletin highlighting the Pakistan regime's support for Maqbool Bhat and its entanglement with terrorism (before the formation of Bangladesh) a deep communal rift is exposed. The minority community condemns hijacking and Maqbool Bhat while the majority cheers the hijackers. A few minutes before they had been gossiping outside, now the pandits suddenly leave the tent.

Over a period of time Abdullah begins using the term *azadi* (freedom), which to the pandit means danger. Shalimar, whose relationship with Boonyi has collapsed, crosses the Line of Control (LOC) with a group, leaving his brother Anees behind, suggesting the divisions among the insurgents and thereupon begins to undertake hit operations. An iron mullah takes a group to a "forward camp" called FC 22, set up by Markaz Dawar for worldwide jihadist activity that is supported by Pakistan's Inter-Services Intelligence (ISI). With the Russians in Afghanistan, there has been support for the mujahidin and Taliban from the Central Intelligence Agency. There are raids on villages in Rajouri district and LeP (Rushdie's version of a radical Islamist, Lashkar-i Tayyaba type formation) posters appear asking women to wear the burka. President's Rule is declared and terms such as *mukhbir* (informer) and *kafir* (infidel) for pundits come into circulation propagated by the Jamaat-i Islami of Kashmir. A Muslim insurgency is launched and posters asking the pandits to leave Kashmir appear. Temples are attacked including the famous one dedicated to the goddess at Kheer Bhawani. In the ensuing exodus some 350,000 pandits flee. There are 600,000 troops in Kashmir but the pogrom is not prevented. The village dance troupe crumbles.

Rushdie's account intimates civilizational cosmopolitanism but also the tragic de-cosmopolitanism embedded in the two nation-states of the subcontinent born out of the partition as also from Islamist civil society. It augurs a civilizational tragedy, no less. In the section that follows I move to an argument about the two paradoxes of the Indian state and to a discussion of the most recent events in Kashmir and the question of the "tribal" insurgency.

THE DOUBLE PARADOX OF THE INDIAN PUBLIC SPHERE

The Indian public sphere is characterized by a double paradox. The first is the co-presence of political religion and political secularism. In this respect India is not unique. This is the case with many modern societies in which political and (trans)nationalized versions of religion have begun to play a growing role in the public sphere. In India, however, this has resulted not only in the erosion of political secularism but in the manifestation of both majority and minority communalism because of the mediating factor of electoral democracy.

Post-colonial India is the largest territorial region of South Asia, a liberal democracy, an emerging world power, and one of the most religiously diverse countries of the world. It has seen the rise of Islamism, political Hinduism and Sikhism, which have become transnational and diasporic religious movements. Besides these, there are variations of region and language and dalit/bahujan or so-called low caste and indigenous peoples or tribal theologies, which are becoming increasingly self-aware.

The colonial government in India had recognized religion as a fundamental category of administrative classification (Manchanda 2009). This was in consonance with the idea of religion imported from Protestant Europe. The perspective fuelled versions of nationalist thought that saw India as consisting of religious nationalities. It was not only Mohammad Ali Jinnah, widely regarded as the founder of Pakistan, but also Veer Damodar Savarkar, who two decades preceding Jinnah articulated the two-nation theory. While Jinnah was an arch liberal-constitutionalist and an advocate of provincial decentralization and the parity of nationalities, Savarkar and Madhav Sadashiv Golwalkar, the second chief of the Hindu right-wing organization, Rashtriya Swayamsevak Sangh, fostered a particularly violent majoritarian ideology activated in the state pogrom against Muslims in Gujarat in 2002 and against Christians in Orissa in 2008. A third one against another minority, the Sikhs, had already taken place in Delhi in 1984.

Secondly, the Indian state represents also a coercion/democratization paradox. On the one hand, it is democratic-secular constitutionally, institutionally and in many other respects. On the other hand, like all modern states, it has displayed unabashed coercive power particularly in regions that have been seen as representing "danger" to national unity and integration. This has been the case particularly in the regions regarded as "frontiers" including the northwest, north, and northeast of India. These "frontiers" have long been the sites of "old and new great games," extensively documented by the colonial foreign policy archive and in literary works such as Rudyard Kipling's novel *Kim*. In Kashmir-Afghanistan-Pakistan (abbreviated more recently as Af-Pak by the US security establishment) there has been a long history of conflict over power, territory, and natural resources between the great powers of England, Russia, and later, the USSR and the USA. India is currently also one of the five major foreign players in Afghanistan.

In addition, India has had "inner frontiers." Indian empires including the Turko-Afghan Sultanate, Mughals and the British were involved in continuous conflict with the "wilderness" (the *mawas* or "wastes"). This hinterland is the region with a high concentration of "tribal" peoples and is currently in the grip of Maoist insurgency. Decades of underdevelopment have produced a civil war in India's heartland affecting some 220 of India's 626 districts in the states of Chattisgarh, Jharkhand, Bihar, Orissa, and Andhra Pradesh. These are the areas under the influence of the Communist Party of India (Maoist), where the insurgents, popularly known as Naxalites, exercise influence among tribal/indigenous/Adivasi groups and seek to protect land alienation, erosion of natural resources, but use extremely violent methods. Some 90 per cent of the Naxalites comprise Adivasis, although the leadership tends to be from outside.

As distinct from the Adivasis of what are called the VI Schedule Areas, are those listed in the V Schedule, mostly lying in the northeast of India comprising the seven states of Assam, Arunachal Pradesh, Manipur, Mizoram, Nagaland, Sikkim, and Tripura. The Ministry of Home Affairs mentions 200 ethnic groups with distinct languages and identities. Other sources, however, mention as many as 400 tribal and sub-tribal groups (Ministry of Home Affairs 2003; Sahni 2002). All of Assam, most of Manipur and Nagaland, and parts of Arunachal, Meghalaya, and Tripura have been declared "disturbed areas" under the Armed Forces (Special Powers) Act, 1958 (amended in 1972). While the state now emphasizes a political solution with respect to Kashmir this is not the case with respect to the northeast. State violence has currently created a failed state within the Indian Union, in the case of Manipur.[6]

Democracy and secularism rest uneasily on a highly coercive state. The national movement whose central principle was non-violence has been replaced paradoxically by a particularly violent state apparatus. But it must also take into account the dark side of the state, including militarization, nuclearization, and internal conquest.

KASHMIR

In terms of India's multiculturalism one needs to raise the question of whether the civilizational history of living together was cognized adequately by the nation. Certainly the Indian state provided for a federal structure with multi-ethnic units and for statehood for major linguistic groups. Manchanda (2009) refers to India's innovative experiment in ethnically delimited autonomous "homelands," and even the experiment with shared sovereignty. The state of Jammu and Kashmir was given autonomy and right to self-governance by the Indian Constitution's Article 370-1.

The idea of a Kashmiri nationalism based on region rather than religion had originally been articulated by Sheikh Abdullah in the 1920s. The Congress supported the National Conference (NC) resistance against the princely monarch. An ambivalent relationship existed between Jawaharlal Nehru and Sheikh Abdullah. There was the common belonging to a cultural and linguistic region and possibly a friendship: in July 1946 Nehru had personally defended the Sheikh in his sedition and treason case against the Dogra Maharaja Hari Singh (Behera 2006, 1.9n).

The term Kashmiriyat was brought into circulation by Sheikh Abdullah in the 1940s to describe the region's vernacular nationalism. Sheikh Abdullah had formed the Kashmir Muslim Conference in the face of the maharaja's anti-Muslim rule (he himself had been denied a teaching position). He did not join the Muslim League despite Jinnah's efforts to persuade him, and indeed, rejected the two-nation theory (on grounds that it was spreading poison and leading to communal killings in Punjab and Bengal). He declared his preference for the secular democratic struggle of the Congress and renamed the Muslim Conference as the National Conference so that all people could join it. One of his speeches points out that there had been no partition-related killings in Kashmir, which had "raised its voice of Hindu-Muslim unity" and assured protection to Hindu and Sikh minorities. Sheikh Abdullah expressed a strong support for secular democracy rather than for a religious state.

Sheikh Abdullah's New Kashmir Manifesto entailed radical legislation giving rights to women in education and employment and a land ceiling of 9.2 hectares. But this major land reform measure was seen as antithetical by the landed elite and was opposed by the Praja Parishad (the institutional equivalent of the Indian National Congress in the princely states) led by Shyama Prasad Mookerjee.

The question of the legitimacy of the accession has been recently debated. Badri Raina contests Arundhati Roy's argument about the illegality of accession and annexation of Jammu and Kashmir by the Indian state to the Union of India in 1947.[7] The uniqueness of Jammu and Kashmir, Raina points out, lies in its accession, in its popular national movement, and *in the heroically principled declaration of allegiance to a prospectively secular and democratic Hindu-majority India by a Muslim Kashmiri leader of a Muslim-majority state, Sheikh Abdullah*" (italics in original).

The maharaja wrote to Louis Mountbatten that the invasion of tribesmen from the northwest frontier most likely had the support of the provincial and national government of Pakistan, and given the circumstances, agreed to accession. Ambivalence was coded into the Instrument of Accession, however, as it stated that the maharaja was not bound to accept any future Constitution of India (Clause 7), and that "Nothing in this instrument affects the continuance of my sovereignty in and over this State" (Clause 8).[8] These stipulations continue to this day to colour the fraught history of tensions between the Union and the state, although later Kashmir clearly accepted the sovereignty of India implicit in the special status of Jammu and Kashmir and in Sheikh Abdullah's own statements of tying the destiny of Kashmir with India.

The first phase of the post-colonial state involved divided and shared sovereignty, but also conflicting nationalisms and centrist anxiety. The Instrument of Accession specified that the "internal autonomy and sovereignty of the Acceding States shall be maintained except in regard to three subjects which will be under the Central government (namely, Defence, Communications, and Foreign Affairs)." Jammu and Kashmir was granted a special status in constitutional law and Article 370 specifies that except for the subjects specified in the Instrument, the Indian parliament needs the state government's concurrence for applying all other laws.

The Delhi Agreement between Sheikh Abdullah and Nehru in 1952 reiterated its commitment to Article 370, that Jammu and Kashmir would have its own flag; that the state legislature could confer special rights on "state subjects;" and that the Sadar-i-Riyasat (later governor) would be elected by the state government. Jammu and Kashmir had its own Constituent Assembly and its Constitution was adopted and enacted on 17 November 1956. According to Article 3 of its Constitution, the "State of Jammu and Kashmir is and shall be an integral part of the Union of India." Article 5 states that the executive and legislative power of the state does not extend to matters "with respect to which Parliament has power to make laws for the State under the provisions of the Constitution of India." These provisions cannot be amended.

Behera (2006) maintains that while the Centre saw Article 370 as a temporary provision, Sheikh Abdullah in contrast saw the Instrument of Accession as a division of sovereignty whereby the state would retain internal sovereignty. He saw the pressure of the Central Government for closer federal integration as an encroachment on Kashmir's political autonomy. "Sheikh Abdullah began exploring the idea of an independent Kashmir" (40).[9] He shifted from a position of endorsing accession to India in 1947 to insisting on the self-determination of Kashmiris by 1952 and looked for support to the US and UK. Sheikh Abdullah was unsure of the longevity of secularism and of what the future political scene would be in Delhi, and Delhi was unsure of his strategy. Behera points out that India retreated from its commitment to provide a federal, democratic, and secular model of self-governance in Jammu and Kashmir. She also asserts that India has since adopted a corrective course, but that autonomy and internal sovereignty continue to be elusive.

A second phase of direct interference in Jammu and Kashmir was inaugurated in the early 1950s. In 1953, Sheikh Abdullah's government was dismissed and he was arrested on grounds of hobnobbing with Americans and plotting to secede and declare independence (according to A. G. Noorani, with the consent of Nehru). For Nehru "national interest was more important than democracy." Sheikh Abdullah was replaced by "Delhi's man," Ghulam Mohammad Bakshi, who began the process of dismantling Article 370. Bakshi began the process of closer federal integration and presided over an undemocratic, coercive, and centralized state apparatus with a corrupt administration whose economic development benefitted an elite minority. In 1959 the jurisdiction of the election commission was extended to Jammu and Kashmir.

After Nehru's death, Sheikh Abdullah became more intransigent and insisted on intervention by Pakistan to guarantee Kashmir's rights. Thus far Kashmiri Muslims had supported the democratic NC rather than the Islamist, Jama`at-i Islami (JII) that saw India as an "occupation force in Kashmir."

A third phase involved subverting the vision of autonomy. Under the 1974 Indira Gandhi-Sheikh Abdullah Accord, Sheikh Abdullah accepted Jammu and Kashmir as a "constituent unit of the Union of India" and that Article 370 could not be restored to its original form. Not even symbolic political concessions were given, such as changing the title of governor to Sadar-i-Riyasat and prime minister to Wazir-i-Azam. The promised review of parliament laws that had been extended to the state after 1953 never took place. Instead parliament acquired jurisdiction over union subjects rather than the three original subjects as per the norm.

In the 1977 elections contested by the NC, Sheikh Abdullah defiantly declared, "Kashmir was a part of India and Kashmiris were Indians. [But] If we are not assured a place of honour and dignity in India, we shall not hesitate to secede." Sheikh Abdullah's son, Farooq, led the NC in the elections of 1983 but saw Kashmir's future with India. Farooq's government was destabilized and dismissed by Indira Gandhi in 1984.[10] A fourth phase involving compromised democracy and insurgency followed the Farooq Abdullah-Rajiv Gandhi Accord of 1986 in the wake of which the elections of 1987 were rigged and the constitutional process compromised. Behera (2006, 47) comments, "It was in police control rooms and Kashmiri jails that the first generation of Kashmiri militants was born." Insurgents preferred the bullet when they saw that the ballot had failed. The Jammu Kashmir Liberation Front (JKLF) spearheaded an underground militant movement to secure freedom (azadi). It sought to paralyze the state apparatus including the police, paramilitary, and intelligence. The insurgency became full blown in 1990 having been transformed from an indigenous underground movement of young people into a mass movement for azadi. In the second phase the uprising split along two lines, one in favour of secession and accession to Pakistan, the other in favour of an independent state. The Muslim United Front was formed, which included the JII, Ummat-e-Islami, and the Anjuman Ittehad-ul-Musalmeen.

After Jagmohan was appointed governor and Farooq Sheikh Abdullah resigned as chief minister, state repression was launched including cordon and search operations, curfews, road blocks, torture, rape, detention, and shootings at public processions and in markets. No distinction was made between militants, sympathizers of militants, and innocent civilians. The Armed Forces Special Powers Act (AFSPA) was imposed in 1990. Militancy was contained by the mid-1990s, but not eliminated. Meanwhile Azad Kashmir also underwent a state of internal colonialism.

The liberation struggle of the second generation following independence was critical of Sheikh Abdullah for having surrendered the demand for a plebiscite in favour of power in 1975. His death anniversary was commemorated as *yome-i-nijat* or day of deliverance. In the insurgents' historiography, Accession Day was denounced as the day of occupation and Nehru's birthday as *yome-i-siaht* (black day).[11] Police stations, the Central Reserve Police Force, and intelligence officials became targets of attack.

While the JKLF was an advocate of Islamic democracy and socialism, the Hizb-ul Mujahidin and its parent political party, the JII, sought to provide an Islamist frame and to discredit and displace the JKLF. Pakistan emerged as the locus of state-sponsored jihad and support for non-state armed groups in the Valley. Its intelligence agency, the Inter-Services Intelligence, supported the Hizb-ul Mujahidin rather than the more secular JKLF. The first set of Afghan and Pakistani militants sent to Kashmir were attached to the Hizb-ul Mujahidin. In 1990 some 10,000 Kashmiris crossed over to Pakistan. Deobandi jihadi organizations included the Harakatu'l-Ansar (Movement of the Helpers [of the Prophet]) in Kashmir and the JII. Later the ISI began giving greater support to the Markaz Dawa ul Irshad and its militant wing, the Lashkar-i Tayyaba (Army of the Pure). A ripe apple theory that India would bleed and Kashmir would fall came into circulation. A 1995 BBC documentary showed evidence of camps in Azad Kashmir and Pakistan supported by the JII where fighters were being trained.

Yasin Malik of the JKLF and Shabir Shah of the People's League were released in 1994 and the All Parties Hurriyat Conference was formed, but the moderates were marginalized, including Yasin and Shabir who were expelled in 1996. The pro-Pakistan JII chief, Syed Ali Shah Geelani who became Hurriyat chairman in 1998 urged Kashmiris to view themselves as a part of the *millat* or Islamic community. Yasin Malik lambasted Pakistan for Islamicizing the Kashmir movement even though Kashmiri Muslims had historically struggled "to safeguard their mystic Muslim culture based on the universal principles of love, brotherhood and philanthropy" (Behera 2006, 165, also 82–3, 152, 157). Processes of dialogue were underway: George Fernandes was negotiating with the Hizb-ul Mujahidin when the highly respected Mirwaiz Maulvi Farooq was killed.[12] Reconciliation efforts were purportedly discouraged by Jagmohan. There was a marked deterioration as warnings appeared on posters creating an atmosphere of insecurity and loudspeakers from mosques proclaimed Nizam-e-Mustafa or an Islamic state. Most of the 162,500 strong Hindu population fled the Valley including virtually the entire Kashmiri pandit community.[13] More recently Sikhs have also been targeted.

The institutionalized impunity and the constant violation of human rights along with prosecutions have been repeatedly pointed out (Sharma 2010). The report of the Srinagar-based Association of the Parents of Disappeared Persons, 2008, highlighted the 8,000 persons who were missing since 1989. It also reported multiple graves in the LOC, an area to which the military has access.[14] Despite the promise of State Human Rights Commission to investigate disappearances, it was unable to either investigate or order any prosecutions against members of the security forces since this requires prior sanction from the Home Ministry. India is not signatory to the United Nations (UN) Convention against Torture. It signed the International Convention from Enforced Disappearances in 2007, but does not allow the UN Special Rapporteur on Torture or Working Groups on Arbitrary Detention and on Enforced or Involuntary Disappearances to visit India (Behera 2006). Sharma (2010, 61) comments, "Torture does not stop terror. Torture is terror." He also points to the attacks by non-state armed groups such as Harkat-ul-mujahidin in Kashmir along with United Liberation Front of Asom and Kuki Revolutionary Army and Muslim United Liberation Tigers Front in Assam, in the northeast, whose violence involves civilian killings, abduction, and torture.

The most recent round of violence was associated with fears of the disappearance of an entire generation of young Kashmiri males. It left in its wake some 112 dead, mostly young boys who had come of age during the insurgency and who had experienced violence. It began with the Amarnath Shrine Board street protests that indicated the emergence of Syed Ali Shah Geelani of the Tehreek-i-Hurriyat as the primary secessionist voice in Kashmir. The Muslim United Front is a coalition of urban petty bourgeoisie and rural orchard-owning elite supported by disenchanted youth – children witnessing the decline of artisanal and trading occupations of their parents who lack skills and resources to compete in a new world. The controversy over Amarnath widened the intra-region divide between Jammu and Kashmir but also marked a split on religious lines. Reports of the transfer of 39.88 hectares or 800 kanals of forest land to the Shri Amarnath Shrine Board to build facilities for Hindu pilgrims were in circulation.

The elections had been read as a success story for Indian democracy although some two-thirds of the political spectrum had excluded themselves from the process – there was little realization that the core issues of the status of Jammu and Kashmir remain unsettled. In 2000 the State Autonomy Committee Report was discussed and a resolution adopted recommending restoration of Article 370 to the pre-1953 status and limiting Indian jurisdiction to defence, foreign affairs, and communication. It was, however, rejected by the Indian Cabinet. In 1998 Farooq Sheikh Abdullah had set up a Regional Autonomy Committee that proposed devolution, but the state government instituted division into eight autonomous units on ethnic-religious lines without any political and economic devolution.

There is the question of autonomy and self-rule that remains to be resolved, but also that of the autonomy of the regions within. The NC and the People's Democratic Party (PDP) have proposed two models, but in the wake of the protests and deaths of young stone throwers in the summer of 2010, any discussion on these has been sidelined. The Central government sought to break the political impasse with a visit by an all party and the work of three interlocutors. Jammu and Kashmir urgently requires a Truth and Reconciliation Commission, and justice for those who have suffered. Sharma suggests a process of truth, justice, and restitution (including compensation, rehabilitation, and satisfaction and guarantees of non-repetition).

FROM THE MARGINS OF INDIAN RELIGIONS AND CIVILIZATION

The second civilizational tragedy in contemporary India threatens cultures that are three millennia old.[15] On the margins of Hindu civilization have lived the peoples that have been disparagingly called "tribes" by many colonial anthropologists even though several of them have been authors of highly diverse and creative cultures.

Their marginality has been highlighted most recently by the predicament of the Dongria Kondh. This is an Adivasi group that has been recently involved in an "epic" battle with a mining company, Vedanta. Unlike most such battles over land and resources, the local community won a small round. Consisting of some 8,000 members, the Dongria Kondh, along with the Kutia Kondh, depend on the forests of the upland areas of the Niyamgiri hills in the Kalahandi district of Orissa. They inhabit and have had access to an area that is part of the Community Reserved Forests, according to several forest settlement reports and Working Plans. These lands were leased by the Orissa government to the USD 7.9 billion Anil Agarwal-operated mining giant, the Vedanta Company for bauxite mining to produce aluminium, which also managed illegal occupation of over twenty-six hectares of village forest lands. In Niyamgiri, however, it was the Kondh who were arrested as the company forcibly took them to police.

The Kondh have a distinctive cultural identity and a livelihood dependent on shifting cultivation based on agro-forestry that uses mountain slopes and streams. The Dongria Kondh are described by the report of the N.C. Saxena Committee commissioned by and submitted to the Ministry of Environment and Forests as "endangered" and "primitive" and also as a "polytheistic animist" culture that worships the mountains and the earth, male and female principles that create Kondh prosperity, fertility and health (Saxena et al. 2010, 46). The report points out that the proposed mining would strip seven square kilometres of the Niyamgiri hill top and alter water supply, affecting both ecological systems and human communities. Many Dongria Kondh have already been rendered destitute and can no longer grow vegetables.

While the media projected the Ministry of Environment and Forests' rejection of forest clearance as a victory for the young Congress politician Rahul Gandhi and the ministry, this was clearly an outcome of the struggle of the Dongria Kondh and its organization, the Niyamgiri Suraksha Parishad. Rahul Gandhi's visit was preceded by the descent of goons and then police who beat up Lada Sikaka Majhi, a leader of the Parishad, accusing him of being a Maoist. "What is a Maoist?" he queried tragically (Chikermane 2010a). The ministry's denial was later challenged in the Supreme Court, which ordered the state government to organize gram sabhas under the Forest Rights Act of 2006 to determine the views of forest dwellers on whether mining should be allowed or not. In August 2013 *gram sabhas* (village assemblies) unanimously rejected mining of the forest.

Let us dwell for a moment on the cosmology of the Dongria Kondh. For the community the hill is sacred for it is the abode of Darani Penu, the earth goddess and her husband Kotebali Penu. Their "cosmos" also includes the lower gods: the arrogant Jatrakudi Penu who is the source of drought, Bima Penu who protects crops, and Takrani Penu who protects the Dongria Kondh from disease. The Dongria Kondh see the refinery as *raksasi* or demonic and identify the hill with life itself. As Chikermane (2010b) puts it, the question is not of compensation or corporate social responsibility and whether a few thousand people should be left behind for development of the second fastest growing economy in the country, it is also about something far more complex, multi-layered, that challenges reason itself and has to do with the religious imagination of peoples.

Contrast once again the deep civilizational diversity and the highly plural religious imaginaries of the subcontinent with the "world religions" frame of the Indian polity. The Constitution extended affirmative action to scheduled castes and scheduled tribes listed in the schedules of the Constitution. These categories were seen as clusters of communities that needed special political and economic rights to counter their state of deprivation. They were given reservation in state employment and in educational institutions. Ambedkar, the dalit leader and one of the major drafters of the Constitution did not see these rights as existing in perpetuity. Later, another category, the Other Backward Classes, incorporating socially and educationally backward groups, was also made the object of affirmative action.

If multiculturalism is identified as the problematic of community and equality, quite clearly the STS are among the most deprived and backward sections of Indian society. They are the most underrepresented in the state bureaucracy and legislatures. They have also been ignored in the larger social science discourse on Indian multiculturalism, which focuses on religious community (defined in terms of world religions) and caste, and which has ignored non-canonical religions. As Roy-Burman (2009) points out, the Adivasis were adversely affected by the very fashioning of the sovereignty of the post-colonial state. The nationalization of forests deprived tribes and lineages of their rights to land, the forests, and its produce. Roy-Burman maintains that India follows common law jurisprudence, based on the Roman legal concept of *res nullius* that claims all residual land not assigned by the sovereign as property belongs to the state. In effect this denies the customary law of the tribals or the historically embedded concept of *res loci re sitae*, that is, that what is practised in a place is the law of the place, which has prevailed in most parts of the world.

There is no recognition of the communal/tribal pattern of land holding included by the Planning Commission. Ashis Nandy narrates the account of K. L. Saigol, a retired bureaucrat involved with negotiations with the Naga tribes of northeast India soon after independence. The Indian side insisted that all land belongs to the state, a position that left the Naga leaders aghast. So they refused to come to a settlement and the problem continued for another twenty years (Nandy, personal communication, Delhi, 15 July 2010). Roy-Burman (2009) cites the Expert Group on Prevention of Land Alienation in Tribal Areas, constituted by the Ministry of Rural Development, Government of India, that in its report submitted in 2004 (reprinted in 2006) observed that the "large extent of land in several States over which members of scheduled tribes have had ownership rights or customary rights for centuries has neither been surveyed nor settled with clear proprietary titles for scheduled tribes." In 1987, the Lok Sabha acknowledged that the "communal holdings of tribals had not been recognized," (ibid.). Roy-Burman asserts that Land Survey Acts and Rules in all the states of India should be reviewed and gram sabhas involved in all survey and settlement operations so as to record rights of communities and individuals. The banking law should be amended to enable banks to extend institutional finance to community as land-holding legal person.[16]

The larger problem is that tribal society has been treated as "backward" and "primitive" rather than as endowed with knowledge. As former activist Kishore Saint puts it, what is at stake currently is the very survival of the tribals. There is, in effect, an internal colonialism as a consequence of which most tribal labour has now been reduced to wage labour. There is little regard for their intellectual property rights. Ironically, along with their marginality, as Roy-Burman asserts, tribal peoples are experiencing something like a renaissance, an enormous wave of creativity. There are some one hundred thousand books in tribal languages that ought to be collected. Tribals, he asserts, should be the vanguard of the twenty-first century (Roy-Burman 2010).

The Indian state dominated by the world religions framework continues to efface tribal religiosities. Post-colonial India recognizes several grounds of difference, but has also not recognized others. It has also tended to privilege Hindu and Muslim identities. In a recent landmark volume, *Aadi dharma* [Primeval Dharma], Munda and Kiman (2009, 5) argue that Indian censuses do not *recognize* tribal religious practices, hence tribal peoples are forced to identify themselves as Hindu, Muslim, Christian, or as "other religion." The authors argue that while variants of tribal religious practices might have familial resemblance to Hinduism, Islam, and Christianity, they also have a distinctive character.

The historical injustice to "tribals" appears in the interstices of the law. The Panchayat Extension to Scheduled Areas Act (PESA) was enacted only in the wake of the social movement the Ganv ganrajya, which demanded their hitherto autonomous, self-governing polity.[17] Sixty years after independence a landmark piece of legislation, the Scheduled Tribes and Other Traditional Forest Dwellers (Recognition of Forest Rights) Act 2006, recognized the pre-existing rights of forest communities, which were not a "grant" of the state. The act also records the historical injustice that was an outcome of non-recognition in the colonial period and also in independent India. The notification of the Forest Rights Act is expected to benefit ten million forest dwellers across seventeen states (Saxena et al. 2010).

There has been an interesting discussion recently of what is being called the "new animism." It is invoked in Bruno Latour's critique of the nature/culture binary and in the recognition of the need to tackle the tricky question of animism anew in order to recognize the agency of rivers and mountains. Moderns of the sixteenth century, Latour writes (2010a, 481), poured scorn on "those poor archaic folks, who had the misfortune of living on the wrong side of the 'epistemological break', believed in a world *animated* by all sorts of entities and forces instead of believing, like any rational person, in an *inanimate* matter producing its effects only through the power of its causes." Modernism thus invented inanimism: the idea of an agency without agency. Latour counters the modernization thesis with the idea of compositionism. Sunita Narain's comment on Latour's public lecture pointed to "a million mutinies" in India – important voices as they intimate that outside the dominant narrative there are conceptions of life and livelihood, which challenge the consumer-driven paradigm of growth (Latour Seminar, Delhi University, Delhi, 6 January 2012). This is the difference with the environmental movement of the West, which came in the wake of wealth and was part of the clean up of waste. In India it has come from the other end, from the politics of the people.

Harvey (2005) points out that the new animism is not about primitivism or pre-modernity, but recognizing another way of being human and different ways of speaking, listening, acting, and being and living in the world that are life-affirming. The old animism à la Edward Tylor (popularly regarded as the nineteenth-century founder of anthropology), saw people as investing objects with qualities/souls. This was seen as a mythopoetic primitive tendency involving "belief in spiritual beings," including the attribution of life to inanimate objects and of "souls" to animals. James Frazer, another proponent, referred to trees and plants as having souls. Durkheim saw the origins of religion in totemism, which was countered by Levi-Strauss' argument that natural species are chosen as totems because they are "good to think." Harvey (2005, 12) cites Deborah Rose's comment in the context of her work on Aboriginal people that "totemic relationships connect people [human and other-than-human] to their ecosystems in non-random relations of mutual care." Harvey (2005, 25) argues that in Gabriel García Márquez's *One Hundred Years of Solitude*, the gypsy artist Melquíades provides a statement of the core of animist belief when he drags two metal ingots from house to house, attracting all kinds of magnetic objects to follow him and says, "'Things have a life of their own ... it's simply a matter of waking up their souls.'" Animism then is minimally understood as recognition of personhood in a range of human and other than human persons. There is also the question of the categories animism and pagan, and whether pagan might better describe Indian non-anthropocentric cosmologies. Pagan is described as the idea of a religious culture for which there is no creator and no place, no time, no language where truth has not expressed itself (Sharma 2012).

While the Indian state has not challenged the conception of "world religion," and has chosen to ignore these rich worlds of animist/pagan practice, it is interesting to mark a small, dialogic space opened up by the N. C. Saxena Committee that recognizes the importance of the sacred, of the animistic in environmental debates.[18] But the larger story is of political and intellectual incomprehension of the deep plurality of civilizational multiculturalism and of Indian religio-cultural-political imaginaries. These certainly involved hierarchies of various kinds but also did not have the asymmetries fostered by capital. Modernization has involved a huge displacement of pastoral and tribal worlds and of peasant cultures by an onslaught of urbanity.

An understanding of the Indian nation-state in relation to secularism and multiculturalism must be predicated on its high capacities in terms of constitutionalism and institution building, that is, the inclusive dimension of power. But it must also take into account the dark side of the state, including militarization, nuclearization, and internal conquest.

POSTSCRIPT

Much has happened in JK for which the ruling elite of both India and Pakistan and the Kashmir Valley are responsible. Nonetheless, it is difficult to agree with the assertion that Kashmir is Palestine, a parallel that was drawn after a summer of stone throwing by Kashmiri youth. There are several reasons why the comparison fails to hold despite considerable similarities such as the early visual representation of the landscape as bereft of people and these lands as territories of "desire" (see Rai 2004; Kabir 2009). More specifically this has to do with the specificity of state formation in India and Israel. Jammu and Kashmir does have a functioning democracy however impaired it is by the state's coercive power, whether from the national or regional level, and restricted as the political space is by the fact that a section of the political spectrum has boycotted elections. Richard Mahapatra argues that the first panchayat polls in thirty-four years were a vote for self-governance, not self-determination, with a 79 per cent voter turnout, double that of the 2001 panchayat polls. The members of the Panchayati Raj institutions have been demanding genuine devolution of powers for a third tier and bargaining with the state government. Given the demonstration of their stake in the Republic they have been targeted by militants and some 900 representatives have resigned (Mahaptra 2012). Further, political proposals envisage a future for Kashmir, which take it beyond the "zone of conflict."[19] The People's Democratic Party has proposed a model of "self rule" involving a confederal model of autonomy and shared sovereignty invoking an older territo-cultural model of Kashmir as a zone of encounter between cultures. The National Conference in a somewhat less sophisticated fashion has proposed autonomy, but also a receding role for the army and the dreaded AFSPA, and a soft border with Pakistan. It is interesting that Syed Ali Shah Geelani, the leader of the "pro-Pakistan" faction of the Tehreek-i Hurriyat, should cite the Mahabharata, and indeed the Gita, in expressing his concern that the pandits should return to the Valley, as he does in a 17 April 2011 Hindustan Times article. His efforts to participate in a dialogue with members of Indian civil society suggest a shift in his position.[20] Interestingly, Geelani denies to minority Hindus and Buddhists the same right to azadi that he demands vis-à-vis the Indian state.

Middle India with its (de)tribalized communities continues, however, to be a zone of escalating insurgency and state and non-state terror. Clearly the model of "Indigenous peoples" of Canada, the Americas, and Australia does not apply since in these areas a simpler situation obtains in which the "politics of recognition" involves recognizing them as "First Nations." Although these countries decimated their Native populations, India could do well to learn from them, for example from Canada's *Charter of Rights and Freedoms*, which could renew the social contract with "tribal" peoples and also go beyond this by envisioning a new future for them.

NOTES

1 My thanks to participants at the conference on "Multiculturalism and Religious Identity: Perspectives from Ottawa and Delhi," University of Ottawa, 22–25 September where this paper was first presented, and also to the considered comments of my colleagues following the presentation of the paper at the Centre for the Study of Developing Societies (CSDS) faculty retreat, Orccha, from 29 November to 1 December 2011, particularly to Ankur Dutta, who was discussant, and to Deepak Mehta, D. L. Sheth, Sonia Sikka, Arvind Mayaram, and Madhu Kishwar for specific discussions. One of my Kashmiri students, Farukh Faheem, first drew my attention to how Rushdie's novel *Shalimar the Clown* is able to capture the ethos of Kashmiriyat or Kashmiri-

ness as well as the tragic fate of Kashmir, even though we are all aware of the many faces of Kashmiriyat.

2 In a recent dialogue Bharucha stated that we need the term "interculturalism" because "it is politically necessary for us as artists, as citizens, to find ways of countering the dominance of official state-determined 'multiculturalism.'" But he also acknowledged that "even as 'multiculturalism' is being discredited these days by conservative politicians in favour of 'integration,' it has played a huge role in mobilizing the lives and cultural futures of immigrants in countries like Canada, Britain, Australia, and, marginally, the U.S." (Bharucha 2011).

3 Exhibition *Drawing Trails*, Galerie Espace, New Delhi, 17 April–30 May 2009.

4 The Muslim Rishis were an indigenous mystical order founded by Hazrat Nuruddin Nurani (1356–1440), which spread Islam but was highly regarded by both Hindus and Muslims. It spearheaded a movement critical of caste hierarchy and oppression, which distanced itself from the ruling elite and was close to the people. One can identify in the verse of Nund Rishi, the founder of the Muslim Rishis, the only Kashmiri indigenous Sufi order, its grounding in the Kashmir philosophical-theological school of non-dualism, which came to be described as Kashmir Saivism.

> Children of the same parents,
> When will Hindus and Muslims cut down the tree of dualism?
> When will God be pleased with them and grant them His grace?
> We belong to the same parents
> Then why this difference?
> Let Hindus and Muslims worship God alone.
> We came into this world like partners.
> We should have shared our joys and sorrows together.

5 See M. K. Raina's account of the tradition, which incorporates elements of Sanskrit theatre. http://www.koausa.org/BhandPather/index/html.

6 Bimol Akoijam feels that popular support for insurgent groups has expanded from a fringe in his father's time, which he estimates at 4 per cent to something like 40 per cent (personal communication, 30 September 2009).

7 http://www.outlookindia.com/article.aspx?266685. See also http://www.thehindu.com/opinion/open-page /article961441.ece and "Kashmir Now or Never," the cover story of *Communalism Combat* (July-August 2010).

8 http://www.jammu-kashmir.com/documents/instrument_of_accession.html.

9 Behera (2006, Ch. 2, n37) cites Balraj Puri that Sheikh Abdullah had claimed that we can sever our relations with India even today, if we wish to do so. This right is given to our state and not to others.

10 Farooq Abdullah allied with Mirwaiz Farooq's Awami Action Committee, which had Islamist leanings. The Congress also used the JII to undercut the NC (Behera 2006, 45–6).

11 Madhu Kishwar pointed out to me the great disillusionment of Kashmiris with Sheikh Abdullah between 1948 and 1953 after some 10,000 persons were thrown across the LOC and a similar number into jail. She maintains that his grandson, Chief Minister Omar Abdullah, has been stoking the fires of secession; take, for instance, his recent statement on accession. Omar takes credit for holding Panchayat elections after over 30 years in JK, but what is the meaning of these partyless elections, Kishwar asks (personal communication, 16 July 2011).

12 In an article on 4 January 2011 in *The Times of India*, Kashmiri leader Abdul Ghani Bhat stated that it was "our own people" who killed Mirwaiz Muhammad Farooq. Likewise, Abdul Ghani Lone refers to terrorists, thereby imputing a critique of Syed Ali Shah Geelani and reasserting the "moderate" position. Sajjad Lone has subsequently reiterated the statement he made nine years ago following his father's shooting that held the ISI and Geelani responsible. "Bitter truth must prevail," Lone stated. "Bhat's statement (is) yet another chance for the nation to evolve. The least we owe to the people is the right to know who killed whom," Lone quipped on Facebook.

13 http://www.indiatogether.org/peace/kashmir/intro.htm.

14 Another estimate is of 150,000 dead, 5,000 orphans, 15,000 missing, 10,000 rapes, 20,000 jailed, and 30,000 widows. Human Rights Watch/Asia Watch reports 12,000 killed between 1989 and 1993 (Asia Watch 1993). A special investigating team of Human Rights Commission produced a report following 3 years work confirming unmarked and mass graves, identifying 2,373 graves in 55 villages, writes Kalpana Sharma in "Unearthing the truth," in *The Hindu* on 3 September 2011. See also Shabnam Ara's film, *Waiting*.

15 For a recent statement of two competing perspectives see Arundhati Roy's essay in *Outlook India*, "Walking with the Comrades" from 29 March 2010 and Minister of Rural Development Jairam Ramesh's Sardar Patel Memorial lecture (http://naxalrevolution.blogspot.com/2011/10/jairam-ramesh-on-naxalite-maoist.html#more).

16 For this some preliminary work was done by a committee jointly set up by NABARD and Nagaland government in 1989–90.

17 The NC Saxena Committee also recognizes the integral relation between ecosystems and governance (gram sabhas) whose consent/refusal is required for development projects.

18 The functioning of the Ministry of Tribal Affairs has been criticized for failing to spend the funds allocated to it, focusing largely on funding NGOs

and for failing to finalize a National Tribal Policy, which it had announced six years ago. See NC Saxena, "Tribal Neglect and Limitations of the Budgetary Approach to Development," submitted by Saxena to National Advisory Committee (Saxena et al., 2010).

19 According to Chakraverti Mahajan, doctoral fellow at the Institute of Economic Growth, Delhi, militants used to be called mujahidin, but are now called "terrorist" as there is a widespread sense of disillusionment with extremist violence. He found this from a number of interviews in the border villages of the state of JK (personal communication, 13 January 2011).

20 I attended two such dialogues with Geelani held in Delhi organized by the Kashmir Committee one on 3 February 2013 and the other on 26 March 2012 held at CSDS.

REFERENCES

Ali, Agha S. 1997. *Country without a Post Office: Poems*. New York: W.W. Norton.
Asia Watch. 1993. *The Human Rights Crisis in Kashmir: Patterns of Impunity*. Boston: Physicians for Human Rights. http://www.hrw.org/sites/default/files/reports/INDIA937.PDF
Behera, Navnita C. 2006. *Demystifying Kashmir*. Delhi: Pearson Longman.
Bhargava, Rajeev, ed. 1988. *Secularism and Its Critics*. Delhi: Oxford University Press.
– 2007a. "The Distinctiveness of Indian Secularism." In *The Future of Secularism*, edited by Thirukodikaval N. Srinivasan, 20–53. Delhi: Oxford University Press.
– 2007b. "How Should Secular States Deal with Deep Religious Diversity? The Indian Model." In *Governing Diversity: Democratic Solutions in Multicultural Societies*, edited by Razmik Panossian, 47–54. Montreal: International Center for Human Rights and Democratic Development.
Bharucha, Rustom. 1999. "Interculturalism and Its Discriminations: Shifting the Agendas of the National, the Multicultural and the Global." *Third Text* 13(46): 3–23.
– 2011. Dialogue with: Erika Fischer-Lichte. *Textures*. http://www.textures-platform.com/wp-content/uploads/2011/08/Dialogue_Fischer-Lichte_and_Bharucha.pdf.
Harvey, Graham. 2005. *Animism: Respecting the Living World*. Australia: Wakefield Press.
Kabir, Ananya Jahanara. 2009. *Territory of Desire: Representing the Valley of Kashmir*. Minneapolis: Minnesota University Press.

Latour, Bruno. 2010a. "An Attempt at a 'Compositionist Manifesto.'" *New Literary History* 41 (3): 471–90.

Latour, Bruno. 2010b. "The Politics of Nature: East West Perspectives." Paper presented at Delhi University, Delhi.

Mahajan, Gurpreet. 2002. *The Multicultural Path: Issues of Diversity and Discrimination in Democracy*. New Delhi: Sage.

Mahapatra, Richard. 2012. "The Panchayat Outrage." *Down to Earth*, November 30, 2012. http://www.downtoearth.org.in/content/panchayat-outrage?quick tabs_1=1.

Manchanda, Rita. 2009. *The No Nonsense Guide to Minority Rights in South Asia*. New Delhi: Sage.

Mayaram, Shail. 2010. "Interculturality and the City." In "Living together," special issue, *Seminar* 610.

Ministry of Home Affairs. 2003. *Committee on Reforms of Criminal Justice System: Report*. Bangalore: Government of India. http://mha.nic.in/hindi/sites/upload _files/mhahindi/files/pdf/criminal_justice_system.pdf

Ministry of Home Affairs. 2009. "Annual Report." New Delhi: Government of India. http://mha.nic.in/hindi/sites/upload_files/mhahindi/files/pdf/AR(E)0809 .pdf

Munda, Ram Dayal and Ratan Singh Kiman. 2009. *Aadi dharma: bhartiya adivasiyon ki dharmik asthayein* [The Eternal Moral Order: The Religious Beliefs of India's Adivasis]. New Delhi: Rajkamal Prakashan.

Raghuramaraju, A. 1998. "Secularism and Time." *Social Scientist* 29 (11–12): 20–39.

Rai, Mridu. 2004. *Hindu Rulers, Muslim Subjects: Islam, Rights and the History of Kashmir*. Princeton: Princeton University Press.

Roy-Burman, B. K. 2009. "What Has Driven the Tribals of Central India to Political Extremism?" *Mainstream* 47: 11–26.

Roy-Burman, B. K. 2010. "Interface with Militant Left Radicalism." Seminar, CSDS, Delhi.

Rushdie, Salman. 2005. *Shalimar the Clown*. New York: Random House.

Sahni, Ajai. 2002. "Survey of Conflict and Resolution in India's Northeast." *Faultlines* 12: 39–112. http://www.satp.org/satporgtp/publication/faultlines /volume12/Article3.htm

Saxena, N. C., S. Parasuraman, Promode Kant, and Amita Baviskar. 2010. "Report of the four member committee for investigation into the proposal submitted by the Orissa mining company for bauxite mining in Niyamgiri." Submitted to Ministry of Environment and Forests.

Sharma, Mukul. 2010. *Human Rights in a Globalised World*. Delhi: Sage.

Sharma, Suresh. 2012. "Adhunikta aur pagan sabhyatayain [Modernity and Pagan Civilizations]." Suresh Sharma in conversation with Udayan Vajpeyi, *Samas*, 9–58. Bhopal: Vani.

Sikand, Yoginder. 2003. "Nund Rishi, the 'Flag-bearer of Kashmir.'" In *Shared Spaces: Exploring Traditions of Shared Faith in India*, 246–68. Delhi: Penguin.

13

An Exploration of Multi-Religiosity within India: The Sahebdhani and the Matua Sects

SIPRA MUKHERJEE

With a nation like India and a religion like Hinduism, characterized more by multiplicity and fluidity than by definitiveness, multiculturalism would appear to come easy. Recent history, however, points to complications that suggest that even a multicultural and multi-religious nation like India may encounter difficulties in concretizing these concepts. This is despite the fact that India has both a tradition of, and official policies supporting, multiculturalism and multi-religiosity. Any policy of multiculturalism usually requires a naming and demarcation of the many cultures, or at the very least a clarification of characteristics that could constitute a culture/religion. This makes a faith like Hinduism extremely difficult to outline, with the consequence that the name becomes a kind of umbrella term capable of including almost any faith that is born on Indian soil and that includes some who are born Hindus, but convert to religions like Buddhism, Jainism, or Sikhism.[1] This widely permitted diversity may have two consequences. First, diversity and plurality of faiths and cultures are encouraged within its scope, as long as some very cardinal principles (remarkably few, if any, in the case of Hinduism) of the faith are not flouted. Second, this ability of a faith to include cultural differences may lead to a dilution of, or even a negation of, the challenge that a breakaway sect poses to the mainstream religion. The differences will simply be appropriated within the faith as yet another form of plurality that characterizes it.

My case studies are two religious sects and a closely related third, from the east of the Indian subcontinent. The area was known as (undivided) Bengal in colonial times, and is now Bangladesh and West Bengal in post-colonial times. Though the two sects emerged at approximately the same time, the early nineteenth century, and drew their following from similar groups, the lower castes of Bengal, they have had very different trajectories of development over the past two centuries. Each of these sects chose a particular framework within which to articulate beliefs and objectives. The Sahebdhani sect drew upon the equality of faiths/religions as the rationale for its being, while the Matua sect drew upon the equality of man for its existence. Over the last two centuries, the Sahebdhani and the Matua sects have gone through the twists and turns of history in India to emerge as a failed and a successful sect respectively.

In the context of the Indian subcontinent, multiculturalism has largely been seen as a desirable strategy in colonial and post-colonial India. The fact that multiculturalism has been chosen both by custom and by law, officially and unofficially, would seem to affirm the country's belief that a shared set of resemblances exists in the community, which allow the nation to bond, despite its many cultures. Through its Constitution in post-colonial India, the country articulated its commitment to evolving legislative and social policies that would allow its citizens the right to retain and express their distinct cultural and religious identities while participating in the common public life of a wider society. Within this framework, the inclusion of the many identities as a part of multiculturalism in India is seen as desirable. However, as Bruner (1986, 122) emphasizes, "a culture itself comprises an ambiguous text that is constantly in need of interpretation by those who participate in it ... Meaning, therefore, is in interpersonal negotiation." The most dynamic and fluid texts of a culture are possibly its religious identities which are shaped by, and which in turn shape, the other identities thrown up by history. It is with this fluidity in mind that this chapter will look at the way in which the two faiths of the Sahebdhani and the Matua have emerged over the past two centuries.

THE SAHEBDHANI SECT

The Sahebdhani sect appeared in the Dogachhia-Shaligram area in the district of Nadia in the eighteenth century. The first documented reference that we have to this sect is by Akshaykumar Dutta published in 1870. He writes: "Legend has it that in the jungles bordering Shaligram, Dogachhia and other villages, there lived an Udasin[2] ... Raghunath Das, inhabitant of Bagare, Dukhiram Pal, inhabitant of Dogachhia, a few other Hindus and one Mussalman became his disciples. The name of the Udasin being Sahebdhani, the sect came to be called the Sahebdhani sect" (Dutta 2009, 230). Since then, references to the sect have been made by scholars Dineschandra Sen and Ramesh Chandra Mazumdar. With followers from both the Hindu and Muslim communities, the teachings of the Sahebdhanis were an eclectic mix from diverse religions. Kuber Gosain (1787–1879),[3] one of the earliest leaders of the sect, dissolves the barriers between the two in his song: "Allah Muhammad Radha Krishna / merge into the same body and soul ... / Father is Allah, and Mother is Allahdini,[4] / What do I make of this" puzzle?"[5] (Chakraborty 2003, 24). This sect does not generally recognize the divisions between the Hindu and Muslim, and a Hindu Sahebdhani can take a Muslim as his guru, or vice versa. The only difference, intriguing because it is almost alien to the rest of their religious practice, is that a Muslim disciple is initiated with the mantra "Dindayal Dinbandhu" and the Hindu disciple with the mantra "Kling Dinadayal Dinabandhu" (Dutta 2009, 230). That the sect had its beginnings among the poorer people is evident in the names they gave the God they worshipped: Dinadayal and Dinabandhu, meaning "He who is merciful to the poor" and "He who is a Friend of the poor."

Begun in the early nineteenth century, the Sahebdhani grew in popularity among the lowest of the low castes. Its followers included people from the untouchables and other lowly castes. The Bagdi, Dhopa, Chandal, Dom, Shnuri, Gnoral, Chamar, and others were followers of this sect. A significant fraction of the followers were Muslim. In fact, a list of the fakirs who assembled at the 1914 annual fair held in Agradwip shows an almost equal ratio of Hindus to Muslims. There were, however, no disciples from the caste Hindus. This finding is not as predictable as it may first appear. Religious sects begun entirely by the lower castes did sometimes include caste Hindus. The Kartabhaja sect, for example, had followers from among the Brahmins, Kayasthas, and Baidyas. This sect, both contemporary to and from the same geographical area as the Sahebdhanis, serves as a perfect foil to the Sahebdhani sect. Their early followers from the same caste hierarchy as that of the Sahebdhani, the Kartabhaja sect was in fact so similar to the Sahebdhani that the two are sometimes mistaken as being branches of the same original sect. Upper-caste elite from the neighbouring metropolis of Calcutta were however supporters of this sect in the second half of the nineteenth century. The maharaja of Bhukailash, Jainarayan Ghoshal, though a Vaishnav himself, patronized the sect. Like the Sahebdhanis, the Kartabhajas too rejected the Vedas and were articulate against Brahminical Hinduism. But the increasing number of upper-caste devotees affected the original eclecticism of the Kartabhajas, gradually transforming them into a sect now known as a deviant but Hindu sect. A movement toward Vashnavism begun by one of its leaders, Dulalchand, who consolidated and established the sect in the early nineteenth century, grew stronger in late nineteenth century. The Sufi fakir Awlchand who had begun the sect was transformed into an avatar of Shree Chaitanya. As one Kartabhaja song goes: "Krishnachandra, Gourchandra,[6] Awlchandra, / Are three in one, one in three" (Dutta 2009, 222).

Writing in 1870, Akshaykumar Dutta (2009, 227) notes that the Kartabhaja sect was "in all probability" a branch of the Chaitanya sect. Though the eclectic nature of the religious practice remained to some extent, the sect had begun to be counted among the many Hindu sects, thus increasing its acceptability to the larger majority. There is much debate on whether the Kartabhaja followers practice Sahajiya and Tantric rites or not. The truth possibly is that more than one Kartabhaja tradition exists, with the most well-known one at Ghoshpara, Kalyani, which has rejected the Sahajiya and Tantric practices for a mode of worship more acceptable to the *grihastha* (householder) followers. By the 1870s in fact, the Kartabhaja sect had become one of the largest popular religious sects in Bengal. Of the Sahebdhani sect, Dutta 2009, 230) writes: "They do not believe in discrimination. Whether Hindu or Muslim, both are accepted into the community." Dutta, in his description of the many religious sects of India, devotes almost ten pages to the Kartabhaja sect, while the Sahebdhani sect gets about a page and a quarter. But there was still usually a secrecy maintained by the followers of both these sects about the practice of their religion, since their opposition to established rules of commensality, untouchability, and social intercourse angered the orthodox Hindus. They were condemned by the orthodox as dirty, morally degenerate, and sexually promiscuous. The Ghoshpara Kartabhajas, however, who had intrigued the Serampore Christian missionaries Ward and Carey with their idol-less and ritual-less egalitarian faith, dissociated themselves from the Sahajiya versions, purifying their songs of the physical (*dehatattva*) and emphasizing the more "acceptable" spiritual. By the late nineteenth century and beginning of the twentieth, with the century-long social reform carried out in Hindu society, Hinduism was more pliable about the observance of caste rules. The Ghoshpara Kartabhajas had by then also earned the respect of many of the caste Hindus and educated people from Calcutta. The number of followers of the sect greatly increased and the Kartabhaja sect grew increasingly institutionalized. Their annual festival at Ghoshpara grew more ritualistic now, and followed the purity-impurity discrimination of the Hindu dharma.

Unlike the Sahebdhani sect, which has remained poor with little recognition from society, the Kartabhaja sect has grown increasingly well-organized and institutionalized in its rituals and assemblies from the late nineteenth century. There are trustees and *Mohantas* of the sect who communicate with the government and other authorities to manage their annual festivals. The colonial government granted permission to this, by then, Vaishnava sect to hold its annual fair on a ground of about 600 bighas (about 80 hectares). Post-independence, however, in the more secular-spirited and socialistic ambience of Bengal, the allotment of land by the government is smaller compared to the pre-Independence scenario, but there is still an allotment. For the Sahebdhani sect however, with its strong associations with both Islam and Hinduism, its location *between* the established faiths manifest, and its significant number of both Hindu and Muslim followers, its numbers have dwindled.

It is not very difficult to understand the trajectories that these two closely related sects have taken over the last couple of centuries. Despite the diverse circumstantial elements that must have influenced the rise or fall of the sects, certain lines of association can be drawn between the development of the sects and the overriding moods of the times through which Bengal passed during these years. Geoffrey Oddie (1995, 328) surmises that these sects "arose in the flux and turmoil of rapid political, social and economic change in Bengal." Sudhir Chakraborty concludes that both the Sahebdhani and the Kartabhaja were sects born out of the social and political breakdown that occurred in Bengal in the early eighteenth century. The long-drawn out domination of the Brahmins had led to an extreme marginalization of the Shudra and other lower castes. The egalitarian Vaishnavism preached by Chaitanya, which had eased the lives of the marginalized, had gradually come under the stranglehold of rituals and the *shastras* again. The Bengali Muslims, too, with their large numbers of agricultural laborers, were frustrated by the Urdu and Arabic-speaking Muslim *maulavis* who demanded obeisance and servility, refusing to treat the Bengali Muslim as belonging to the Islamic faith. This was also the time when the Sufi preachers came to the areas in and around the Nadia district (Chakraborty 2003, 31). They frequented the towns of Kushtiya, Jessore, and Murshidabad, preaching a simple message of love and tolerance that attracted the lower castes who had grown dissatisfied with the discrimination and inequality practiced by established religions. The late eighteenth and early nineteenth century Nadia and its surrounding areas also saw the rapid transition from one economic-political order to the next as the British East India Company took over power in the markets of

Bengal, ushering in capitalism. In this time of a rapidly changing society, there was a need for a faith that would offer stability and solace to the lower castes who were increasingly marginalized by religion, politics, and economy.[7] Oddie (1995, 329) describes the early Kartabhaja: "Members [of these sects] were low caste, poor, illiterate people engaged in agricultural operations ... Change was in the air ... Because of chronic rural indebtedness, landlord oppression and famine ... thousands of the poor low-caste people were seeking something better." After almost three-quarters of a century, however, in the late nineteenth century scenario of colonial Bengal, the needs were changing. Though this change was felt most strongly in the cities, the effects spread rapidly to rural Bengal. With the growing disaffection with British rule, and the gradual building up of anti-colonial efforts, the nationalist discourse shifted its emphasis to that of the *Indian* identity, clearly marking the colonizer as its Other. The politics of this time recognized both the Hindu and the Muslim as "Indian" identities as against the colonizers' foreignness. Both Hindus and Muslims being anxious to include within their flock as many as possible, the identities of the two were made eminently stretchable. This was also in reaction against Christian evangelization and in response to the census which delineated each community by numbers, eventually leading up to political representation in the colonial government. Comparatively less attention therefore was paid to rebellions against orthodoxy. The efforts of the Hindu social reformers in the early nineteenth century to reform and modernize orthodox Hinduism are well known, and Rafiuddin Ahmed writes about the Islamization that occurred in Bengal toward the end of the nineteenth century (Ahmed 1981). The anti-imperialist discourse emphasized fraternity *between* the two Indian communities and Hindu and Muslim Indianness against the foreign colonizer. This made the more nuanced differences *within* each community less important. The position of marginalized groups within a community was sought to be addressed through reform of the religion itself. This also explains the gradual easing of the early nineteenth-century persecution that the followers of these sects had faced from both the Muslim *maulavis* and the Hindu Brahmins. None of that earlier intense resentment is palpable anymore in contemporary Ghoshpara. There may occasionally be derisive laughter toward followers, but the derision and contempt remain on this side of tolerance. "That severe storm of conflict is peaceful today," comments Chakraborty (2003, 83). The once-strong Islamic features have been lessened and the few Muslim followers of the Kartabhaja sect have names which are distinctly Hinduized, or at least not obviously Muslim, as in Shashisekhar Mondol. By

drawing gradually closer to the mainstream, the sect has softened its rebellion against orthodox Hinduism, and, in the modern, more liberal society where discrimination by caste is unconstitutional, is seen as one of
the successful popular Hindu sects that incline toward Vaishnavism. The
Sahebdhani, however, is a sect that was fast disappearing. The guru of this
sect was still called the fakir, holding the fakir's staff in his hand as symbol of his spiritual authority, and the sect displayed an inability or disin-
clination to align itself with either Hinduism or Islam.

Multiculturism, as Peter Caws (Goldberg 1994, 1) emphasizes, stands
for a wide range of social articulations, ideas, and practices that the "-ism"
reduces to a formal singularity, fixing it into a cemented condition, the
ideology of "political correctness." The Sahebdhanis and the Kartabhajas
sects had originated from the need of the marginalized to articulate a faith
which would recognize their humanity and dignity. Unable to concretize
this within the parameters of either of the two established religions of
Hinduism and Islam, they created their own faith, rejecting the bounds
and identities of the major faiths. But with the religious reforms that were
carried out on the Indian subcontinent, the severity of the earlier hierarchy lessened as did the consequent marginalization. The changed circumstances made a few of the sects' earlier protests irrelevant to some extent,
and the need for amity between the two faiths was more keenly felt than
the need for creating a separate space that concretized the equality of the
faiths. Since this need was entirely in keeping with the teachings of the
sects, there was no tangible conflict felt between the objectives of the sects
and that of the mainstream. But plotted on the singularity of a binary, as
it were, the language used by the mainstream dealt in absolutes, treating
as solid monoliths the two religious cultures of Hindu and Muslim, concerned as it was about harmony between the two. The finer differences,
discriminations, and marginalizations within the community were seen as
less significant and were consequently given far less importance. This
problem of reductiveness caused by ahistorical simplifications about the
experience of an identity denies space to the pluralities, nuances, and
shifts that occur and are present within these identities. Inducting identities and cultures into an established (accepted by state or society) framework consequently tends to treat them as anthropological givens of a
culture. This way of viewing may be a consequence of internalizing the
way in which Indian culture was viewed through colonial lenses, as
Nicholas Dirks (1992, 3) writes, assimilating culture to the land itself,
"fixed in nature, and freed from history." In the process of its working
therefore, multiculturalism as policy may both enable and limit the agen-

da of liberalism. While it consciously and deliberately seeks to encourage
and even support difference, the documented and fixed nature of the differences may, in practice, lead to other "unregistered" differences being
wiped out.

THE MATUA SECT

An interesting example of the official multicultural discourse encouraging and strengthening a "small" faith can be found in the case study
of the Matua sect. This sect too was begun in the early nineteenth century in Faridpur, now in Bangladesh and very near the district of Nadia
in Bengal. Founded upon the belief in the equality of man, the Matua
emphasized equality among castes. Begun among the untouchable caste
of the Chandals, the Matua sect was a religious movement, the word
Matua meaning one who is *motto* or obsessed with something, here possibly referring to the Matua's passionate spirituality and devotion to the
Maker. But the sect had a distinctly socio-economic accent in its teachings and the founder, a visionary by the name of Harichand Thakur, actively promoted education, encouraging the lowly caste to rise above
the socio-economic peripheries into which it had been thrust by the
dominant Hindus. In association with the Baptist missionary C. S.
Mead who worked in the Faridpur area, Guruchand Thakur set up
schools, encouraged literacy, and preached the dignity of all men (Mead
1997). But the Matua order, based on the equality of all men, encouraged the seeds of rebellion. Moreover the belief that Harichand Thakur
was the son of God gave him supernatural powers that enabled him to
judge and punish the evil landlords and priests, thus tending to subvert
the hegemony. The Matua faith gave the lower-caste community emotional sustenance as they came together in a struggle to challenge the
hegemonic powers of society. Sekhar Bandyopadhyay (1990, 2563), in
his study of the Namasudra-Muslim disturbances in Bengal, writes
about the Matua sect:

> Collective action was imperative for submerged groups to establish
> their self-image … the emergence of a protestant Vaishnava religious
> sect called *Matua*, with its headquarters at Orakandi in Faridpur, lent
> further cohesion to the community. Both its preceptors and followers
> belonged to the same community and as the high caste Vaishnavas re-
> fused to have any social interaction with them, the latter acquired a
> greater sense of group solidarity. *'Jar dal nei tar bal nei'* [those who do

not form a group do not have power] was one of the principal teachings of its guru to his disciples.

The sect remained a small, insignificant and entirely religious one until 1872 when the Chandals made the first attempt to subvert the ritual order of Hindu society. It was in this decade that the Matua faith really spread among the lower-caste Chandal community, who consciously "articulated a new 'Namasudra' caste identity, constructed on the basis of an ideology of protest against caste domination" (Bandyopadhyay 2011, 239). A reasonably well-off Chandal headman of a village disregarded the norms of commensality and invited his upper-caste neighbour to the funeral ceremony of his father. This invitation, interpreted by the caste Hindus as an act of arrogance and defiance, angered the Kayasthas of the neighbourhood who forbade the acceptance of this invitation and any intermingling with their community. They cited various reasons and ways by which the men and women of the untouchable community were "below" them and of a disrespectable stature. Among the "signs" of disrespectability were the occupation of the men who cleaned human filth and the customs of the women who visited public places like the market to sell their wares. Significant to this discussion is the fact that the upper-caste Hindus supported their accusation of the Matuas being disreputable with the argument that even the government acknowledged the unclean nature of this caste because in the prisons only the Chandal inmates were made to work as scavengers to clean the human waste. In protest, the untouchables declined to continue these activities, which had thus tainted them in the eyes of society. Their refusal to work as scavengers in prisons was communicated to the government officials who came to enquire into the reasons for this "strike" by the Chandals. Bandyopadhyay (2011, 34) reads this organized refusal to work by the Chandals as the Chandal leaders' attempt "to invoke the notions of communal solidarity as an alternative source of power." The strike was continued for over four months, making life very difficult for both Hindus and Muslims of the community because of the unremoved waste, the untilled fields, the empty markets. But the poorer Chandals found it difficult to sustain the strike, and it had to be called off. The Chandals returned to their early jobs at conditions worse than before. In the prison houses, though, the job of the scavenger was no longer to be thrust upon the Chandals, but they were "only to be persuaded and not forced to do [it]" (Bandyopadhyay 2011, 35).

There were two groups in conflict here: that of the caste Hindus and that of the Matua Chandals. But the third entity called upon by both parties to strengthen either side was the government with its official discourse of egalitarianism. This third discourse became increasingly important to the lower castes as it appeared to hold out the promise of a society free from the caste discrimination that had crippled it for centuries. The community therefore looked to the government policies as more egalitarian and beneficial for it. Strengthened and united by the Matua faith, and supported by the official policies, the community structured its identity as separate from that of the caste Hindus. Bandyopadhyay (2011, 55) suggests that this alienation from the high-caste Hindus and the goodwill toward colonial governance may also have been encouraged by "the philanthropic work of the different government agencies and of the Christian missionaries, who had long been trying to win over such depressed communities." The editorial in the *Pataka* journal reads: "The blind Hindu kings have kept us slumbering as they ruled Hindu society. Today we have awakened from that slumber with the aid of the powerful British who believe in equality of man. Not in the discrimination of caste" (Bose 1959, 200).

The British government's policy of "special protection" to the backward castes assured the Namasudras some respite from the unequal competition that they faced with the privileged upper castes. This policy of the colonial government may have been partly to elevate the condition of the depressed classes, but was also to thwart the anti-colonial nationalist movement rapidly gaining ground among the upper-caste Hindus and upper-class Muslims. At this point in history, therefore, both the lower castes of Bengal and the colonial government were united in their hostility toward the Bengali upper castes. Bandyopadhyay (2011, 59) traces how the "calculations of the colonial government and the aspirations of the Namasudra elites thus perfectly coincided." The journal *Chaturtha Duniya* (meaning "The Fourth World"), a publication by a press run by members of the Namasudra community states that the Namasudras, like the Muslims, did not join the nationalist movement in early twentieth century because they believed the discrimination of the higher-caste Hindus, who were dominant in the nationalist movement, were responsible for the backwardness of the lower castes and the poor Muslims of Bengal (Biswas 1997, 38–9). From around 1908, however, the nationalist discourse came to be increasingly dominated by a more egalitarian and liberal outlook. As the resolutions taken in the Bengal Provincial Conferences of 1908 show, the Namasudras were beginning to secure for themselves a space of greater political power than they had occupied in the nineteenth century. By this time, the Matua faith included, besides the Namasudras, other lower castes like the Teli, the Mali, the Kumb-hakar, Mahishya, Chamar, and others. With its message of equality and dignity for all, the Matua faith cemented together the many lower-caste communities marginalized by upper-caste domination. Their gatherings became the rallying point for all the untouchable and lower-caste com-munities of the area. Though the appeal of nationalist leaders like Sub-has Chandra Bose with his call for social upliftment, along with political empowerment, was strong, Bandypodhyay notes that it was not till 1917 that the leaders actively thought of accommodating the political ambi-tions of the lower castes. Subhas Bose's words as quoted in the journal *Chaturtha Duniya* are: "Our social and political struggle must continue si-multaneously. The political party which will be successful in bringing political freedom will be the party which will also free the people eco-nomically and socially" (Biswas 1997, 49). By the second decade of the century, the Matuas connected with, and were strengthened by, the pan-Indian Dalit discourse powerfully voiced by leaders like Ambedkar. Namasudra leaders like Jogendra Nath Mondol were associated with Ambedkar and actively worked for the organization and empowering of the community. However, with a diversity of identities and alignments becoming possible in the 1940s, prior to the Independence and partition of India, the united community began to fragment, and many of the more successful Namasudras joined the dominant political structure. With political and economic power becoming accessible, the subversive edge of the Matua faith tended to be "often blunted by an urge for ac-commodation and acquiescence" (Bandyopadhyay 2011, 240). Partition displaced the majority of the Matua community, many of whom were Hindus living in areas that were to be included in East Pakistan. Manoranjan Byapari (2007, 4116), the Dalit novelist writes:

Prior to 1947 almost 90% of them lived in East Bengal in the districts of Khulna, Faridpur, Jessore and Barishal … The fear of communal vi-olence (during Partition) drove them away from their villages. In the darkness of night they crossed the border, leaving behind their land, houses and all material possessions. Year after year they lived under trees, on pavements, on railway platforms, in refugee camps – existing at a subsistence level. In the name of rehabilitation, some were sent to uninhabited islands in the Andaman region, some were packed off to the forests and the unproductive terrain of Dandakaranya in Madhya Pradesh and other barren pockets of the country. Thus an organised and cohesive community got fragmented and lost its strength.

This, however, was only a temporary lull, and by the 1960s and 1970s, the Namasudra community and other marginalized castes organized themselves as a powerful community in Bengal (now the West Bengal state of India) once again. The communities were now clearly aligned with the pan-Indian Dalit movement, and Byapari (2007, 4118) identifies the Matua movement as "the first organized Dalit activity in Bengal." Today, with the significance of the Dalits increasing across the country, the Matua sect is now actively courted by the political powers of Bengal. The Constitution of Free India forbids discrimination according to caste and grants reservations for employment and education to members of caste groups who have faced centuries of marginalization and discrimination. Listed as the scheduled castes or scheduled tribes, the followers of the Matua faith have vastly increased their numbers. The faith now has a total of about 12.5 million followers living in West Bengal. While the faith has strengthened and liberated the depressed castes, the caste identity of the Matua followers has been emphasized. The struggle for liberation from the bonds of caste has ironically reinforced their identity as a group, sometimes elevating the caste identity to one above the national identity. Byapari emphasizes the need for the mainstream to recognize the works of Advaita Maalbarman or Benoy Majumdar as writers belonging to the Namasudra community. The writings of these two authors, Byapari (2007, 4119) writes, have secured them "a durable place in the history of Bangla literature and many readers do not even remember his caste identity." Kalyani Thakur resents the fact that their poetry is more often than not seen as part of a tradition of "progressive" writing. She has therefore, to assert her identity, added the word "Charaal" (the colloquial form of "Chandal") to her own name on the cover of her books.[8] Their struggle is different, they feel, and their writings must be seen in context to be properly understood and appreciated. Byapari (2007, 4117) writes:

> Some people are unwilling to grant this recent writing a separate status by designating them as "dalit." They point to the long tradition that existed in Bengal of writing about the deprived and the underprivileged. The writers who have contributed to this tradition include names like Rabindranath Tagore, Bibhutibhusan, Tarashankar and Manik Bandopadhyaya, Satinath Bhaduri, several other "progressive" writers and those who belonged to the Kallol and Kalikalam groups in the 1930s and the 1940s. What the dalit writers are doing today are seen by these critics as merely an extension of that tradition.

The Dalit identity taken consciously, deliberately, and determinedly by the Matua followers has blended the aims of the faith with the socio-political aims of the Dalit community. While this is entirely in keeping with the injustice and neglect faced by the community, it determines the trajectory of growth in accordance with preconceived notions of development, restricting the possibility of free interplay between and within cultures. The practice of the Matua faith may then become the expression of certain chosen aspects of their identities, or certain aspects chosen "on the basis of some external given" (Caws 1994, 384). Though the choices made by the Matuas are driven primarily by the ideal of egalitarianism, this choice also includes a rejection of Brahminical hegemony and ritualistic Hinduism, and a conscious embracing of the caste identity of the lower caste. In the process, caste has become the chosen form of identity, ranked higher than that of their other identities like national identity, with its nationalist discourse dominated by the upper-caste Hindus, or linguistic identity. While this strengthens the Matua struggle by narrowing its focus, it also foregrounds and privileges a certain part of the self, isolating it from the network of diverse dialogues that shape an identity.

Strengthened by its history, the Matua is a sect that has seen a positive outcome with its struggle to achieve egalitarianism. But the similarly constituted sect of the Sahebdhani is disappearing. The Sahebdhani sect, also preaching brotherhood and amity, cannot be slotted into the categories allotted by policies, multicultural or otherwise. By delineating cultures clearly, multiculturalism encourages difference, but difference only of a given kind. It tends to smooth out the nuances, mutations, disparities, and variations *within* a culture. As Anne Vallely shows in her chapter on the Indian Jain community in this volume, the issue of a separate identity appears to revolve around how much difference makes a "difference." In the case of the Sahebdhani community, small and insignificant in number to start with, the difference has not been seen as substantial enough to warrant definition as a distinct faith. Unlike the section of the Jain community whose cautious integration with the Hindu community has been noted, the Sahebdhanis' merging with the two dominant faiths, Islam and Hinduism, has gone unobserved and unheeded. Integration with the larger recognizable identities has been voluntary in cases, and fortuitous in others, since the multicultural discourse of the Indian nation does not identify the Sahebdhani among its many listed faiths. The Sahebdhani sect has consequently all but disappeared.

CONCLUSION

Over a span of time, multicultural policies, by laying down and defining the possible religions and figuring each culture as a block with differences existing only between and not within cultures, can lead to homogenization of the community and to suppression of dissenting voices within the culture. By lessening intra-communal differences, *inter*-communal differences are heightened, as each culture defines itself through its dissimilarities with other cultures. Bhikhu Parekh (2000, 256) writes:

> Every culture is internally plural and reflects a continuing conversation between its different traditions and strands of thought. This does not mean that it is devoid of coherence and identity, but that its identity is plural, fluid and open. Cultures grow out of conscious and unconscious interactions with each other, define their identity in terms of what they take to be their significant other, and are at least partially multicultural in their origins and constitution. Each carries bits of the other within itself and is never wholly *sui generis*. This does not mean that it has no powers of self-determination and inner impulses, but rather that it is porous and subject to external influences which it assimilates in its now autonomous ways.

Multiculturalism, when articulated as an official policy, will need to define clearly the identity of each culture. Such a definition has the unfortunate tendency to think of religions as fixed and unchanging, thus essentializing the inherently fluid nature of cultures. The answer to the conflict between rigidity and fluidity, between essentializing reductiveness and indefinable openness does not, however, lie in doing away with the idea of multiculturalist policies, but in remaining aware that official policies of culture and religion may encourage restrictive views of cultures and faiths. Sonia Sikka in her chapter in this volume speaks about the role that public education could play in challenging the essentialist assertions of religions that may arise in a multicultural society. She points to the possibility of including the histories of religions as part of education. An awareness of how the teachings of religions, though seemingly carved in rock, have adapted over time to the needs of its community, changed with history, and shifted its emphases, would add a dimension of fluidity to the concept of religion. Unless the processes of historical change integral to all faiths are recognized and articulated in official policy, there will be a tendency to essentialize religious identities, treating them as permanent and fixed, erasing the heterogeneity within and the dynamic nature of the faiths. Seeking to capture the spirit of pluralism in the black and white of official policies may consequently have unintended consequences.

NOTES

1 This is complicated by the fact that the Hindu Personal Law applies to the Sikhs, Buddhists, and Jains, and in two different contexts given in Article 25 of the Indian Constitution, they could be treated as Hindus. The situation is aggravated in the case of smaller sects, where the separate-ness from Hinduism can scarcely be acknowledged explicitly. An interesting case in this context was the attempt by the Ramakrishna Mission to declare itself non-Hindu and hence a minority sect, and its consequent legal failure (see Mukherjee 2012).

2 Udasins, sometimes recognized as belonging to a particular religious sect, are wandering mendicants who believe in the monastic tradition and live as solitary ascetics, indifferent to the attachments of the material world. Chakraborty (2003, 31) concludes that this Udasin was possibly one of the many Sufi saints, belonging to the Qaderiya or the Chisti sect, who frequented Bengal at this time. Dineschandra Sen comes to the same conclusion.

3 Dates regarding Kuber's birth and death as indicated in the transcript of Kuber Gosain's songs made by Ramlal Ghosh (Chakraborty 2003, 30).

4 Allahdini literally means "the beloved girl." In this song it refers in all probability to Radha, the beloved of Krishna. Many Sahebdhani songs include references to Radha, a finding that has led scholars to surmise that one of the foremost teachers of the early Sahebdhani sect may have been a woman.

5 "Allah Muhammad Radha Krishna/Ekange ekatme holo shar/Pita Allah Mata Allahdini, mormo bojha holo bhar."

6 Krishnachandra means Krishna, an Gourachandra is Gouranga or Sri Chaitanya.

7 Hugh B. Urban discusses how the changed economic and political scenario entered into the songs of the Kartabhaja sect, introducing metaphors and idioms usually associated with the material world. Thus the East India Company is referred to as the Poor Company (garib Company) because it cannot support or benefit the poor of these rural areas. The superior Company, the songs suggest, is that egalitarian faith preached by Gauranga, which will "buy" and "sell" the richer wares of the soul (Urban 2003).

8 Conversation with Kayani Thakur, a Matua poet and activist, at Bhawani Dutta Lane, Kolkata, on November 25 2010.

REFERENCES

Ahmed, Rafiuddin. 1981. *The Bengali Muslims, 1871–1906: A Quest for Identity.* Delhi: Oxford University Press.

Bandyopadhyay, Sekhar. 1990. "Community Formation and Social Conflict: Namasudra-Muslim Riot in Jessore-Khulna." *Economic and Political Weekly* 17: 2563–8.

– 2011. *Caste, Protest and Identity in Colonial India: The Namasudras of Bengal, 1872–1947.* New Delhi: Oxford University Press.

Biswas, Anilranjan. 1997. "Antayja Banglar Nabajagarane Guruchander Bhumika." In *Chaturtha Duniya*, edited by Antyaja Samaj Jagoroner Patikrit, Guruchand Thakur, and Shardhashatabarsha Sankhya, 22–62. Calcutta: Ember.

Bose, N. K. 1959. "Some Aspects of Caste in Bengal." In *Traditional India: Structure and Change*, edited by Milton Singes, 191–206. Philadelphia: American Folklore Society.

Bruner, Jerome. S. 1986. *Actual Minds, Possible Worlds.* Cambridge: Harvard University Press.

Byapari, Manoranjan. 2007. "Is there Dalit Writing in Bangla?" Translated and introduced by Meenakshi Mukherjee. *Economic and Political Weekly* 42 (41): 4116–20.

Caws, Peter. 1994. "Identity: Cultural, Transcultural and Multicultural." In *Multiculturalism: A Critical Reader*, edited by David Theo Goldberg, 371–87. Cambridge: Basil Blackwell.

Chakraborty, Sudhir. 2003. *Banglar Gouna Dharma: Shahebdhani o Balahari.* Calcutta: Pustak Bipani.

Chatterjee, Partha. 1988. "Caste and Subaltern Consciousness." In *Subaltern Studies VI*, edited by Ranajit Guha, 169–209. Delhi: Oxford University Press.

– 1993. *The Nation and Its Fragments: Colonial and Postcolonial Histories.* Princeton: Princeton University Press.

Dirks, Nicholas B. 1992. *Colonialism and Culture, the Comparative Studies in Society and History Book Series.* Michigan: University of Michigan Press.

Dutta, Akshaykumar. 2009. *Bharatbarshiya Upasak Sampraday.* Kolkata: Karuna Prakashani.

Goldberg, David Theo. 1994. "Introduction: Multicultural Conditions." In *Multiculturalism: A Critical Reader*, 1–43. Cambridge: Basil Blackwell.

Mead, C. S. 1997. "Smritikatha." In "Antyaja Samaj Jagoroner Patikrit, Guruchand Thakur Shardhashatabarsha Sankhya," special issue, *Chaturtha Duniya* December: 9–16.

Mukherjee, Sipra. 2012. "The Curious Case of the Ramakrishna Mission: The Politics of Minority Identity." In *Minority Studies*, edited by Rowena Robinson, 227–48. Delhi: Oxford University Press.

Oddie, Geoffrey A. 1995. "Old Wine in New Bottles? Kartabhaja (Vaishnava) Converts to Evangelical Christianity in Bengal, 1835–1845." *The Indian Economic and Social Review* 32 (3): 327–42.

Parekh, Bhikhu. 2000. "Theorizing Political Theory." In *Political Theory in Transition*, edited by Noël O'Sullivan, 242–60. Routledge, London.

Urban, Hugh B. 2003. "Songs of Ecstasy: Mystics, Minstrels, and Merchants in Colonial Bengal." *Journal of the American Oriental Society* 123 (3): 493–519.

14

The Difference "Difference" Makes: Jainism, Religious Pluralism, and Identity Politics

ANNE VALLELY

INTRODUCTION

Upon hearing the oft-touted assertion of India being "the world's largest democracy," the Jains of India either beam with pride as living exemplars of its success, having long thrived on the fertile soil of India's religious pluralism, or they cast their eyes to the sky, considering such declarations to be nothing more than propagandistic whitewashing, masking a fraudulent state policy of Hinduization.

In this chapter, I bring Jain voices into our discussion of religious pluralism, multiculturalism, and secularism, particularly as they relate to issues of minority status recognition. My intention is not to attempt any evaluation of Jain identity claims, but rather, more modestly, to contextualize these claims within India's recent history, and to draw attention to the way competing identity claims reveal important features of Jainism in the contemporary period. I also want to highlight the challenges these forms of identity politics pose for religious pluralism in this historical moment, which, ironically, boasts religious pluralism as its defining trait.

The contemporary postmodern period of the last thirty years or so is characterized, among other things, by the rise of a particular type of adversarial identity politics in which self-conscious allegations of a marginalized identity against a dominant discourse are now the norm. Indeed, identity politics is one area where delineations between the modern and postmodern can be made fairly straightforwardly. Where modern/postmodern boundary making can often appear arbitrary and largely academic, here the distinction helps to identify the shift in identity politics over the last few decades. The shift – which has been described by Christopher Butler (2002) as a move away from a concern with content to that of context – is one in which self-identification is not focused so much on identifying a particular cultural essence, as it is on one's relative position within the political arena of recognition. Self-identification depends here on the use of a particular type of discourse that highlights grievance, and that situates grievance in a contextual relationship vis-à-vis a hegemonic Other. This chapter does not weigh in on these questions of religious rights and wrongs, nor on issues of cultural subordination or injustice. Instead, it looks to identify how this discourse is being employed by Jains, and the challenges its use imposes for a harmonious working of multiculturalism, secularism, and religious pluralism.

BRIEF BACKGROUND

Jains remain a little known religious community outside of India, even though their present economic influence within the country is considerable, and their religious and cultural influence has been historically immense. Jainism appeared in the historical record at roughly the same time period as Buddhism, and shared many of its early tenets and practices, as well as its basic orientation to worldly existence. Of the two, Jains put a greater emphasis on the role that violence plays in human suffering, and the role that non-violence plays in our ultimate liberation (moksha). However, the socio-political history of the two traditions diverged after the first few centuries, with Buddhism expanding beyond India and eventually becoming a world tradition, and Jainism remaining small in numbers and mainly geographically confined to India.

The overwhelming attention Jainism placed on ahimsa (non-violence) as the key to salvation distinguished it from other *shramana* (world renouncing) traditions of ancient India. Avoiding harm to all life forms – humans, animals, plants, and singled-celled beings – informed the austere ascetic practices by which Jain mendicants became renowned. The centrality of the concept of ahimsa can also be seen throughout the medieval and early modern periods, in that debates over the "true" meaning and practice of ahimsa were the primary cause of many schisms within mendicant lineages. In the modern period, the words "ahimsa paramo dharma" ("non-violence is the supreme path") are commonly heard among Jains to encapsulate the essential teachings of their tradition, and they have, in recent years, taken on near creedal authority. Today Jains readily present their commitment to ahimsa as their single most defining characteristic, and as their most important contribution to the world.

THE EMERGENCE OF MODERN JAINISM

Modern Jain communities have strongly defined social identities. The degree to which anything similar, in terms of social cohesiveness, can be said to have existed in the past is a matter of considerable dispute, and is fuelling some of the contemporary identity politics within the community. Certainly there is evidence for the existence, for nearly three millennia, of a community of followers devoted to the teachings of the Jina, but the way in which these followers have understood and defined themselves throughout this long period is far from obvious. I make this point in an earlier discussion of contemporary Jainism: "Being 'a follower of the Jina' (from which the designation Jaina was eventually derived in the nineteenth century) may or may not have been a salient identity marker. Outside the writings of the philosopher-acharyas, it was not likely predicated upon an ideological exclusion of non-Jain ideas and practices" (Vallely 2009, 331).

A self-conscious identification as "Jain," as someone who belongs to a tradition that proffers a total, self-contained way of life distinctive among the religions of the world, is a modern phenomenon, rooted in the political and historical developments of nineteenth century India. Prior to this period, and stretching back to at least the time of Mahavira in the sixth century before the Common Era (BCE)[1], if not to his predecessor Parshvanath in the ninth century BCE, there were certainly mendicants and lay devotees who sought to emulate the lives of the Jinas, but their religious identification would have likely been to particular ascetic-teachers or to a community of mendicants which, for the lay followers at least, would not preclude simultaneous engagements with other religious disciplines and devotions.

In the decades following Mahavira's life, it is likely that followers of the Jina would have included both clothed and naked ascetics – markers that have since come to define the watertight sectarian identities of Svetambara and Digambara Jains. The literal translations for the Sanskrit words "Svetambara" and "Digambara" are "white clad" and "sky clad" (i.e., without clothes) respectively. Mendicant and lay Jains who follow the path of the Jina as represented by the white-clad mendicants call themselves Svetambaras, and those who follow the path as it is represented by naked mendicants call themselves Digambaras. Although the distinctive mendicant practices are now long-established ones, they did not originally emerge in opposition to one other, or in response to doctrinal disagreement. As Paul Dundas (2002, 48) states: "archeological and inscriptional evidence suggests that there was a gradual movement among Jain monks towards a differentiation on apparel, or the lack of it, rather than any abrupt doctrinal split."

It is worth stressing that the sectarian designations of Svetambara and Digambara do not represent breakaway movements from some original state, but rather represent different traditions of religious transmission. The Sanskrit word *sampradaya*, which denotes the conveyance of teachings from one teacher to another, better captures the sense of Digamabara and Svetamabara distinctiveness than does the word "sect" (Dundas 2002, 45). Nevertheless, both terms are regularly used by Jains themselves and for this reason I have chosen to employ the word "sect" here.

The differences in practice now defining the sects were likely part of the more fluid and flexible ways in which one could be a "follower of the Jina" in the decades after the death of Mahavira (fifth century BCE). But the gradual geographical shift of Jain mendicants and their lay followers from the area of Magadha (modern day Bihar) toward southern and western India set the stage for the emergence of two distinctive patterns in Jain practice. Their eventual establishment in the south (e.g., Karnataka, Tamil Nadu) and in the west (Gujarat, Rajasthan, Maharashtra), combined with the absence of any central authority to establish and enforce conformity between them, resulted in the emergence of the distinctive practices and beliefs that today constitute Jainism.

In the mid-fifth century Common Era (CE), an important gathering of the clothed mendicants occured in the Saurasthran town of Valabhi, Gujarat (which has come to be known as the Council of Valabhi), with the goal of compiling and codifying their scriptural tradition. This gathering marks the first authoritative classification of Jain monastic discipline, and therefore the first concerted effort to establish a particular way of being a "follower of the Jina" as normative. The mendicant practice of wearing white clothing received formal sanction at the council. Although the practice of nudity is the most striking difference upheld by the Digambaras, other important issues also divide the groups, such as their views on the capacity of women to attain liberation (Digambaras deny this possibility whereas Svetambara accept it), and whether or not an embodied omniscient being (*kevalin*) requires the intake of food (Svetambaras claim they do; Digambaras claim they do not). The Svetambara codification of correct practice and doctrine at the Council of Valabhi was, naturally, rejected by the naked ascetics as unorthodox.

We see from this that the sectarian classifications of Svetambara and Digambara, which today represent the most basic categories of identification within Jainism, only developed an ideological component gradually, nearly a 1000 years after the death of Mahavira. And although the categories were of obvious importance to the acharyas (mendicant leaders) preoccupied with establishing correct discipline, it is unlikely they played any significant role among the lay followers whose religious lives were firmly entrenched in the specificity of their own traditions, and who had little interaction with Jain communities in other parts of the country, and certainly little knowledge of the many minor doctrinal differences that existed between them.

Today, Svetambara and Digambara communities exist side by side, although the traditional patterns of Svetamabara dominance in the northwest and Digambara dominance in the south endure. Sectarian temples are easily recognizable: the Digambara aesthetic in temple architecture and interior space is evocative of a subdued, quiescent mood, depicting Jina *murtis* (idols) without clothing and in a state of deep meditation; the Svetambara aesthetic by contrast works to enliven the senses, with ornate temples and lavishly decorated, clothed, and wide-eyed Jina *murtis*. As such, the Svetambara aesthetic is comparable, on some levels, with Hindu temple ornamentation, and indeed may have arisen as a result of the greater religious fluidity and caste heterogeneity among Svetambaras (than among Digambaras) with their Hindu neighbours. Despite the sectarian differences related to temple worship, and those of mendicant practice (naked/clothed), the categories "Digambara" and "Svetambara" remain general ones that carry little emotive force. They communicate little about the practices and affiliations that are meaningful to Jains on a day-to-day basis. It is at the level of the sub-sectarian divisions (e.g., Sthankavasi Svetambaras or Terapantha Digambaras), or caste loyalties (e.g., Oswal Deravasi Svetambara) that identification is more forcefully expressed. Like Russian dolls, as one moves through the various "personas" and gets closer to the centre, one approaches what expresses itself as the non-reducible core of identity. The sub-category, or even sub-sub-category, is the space of most meaningful engagement precisely because it emerges out of the lived experience of an intimate religiosity, grounded in the "particular" – in a particular place, within a particular community, using a particular language, and entering devotional space through particular rituals. Peter Flügel, in his chapter "The Invention of Jainism," discusses the considerable variability that has always existed within the sects, and how efforts to establish unified sectarian fronts were being pursued in the late nineteenth century, at the same time that a collective trans-sectarian identity as "Jain" was emerging. He writes, "the national Conferences of the 'Digambaras,' 'Śvetambaras,' and 'Sthanakavasis,' which were founded around the turn of the century, agitated for sectarian unity within their equally divided 'sub-categories'" (2005, 5 fn21). Despite the fact that meaningful religious engagement primarily operates at the level of the particular, all Jains today understand themselves to be either Svetambara or Digambara,[2] and their religious lives largely unfold within these broad sectarian boundaries. As alluded to above, sectarian affiliation is reinforced by experience since Jains unavoidably engage with particularized expressions of religious ideals: the temples with which they affiliate, the *murtis* with which they ritually engage,[3] and the mendicants with whom they identify, all fall along sectarian lines. By contrast, identification with trans-sectarian "Jainism" is an engagement with an idea. Because there is no such thing as a trans-sectarian temple, murti, or mendicant (and there is only one text that can claim such status),[4] to adopt an identity as "Jain" that transcends sect and caste affiliation unavoidably becomes a conceptual sort of affiliation, requiring a degree of abstraction that is not an integral part of the religious experience.

The colonial period provided the context and impetus for the development of such a conceptual, rationally construed sense of identity. Sociopolitical events conspired with the scholarly endeavours of the Orientalists to produce, among a group of reform-minded and largely Western-educated Jains, a sense of urgency and righteousness in establishing Jainism as an independent tradition, on an equal footing with Hinduism, Buddhism, Islam, and Christainity. These reformers feared that, in the absence of a non- or trans-sectarian Jain identity, on par with the other religions, the followers of the Jina would continue to be considered as an offshoot of either Hinduism or Buddhism.

Jainism failed to receive recognition as an independent tradition by the colonial government due mainly to the lack of textual evidence to support such a claim. According to the Jain reformers, the blame for this rested squarely with the extremely conservative (or "backward") position of the mendicants who acted as wardens of the texts. As a consequence of their judgment, the sacred texts of both the Svetambara and Digambaras were largely off limits to all but senior mendicants. Most crucially, they were strictly forbidden from appearing in public courts of law, despite the pleas of the reformers who claimed they needed the scriptures to prove the uniqueness of Jainism. The mendicants feared that public access to the sacred scriptures would result in their debasement, for instance, they were concerned that thumbing though the texts would result in their contact with saliva. To add insult to injury – or injury to insult, as the case may be here – the mendicants objected to the printing of the texts, citing the violence of the printing press, which they claimed resulted in the death of innumerable microorganisms.

A turning point came in 1879 with the publication of Hermann Jacobi's scriptural translations. Flügel (2005, 2) writes:

> Because no textual evidence was presented by the Jains in public, Jainism/Jinism was not recognised as an independent "religion" until 1879 when Hermann Jacobi in the introduction of his edition of the Kalpasutra of Bhadrabahu furnished for the first time textual proof that the ancient Hindu and Buddhist scriptures already depicted the nigganthas as a separate "heretical" (tirthya) group. With this, Jaina Studies was established as an independent field of academic research. Before Jacobi, the Jains were regarded either as "Buddhists" or as a "Hindu sect." After Jacobi's publication, Jainism became gradually recognized as a universal or "world religion."

Jacobi's translations provided the textual proof necessary to persuade the colonial government of Jainsim's historic existence as an independent tradition and bolstered the reformers' efforts to persuade the "followers of the Jina" to self-consciously identify as "Jain." I once again cite Flügel (2005, 5):

> To raise the communal self-awareness amongst Jains, British educated Jain reformers campaigned from the mid nineteenth century onwards for the public self-identification of the Jains as "Jains," particularly at the time of the Census when many Jains, for one reason or another, still identify themselves as "Hindu." The incentive of gaining separate representations and other privileges that were granted by the colonial and post-colonial governments to recognised religious communities promised new avenues for the advancement of the political and economical interests of the educated Jain elites and for the preservation of the Jain religion.

The momentum created by Jacobi's findings, combined with knowledge of the privileges that would accrue from having public recognition, and the perceived insult (at least for the reformers) of having Jainism subsumed within the broader ambit of Hinduism and Buddhism, chipped away at the conservatism of the mendicants, and gradually led to the printing and dissemination of Jainism's sacred texts. The efforts of the reformers met quick success: the category "Jain" was included for the first time in the census of India of 1881. However, it is important to stress that the general acceptance of the existence of an independent tradition of Jainism did not, at that time, carry an exclusivist orientation.

Indeed, scholars of Jainism[5] are largely united in their view that, until as late as the mid-twentieth century, the label of "Jain" did not contain within it an inherent antipathy to Hinduism. Paul Dundas (1992, 4) discusses how most Jains, in the earliest Indian census reports, were even reluctant to be excluded from the general Hindu classification: "The earliest censuses of India suggest that many Jains and members of other religious groups saw themselves as in fact constituting varieties of Hinduism and, according to the Census Report for the Punjab of 1921, 'in view of the unwillingness of large numbers of Jains and Sikhs to be classed separately from Hindus, permission was given to record such persons as Jain-Hindus and Sikh Hindus.'" Because the social and even much of the religious life of Jains overlapped (and continues to overlap) with their Hindu neighbours, most Jains did not consider Hindu and Jain identities to be incompatible (Scott Clark, 2007). According to the Jain scholar Padmanabh S. Jaini (1979, 292), such an open, non-restrictive engagement with religious others was a deliberate strategy of "cautious integration," pursued by the minority Jain community concerned with its survival. Others point to the non-discursive, spontaneous "polytropic"[6] identity characteristic of much South Asian religiosity, marked by pratical inclusivism rather than ideological exclusivism. As an example of the pervasiveness of the latter, Michael Carrithers describes a scene at a Digambara Jain political rally at which a Jain farmer began his speech with a prayer to the Hindu god Hanuman. Only one man complained to Carrithers of the behaviour of such "ignorant villagers." Carrithers (2000, 838) writes: "The farmer lived among fellows for whom such polytropy is unremarked and unremarkable, and his mistake was to assume that sensibility to be shared by all present. Throughout the twentieth century Jain educated and urbanized reformers have had a vivid sense of this village milieu as a sink of 'ignorant' and 'false' views and as a target of Jainizing campaigns." Whether due to natural polytropy or a deliberate strategy of "cautious integration," it would appear that most Jains (with the obvious exception of mendicants for whom the pursuit of a narrowly defined religious path is consciously embarked upon) were unlikely to understand their identity in absolute terms. Efforts by Jains to define their tradition in exclusivist terms, that is, as a historically, legally, and religiously distinct tradition, form a relatively recent development, emerging within the same context as that of Hindu and Sikh revivalist/reform movements of the nineteenth century.

Beginning in that period and continuing into the present, prominent reform Jains have been orchestrating a steady campaign to raise awareness about the independence of the Jain tradition, and to have individuals proudly identify with it. For example, vigorous "Jain-izing" campaigns have been undertaken since the 1981 census, after it was discovered that many Jains treated their Jainism as only a secondary identity-marker. Campaigners were successful in urging the community to register first and foremost as "Jains" on their census forms, with over a million "new" Jains appearing in the 2001 census. These numbers do not represent converts to the tradition (Jainism has since its early centuries been a largely non-proselytizing tradition). Instead they reflect a growing willingness among those who identify with Jainism to do so in more exclusivist terms, and to identify "Jainism" as their primary mark of identity.

The use of an exclusionary ideological discourse is also now commonplace within Jain social, educational, and cultural groups. The move from a non-discursive and inclusive religio-socio-cultural identity to that of an ideologically informed and exclusively religious one is a phenomenon of many contemporary religious traditions, as each seeks to define itself as distinct from all others, as well as from social institutions such as politics, economics, or culture (Beyer 1998, 1).

One recent event has tested the limits of this move toward exclusivist identity within the Jain world: in a professed effort to redress problems of systematic inequality and discrimination of minority communities, the Indian government's Ministry of Home Affairs set up, in 1991, a Minorities Commission to find institutional solutions in order to preserve (in its words) "the country's secular traditions and to promote National integration."[7] In 1992, the National Commission of Minorities Act was put into effect, with the official recognition of Muslims, Sikhs, Buddhists, and Parsis as national minorities. National Minorities would henceforth have the constitutional right to minimum welfare programs and to establish and manage their own educational institutions.

The absence of Jains from this list has become a central issue of contemporary identity politics and a source of dispute within the community.[8] A large segment of the community remains outraged for being excluded from the list, while another large segment is determined to stay off it.

This internal dispute over religious identity falls (almost perfectly) along the fault lines of Jain sectarianism, with Digambara Jains largely seeking minority status, and Svetambara Jains largely opposing it. It is important to note that both sects – Digambara and Svetambara – understand Jainism to be a unique religious expression. And, since 1993, so too does the National Commission for Minorities which has acknowledged, and made pronouncements on, the historical uniqueness of Jainism and its distinctiveness from Hinduism. So the distinctiveness of Jainism does not seem to be in contention, but nor is it the linchpin some Jains hoped it to be, guaranteeing minority status. Instead, the issue seems to revolve around how much difference "difference" makes. Within the tradition of "Hinduism" – itself widely recognised as a totality (and certainly not unanimously) only since the nineteenth century – accepting high levels of difference within the fold is the norm. As South Asian scholars are quick to acknowledge, the ideological construct of Hinduism contains within it a dizzying number of sectarian affiliations, many of which share very little in common. Given this cultural tolerance, or even predilection, for plurality, the "differences" that Jainism shares with other traditions are not, in and of themselves, enough to assure (or warrant) minority status.

THE PRO-NATIONAL MINORITY STATUS ARGUMENT

Pro-National Minority Status (NMS) Jains, who are mainly from the Digambara sect, argue that "minority status" should not be dependent upon community consensus, but rather should be determined on a numerical criterion: According to the Government of India's 1981 census, "the religious minorities constitute about 17.4% of the population of which Muslims are 11.4%, Christians 2.4%, Sikhs 2%, Buddhists 0.7% and Jains 0.5%. It means that per 10,000 persons in India 8,264 are Hindus, 1,135 are Muslims, 243 are Christians, 196 Sikhs, 71 Buddhists and 48 are Jains" (quoted in Bal Patil's online speech, 2010). Jains are the majority population nowhere. In this, they are different from other minorities – for instance, Sikhs are a majority in the Punjab; Muslims are in Kashmir, and yet both have gained National Minority Status. NMS recognition would provide Jains access to state scholarships, and (crucially) allow Jainism to be taught in state-supported Jain schools.

Furthermore, those who support NMS argue that differences between Jainism and Hinduism are very significant and are in urgent need of recognition lest the numerically tiny tradition become fully absorbed in an ever-encroaching Hinduism. Bal Patil, a Jain journalist, social activist, and fervent supporter of NMS for Jains, writes: "The denial of the minority status to the Jains will mean their death warrant as a distinctive religious cultural group especially when all other minorities are going to be recognised ... *Although the Jains hold important positions in industry and commerce and other spheres of life, as a community the Jains are backward"* (Bal Patil 2010; italics added). Bal Patil[9] had almost single-handedly spearheaded the massive campaign for Jain NMS. In 2002, he petitioned the Supreme Court to have the Government of India declare Jains a national minority in accordance with the recommendation of the NMS. In the name of a prominent Digambara activist organization,[10] he presented the Supreme Court of India a document whose title, *Jainism: A Distinct Religion: Not a Branch or Sect of Any Other Religion*, leaves no room for ambiguity in its objectives: The document affirms that "Jains have been continuing as a religious community separate from the Hindu religious community," and that "the theology, metaphysics, logics, ethics, rituals of the Jains are fundamentally different from other religions" (Bharatvarshiya Committee 2006, 2).

It enumerates evidence of Jain distinctiveness, particularly vis-à-vis Hinduism. For instance, it states:

- Jainism is a self-contained system. Its source is its own shastras.
- Historians, orientalists and Indologists are almost unanimous that Jainism is an original, separate and an ancient religion of India and is quite distinct and self-contained.
- Jains do not recognise the scriptural character of the Vedas.
- God, as the creator and preserver of the universe, is repugnant to the Jain philosophy.
- Jains do not believe in avatarvada (theory of avatars).
- Jain shastras make it impermissible to worship anyone except the Tirthankaras.
- The ultimate goal of Jain ethics is moksa. Its path is renunciation and, therefore, according to Jainism, final liberation cannot be attained by the intermediation of any third force or, by merely doing good and meritorious acts. (2006, 2)

In 2005 the Supreme Court ruling failed to provide Jains with nationwide minority religious status. It recognised Jainism's distinctiveness, but argued it to be part the larger Hindu family, and appointed state-level courts to individually determine whether or not the Jains are minorities within their respective states. NMS supporters accuse the government of pandering to Hindutva's Hinduization policies and dogma.

Thus far, Jains have been declared a religious minority in Karnataka, Madhya Pradesh, Uttar Pradesh, Jharkhand, West Bengal, Rajasthan, Uttaranchal, Maharashtra, and Delhi. Significantly, Jains have not being declared a minority in Gujarat – the state with the largest Jain population (though still a numerical minority). The reasons for this are illuminating and will be taken up under the following section.

THE ANTI-NATIONAL MINORITY STATUS ARGUMENT

The minority status petition is by no means universally supported by Jains themselves, and some Jain groups and acharyas (mendicant leaders) have spoken out against it. Pragmatically, stressing the overwhelming social fact of cultural integration between Jain and Hindu groups, and the harmonious relations that have existed between the groups throughout history, they wish to maintain the status quo. They argue that formal delineation from Hinduism is unnecessary given the de facto recognition that Jains already possess, and given the historical success of the community in the absence of restricted identity-markers.

Socially, to distinguish between Jains and Hindus would, in many cases, be impractical as well as potentially disruptive. In Gujarat, for instance, the state with the greatest proportion of Jains, Jain-Hindu marriages are commonplace. It is customary for members of the Jain Agrawal caste to regularly intermarry with the Hindu caste of the same name (Hindu Agrawals); more common even than intermarriage with members of the other major Jain caste in Gujarat, the Oswals. Caste heterogeneity is more common among Svetambara Jains than it is among Digambara, resulting perhaps in a weaker commitment among Svetambara to an exclusively Jain identity.[11] Indeed, many Svetambara Jains readily identify as Gujars or Marwaris – an identity that suggests a cultural or even trade identification that transcends religion.

Economically, Jain and Hindu trading castes in Gujarat have shared a long historical relationship of amicable interdependence. And, as with the trading castes more generally, they tend to be ideologically conservative. Many Jains, for instance, express sympathy with Hindutva's conservative ideology, and adopt its claims to ancient greatness and its sense of historical victimization at the hands of "foreign invaders" as their own. Those who oppose minority status recognition, while not denying differences of a theological or religious nature between Jains and Hindus, consider the social, cultural, and ideological commonalities between the communities to supersede them. Their distinctive religious identity as Jain is subsumed under a broader shared geography and common culture (*sanskriti*).

CONCLUSION

In the introduction to his 1985 text "Modern Indian Responses to Religious Pluralism," Harold Coward laments the absence of a chapter on Jainism. The significance of the omission is, however, lessened, Coward writes (1985, xi), because "The Jaina community does not seem to have been much involved in the dynamics between religions in the recent past." Today, this would a difficult statement to make; much has changed since the mid-1980s. The nineteenth-century goals of Jains to have their tradition recognized as an ancient and enduring one have given rise in the second half of the twentieth century to far more politicized efforts (mainly within the Digambara sect) to have it crystallized around an explicit minority identity, distinct and protected from the dominance and pervasiveness of "Hinduism."

In the modern period it is common for religious communities to understand and express themselves in a global religious arena in a highly characteristic way: self-articulation is hinged, not just on the expression of distinctiveness, but on how that distinctiveness is potentially undermined or threatened, and on how it needs to be protected through legislation. This is typically a politicized discourse that denies similitude, and treats discourses on congruity as cynical efforts of the powerful to obscure important cultural and religious distinctiveness.

Although Jains are divided about how to understand themselves, they are not divided on the effectiveness of this form of self-expression: Jains in the contemporary period are awash in the discourse of identity politics; both communities use it to construct their religious identity – though the characters playing the key roles in the drama are different. For Digambara Jains, Jainism is besieged and its main threat is Hinduism; for Svetambara Jains, who cherish being part of the great Hindu community, Hindu culture is besieged and the threat comes from those seeking to weaken Hindutva.

Minority issues and religious differences are the concerns of the day, with the ostensible and laudable goal of fostering greater religious harmony. It would appear, however, that more often than not, such concerns lead to further divisive identity politics. Perhaps it would be more accurate to argue that concerns with minorities and with differences are the issues that shape the discourse of the day, and to which all must respectfully submit if success in the court of public opinion is to be had. As argued in this chapter, within the world of Jainism, what constitutes a minority is difficult to ascertain, and how much difference a difference makes depends on who is making the claim. Furthermore, the fact that these debates are taking place within the dramatically diverse, inclusive, and difficult-to-demarcate context of "Hinduism" complicates matters. Since the delineation of Hindu from non-Hindu is unstable and dynamic, definitively determining whether Jains are insiders or outsiders may be an impossible, and ultimately undesirable, endeavour.

Whatever the causes and possible outcomes, the Jain community is undergoing changes in the way it talks about itself. Jains today are increasingly concerned with questions of recognition and identity, eager to stress their cultural oneness with the Hindu nation, or their religious distinctions from it. The extent to which ideologies of oneness or separateness are impacting on the lived practices of Jains, and limiting the once "polytropic" nature of lived Jain religious practice, remains to be seen.

NOTES

1 The traditional Svetambara dating for Mahavira is 599–527 BCE. The Digambara date his death in 510 BCE.

2 It is possible to identify with both, if for instance one's parents were from each sect, but this is very rare.

3 The Sthankavasi and Terapanthi sects – both within the Svetambara fold – do not have temples nor support *murti* worship, considering such practices as forms of attachment and violence.

4 Umasvati's Tattvartha sutra (second century CE) is hailed as authoritative by both Svetambaras and Digambaras. It is not so much non-sectarian as it is simultaneously Svetambara *and* Digambara, as both sects claim it to be of their own sect.

5 See for instance Dundas (1992), Carrithers (2000), Flügel (2005), Menski (2006).

6 Michael Carrithers uses the term "polytropy" to refer to the fluidity of South Asian religiosity. He writes, "I coin the word from the Greek poly, 'many', and tropos, 'turning', to capture the sense in which people turn toward many sources for their spiritual sustenance, hope, relief, or defence" (2000, 834).

7 No.F.8-9/93-SC/ST dated 28-7-95 of the Ministry of Human resources Development, Dept of Education, SC/St Cell, constituting a National Monitoring Committee for Minorities Education (Published in Part I, Section I of the Gazette of India).

8 On 21 January 2014, the Jains were granted national minority status by the central government.

9 Bal Patil died on 2 October 2011 in Mumbai at the age of 78.

10 Bharatvarshiya Digambar Jain Teerth-Kshetra Committee, Mumbai.

11 By way of contrast, the continuing influence of the institution of the Bhat-
tarak – an office of preeminent spiritual and social authority among Digambara Jains – is one reason cited for the maintenance of homogenous Jain
castes among this sect.
Some of these subjects were the focus of a follow up seminar held at the
India International Centre in Delhi in February of 2013 (see www.livingwith
religiousdiversity.com).

REFERENCES

Bharatvarshiya Digambar Jain Teerth-Kshetra Committee. 2006. *Jainism: A Distinct Religion: Not a Branch or Sect of Any Other Religion.*

Beyer, Peter. 1998. "The Religious System of Global Society: A Sociological Look at Contemporary Religion and Religions." *Numen* 45 (1): 1–29.

Butler, Christopher. 2002. *Postmodern: A Very Short Introduction.* Oxford and New York: Oxford University Press.

Carrithers, Michael. 2000. "On Polytropy: Or the Natural Condition of Spiritual Cosmopolitanism in India: The Digambar Jain Case." *Modern Asian Studies* 34(4): 831–61.

Clark, Scott. 2007. "Jain Identity Politics: Karma, Dharma and Moksha in a World of Others." Paper presented at the Dharma Traditions of North America/AAR meetings in San Diego, California, November 16–18.

Coward, Harold G. 1985. *Modern Indian Responses to Religious Pluralism.* Albany: Suny Press.

Dundas, Paul. 1992. *The Jains.* London: Routledge.

Flügel, Peter. 2005. "The Invention of Jainism: A short History of Jaina Studies." *International Journal of Jain Studies* 1 (1): 1–14.

Jaini, Padmanabh S. 1979. *The Path of Purification.* Delhi: Motilal Banarsidass Publishers.

Menski, Werner. 2006. "Jaina Law as an Unofficial Legal System." In *Studies in Jaina History and Culture*, edited by Peter Flügel, 419–437. London and New York: Routledge.

Patil, Bal. 2010. "The Jaina and the British: Jain Minority Issue." A lecture given at Tuebingen University, February 19.

Vallely, Anne. 2009. "Jainism." In *The World's Religions: Continuities and Transformations*, edited by Peter Beyer, and Peter Clarke. Abingdon: Routledge.

Cases

Bal Patil & Anr Vs. Union of India & Ors [2005] Insc 399 (8 August 2005).

15

Religion Education in a Multicultural Society[1]

SONIA SIKKA

RELIGIOUS DIVERSITY AND THE BACKLASH AGAINST MULTICULTURALISM

Over the years, multiculturalism, as a social and political model for managing diversity, has often come under attack for allegedly generating a host of social ills: for increasing social fragmentation, creating ethnic ghettos, eroding respect for liberal democratic values among minority communities, and so on. In the context of the recent backlash against multiculturalism in the UK, continental Europe and, to a lesser degree, Canada, a number of analysts have argued cogently and carefully against the factual assumptions underlying reactions against multiculturalism expressed in the popular media and in political rhetoric, as well as in the partial retreat from this model at the level of public policy.[2] In Canada, the birthplace of official multiculturalism, anyone who has been following the career of this much-maligned social and political model over the past two decades might well experience a sense of déjà vu. For we have been here before; it has had to be argued more than once that, in spite of widely known (although not necessarily widely shared) alarm about the purported dangers of multiculturalism, Canada's multicultural experiment has largely been a success. The fears voiced by popular critics have simply not come true. There is no evidence that multicultural policies, or the general set of attitudes associated with multiculturalism – what Kymlicka (2007, 150) has called the "ethos of multiculturalism" – has led to a lack of social cohesion, or has eroded respect for the fundamental ethical and political values that inform Canada's laws and institutions.

In an older round of this reiterated pattern of backlash and defence, representative worries about multiculturalism were presented, in a strident and alarmist tone, by Neil Bissoondath in his best-selling book, *Selling Il-lusions: The Cult of Multiculturalism in Canada*, first published in 1994. Kymlicka (1998, 20) responded to the claims made in this book a few years later, pointing out that "whether we look at naturalization, political par-ticipation, official language competence, or intermarriage rates, we see the same story"; namely, that "there is no evidence to support the claim that multiculturalism has decreased the rate of integration of immigrants, or increased the separatism or mutual hostility of ethnic groups." Yet Bis-soondath's book was republished in a second edition in 2002, and the mis-conceptions underlying its account are, if anything, more prominent now than ever before (see Ryan 2010, 22), although, at the same time, support for multiculturalism remains quite high in Canada among the general population.

These misconceptions about the putative negative consequences of multiculturalism have fused in unfortunate ways with an increased suspi-cion and hostility toward religious minorities in the wake of 9/11, pri-marily toward Muslims but not exclusively so. Once again, a critical response based on actual evidence was needed, and was provided by Michael Adams in *Unlikely Utopia: The Surprising Triumph of Canadian Plu-ralism* (2007). Adams points out that Canada actually does a rather good job of integrating immigrants, in comparison with European nations, and that "Canadians of diverse backgrounds do, by and large, appear to be liv-ing fairly successfully together" (xv), "although they do not recognize this success as well as they should" (28). Similar points are made by David Ley (2010) and Phil Ryan (2010).

At the same time, however, there are also some worrying statistics pre-sented by Adams, drawn from polling conducted by his own firm, Envi-ronics. These pertain to the integration of religious minorities, especially Muslims, and give some legitimate cause for concern, in relation both to views expressed by members of those minorities, and views expressed about them by others. For instance, according to one Environics poll, Adams (2007, 41) tells us, "about three in ten [Muslims] report a negative experience related to their race, religion or ethnicity in the past two years." Another Environics poll, of a representative sample of Canadians, found that 57 per cent believe that Muslims want to remain distinct from Cana-dian society rather than adopting Canadian customs and the Canadian way of life (93), whereas 57 per cent of Canadian Muslims say they believe most Muslims want to adopt Canadian customs. The situation is rather worse in Quebec than in the rest of Canada, for reasons presumably hav-ing to do with the province's own historical struggles surrounding identity, on the one hand, and religion, on the other.[3] Adams reports that 70 per cent of Quebecers agree that "there are too many immigrants coming into this country who are not adopting Canadian values" (119), a higher proportion than in the rest of the country. In comparison with other Canadians, Quebecers are also more likely to believe that Muslims wish to remain apart (119). In addition, Adams reports, while arguably underemphasizing, some disconcerting views among Muslims themselves; for instance, in response to a hypothetical question about the arrest of eighteen Muslim boys and men in Toronto on suspicion of plotting terrorist attacks on Canadian targets. A full 12 per cent of the (Muslim) respondents said the attacks would have been at least somewhat justified had they been carried out, and 5 per cent that they would have been completely justified (104). These percentages are small, but not insignificant.

A number of authors have noted that a major reason for the negative attitudes toward Muslims, along with some other religious minorities in Canada is simply ignorance, and the fearful stereotyping that often accompanies it. Natasha Bakht (2005) stresses this point in the context of her discussion of the proposal, in Ontario, to recognize the decisions of Islamic courts concerning matters of family arbitration, which generated a huge amount of hysteria but very little reasonable, informed discussion. As Amin Malak (2008, 80) observes: "Despite Muslims' roots dating back to more than a century in Canada, despite their number in Canada approaching a million, and more importantly, despite Islam being constantly in news headlines, it is surprising that not much gets told here about the genesis and spread of the world's second largest religion. Apart from exotic and sensational stories, there is a dearth of profound and serious knowledge about Islam that is available in the Canadian media, educational institutions, and official policy pronouncements." In light of these points, it does seem that Canadian multiculturalism, in spite of its successes, has fallen short in educating citizens about the cultures, including the religions, of the diverse groups of people that make up the nation. Contrary to the claims made by some of its detractors, there is no good reason to believe that multiculturalism has been positively harmful, at least in Canada, in regard to encouraging communitarian insularity and a lack of dialogue. To make this case, one would need to show that nations with multicultural policies generally suffer from such flaws to a greater degree than nations without them – Canada, for instance, in comparison with France – and the evidence does not support this thesis. But it does indicate that multiculturalism in Canada, and probably elsewhere, has not fostered an adequate level of knowledge about the histories and cultures of the various civilizations with which many citizens of non-European ancestry feel themselves to be connected. The problem is that a genuinely held commitment to pluralistic tolerance and formal respect for others can co-exist with profound ignorance about the content of what is supposed to be respected or tolerated. And such ignorance can in turn leave the commitment fragile, vulnerable to corruption through unjustified fears, stoked by sensationalist and distorting media coverage as well as political demagoguery.

RELIGIOUS ILLITERACY AND THE NEED FOR RELIGION EDUCATION IN SCHOOLS

A number of religious scholars and educators, moreover, have recently drawn attention to the lack of knowledge about religion generally in some Western societies. In the US, for example, Stephen Prothero (2007) complains about the widespread "religious illiteracy" among Americans, and proposes that courses on religion be mandatory in American high schools. He argues that the taboo on the subject of religion in public schools is based on misunderstandings about the separation between church and state (9), drawing a distinction between "academic offerings *about* religion" and "devotional courses *in* religion" (170).[4] Diane Moore echoes and expands upon a number of Prothero's assertions in *Overcoming Religious Illiteracy: A Cultural Studies Approach to the Study of Religion in Secondary Education* (2007). She notes that "though the United States is one of the most religiously diverse nations in the world, the vast majority of citizens are woefully ignorant about religion itself and the basic tenets of the world's major religious traditions" (3). She also claims – rightly, I believe – that "religious illiteracy has helped to foster a climate that is both politically dangerous and intellectually debilitating" (4). Although the political dangers of this ignorance about religion may be less starkly evident in Canada than in the US, the negative repercussions of the religious illiteracy Moore identifies, including misunderstanding and prejudice toward minority religions, are certainly visible north of the border as well.

In this context, Quebec's controversial new Ethics and Religious Culture (ERC) program, first taught in 2008–9 and at the time of writing the subject of a Supreme Court challenge, is worth examining as a possible model for non-denominational instruction about religion. The course has been implemented at both the elementary and secondary school levels, and is mandatory for all schools, including even denominational schools, both public and private. As the Quebec government has been unwilling to grant exemptions from the course either to individuals or to schools, it is not surprising that legal challenges to its mandatory character have been launched, appealing to freedom of conscience and religion.[5] The principles of the program reflect Quebec's established commitment to "interculturalism," a model of cross-cultural relations that is supposed to emphasize interaction and dialogue leading to integration (not assimilation) within a revised common culture, rather than to the preservation of separate communities that is supposedly promoted by Canadian multiculturalism. Regardless of whether or not multiculturalism, as implemented in the rest of Canada, actually does promote such a state of affairs (and there are specific historical reasons, rooted in its own status within Canada, for Quebec's rejection of the multicultural paradigm), the principles of the ECR program are worth examining as providing a possible model for the kind of public education about religion that is needed in modern secular societies comprising diverse religious traditions and affiliations.[6]

The program does address both of the shortcomings I have been highlighting: first, the lack of genuine intercultural understanding in Canada, particularly with respect to non-Western traditions, and, second, the lack of knowledge about religion. According to the description released by the Quebec ministry responsible for the program, it aims to develop three competencies, namely: "Reflects on ethical questions," "Demonstrates an understanding of the phenomenon of religion," and "Engages in dialogue" (Gouvernement du Québec 2008, 296). A good deal of emphasis is placed on this third element, education for dialogue. The guidelines emphasize the need for "respecting conditions that are conducive to exchange" (297), and call for "dialogue that is characterized by listening and discernment, and that has no room for attacks on personal dignity or actions that might compromise the common good" (296). Indeed, it might be argued that such civility should be a feature of wider public discourse about religion, providing an alternative and counterweight to the kind of polemics offered by authors like Christopher Hitchens and Richard Dawkins. The broad aim of the Ethics and Religious Culture program is stated in the following terms: "while endeavouring to form autonomous individuals, capable of exercising their critical judgment, this instruction also has the objective of fostering dialogue and community life in a pluralistic society" (293).

Respect for pluralism, in fact, defines the secularity of the education being provided by the program. Thus, its design is informed by a certain understanding of what secularism means, or should mean, in a society like Quebec. It is what Bouchard and Taylor define as "open" rather than "rigid" secularism, in their report on reasonable accommodation in Quebec, which is strongly supportive of the ECR program (Bouchard and Taylor 2008, 20, 134–53). Open secularism, as the Bouchard-Taylor Report describes it, is committed to the basic principles of any form of secularism, including separation of church and state, as well as the neutrality of the state toward religion. But it applies these principles in a flexible manner, and in one that accords with the values and goals of interculturalism. It does not strive to emancipate people from religion, for instance, nor does it ask them to keep their religious identities hidden. Rather, it seeks to achieve a balance between state neutrality and religious freedom, while recognizing the profound meaning of religion in the lives of many citizens, and approaching religious diversity in a spirit of tolerance and respect (20, 131–54).[7]

Adapting this understanding of secularism to the context of the ECR program in particular, George Leroux (2007, 14; my translation) writes, in *Éthique, culture religieuse, dialogue: Arguments pour un programme*: "*laïcité* does not signify a rejection of religion or conviction, but a welcoming of difference in a world of respect and right."[8] A little later in the book, Leroux remarks (19; my translation) that "the new program does not intend to leave empty the place of religion and symbolism, but to occupy it differently."[9] These statements suggest an interpretation of secularism, in the sense of "*laïcité*," which does not involve a wholesale exclusion of religion from public life, and therefore from schools, let alone hostility or contempt toward religion. To be sure, the latter stance is not usually a component of the avowed commitments of modern secular states. But disdain for religion, combined with an expectation of its disappearance in the near future, does characterize the standpoint of some citizens who think of themselves as advocates of secularism. In addition, and perhaps more importantly, this view of religion may be the one received by religious citizens as an effect of certain kinds of policies, even if that is not the intent of the policies. An awareness of these realities, I think, underlies Leroux's (16; my translation) insistence that "the secular school is not in effect the school of those who have renounced religion and who tolerate, while despising, those who preserve a place for it in their life; it is the school of respect of the the freedom of religion and the freedom of conscience of all."[10]

Leroux's (2007, 45; my translation) defence of the Ethics and Religious Culture program also expresses an ideal for managing religious, as well as cultural, diversity that rejects the multicultural approach on the grounds that "confining each person within a circle of customs and common practices does not contribute to the emergence of the common city."[11] As I have noted, it is doubtful that multiculturalism per se, as applied in Canada, actually promotes such cultural insularity, especially in comparison with policies of formal equality and assimilation. But that is clearly not the comparison Leroux has in mind, for those are not the ideals on which the Ethics and Religious Culture program is modeled. And a case can be made that the theory and practice of multiculturalism in Canada have not included an adequate focus on understanding and dialogue. Thus, Leroux's point is well-taken, given that the "cité commune" of which he speaks is not a pre-existing majority culture, but the product of a properly inclusive deliberative conversation between diverse groups of citizens. As stated in the official description of the program: "In order to be viable, a pluralist society in which there is a profusion of ethical questions and where diverse beliefs and ways of thinking, being and acting coexist needs to define itself as open and tolerant. In order to foster community life, such a society cannot circumvent the need for dialogue that is imbued with listening and reflection, discernment and the active participation of its members" (Gouvernement du Québec 2008, 320). The message here is that the right way to manage diversity in a pluralistic society is by encouraging participation in a common conversation, not merely by granting symbolic recognition and then leaving one another alone.

In this context, the critical dimension of the Ethics and Religious Culture program is highly significant. While the program does aim to "respect" plurality, as well as religious freedom, in a certain manner, teachers are also supposed to "help students develop a critical sense that will enable them to understand that not all opinions have the same worth" (Gouvernement du Québec 2008, 307). A government pamphlet discussing the proposal for the program, released in 2005, makes it clear that the notion of respect on which the program is based does not exclude critical evaluation. Section 2.3 of the pamphlet, titled "Learnings that Respect the Freedom of Conscience and Religion," states that "students studying ethical or religious issues should aim to understand them without negative prejudices or blind submission" (Gouvernement du Québec 2005, 6). A distinction is drawn, however, between the aims of the instruction offered at elementary and secondary school levels, with the critical element being confined to the latter: "In elementary school, emphasis will be placed on the values, beliefs and convictions that the students have in common in order to foster recognition of others and to develop their respect and tolerance. At the secondary level, students will broaden and consolidate their knowledge in order to address ethical or religious issues with objectivity and discernment" (Gouvernement du Québec 2005, 6). The final text of the official program description is more cautious on this point. It carefully directs the critical element of the instruction toward the ethics component alone, while using the language of understanding for the religion component. But there is overlap between these components, as the document itself recognizes and stresses, and the fact that the broad aims of the program include developing a capacity for critical reflection is inescapable. In practice, it is unlikely that such reflection could be wholly limited to instruction on "ethics" while being excluded from the study of "religion." One might argue, moreover, that encouraging students to adopt a critical perspective on their religions is not the legitimate province of schools, and violates religious freedom. Nonethless, I believe this critical component of the program, implemented in some fashion, is valuable and necessary. This is partly because I want to add a justification for the existence of public education programs like this one that is different from the ones I have been outlining.

Elsewhere, I have argued that both the liberal and the multicultural paradigms of public and political reasoning tend to encourage a view of religions as fixed bodies of belief, accepted by faith and exempted from processes of critical reflection. Because they allow justificatory appeals to either religious freedom or identity, while disallowing public critical reflection on the substance of religious views, these political paradigms may inadvertently create a climate conducive to the flourishing of fundamentalist forms of religion, as well as rigid constructions of identity. Although there are good reasons for insisting on neutrality about religion in select public and political spheres (within judicial reasoning, for instance), it is important that the ideal of neutrality appropriate to these spheres not spill over into a general taboo on the substantive evaluation of particular religious claims. There must remain public spaces in which the content and history of religious belief, symbolism and practice can be both learned and debated, not least because citizens should not come to think that reasoning and critical debate are alien to the very nature of religion (which is not true) (Sikka 2010).[12] Education about religion in public schools can be a partial solution to this problem, but only if it helps to counter the conception of religion as a system of dogmatic and unrevisable belief, and if it acquaints students with processes of theological reasoning.[13]

Yet one should hesitate to ask that mandatory instruction about religion in schools include direct critical assessment of religious claims, let

alone a comparative evaluation of the merits and shortcomings of different religions. A proposal to include such instruction in schools would be
extremely contentious, and possibly unconstitutional. Actually providing
the instruction would place an impossible burden on teachers, lead to
fraught situations in the classroom, and therefore do more harm than
good. There is, however, a more indirect route, one that does not require
compromising neutrality on the part of teachers, or setting up emotional-
ly charged debates in the classroom. Ironically, it is indicated by Diane
Moore (author of *Overcoming Religious Illiteracy*), in a passage where she
describes her experience of explaining to secondary school students the
difference between a theological and a religious studies approach to religion. She tells us:

> Because so many students associate religion with devotional practice,
> initial exposure to diverse and sometime competing claims about God
> can be both conceptually and theologically challenging ... In my expe-
> rience, students are eager to discuss the relevant issues that arise in the
> face of such encounters with diverse views but have limited tools to
> do so in thoughtful, respectful, and critically engaging ways ... The no-
> tion that there could be legitimate differing (and even competing)
> claims within and between religious traditions was a difficult concept
> for students to grasp. It took time for them to recognize that questions
> about the veracity of one interpretation over others arose out of a the-
> ological ... as opposed to a religious studies framework. (Moore 2007,
> 150)

There are several interesting points to notice about this narration. One is
that Moore's students were initially unfamiliar with the very idea of theological disagreements and differing interpretations of sacred texts, and did
not know how to engage with these. This suggests that these students had
absorbed an idea of religion as a rigid set of beliefs and practices. The social prevalence of this idea of religion is amply confirmed, unfortunately,
by my own experience of teaching philosophy of religion at the university level. Many students in the classes I have taught (but not usually those
majoring in Religious Studies) are simply unfamiliar with forms of debate
couched within religious discourse – in other·words, with modes of theological reasoning. The second point I would draw out from Moore's account of her experience, though, is that, although she is differentiating
theology from religious studies, her students are actually learning about
theology through the religious studies approach that she has adopted. Ed-

ucating students about religion in a way that pays appropriate attention to history and culture also educates them about how one may debate religious theses with an orientation toward truth, even if establishing the veracity of those theses is not the direct aim of the instruction. The history of religion, after all, includes such debates, and one cannot tell it accurately without rehearsing them.

A major shortcoming of the "world religions" approach adopted in many secondary school level courses in the past is that it had tended to communicate a view of religions as static and homogeneous, giving tidy descriptions of "what Buddhists believe," and the like. Instruction about religion in schools should be working to break down such ideas of religion, which are false to the historical and present reality of religion, rather than reinforcing them. As Robert Jackson (1995, 286–7) argues, "some deconstruction of received ideas about the nature of 'religion' and 'religions' needs to be undertaken in order to enable new models to be developed which avoid the simplistic portrayal of religions as discrete systems of belief and which also accommodate internal diversity and change." A good deal of the diversity and change within religions, moreover, is generated by points of contestation, by substantive objections raised against particular interpretations, beliefs and practices, and arguments on behalf of alternatives asserted as better. While we need, as a society, to inculcate and practice the virtue of civility in our conversations across difference, the political values of toleration and respect for plurality should not come to monopolize all of our public discourse about religion. Accordingly, school instruction should help to educate students about the possibility of debating the content of religion with an orientation toward truth, which it can do in a non-sectarian manner simply by relating examples.

INFORMAL AND POST-SECONDARY RELIGION EDUCATION

One reason why critical reasoning in relation to religion is necessary in a democratic society is that such societies cannot help but make decisions that conflict with the religious beliefs of some citizens. It cannot help but make what are in fact substantive judgements that may not respect certain religious claims, about homosexuality, for instance, or abortion. We need to be honest that substantive judgments are being made in these cases, and that these are arrived at not purely through the application of neutral liberal principles, but through processes of deliberation in which conclusions were reached. Because of this, relations to secularism that neglect the dimension of deliberation, and jettison truth altogether, are problematic.

Veit Bader (2009, 114), for instance, in his critique of secularism, argues that "modern liberal democracy requires that all opinions and voices, ultimately expressed as votes, have to count equally when it comes to final decision-making." Consequently, a properly democratic politics "requires that all defenders of 'truths', whether religious or secular (philosophical, scientistic or professional/ 'expertocratic'), should learn how to resolve their respective 'fundamentalist dilemma'" (ibid.), that is, their wish to impose their views in an authoritarian manner. Now, it is just a fact that in a democratic society all votes count equally (though this does not by any means ensure that all citizens have an equal voice in the decision-making process). And I strongly agree with Bader that religious reasons should not be excluded in principle from public forums. But these considerations should lead to an even greater recognition of the need for critical *deliberation* within a democratic society – for public reason, in effect, with its requirement that people be prepared, and able, to give reasons on behalf of their claims if they wish these to be given weight in the formulation of public policy. We should indeed be suspicious "scientism" and "expertocracy," but we need equally "to understand that not all opinions have the same worth," as the ECR program description puts it (Gouvernement du Québec 2008, 307), even while being sensitive to, and critical of, the biases, inequalities, and distortions characterizing the rules of the game in public arenas. In this regard, some complex distinctions will need to be drawn: about the relation between science and religion, for instance, and the question of what counts as "scientism." It is one thing to say that the mathematical formulae of physics do not capture the whole of reality. It is quite another to say that the law of momentum is just a matter of opinion (likewise, biology and the theory of evolution). Bader (2003, 15) explicitly states that he does not support an "anything goes" form of democratic politics, but neither does he pay enough attention to the processes through which what does and does not go might be determined in a democracy. These processes need to include critical reflection seeking to separate truth from error, at least provisionally, as best as one can, and in a humble and fallibilistic spirit. The education of a well-informed citizenry capable of reasoning and evaluation on matters of religion, conducted in a civil manner, will therefore be doubly necessary in the "moderately agonistic democracy" that Bader favours over secularism.

There are, however, social contexts within publicly funded schools in which it may not be feasible to include mandatory education about religion and religions, at either the elementary or the secondary levels. The subject could be too divisive and its implementation too risky, as may be the case in India, or there could be an insufficient level of interest and/or will on the part of a substantial proportion of citizens, as may be the case in parts of Canada. In such circumstances, other avenues for public education about religion, including respectful critical conversations on religious topics, will need to be sought. I cited at some length the defence of Quebec's Ethics and Religious Culture program offered by Georges Leroux primarily in order to highlight the principles that he, among others, advances for developing appropriate models of citizenship education and dialogue in societies marked by cultural and religious diversity. While formulated to justify the design of a specific school curriculum, these principles have broader applications. They include the claim that symbolic recognition of cultural and religious difference is not enough, but must be accompanied by a genuine knowledge and understanding of one another. They reject practices of accommodation that would leave different communities alone to follow separate paths, in favour of measures encouraging a common, but genuinely inclusive, conversation. While insisting on civility and respect in the manner of conducting this conversation, they propose that it must include critical evaluation.

Thus, the principles Leroux identifies as being the basis for the ERC program manifestly articulate ideals for the management of religious and cultural diversity in general. Their focus on education and dialogue, moreover, acknowledges the importance of everyday interactions in determining the social and political choices citizens make. Constitutional and legal provisions do, of course, have an impact on shaping that everyday world. But the reverse is also true, and formal rules of justice, applied at the level of law and the courts, cannot accomplish everything. One should also not become complacent about the stability of these rules, believing they will necessarily be supported by social consensus in liberal democratic countries, or that they could survive the loss of such support. Courts and constitutions are an important check on the potential pitfalls of majority rule, but there is no way of escaping the fact that a democracy is ultimately dependent upon the character of its *demos*.

In a poly-ethnic and multicultural democracy like Canada, therefore – one comprised of people connected to histories, customs, and religions originating from different parts of the world – one cannot escape the need for a public education that would seek to bridge these differences. That is equally true for a nation like India, which is "multicultural" in its own way. But such education does not occur only within schools. Public discussion and debate are equally important sources of continuing education for citizens and residents of liberal democratic nations. In relation to religion it is therefore important that legitimate secular bans on appeal to substantive religious views, or criticism of such views, within select public spheres such as the judiciary not be allowed to spill over into a tacit taboo on *all* public discourse about religion (see Sikka 2010). One should note that in India it is not only self-proclaimed anti-secularists like Ashis Nandy who complain about attempts to exclude religion from public life (e.g., Nandy 2007). Meera Nanda (2008), for example – a staunch secularist if there ever was one – also argues for the right to make substantive assertions about religion. In an obvious sense, these two are resolutely opposed, since Nandy wants to make space for positive religious discourse, while Nanda wants the right to criticize religion, to which she is unambiguously hostile. Both prescriptions seek to allow substantive claims about religion within public life, though, and the voicing of such claims, along with the debates they generate, is an important component of informal public education about religion.

Furthermore, the fact many individuals in India who are hostile to religion are perfectly able to articulate their views in public without fearing for their safety shows that this possibility exists, although one would perhaps like to see more measured and complex analyses, as well as ones that could reach beyond a narrow intellectual circle. It might be objected that dangers arise precisely when one seeks to reach beyond that circle. But what lesson should one draw from this? That Indian citizens should always be careful not to raise critical questions in relation to religion publicly, for fear of reprisals? If that is the situation at present, it is a sad comment on the state of Indian democracy, and ameliorative measures need to be adopted. Education can play an important role here. The inclusion of appropriate education about religion at the school level in India may, in the current circumstances, be asking too much, but one should at least work toward establishing a public culture in which it is possible to debate questions about religion, with civility and without violence.

One should also work toward having the academic and critical study of religion recognized as a subject at the post-secondary level, and creating the conditions that would make this possible. Universities in India do not as yet include religious studies departments. The establishment of such departments could help to move critical discussions of religion beyond the narrow and impoverished analyses offered by authors like Nanda, who consider religion to be nothing but superstition and ideology, toward richer and more balanced appraisals of the nature and function of religion, as well as of particular varieties of religious belief and practice. Martha Nussbaum (2010, 131) draws attention to this issue in *Not for Profit: Why Democracy Needs the Humanities*, specifically noting that "the study of comparative religion and the history of religions is not an academic subject in Indian universities." Nussbaum makes this point as part of a wider critique of the weakness of humanities education in India due to an exclusive focus on science, economics, and technology. She connects the ignorance and lack of critical ability resulting from this shortcoming of the Indian education system with a vulnerability to propaganda and distortion, and connects the latter, in turn, with episodes of religious violence, as in the case of Gujurat (Nussbaum 2010, 142; see also Nussbaum 2007, 178).

Indeed, in the same work, Nussbaum suggests more generally that "the understanding of the world's many religious traditions" is "crucial to the success of democracies in our world" (Nussbaum 2010, 83). Consequently, appropriate education about religions should be included in US school curricula, Nussbaum argues, as exposure to different religious traditions will foster both better global citizenship and better US citizenship (ibid.). I would add that in Canada and the US, post-secondary institutions could also do a better job than they currently do in educating students about this topic. There are departments of religious studies in both countries, but these need not be the only locus of education about such an important aspect of human culture across the world. It is true that courses in other humanities disciplines – literature, philosophy, history, and art history, to name a few – may indirectly treat matters associated with religion. Judging by results, however, these courses do not suffice. In Canada, I have frequently been astonished at the level of ignorance about religion even among individuals who have obtained advanced humanities degrees. Somehow, they do not connect the ideas they have encountered through their study of literature, art, or philosophy with religion, even when in fact these ideas are historically inseparable from religion. And the studies of religious illiteracy in the US cited earlier suggest that what is being currently provided there is also not working. The situation is only worse in India.

In Western democracies, a greater focus on religion in humanities courses at the university level might help, along with – crucially – less Eurocentric curricula. These suggestions again accord with the broader goals of Quebec's Ethics and Religious Culture program, which seeks to educate students about the topic of religion in a manner that recognizes cultural diversity. In my own discipline, philosophy, a survey of areas of specialization among faculty members in departments across Canada, as well as of course offerings and descriptions, will quickly reveal that, with a few exceptions, little attempt is made to include non-European philosophical traditions. Philosophy is not religion, but historically it has been, at the very least, a neighbouring discipline, and many of the topics it treats do overlap with religious and theological concerns. An engagement with non-Western philosophical traditions – with Arabic and Asian philosophy, for instance – would help to educate students about aspects of the religions that originated in these regions. Furthermore, philosophy brings to bear on its topics exactly the kind of critical engagement that is needed in the sphere of education about religion. In the first place, philosophical engagement with the history of ideas focuses primarily on critical debates. In relation to religious and theological ideas, such a historical focus can help to challenge the notion that religion – *any* religion – has ever been a clear, stable, and uncontested body of belief. And second, philosophical approaches directly involve the critical assessment of ideas, familiarizing students with modes of argumentation and reasoning.

Courses specifically in philosophy of religion naturally have a special role to play in helping to educate students about these topics. However, in order to fulfill this role effectively, such courses need both to be sensitive to the history of ideas within religious traditions, and they need to reflect the multiplicity of such traditions across the world. As a professor who teaches philosophy of religion regularly, I have been frustrated with the exclusive orientation toward Christianity of almost all English-language textbooks and anthologies on the subject, as well as their lack of attention to historical debate and variation. These shortcomings reflect flaws in the way that the subject is generally taught at universities. They send the message to students that (1) "religion," of the sort that matters, is synonymous with the Abrahamic faiths, and in particular with Christianity, and (2) its basic character is clear and stable, so that critical questions about religious belief need not be concerned with variations in its content, or with theological debates about that content. An approach of this sort is actually counter-productive rather than helpful for the purposes of communicating information about the world's different religious traditions, familiarizing students with modes of theological reasoning, and alerting them to the fact that contestation and change have been an intrinsic part of the history of religion.

THE PROBLEM OF "RECOGNITION"

Instruction about religion that respects these goals, on the other hand, can aid not only in cultivating critical engagement, but also in countering the problem of essentialism set up by the logic of "recognition." With respect to India, Shail Mayaram has highlighted this problem in an especially concrete and powerful fashion through her work on minority Muslim and *Mer* identities. Her book, *Resisting Regimes: Myth, Memory and the Shaping of a Muslim Identity*, provides a detailed historical study of a Muslim community pressed to conform itself to a specific understanding of Islam through acts of religio-political coercion and violence (Mayaram 1997). In light of such acts, past and present, Mayaram (1999, 397) suggests in a later essay that "multiculturalists in India must ... ask themselves the question, 'recognizing what and whom?'" Pointing out that "pre-modern Indian identities were both fluid and complex" (Mayaram 1999, 385), she raises concerns about cases where the modern Indian state, operating within the logic of recognition, "helps create religious boundaries and sustains ideologies of anti-syncretism," practices in which religious organizations and institutions also participate (Mayaram 1999, 395). Anne Vallely and Sipra Mukherjee, in their contributions to the present volume, also focus on these kinds of practices, which tend, whether by design or inadvertently, to establish and freeze in place singular and mutually exclusive identities.

Admittedly, education about religion can itself promote essentialism if it proceeds by defining distinct religions in terms of fixed sets of beliefs and practices. The message thereby communicated is that "religions" are settled entities separated by clear borders, with no space left for communities and formations that do not fit the established categories, whether these be existing or new ones. But it is in response to precisely this concern that I have argued in favour of education about religion that would be historical, recognizing not merely the existence of distinct religious communities, but also the controversy, contestation, syncretism, and reform that have characterized religion. Learning about the history of religion(s) can thus help to counter some of the negative effects produced by the operation of religio-political practices of recognition. The latter, positioning religion as a matter of "identity," necessarily push religious communities and movements to define themselves in essentialist terms, not least by providing political and economic incentives for them to do so. After all, a group cannot claim the benefits of being "recognized" as a distinct community – a religious minority, for instance, that ought to be accommodated and protected – unless it is able to define the content of its identity clearly, and in such a way as to exclude assimilation to other groups. The history of religions, on the other hand, reveals that as a matter of fact these have always been variegated and changing. It also reveals the role of critical reasoning in relation to this variety and change, whether that be theological reasoning about matters of metaphysics, or ethical reasoning in religious terms, or internal critiques of institutions. Thus, public education about religion, delivered in a manner that reflects these dimensions of its history, can help to challenge essentialist assertions rather than reinforcing them.

Such education needs to take place at an informal level as well, through public dialogue. While the public arena is admittedly not one to which all have fair and equal access, and while minorities of many sorts, including religious minorities, need to be protected from the disadvantages of majoritarian decision making, it is also important that questions of "identity" not monopolize the whole of public reflection on religion. There must also be space for informed and inclusive reflection on matters of substance, in order to promote mutual understanding, and as part of the attempt to achieve at least the minimal level of consensus required to maintain justice and peace in a diverse democratic society. To this end, the careful negotiations of religious plurality instantiated in the principles of Quebec's Ethics and Religious Culture program provide a helpful guide, for religion education both within schools and beyond.

NOTES

1 I wish to thank Avigail Eisenberg, Gurpreet Mahajan, and Shail Mayaram for their critical questions in response to the earlier version of this paper presented at the workshop, "Multiculturalism and Religious Identity" (University of Ottawa, 2009). A number of the points I make in this paper are the direct product of reflection on their questions.

2 See Phil Ryan's *Multicultiphobia* (2010) and, with respect to Europe, the essays collected in *The Multiculturalism Backlash: European discourses, policies and practices* (Vertovec and Wessendorf 2010).

3 See Bouchard-Taylor 2008 for an analysis of these points, and for an account of Quebec's struggles with religious and cultural diversity generally, in relation to immigrants.

4 This is the distinction to which I am alluding in the title of my paper, through use of the admittedly awkward phrase "religion education" rather than "religious education."

5 One of these was filed by parents in Drummondville seeking an exemption for their two children attending public schools at the elementary and secondary levels. This case was argued before the Supreme Court of Canada, which ruled in 2012 that the ERC course does not infringe on parents' char-

ter rights. The other was filed by Loyola High School, a private institution in Montreal, and at the time of writing was before the Supreme Court.

6 Thus, my engagement with the ERC program in the following pages is confined to its general principles, and is guided by the broad question of education about religion in multiple contexts. It is not my purpose to evaluate the details of the program's content, structure, or implementation within the Quebec school system.

7 Unfortunately, recent events in Quebec appear to signal a retreat from the open secularism outlined and recommended in the Bouchard-Taylor Report. The tabling of Bill 94 in 2010, to strong support from a number of groups, is the clearest example. This bill would require women who wear *niqabs* or other face coverings to remove them when delivering or receiving government services. See the objections to Bill 94 voiced by LEAF (the Canadian Women's Legal Education and Action Fund) in its submission to the Quebec National Assembly (LEAF 2010).

8 "*Laïcité* signifie non pas refus du religieux ou de la conviction, mais accueil de la différence dans un monde de respect et de droit."

9 "Le nouveau programme entend ne pas laisser vide la place du religieux et du symbolique, mais l'occuper autrement."

10 "L'école laïque n'est pas en effet l'école de ceux qui ont renoncé à la religion et qui tolèrent en les méprisant ceux qui lui conservent une place dans leur vie; elle est l'école du respect de la liberté de religion et de la liberté de conscience de tous," where "l'athéisme et l'agnosticisme y trouvent une place aussi légitime que la croyance."

11 "Confiner chacun dans un périmètre de coutumes et d'usages ne contribue pas à l'émergence de la cité commune."

12 I make parallel points in relation to India in my article "The Perils of Indian Secularism" (Sikka 2012).

13 In "Liberalism, Multiculturalism and the Case for Public Religion," however, I suggest that critical instruction about religion can be optional, and does not lose its value if it is so, as students will still be surrounded by peers who are receiving this instruction, and both parents and students will be sent the message that this is a normal way of engaging with religion (Sikka 2010, 602, 606n25). For similar reasons, I would argue in favour of granting exemptions from the ECR program for individual students in public schools, and for private institutions. Forcing this form of religious education on resistant students and parents is, in my view, counter-productive.

REFERENCES

Adams, Michael. 2007. *Unlikely Utopia: The Surprising Triumph of Canadian Pluralism*. Toronto: Viking Canada.

Bader, Veit. 2003. "Religions and States. A New Typology and a Plea for Non-Constitutional Pluralism." *Ethical Theory and Moral Practice* 6(1): 55–91.

– 2009. "Secularism, public reason or moderately agonistic democracy?" In *Secularism, Religion and Multicultural Citizenship*, edited by Geoffrey Brahm Levey, and Tariq Modood, 110–36. New York: Cambridge University Press.

Bakht, Natasha. 2005. "Were Muslim Barbarians Really Knocking on the Gates of Ontario? The Religious Arbitration Controversy - Another Perspective." *Ottawa Law Review, 40th Anniversary* Summer: 67–82. Available at http://papers.ssrn.com /sol3/papers.cfm? abstract_id= 1121790.

Bouchard, Gerard, and Taylor, Charles. 2008. *Building the Future: A Time for Reconciliation*. Report of the Commission de consultation sur les pratiques d'accommodement reliées aux differences culturelles. Final Report – Complete (English). Available at http://www.accommodements.qc.ca/index-en.htm.

Gouvernement du Québec, Ministère de l'Éducation, du Loisir et du Sport. 2005. "Establishment of an ethics and religious culture program: Providing future direction for all Quebec youth." Available at http://www.mels.gouv.qc.ca /fileadmin/site_web/documents/publications/BSM/Aff_religieuses/prog _ethique_cult_reli_a.pdf.

– 2008. "Ethics and Religious Culture: Elementary Program." Available at https://www7.mels.gouv.qc.ca/DC/ECR/primaire/index_en.php?page=accueil.

Jackson, Robert. 1995. "Religious Education's Representation of 'Religions' and 'Cultures." *British Journal of Educational Studies* 43(3): 272–89.

Kymlicka, Will. 1998. *Finding Our Way: Rethinking Ethnocultural Relations in Canada*. Toronto: Oxford University Press.

– 2007. "Disentangling the Debate." In *Uneasy Partners: Multiculturalism and Rights in Canada*, edited by Janice Stein, David Robertson Cameron, John Ibbitson, Will Kymlicka, John Meisel, Haroon Siddiqui, and Michael Valpy, 137–56. Waterloo: Wilfrid Laurier University Press.

LEAF (Women's Legal Education and Action Fund). 2010. "Submission to the Quebec National Assembly on Bill 94." Available at http://www.leaf.ca /features/documents/C3/LEAF%20Submission%20to%20Quebec %20National%20Assembly%20on%20Bill%2094%20(Final%20-%20English).pdf.

Leroux, Georges. 2007. *Éthique, culture religieuse, dialogue: Arguments pour un programme*. Quebec: Éditions Fides.

Ley, David. 2010. "Multiculturalism: A Canadian Defence." In *Multicultural Backlash: European Discourses, Policies and Practices*, edited by Steven Vertovec, and Susanne Wessendorf, 190–206. New York, Routledge.

Malak, Amin. 2008. "Towards a Dialogical Discourse for Canadian Muslims." In *Belonging and Banishment: Being Muslim in Canada*, edited by Natasha Bakht, 74–84. Toronto: TSAR Publications.

Mayaram, Shail. 1997. *Resisting Regimes: Myth, Memory and the Shaping of a Muslim Identity*. Delhi: Oxford University Press.

– 1999. "Recognizing Whom?: Multiculturalism, Muslim Minority Identity and the Mers." In *Multiculturalism, Liberalism and Democracy*, edited by Rajeev Bhargava, Amiya Kumar Bagchi, and R. Sudarshan. Delhi: Oxford University Press.

Moore, Diane L. 2007. *Overcoming Religious Illiteracy: A Cultural Studies Approach to the Study of Religion in Secondary Education*. New York: Palgrave Macmillan.

Nanda, Meera. 2008. "God Delusion at Work." *Economic and Political Weekly* 18: 15–19.

Nandy, Ashis. 2007. "Closing the Debate on Secularism: A Personal Statement." In *The Crisis of Secularism in India*, edited by Anuradha Dingwaney Needham, and Rajeswari Sunder Rajan, 107–17. Durham and London: Duke University Press.

Nussbaum, Martha. 2007. *The Clash Within: Democracy, Religious Violence, and India's Future*. Cambridge: Harvard University Press.

– 2010. *Not for Profit: Why Democracy Needs the Humanities*. Princeton: Princeton University Press.

Prothero, Stephen. 2007. *Religious Literacy*. New York: HarperCollins.

Ryan, Phil. 2010. *Multicultiphobia*. Toronto: University of Toronto Press.

Sikka, Sonia. 2010. "Liberalism, Multiculturalism and the Case for Public Religion." *Politics and Religion* 3: 580–609.

– 2012. "The Perils of Indian Secularism." *Constellations* 19 (2): 288–304.

Vertovec, Steven, and Susanne Wessendorf, eds. 2009. *The Multiculturalism Backlash: European Discourses, Policies and Practices*. London: Routledge.

16

Doing Caste, Making Citizens: Differing Conceptions of Religious Identities and Autonomy in Hindu Law[1]

GOPIKA SOLANKI

Debates rage between feminists and proponents of group rights over the question of whether multiculturalism is antithetical to gender equality. These contentions are particularly sharp around the question of recognition of religious family laws, as these shape gender roles, as well as ethnogender identities and subjectivities within the family, and impact on the distribution of resources within the family. Feminists further argue that the recognition of religious family laws consolidates intra-group hierarchies, essentializes the boundaries of religious groups, denies women equal citizenship rights by concretizing gender inequality within the family, and violates individual liberty (Cook 1994; Moghadam 1994; Nussbaum and Glover 1995; Okin 1999; Phillips 2007).

In addition, feminists also point out that policies such as the recognition of religious family laws, which allow ethnoreligious groups to control the family, adversely impact the autonomy of women, as conceptions of conjugality and the rights accrued to women in the family under religious family laws do not recognize women's personhood in law; these ethnoreligious groups, through their laws, demand women's uncritical subjection to group norms and also influence ethnogendered intra-group socialization. These debates are particularly relevant for India as the state recognizes religious laws of majority and minority religious communities. This state policy has been criticized by a majority of scholars who argue that the Indian state's recognition of religious family laws has violated women's rights within the family, and further cemented religious identities (see Parashar 1992; Rajan 2003; Parashar and Dhanda 2008).[2]

I investigate the above question by assessing the Indian state's policy of legal pluralism[3] in the governance of the conjugal family in religious family laws. By drawing from John Griffiths' (1986) definition and typology of legal pluralism,[4] I define legal pluralism in India as the way that the state recognizes and checks non-state laws that are used to govern the family. To elaborate, two aspects characterize the Indian variant of legal pluralism in the regulation of the family. First, the Indian state recognizes religious family laws, and as a result, religious groups such as Hindus, Muslims, Parsis, and Christians are governed by their own religious family laws, that is, laws governing marriage, divorce, maintenance, adoption, and inheritance.[5] Inter-religious marriages are regulated by secular law, the Special Marriage Act, 1954, and any Indian citizen can choose to marry under secular law. The second aspect of this policy is shared adjudication, in the sense that the state splits its adjudicative authority to govern marriage and divorce with societal groups, including caste councils and civil society organizations. For example, Section 29 (2) of the Hindu Marriage Act, 1955[6] allows both state courts and the caste-councils (panchayats[7]) to adjudicate in laws governing marriage and divorce among Hindus. The state does not establish or fund religious or customary courts. Nevertheless, this state policy permits what David Sugarman (1983, 216) calls "facilitative law making," the state legitimization of law production in non-state domains. Scholars have discussed different imaginaries of law, family, and gender and religious membership that prevail within the socio-legal sphere and have pointed out similarities and differences in the normative constructions of the conjugal family and gender roles between the state-authored Hindu law and the laws and practices of various castes (see Chowdhry 2004; Holden 2008; Kapila 2004; Parry 2001; Solanki 2011).

This chapter pursues this line of inquiry by highlighting different conceptions of religious identity and autonomy of legal actors that emerge in the state-constituted Hindu law and the caste laws of Meghwals, a Dalit[8] group in Mumbai,[9] as well as the agency of women in building the autonomy-enhancing capacity of legal subjects within caste laws.[10] The first section of the chapter outlines the construction of the normative "Hindu" conjugal family through the textual analysis of state-authored Hindu law governing marriage between 1955 and the late 1970s. The second section traces caste formation and law making among the Meghwals during the same period, focusing on the conditions that undergirded two democratic moments during caste formation that spurred the codification of Hindu law within the caste in a specific direction.

The chapter argues that although the state-authored Hindu law potentially entrenches the difference between Hindus and non-Hindus, and does not guarantee gender equality in law, in the shared adjudication model, marginalized groups can creatively utilize this model to debate and craft varied conceptions of conjugal family, religious identity, and gender roles that differ from the state schema. The process of caste formation and law making outlined here demonstrates that at different points in caste formation, the caste group, which was classified by the state as "Hindu" and governed by Hindu law, adopted and discarded various religious identities, privileged hybrid religious identities, and recognized and regulated different conceptions of more egalitarian gender roles and rights within marriage. In addition, the data also counters the feminist criticism that ethnoreligious communities are inherently patriarchal and violate women's rights and autonomy. Indeed, the data shows that during ongoing processes of caste formation, the caste group facilitated democratic law-making processes and women's participation in these enabled the group members to collectively craft conjugal relations in ways that enhanced women's autonomy within the conjugal family. The caste group fashioned legal subjects that were autonomous, yet socially responsible and organized their conjugal family to facilitate this manner of "doing" conjugality.

Digressing from exclusively state-centred conceptions of agency, this chapter suggests that while the policy of recognition of religious family laws allows the Indian state to ascertain the extent of group rights to govern the family, outline permissible norms and forms of conjugality, and fashion women's rights within the conjugal family, it is critically important to also highlight the role of the societal agents in interpreting, shaping, and at times, subverting state law and policy on the ground. In addition, although the argument here is based on a detailed case study of an urban caste group, the findings based on this individual case study are generalizable as these point to the conditions under which ethnoreligious groups can craft hybrid religious identities and promote family laws that prioritize women's autonomy. In other words, it is suggested here that the caste members' exposure to anticolonial and democratic politics, interactions with different political parties and social movements, along with the growth of a civic sphere within the caste, the substantive citizenship rights enjoyed by the group as public sector workers, and the high level of women's participation in the labour force provided enabling conditions that allowed the group to build intra-group democracy and impacted caste making and gender making within the conjugal family.

STRUCTURING MARRIAGE AND DIVORCE
IN STATE-AUTHORED HINDU LAW

In this section, I discuss the structure of marriage and divorce in the state law in roughly the first three decades of post-colonial India. The Hindu Marriage Act, enacted in 1955 and amended in 1976,[11] governs marriage and divorce among Hindus, and this law is interpreted in state courts. The body of Hindu family law is not unified, and contradictions exist among various laws and judgments in various courts.[12] However, the state law establishes the framework for deciding the criteria for the "legitimate" Hindu conjugal family and also reproduces religious identities.

Marriage ensures the perpetuation of religious/ethnic groups and castes. The Hindu law defines a *Hindu* as a person who is not a Muslim, Parsi, Christian, or Jew (Mulla 1966, 616). Buddhists, Jains and Sikhs are subsumed under the category "Hindu." Thus, Hindu law links the religious and legal identities of citizens. The Hindu law makes a distinction between marriage and non-marriage;[13] the state law specifies that marriages are to be authorized either by custom, religious authority, or state officials.[14]

Under Hindu law, the state privileges heterosexuality[15] and monogamy,[16] criminalizes polygyny,[17] and forbids polyandry and group marriage. As a ground for divorce, an irreconcilable breakdown of marriage is not recognized; Section 13 (a) of the Hindu Marriage Act, 1955 specifies the grounds for divorce under certain conditions.[18] The guiding principle of this provision is that divorces are granted on the basis of the commission of a matrimonial offence. Divorce by mutual consent is possible under Section 13 (b) of the Hindu Marriage (Amendment) Act, 1976. Thus, Hindu law is not monolithic, and in most cases, the notion of divorce as harmful to public order and morality, the institution of the family, and women's status coexists in tension with the notion of individual freedom.

The Hindu law of marriage illustrates the tensions between elements of contract and a sacrament. For instance, the implicit consent of the parties is necessary for Hindu marriage, since a lack of consent invalidates the legality of a Hindu marriage.[19] The provision of a mutual consent divorce in the Hindu law also evinces the contractarian character of the Hindu law. However, the legal acceptance of child marriage as a valid marriage challenges the notion of autonomy within the conjugal family.[20] Under section 5 (iii) of the Hindu Marriage Act, 1955, child marriage is valid but punishable. The wife in such a marriage can obtain a divorce under section 13 (2) (iv) of the act if her marriage was solemnized before she was fifteen years of age, and she has repudiated the marriage after attaining that age but before attaining the age of eighteen. The Hindu law also authorizes the husband as a natural guardian of a Hindu wife if she is a minor under the law. In addition, the Hindu wife's autonomy as a citizen is questionable, since the state law does not explicitly criminalize rape within marriage,[21] except in cases where the parties have received a decree of judicial separation.[22] The state also provides the matrimonial remedy, such as the restitution of conjugal rights under Hindu law, which challenges notions of consent and individual freedom as a basis of marriage, as the decree calls upon the respondent of either sex to return home to the petitioner within a specified time period.[23] This order of cohabitation is not legally enforceable, and though the failure to comply with the decree does not carry legal sanctions, it is interpreted in courts as a demonstration of unwillingness of the party to continue with the marriage.

The parties to Hindu marriage are positioned as equal actors with respect to maintenance. Maintenance is an ancillary remedy under the Hindu Marriage Act, 1955. This law is gender neutral, and as a result, in theory, either spouse can claim maintenance or alimony in cases filed under mutual consent or contested divorce. Maintenance is an independent remedy under the Hindu Adoption and Maintenance Act (HAMA), 1956. The Hindu law on maintenance grants both partners the same rights to maintenance, privileges the notion of equality as sameness, and does not take into account the structural asymmetry of property rights in Indian society (Basu 1999). The Hindu law does not explicitly govern the distribution of matrimonial property, although financially dependent wives are entitled to maintenance if they prove their legal innocence. For instance, as per Section 18 of the HAMA, 1956, a Hindu wife is entitled to claim maintenance from her husband if he is guilty of cruelty, conversion, desertion, adultery, polygyny, or has a communicable disease. While the law maintains the sexual division of labour in the family, the Hindu wife is considered an equal citizen under Hindu law with respect to maintenance. The Hindu law makes the patrilineal family the norm. According to the law, the father is the natural guardian of a child[24] conceived in marriage, and the mother is the natural guardian of a child born out of wedlock.[25]

Thus, the state-crafted laws conceive a particular version of religious identity, as well as notions of moral competency and the autonomy of legal subjects. These frame the ideological and material realms of possibilities and actions for individuals governed under Hindu law. However, in the shared adjudication model, different conceptions of law exist simultaneously; state and societal laws can also cohabit as distinct and parallel normative universes in the same socio-legal sphere.[26] In the following section, I trace the construction of the religious identity, conjugal family, and legal subjectivity among Meghwals, a Dalit sub-group in Mumbai and discuss the implication of state-crafted informalism in law.[27] Against the backdrop of socio-political processes leading to caste formation, law making, and regulation within the caste, this chapter highlights two democratic moments in the history of caste formation among Meghwals. In the 1950s, the caste outlined a caste constitution through the codification of its practices, rules, rituals, and opinions on the ground and charted a plan for democratic internal governance of the caste. Between 1974 and 1975, the caste constitution was amended after collective deliberation by varied caste clusters and implemented with the consensus of the caste members. The 1970s process of codification and reform of caste laws saw the emergence of women as autonomous legal subjects of law and as law makers, participating in broad processes of collective reflection on the content of the law. This chapter discusses how the caste laws as envisaged in 1953 and 1974–75 challenge the statist construction of religious identities under Hindu law and construe notions of personal and collective freedom in law from below.

THE MEGHWAL: OUTLINING THE STATIST CONSTRUCTION OF THE CASTE AND LAW MAKING IN 1953

The city of Bombay was strategically built by the British from the seventeenth century as a port, and as the city developed, its infrastructure and sanitation, privately managed until then, came under the jurisdiction of Bombay Municipal Corporation (henceforth BMC). During that time, persistent famines, plague epidemics, crop failure, and greater connectivity through railways and ports ensured an inflow of individual migrants belonging to different castes and religions[28] from Kathiawar and Gujarat; the BMC hired male and female[29] workers in large numbers. The male and female migrants from Gujarat and Kathiawar who were employed by the BMC as sweepers were classified in state records as Dher,[30] a sub-caste of a group of people previously classified as "untouchables."[31] They resided in chawls[32] constructed by the Khoja Muslims and the Methodist Episcopal Church, and later, the BMC. They shared residential space and occupation as sweepers, scavengers, industrial workers, and in the municipal transport system of the city as coolies. The experiences of caste discrimination and failure to assimilate with other groups of similar occupational status due to competition for employment with the Mahars, Chamhars, or Mangs brought these workers from different religions and castes together to form endogamous circles and, over time, a section of these workers began to call themselves "Meghwal." After the 1920s, they began to be active in the nationalist movement and aligned themselves with the Congress Party rather than with the faction of Dalits organized by Dr. Ambedkar.[33] The Harijan Sevak Sangh and Congress workers within the BMC mobilized the youth. A greater demand for education for workers and a civic sphere of youth organizations and political party workers began to develop within the caste. Many of these group members were also hired as industrial workers and began to be active in trade unions in the BMC and textile mills as of 1940s.

How was the family structured and governed among these clusters? Until the 1950s, these endogamous circles and groups were loosely organized. Two types of social organizations prevailed among these: the clusters of people who had migrated from neighbouring areas of Kathiawar or Gujarat were governed by a *vada panch*, and the clusters of fifteen to eighteen families living in residential proximity was governed by a *tana panch*. The *panch* were heads of dominant families who could exercise some economic power, and officiated in matters of marriage and divorce. Another type of the organization included a cluster of different, overlapping, and often interchangeable groups called *gnats* which called themselves the Meghwals, Rohidasvanshi, Valmikis, Vanakars, and Marus. These *gnats* were controlled by the *pateliya*, or middlemen, who placed themselves in positions of power by economic means, gifts of gab, or coercive abilities through criminal links. The head of the *pateliya*, called *kotwal*, obtained office through initiative and enterprise and his duty was to summon the *gnat*, declare decisions on internal disputes and play the master of the ceremonies on festive occasions. These positions were not hereditary but were open to power bids among members.[34] Some *pateliya* gave regular feasts to fellow members, some ruled by coercion and often extorted money from fellow caste members or *panch* by insisting on giving judgments on matters of marriage and divorce. The groups had multiple centres of power, excommunication of members was disallowed, and members routinely disobeyed their decisions without social sanctions. During this time, a woman wishing for a divorce would inform two relatives about the intention to secure divorce. They would call a meeting of the *pateliya*, and her father would deposit money toward the expenses of assembly and each person would receive fees and give the verdict. Women did not officiate in these meetings. In this context, the reformist youth,[35] from within these loose groups, along with other modernists from within the group, sought to build a caste, reduce the power of *pateliya*, and codify customs and rituals and laws of varied groups. After a failed attempt to create a caste council and to build a caste in 1935,[36] in 1953, about 10,000 men and women gathered in a public meeting lasting for two days in order to approve the first "caste constitution" of the Meghwal *samaj* (collective). The caste constitution of 1953 defines the caste of "Meghwals" as a group that follows the rules of marriage codified through the consensus of its members and that abides by rules of its caste council (panchayat). The spirit of the caste constitution was to be actualized by the formation of a caste council, which was envisaged as a democratic governing body of the caste.[37]

The caste constitution of 1953 remained "consensually and wilfully silent" (samajpurvak samuhik maun)[38] regarding the religious membership of those who chose to be included in the caste of Meghwals. One reason was historical precedent. In 1935, a group of workers had attempted to form a caste panchayat in order to create a caste and that move was rejected by the majority of workers. A primary reason being that the brief outline of the caste constitution made Hinduism the membership criteria for inclusion in the caste.[39] It stated that men and women who classified themselves as "Hindus" would be eligible to vote and also that literate members of high moral calibre, willing to identify as Hindu, who had not been reconverted to Hinduism could contest elections (The Report of Sri Lakshmi Narain Temple 1935, 23–4). The fusing of religious and caste membership criteria went against the actual practices of many caste members who were converted to and/or practiced Islam and Christianity and also worshipped plants and animals, saints, ghosts, spirits and *pirs*, as well as a range of Hindu gods and goddesses. This religious eccelectism continued in the 1950s. Besides, many caste members also felt that they had more to gain socially, economically, and spiritually by aligning themselves with Christian missionaries and Islamic sects rather than classifying themselves as Hindu (Mehta 1936).

In addition, in the 1950s, the reformist youth were aware that the attempt to centralize caste authority would be challenged by the *pateliya* and *kotwals* on the ground and they could not alienate these sections as well as groups that did not wish to subordinate their own customs and rituals under the broad umbrella of the Meghwal caste. They also made the provisions and process inclusive to increase the numbers and to prevent alienation. As one of the pamphlets (*aelan*) stated: "Caste unity and progress through (the virtues of) compromise, conciliation, and accommodation [*samadhan*] of all group members are primary goals of this caste constitution. This caste constitution will be sensitive to beliefs, rituals, laws, and practices of all members of people who join the caste of Meghwals"[40] (Unpublished Handbill, 11 December 1953, Meghwal Central Panchayat). Thus divisive issues were avoided and as a result, the constitution, as a form of rule by omission, observed "public silence" (*jaher maun*) on the contentious matter of the religious identity of its "caste" and validated the heterodox identity of its members. The meaning of religious identities in caste laws contrasted sharply with the state construction of religious identity of subjects governed by Hindu law enacted in 1955. However, the provisions of state law did not penetrate on the ground between 1950–70. In legally plural societies, different conceptions of law exist simultaneously; state and societal laws can overlap or intertwine, or cohabit in distinct and parallel normative universes in the same socio-legal sphere. These two moments of caste formation demonstrate that caste laws were cordoned off from state laws as provisions of state laws were not discussed in varied forums and concerns of harmonizing state and caste laws were not even considered during this time.

How did the caste constitution structure and regulate conjugality and construct legal subjects? The constitution codified and established a common set of shared norms to judge personal and group conduct during rituals, domestic life, and matters concerning shared living among a set of group members. The caste constitution held marriage without economic transaction as "an ideal type marriage" but recognized custom of bride price as a common practice and sought to standardize and regulate the amount. Child marriage was discouraged, but allowed in exceptional circumstances. The caste laws recognized both cohabitation and marriage, and different types of marriage were legally validated – the ritually sanctioned first marriage, the second marriage by elopement between married and/or unmarried lovers, marriage by insistence (a woman falling in love with a married or unmarried man could insist on living with him and his family and be recognized as his wife) (*Sri Meghwal Gnati Bandharan* 1953, 1, 7–11). Marriage and engagements were sealed by negotiations over bride price, a transaction between the marital family and the natal family. The natal family members received bride price at the time of engagement and marriage. Besides, almost all the transactions of bride price were between husbands and women's natal families: "There were times when decisions about first or second marriages of women were made in arrack shops by their husbands and families. Women's opinions were taken in many cases, but sometimes they were contracted to a man who could pay a higher brideprice and this custom had to be regulated" (Interview with Vishrambhai Waghela, 12 January 2003, Mumbai).

Divorce was quite common and the 1953 constitution recognized several kinds of divorce: divorce due to husband's fault (the husband's family in this case would return bride price), divorce due to wife's fault (the husband's family would not return the bride price), divorce due to mutual culpability (the bride price would be split). The grounds for divorce were mental illness, impotency, and "general unhappiness"; the caste also recognized mutual incompatibility as a ground for divorce. The caste laws also granted divorce by mutual consent, in such cases, the husband's family would pay back the bride price and the wife's family would pay taxes to the caste council and fees to the mediators. The constitution acknowledged that the recognition of fault by either party in practice would result in further negotiations around the exchange of bride price and the constitution standardized this amount (*Sri Meghwal Gnati Bandharan* 1953, 7–12). Each case of divorce was to be registered with the caste council and the parties were to pay a tax to the caste council and to the *pateliya*.

The constitution recognized polygyny under certain conditions, in cases of sterility but not before the elapse of five years, and could only be contracted with the consent of the first wife. The bride price was even higher in case of polygyny (equivalent to two years' salary of an individual sweeper) and served as a deterrent. Public opinion was also against polygyny and it was not a controversial issue as divorce was easily obtained (*Sri Meghwal Gnati Bandharan* 1953, 7). Another type of polygyny was practiced, usually in the form of levirate – older widows facing extreme economic hardship and living without shelter were "married," symbolically, to male members of their immediate or extended family so that their "husbands" and families could ensure their security in old age (*Sri Meghwal Gnati Bandharan* 1953, 6). Thus, the constitution also endorsed the authority and guardianship of male members of the family over women members.

The caste constitution recognized "separation due to incompatibility" (*resamanano samay*) and the husband in such cases remained financially responsible for the wife and the children's everyday expenses as well as extraordinary expenses (such as expenses due to illness). A woman who had been separated for more than six months could obtain a unilateral, ex-party divorce and claim bride price and expenses during separation. The husband did not have the right to reciprocal divorce, especially when a woman was a child bride or when she had young children (*Sri Meghwal*

Gnati Bandharan 1953, 10–11). The mother was the natural guardian of the child and had the custody of children for the first six years. The father could reopen the issue of custody when the child became an adult and make a payment to the mother of the child for the years that she, her family, or her partner raised the child (*Sri Meghwal Gnati Bandharan* 1953, 8). Thus, caste laws in 1953 protected women's rights in laws. In many instances, provisions regulating marriage and cohabitation recognized the choices of women, but they were not envisaged as individuals and equal agents uniformly across caste laws. While women were sometimes seen as choice-making subjects, pursuing their desires and preferences, at times, some choices were also decided for them. While their rights were safeguarded in law, their will was, at times, compliant with and subordinate to the will of the natal family, though not always to the marital family. They were placed under the guardianship of male relatives and husbands.

Since the 1950s, the caste members have further organized as public sector workers and developed links with political parties and trade unions.[41] The caste also had a rich civic sphere, public intellectuals were invited in varied discussion forums, and from 1950s onwards, the Meghwal caste members organized various activities at the local level, such as cricket clubs, blood-donor clinics, public health awareness programs, drama clubs, discussion groups, poetry-reading sessions, *bhajan mandalis* (devotional groups), youth clubs, literacy classes, the publishing of several magazines, and the celebration of festivals. Since 1974, the Dalit Panthers began to mobilize a small section of caste members, especially the youth. Wary of the glass ceiling within the Congress Party, a few militant young caste members abandoned the Party and became members of the Dalit Panthers during this time. They were attracted to the political ideology as well as the poetry of the Panthers. The existing rich cultural sphere now became more political. Young Meghwal poets and writers began to form reading groups and hold poetry workshops, where they discussed questions of social justice, favoured a secular and rational approach, and challenged the existence of God in various forums (Bipin Gohil, personal communication, 2 February 2003, Mumbai).[42]

REFASHIONING LEGAL SUBJECTS: DEMOCRATIC REFORMS OF CASTE LAWS IN 1974–75

The caste constitution of 1953 was not observed fully in practice, and between 1963 and 1965, another committee formed to discuss its provisions; this time around, though, a separate committee of women was formed to discuss the provisions, keeping in mind the interests of women. These rounds of discussions did not evince the diffusion of state law as these caste-based law reform committees did not seek to harmonize caste laws with state laws. The next round of discussions took place in 1974–75[43] and the constitution adopted and then bridged the gap between the rhetorical and the actual caste panchayat. The constitution process was aggressively reformist; the intent was to create the boundaries of the caste, to abolish the system of middlemen, to ensure the autonomy of the panchayat, to build public consensus around internal governance, to cure indebtedness through social austerity, and to work toward the upliftment of women. The process of reform this time around began with the establishment of an election commission initiated by the reformists within the caste. Taking charge, the election commission publicized the dates of elections and the structure of the local panchayats, invited lists of candidates in each area, and announced the dates and places where the election would take place.[44] The local youth held street corner meetings in each neighbourhood,[45] the prominent caste member union leaders, poets, and social workers made "public requests" (*jaher vinanti*) to members, and areas that had elected the *panch* were facilitated as the model pockets of social reforms.[46] Elections were held and soon after, an interim constitution committee was formed and it began a broad, inclusive process of reform.[47] The process of discussion on the caste constitution was twofold. One set of discussions happened in the civic sphere in the caste, in issue-based committees – in cricket clubs, discussion forums, poetry clubs, cultural troupe meetings, readings classes, devotional groups (*bhajan mandali*), and during union activities. The other set took place in various neighbourhoods or area-based committees – the local *panch* divided the neighbourhood under its jurisdiction and formed residential committees in each *chawl* and rows of slums and discussions were held in public corners of these streets and *chawls*. In the first round of discussions participants offered a set of changes and suggestions that were then written on blackboards outside the *panch* offices or in communal spaces outside local temples, welfare centres, and *chabutara* (meeting places) so that all residential members could read them while passing by. These discussions were structured to include other members, especially the more marginalized and invisible members: special committees of the most vulnerable sections of the caste, like the beggars' committees (*magan varg*), were formed to accommodate their social rituals and rites.[48] These area-based and issue-based committees' recommendations were discussed in a series of public meetings where all committees presented their discussions to the larger "public of caste members" and after that, the constitution committee was then subdivided into special committees (*Vishay Vicharana Committees*) that proposed changes and visited various areas for the second round of discussions on proposed amendments.[49]

Women were actively mobilized and participated in large numbers. Why did women come to the foreground during 1963–65 and especially in the 1970s? The gender gap in education and employment among Meghwals was low and their employment in the public sector also politicized them and they had began to discuss law reforms among themselves. The male reformers also sought to include them because they realized that "women were more likely to support progressive laws as these would benefit them the most" (Circular by the Meghwal Hitvardhak Samaj, 16 June 1975). The process began collectively. The first women's (*nari samaj*) public meeting was called on 17 August 1975 and social workers from Mumbai, prominent caste leaders who were pro-women, and politicians were invited to participate in the meeting.[50] Prior to this meeting, groups of women were divided in many separate issue-based committees: wedding rites and expenses, bride price, various ceremonies, *mameru* (a ceremony where the woman's natal family gave gifts to women), celebration of first pregnancy and gift giving, widow remarriage and levirate, polygyny and second marriage, marriage of unmarried women to older men, love marriage, elopement and divorce, committees concerning widowhood, divorce, desertion, issues of single women (especially those who had separated from husbands), maintenance and custody of children and any issues that concerned women at large. These committees also discussed these provisions with other area-based committees comprising general members over the course of the year and then held a collective meeting to discuss contested issues: marriage and divorce, elopement of a widow and fixing of bride price. The final changes approved by women members of the caste were announced in a public meeting of women that was also attended by reformist caste members and prominent women social workers of Mumbai and was chaired by Devji Khuman.[51]

These processes led to three important changes: the abolition of middlemen by common consensus and the emergence of the caste panchayat as the only legitimate regulator of marriage and divorce, the continued negation of twinning Hindu and Meghwal identities, and the emergence of women as autonomous legal subjects within caste laws. Under the new laws, women, as legal subjects, were not under the authority, tutelage, or guardianship of the natal family or the mediators, but subjects in their own right.

How did the new laws construe religious identities in caste-based family law? While the question of religious identities of Meghwals was shelved in the 1950s constitution, it was widely reflected upon and debated within the group this time around and the new caste laws explicitly delink the caste identities and religious identities. While religious practices on the ground continued to be heterogeneous, the rejection of adopting a Hindu identity this time around was also the result of greater exposure of caste members to unions, the mobilization of the youth by communist parties, and the exposure to social movements and anti-caste discrimination movements such as the Dalit Panthers in Maharahstra.[52] The pro-Congress Party lobby moved a motion to identify the Meghwals as a Hindu caste group in order to challenge the rising influence of the Dalit Panthers within the caste. The move was opposed by the younger, radical members who argued against the motion; these debates rose to the surface in the mid-1970s and became far more contentious later, in the 1980s. For instance, a paragraph from a private pamphlet circulated in the caste group reads as follows: "Brothers, the new Hindus of our caste live in fool's paradise. We live cheek by jowl with Muslims, the first school of our caste was opened in a *chawl* owned by a Khoja Muslim, many of us believe in and practice Islam, some of us are Buddhists, and some of us worship Jesus Christ, many of us are atheists — we will not be forced to become Hindus"[53] (Unauthored Pamphlet, entitled "Force in the Name of Dharma," 17 May 1975). In the end, the conservatives amongst pro-Congress Party factions were deterred from superimposing a Hindu identity on the Meghwals by aggressive public campaigns against this move by the above factions. They complied with the "mood of the general public," and this issue did not, in the end, deter from unifying the caste through constitution making. The amended sections of the caste constitution in 1970s explicitly state that Meghwals do not follow a religion and the Meghwals members have the right to belong to and practice any religion of their choice such as Islam, Christianity, or Buddhism. Any attempt to pigeonhole Meghwals into religious identities is condemnable (*nindaniya*).[54]

On the question of the regulation of marriage and divorce, old traditions were examined and scrutinized and some were discarded.[55] The new caste constitution bans child marriage, upholds consent as the basis of marriage, disallows levirate between parties of unequal age, and bans marriages for higher bride price contracted by family members without the consent of women.[56] The practice of easy divorce and remarriage, and elopements between married and unmarried men and women is allowed to continue, as these are not anti-thetical to the notion of consent. The caste sphere validates the companionate marriage as the ideal-type marriage. "Debates during the making of the 1974–5 constitution converged around one point: bride price does not seal marriage, consent and compatibility (*man ni marji ane melap*) are essential for marriage and that was a big shift toward reforms" (Interview with Manjibhai Khuman, 23 January 2003).

There was a consensus between the proponents and the opponents of reform and women's committees around the question of regulating the misuse of bride price within the caste. For instance, the new caste laws explicitly discourage and ban the marriage between older married or unmarried men with younger married or unmarried women in exchange for a high bride price.[57] In a similar vein, the legal changes demonstrate the emergence of women as autonomous, rational, legal actors within caste laws. For instance, the practice of granting economic protection to deserted or widowed women within the family through symbolic polygyny was discarded and instead, the new caste laws consolidate economic rights of women within marriage and post-divorce. As per new caste laws, women retain control over their independent income, over property bought from that income during the course of marriage, and gifts received at the time of marriage upon divorce or desertion. In addition, they are also awarded a lump sum amount as maintenance during the period of separation and at the time of divorce. Thus, economic transactions approved in marriage and divorce now recognize women as legal subjects and secure the economic rights of women. Women are also the natural guardians of children and the children have a right to maintenance and inheritance from the man that the mother cohabits with, not from their biological fathers.

The new caste laws advocate the return of bride price to the woman at the time of divorce, not to the natal family, and thus delegitimize the control of the natal family over adult women. For instance, there were differing views about bride price among women's committees and the moderates and conservatives.[58] The conservatives wished to retain the higher amount of bride price. They saw it as a buffer against desertion of women and reaffirmed the control of the natal family over women. The reformists wished to abolish any economic transaction at the time of marriage and agreed to standardize the amount as a baseline compromise. They argued that the higher amounts of bride price provided economic security to women but also that the repayment of high bride price militated against speedy divorce and that it increased social indebtedness. The women's committees were divided: they agreed with the higher amount of bride price in the interest of women, but also advocated its regulation.

In the end, the different groups struck a compromise: the amount of bride price was regulated, but families that wished to pay a higher amount would do so with the permission of the local *panch*. In cases where a party was unable to repay the bride price, the divorce would not be delayed, nor would women's rights be bargained away, but the husband's family could pay back the amount of the bride price to the woman in instalments. The local *panch* and two caste members would serve as guarantors to ensure the repayment at later dates.

How do we conceptualize the rise of autonomy among women under caste laws? Understanding the emergence of autonomous Meghwal women in law requires us to revisit the discussion on the gap between accounts of autonomy within liberalism that hold that the concept of autonomy hinges on the idea of a unified, coherent, atomist self that detaches itself from social environment in order to reflect upon its conception of the good, and the feminist and communitarian critics[59] who stress the importance of social relations, values like benevolence, love, as well as of emotions in the constitution of selves and argue that autonomy cannot be conceived without attending to the importance of the social as a constitutive element. Feminist accounts highlight the complexity of the relationship between the individual and the collective. They demonstrate that while autonomy is not independent of collective, the rise of autonomy can also be in tension with collective values, goals, or traditions. Indeed, societies that acquire autonomy and competency collectively and critically evaluate their customs, habits, and traditions. In doing so, they may diverge over the meanings and value of their traditions and the result may be the rupturing of social ties. In such conditions, Friedman (2003) makes a case for balancing a community way of life, preserving the importance of social relationships, and pursuing the ideals of autonomy, though she is mindful of the destabilizing impact of autonomy on social ties. Similarly, Nedelsky (1989) identifies the feminist conceptions of autonomy in tension with, as well as constitutive of, the idea of the collective. She advocates democratic procedures that help to arrive at autonomy, though she also recognizes that democracy may at times deter from autonomy, promote collective violence, and legitimize gender injustice.

The data show that while the collective scrutiny of contentious matters and traditions exposed many ideological and political fault lines and private interests within the caste, ultimately, public debates did not prove to be deeply divisive, and these collective processes consolidated caste identities, delegitimized the power of middlemen, and established the caste council as a governing body. What we find here is that the democratic reform process undertaken by caste members between 1963 and mid-1970s provided women with the procedural means to deliberate and reflect. This process allowed men and women to challenge and remove external barriers to autonomy. While democracy does not guarantee a validation of women's autonomy in law, factors such as the presence of a vibrant internal civic sphere within the caste, the participation of caste members in the public sphere, and their exposure to unions, political parties, especially the Communist Party of India, social movements, especially anti-caste discrimination movements, and Meghwal women's participation in the workforce and exposure to unions and social movements ensured the consolidation of ideas of freedom and equality within the caste. These became shared values of women's committees as well as the reformist sections of the caste and this social milieu enabled moral competency among group members, including women.

What is the relationship between the individualistic subject of law and the social sphere of the caste? The process of law reforms, and, specifically in these two moments of legal reform demonstrates that society is not merely a ground for the individual to flourish, and that individualism corresponds with society's need for cohesion, solidarity, and unity. Furthermore, autonomy is compatible with societal goals of harmony and progress. What we see here is the evolution of an idea of autonomy that values personal freedom, but also stresses social responsibility in relationships. To illustrate, the idea of autonomy validated in caste laws in the 1970s balances between two different commitments: individual freedom, and social cohesion as a collective good. For instance, while caste laws upheld and approved of widowed, divorced, or married or unmarried men and women's right to elope with partners of their choice, they recognized that these eloping members may be primary earners and exhorted the eloping members to consider the economic vulnerabilities of the families they left behind. Rather than constraining caste members' freedom to pursue relationships of their choice, the caste constitution asked them to provide compensation and to continue to maintain and sustain the marital families they abandoned in order to pursue relationships of their volition.[60] This outcome was achieved by reconfiguring the notions of conjugality and family – parties choosing to elope were responsible for providing for their ex-marital family, including in-laws and other dependent members, as well as their current conjugal family. Thus, these caste members challenged external barriers to autonomy by means of the dialogue within the caste, but also recognized that choices of legal subjects are rooted in concrete material realities of family life, and as a result, justice within the family, as a moral-legal guarantee, was encoded in the constitution. The new subject of law that emerged was a socially responsible and autonomy-maximizing individual. The process revealed that the social provides a ground for individuals to flourish. The individual assumes social responsibility to constitute and maintain the social on the basis of ideals of social justice within the caste. Refashioning the notion of conjugality and the extension of the idea of the family becomes a route through which parties balance personal freedom and social cohesion.

To conclude, the chapter argues that under certain conditions, the rights of ethnoreligious groups can be designed and creatively utilized by state and societal actors in ways that enhance gender equality and women's autonomy in law and prevent ossification of group boundaries. The chapter discusses the Indian state's policy of legal pluralism in the governance of the family, which allows adjudication in state courts as well as in societal legal sites. This policy, under certain conditions, legitimizes societal initiatives to create participatory conditions by setting up organizational structures and procedures and by initiating intra-community dialogue about family matters. These societal initiatives create legal/moral ideas about law that are contextual, change over time, and vary in application on the ground. In such a situation, state law coexists with other normative legal orders and the comparison of state-constituted law with caste laws from below reveal the differences and similarities in the legal constructions of religious identities and legal subjectivities under Hindu law. While the state-authored Hindu law cobbles together a religious category that clubs together Buddhists, Jains, and Sikhs as Hindus, but distinguishes Hindus from Christians, Muslims, or Jews, the caste laws see religious identities as mutually non-exclusive forms and disassociate caste and religious identities of legal subjects governed under Hindu law in society. We also find that the question of religious belonging remains a contentious political issue on the ground; religious identities are not always tied to religious practice and are, to some extent, malleable in the hands of varied interests and political agendas of group members at different points in the trajectory of caste formation. Similarly, while the state-authored Hindu law remains ambiguous about according equal agency to women as citizens, under certain conditions, caste laws, through societal processes from below, develop mechanisms to enhance the autonomy of legal subjects and create socially grounded yet individuated and responsible subjects of law.

NOTES

1 Sections of this paper were presented at various conferences, and I have benefitted tremendously from the comments, encouragement, and suggestions
of Itty Abraham, Srimati Basu, Rachel Sturman, Sylvia Vatuk and the two editors of this volume.

2 However, some do not pit group rights against women's rights so sharply in
the debates around religious family laws in India. See for instance, Agnes
1999; Holden 2008; Menski 2003; Mukhopadhyay 1998; Solanki 2011.

3 The term legal pluralism refers to the coexistence of multiple systems of law
at many levels in time, space, and knowledge. In contrast, legal centralism is
the idea that all law emanates from the state and is adjudicated and enforced
by state institutions.

4 Griffiths (1986, 2) defines legal pluralism as "that state of affairs, for any social field, in which behavior pursuant to more than one legal order occurs,"
and describes two types of legal pluralism: the strong variant in which the
state law is one among the body of laws, and the weak variant in which state
law recognizes and checks non-state laws (Woodman 1999). The Indian case
fits into the second typology.

5 The residents of Goa are governed by common civil laws derived from the
Portuguese civil code; Hindus in Kashmir are governed under the provisions
of the Hindu Marriage Act, 1980. In general, all other civil and criminal laws
in India are uniformly applied to all religious groups.

6 Section 29 (2) of the Hindu Marriage Act, 1955 reads: "Nothing contained
in this Act shall be deemed to affect any rights recognized by custom or con-
ferred by any special enactment to obtain the dissolution of Hindu marriage, whether solemnized before or after the commencement of this Act."

7 The panchayat, or council, is a governing body to regulate the internal affairs of the caste. Traditionally, it was presided over by five or more male el-
ders of the caste.

8 Literally, the oppressed; a politically reclaimed self-referential term used by
groups classified as former untouchables under the caste order of the Hindus.

9 This case illustration does not represent an ideal-type, nor is it a generalizable
account of caste making in India. This case is not meant to illustrate that
Dalit families privilege and represent a specific form of conjugal family that
is distinct from the family constructed by other castes. I privilege a construc-
tivist account of caste formation, and see communities as products of human
action, moulded by varied socio-economic and political circumstances.

10 This chapter is based on content analysis of state and societal laws and on the ethnographic research I conducted in multiple legal arenas in Mumbai between June 2002 and August 2003. The section on caste laws and procedures is based on interviews I conducted with the Meghwals. I have relied on oral histories and archival records to trace the history of group formation, law making, and the creation of the adjudicative loci within the caste.

11 The Hindu Marriage Act, 1955 has not been substantively modified since its enactment. An important exception is the 1976 amendment (Section 13 [b] of the Hindu Marriage [Amendment] Act, 1976) in which the state sanctioned divorce by mutual consent. This section is based on the textual analysis of Hindu law.

12 For discussions of Hindu law also see Agnes 1999; Derret 1963; Menski 2003.

13 The issue of evaluating the validity of marriage surfaces in decisions determining the status of existing marriages, void marriages, nullity of marriage, restitution of conjugal rights, polygyny, and maintenance.

14 More recently, the Indian Supreme Court has directed all states to frame rules and regulations to make registration of marriage compulsory (see *Smt. Seema v. Ashwani Kumar* 2006 2 SCC 578.) This chapter however deals with legal developments between the 1950s and the late 1970s.

15 The Section 377 of the Indian Penal Code 1860 criminalized male homosexuality. It reads: "Unnatural offences: Whoever voluntarily has carnal intercourse against the order of nature with any man, woman or animal, shall be punished with imprisonment … and shall also be liable to a fine." However, the Delhi High Court, in a landmark judgment, ruled that this section should be read down and that consensual sex in private between adult same sex partners should not be criminalized under this act (see *Naz Foundation (India) Trust v. Government of NCT of Delhi and others*, WPC No. 7455/ 2011, Date of Decision: 2 July 2009). This judgment has been overturned by the Supreme Court since then (see *Suresh Kumar Koushal and Anr. v. Naz Foundation and Ors.*, Civil Appeal 10972 of 2013). Not withstanding these developments, in rare cases, the courts have held that the marriage between a man or a woman and a transsexual person is valid under the Hindu law, and so is the marriage between transsexuals (Diwan 1985, 107).

16 See Section 5, Hindu Marriage Act, 1955.

17 Sections 5 (1) and 5 (11) of the Hindu Marriage Act, 1955 prohibit polygyny as well as polyandry among Hindus. Bigamy is punishable under Sections 494 and 495 of the Indian penal code.

18 The grounds for divorce under Hindu law include adultery, cruelty, conversion, insanity, prolonged absence, leprosy or venereal disease, continuous absence of consortium, and renunciation of the world.

19 Section 5 (ii) (a) of the Hindu Marriage Act, 1955 requires that a person be capable of giving valid consent to marriage.

20 The punishment for child marriage is INR 1,000 or a simple imprisonment for fifteen days or both.

21 See Dave and Solanki 2001. Rape can technically fall under the definition of cruelty under section 498 (A) of the Indian Penal Code – the law on domestic violence that criminalizes physical and mental cruelty. However, studies show that in practice, this law is not used to explicitly criminalize rape within marriage.

22 See Section 376A, Indian Penal Code: "Intercourse by a man with his wife during separation: Whoever has sexual intercourse with his wife, who is living separately from him under a decree of separation or under any custom or usage without her consent shall be punished with imprisonment of either description for a term which may extend to two years and shall also be liable to fine."

23 See Section 7 (a) of the Family Courts Act, 1984.

24 In 1999, however, the Supreme Court ruled that the welfare of the child was a predominant concern and that the mother could also be the guardian of the child. See Githa Hariharan and another versus Reserve Bank of India and another. AIR 1999, 2 SC 228. However, this chapter focuses on state law developments between the 1950s and the late 1970s.

25 See the Hindu Minority and Guardianship Act, 1956, subsection 6: "Natural guardians of a Hindu minor ... are—(a) in the case of a boy or an unmarried girl—the father, and after him, the mother: provided that the custody of a minor who has not completed the age of five years shall ordinarily be with the mother; (b) in the case of an illegitimate boy or an illegitimate unmarried girl—the mother, and after her, the father; (c) in the case of a married girl—the husband." Marriage is an artificial contractual status, and the husband claims the guardianship of his children due to his legal status in marriage as a citizen. However, the wife cannot claim the same privilege. According to Jacqueline Stevens (1997, 69–70), through the construction of marriage, the state "positions itself as constitutive of intergenerational identities ... by arrogating to itself the authority to distinguish ... what is profane (sex as "fornication," children as "illegitimate") and what is sacred (sex within marriage, legitimate children)" [and thus, construes] women as part of nature and men as part of political society. A child born within the course of a Hindu marriage is presumed to belong to the husband due to his legal-political status as a husband. Thus, the husband is the guardian of a child regardless of biology, while the mother is seen to be the pre-political, natural, and biological parent.

26 State and societal laws can also intertwine or overlap; these two moments of caste formation capture the coexistence of state and societal laws as existing in exclusive and compartmentalized normative universes.

27 It is not my intention to view this caste as an exemplary case but to point to ways in which this group challenges some forms of gender inequality that are formalized in state laws.

28 Many famines ravaged Kathiawar in the nineteenth century; there was a plague epidemic in 1814, the year 1855 was known as the year of the rat menace (*oondariyo saal*) when mysterious sandy coloured rats destroyed the crops. The dockyards in Bombay began to be constructed in 1600s and the shipyard was built in 1735 (Mehta 1936). Morris (1965, 73) explains, "before 1864, untouchables were much less likely to move to Bombay than other groups and that afterwards they tended to move in at a slightly more rapid rates than all other groups combined, at least until 1921" (cited in Zelliot 1995, 60).

29 Women workers' job was to remove human excreta from buckets and carry these on their heads to dispose of it at the nearest depots or wells, which fed into the main sewage. (Interview with Gangaben Bariya, September 5, 2002, Mumbai). The gender specific data from BMC records demonstrate that in 1931, 32,700 Dher and Mahar men and 9,600 women were employed in the BMC (Mehta 1936, 9).

30 A derogatory name to refer to the group of people previously categorized as "untouchables."

31 While the chroniclers of Dalit history show that Maharashtrian Dalits, the Mahars, migrated to Mumbai as communities (Zelliot 1995), it is difficult to conceive this group of workers as a community. Several factors point to this. By 1865, the BMC had expanded its services and hired many workers from the northwest frontier provinces and these did not have untouchable castes (see Crawford 1866, 2, cited in Albuquerque 1992, 197). Bob Mehta, who studied the Meghwals in 1936, points out that the group members had belonged to different castes in Kathiawar, migrated individually, and were unwilling to speak of the reasons for migration. "Some of our caste members also came here because they were excommunicated, others had fled persecution at the hand of the Kings, yet others had escaped jail terms by in the Princely States, and possibly, some had fled after disputes with village notables," (Arvind Boricha, personal communication, 3 March 2003, Mumbai).

32 The *chawls* are 3–4 story buildings, structured like barracks with one small room per family and with common toilet facilities outside the building. Each building housed about eighty-five families.

33 The Mahars were the first group to organize politically. Their enlistment in

the colonial army, employment opportunities outside the village system, access to education through Christian missions, and their own political struggles led by Dr. Ambedkar were some reasons for their organizing through public campaigns such as the burning of Manusmriti, drinking water from upper caste areas, challenging the prohibition of Dalits in public spaces and the temple entry agitations (Zelliot 1995).

34 See Mehta 1936.

35 These youth organizations included groups like Digvijay Sports Club, Jai Hind Sports Club, Navjuvan Sports Club, Harijan Vidyarthi Sangh, Meghwal Seva Mandal, Jai Hind Mandal (see Sri Meghwal Gnati Bandharan 1953, 17).

36 In 1935, the "conservative" elements among clusters of workers who chose to identify themselves as Meghwals or Rohidaswanshis invited workers to "form a caste" as a first step to belonging to Hinduism during the meeting of the Laxmi Narayan Temple. This was fiercely contested on the ground and deep disagreements over the imposition of a unified religious identity, allegations of corruption in the management of the Lakshmi Narayana Hindu Temple, and the lack of "social vision" were three main reasons why the caste panchayat could not be formed in 1935 (see Harijano Matena Laxminarayan Mandir no Aheval, 1935).

37 See Sri Meghwal Gnati Bandharan, 1953.

38 Interview with Vishrambhai Waghela. 16 February 2003, Mumbai.

39 This attempt to classify the Meghwals as Hindus is rooted in the broader political environment of these decades. The colonial state's documentation project of enumeration and classification of ethnic groups "fixed" religious and caste identities; caste hierarchy was seen as central to Hinduism. The nationalists, like the colonial state, saw caste hierarchy as intrinsic to Hinduism, though their resistance sought to challenge colonial sovereignty over the social. Thus, and as a result, the question of caste hierarchy and untouchability was linked to the nationalist project. From 1920s onwards, the Indian National Congress, under the leadership of Mahatma Gandhi, raised the question of untouchability as central to reforming Hinduism and to the creation of "Hindu" as a political constituency (see Cohn 1996; Dirks 2001; Rao 2009). In contrast, the Dalit leader Dr. Ambedkar highlighted the "violence of untouchability" (Rao 2009, 6) and cast Dalit as non-Hindu and a cultural and political minority. Within this broader context, the pro-Hindu faction of these workers was aligned with the Gandhian project and this move was a response to these contestations.

40 See the report of the meeting held at Valpakhadi in Mumbai, 11 December 1953. Handbill no. 7 of 1953. Filed in the Meghwal Central Panchayat Committee.

41 The Congress Party won the BMC elections in Mumbai in 1948, 1952, and in
    1961, and remained a powerful presence in some of the Meghwal-dominated
    residential areas in central Mumbai. In the years following the independence
    of India, the Congress Party had strong ties with the Meghwals: "Even an
    inert object, like a lamppost fielded by the Congress Party would win an
    election from the Meghwal dominated residential areas" (Lalitbhai Waghela,
    personal communication, March 8, 2003, Mumbai). A few Meghwal workers
    were members of the Bombay Employees Union (Bombay Kamghar Union)
    at the time of its inception in 1935, but by 1949, their numbers had grown,
    and about 15,000 members of the Bombay Kamghar Union participated in a
    long strike for higher wages. This labour activism was invaluable experience
    that served to politicize many Meghwal members (Sri Jeevraj Koli, personal
    communication, April 4, 2003, Mumbai.).

42 Gohil's anthology, published in 1992, is titled: "Ughad jevo Ughadato
    manas." (The rising dawn, a stirred consciousness, a new (just) man). The
    Meghwal Dalit poet, Bipin Gohil, came into prominence in the late 1980s,
    though his poetry was read and discussed in the reading clubs in the mid-
    1970s.

43 The round of discussions continued till late 1970s and then picked up again
    in 1980s; another round of constitutional changes were introduced in 1987
    and then in 1993. These discussions are now institutionalized within the
    caste and biannual public meetings are held to discuss issues concerning
    substantive and procedural aspects of adjudication in caste laws.

44 See the undated pamphlet titled Programme and Time Table, signed by the
    election committee: Mr. Mulji Gigabhai Koli (Convenor), Mr. Palji Dafda,
    Mr. Keshav Wagh, Mr. Mulji Gangjee Koli., and Kishor Singh. Document
    60D.

45 The Public Announcement (*dhandhero*) of the Discussions around the New
    Caste Constitution. Unpublished pamphlet, accessed from the central office
    of the Meghwal Panchayat.

46 Internal communication between the interim committee and residential
    (*chawl*) committees. Doc. 29 of 1974, undated.

47 See also the circular of the Meghwal Hitvardhak Samaj, 16 June 1975. This
    committee was formed under the leadership of Mr. P. T. Petal and Mr. Palji
    Bariya. See Mumbai Meghwal Madhyashti Samiti. Doc. 7/1975. Unpublished
    and untitled document accessed from the Meghwal Central Panchayat.

48 See Internal Communication, paper 8/75, 10 August 1975, signed by Devji
    Khuman and Karsan Chauhan. Accessed from Lalitbhai Waghela, former
    member of the Meghwal Constitution Committee, on 15 October 2002,
    Mumbai. See also circulars dated 7 July, and 12 and18 September 1975, stat-

ing, "We have held street meetings in every corner of the Meghwal areas ... in order to propagate the provisions of our caste constitution and to ensure their speedy And proper implementation...Remember! Stop unnecessary expenses, adopt and implement our caste constitution, form a local panchayat in every area, rule democratically through the Panchayat! ... abolish obsolete customs!"

49 See the report by a member, 5 March 1975, signed by Mansur Koli. We had called a meeting to discuss legal changes to caste constitution at a public hall in central Mumbai. We had a very fruitful discussion and many useful suggestions emerged. However, given the level of participation, many questions remain unaddressed. As a result, we would like to call a follow up meeting. The issues for discussions are: matters related to fixed bride price, marriage, divorce, remarriage and death ceremonies.

50 See Doc.9/1975. Mumbai Meghwal Panchayat: Issued-based Committee. Women's Public Meeting (*nari samaj ni jaher sabha*).

51 See Doc.21/1975. Mumbai Meghwal Panchayat.

52 See for instance the poetry written by Bipin Gohil (personal communication, 2 February 2003, Mumbai), a Meghwal poet during this time: "I had written this poem during the discussion on caste constitution in 1970s: For the poor who wander, nomads, is there God?; Centuries of unanswered questions, extreme suffering, will there be God?-At that time, we had a reading club in the caste and we used to meet and some of us used to write poetry and plays. I never imagined publishing it then ... papers were strewn around in my small room in the slum; I threw away so many of these poems."

53 From the pamphlet "Force in the name of Dharma" 17/05/75. In addition, as a caste member, Vishrambhai Waghela stated, "After this conflict (*vivad*) successive caste constitutions have refrained from inserting the clause that classifies the Meghwals as Hindus. While more recently since the 1990s, the rise of Hindu nationalism has vitiated the atmosphere and some caste members have began to call themselves Hindus, they remain marginalized" (Vishrambhaibhai Waghela, personal communication, 3 January 2003, Mumbai.).

54 See Jaher Nivedan. Public Statement. Unpublished and undated document accessed from the central office of the Mumbai Meghwal Panchayat. 17/09/1975.

55 See an undated public pamphlet: "It is necessary to hold public meetings to discuss changes ... and for propaganda. People need to know new laws and assess their impact on out traditions. Besides, these public meetings serve as vehicles to push forth reforms. We need to phase out our socially regressive traditions and replace them with new traditions and these need to be discussed with people at large. We also need to discuss the structure of the panchayat and ensure that it is democratic. We need to generate an environment

wherein our administration is democratic and we are accountable in the collection, maintenance, and use of our social revenue." Signed by Karsan Chauhan and Devji Khuman.

56 See Doc.21/1975. Public Announcement (*dhandhero*) of New Constitutional Changes, 1975, 3–4, Mumbai. Unpublished and undated document accessed from the central office of the Mumbai Meghwal Panchayat.

57 See Doc.21/1975. Public Announcement (*dhandhero*) of New Constitutional Changes. Unpublished and undated document accessed from the central office of the Mumbai Meghwal Panchayat.

58 See the Report of Women's Issue-based (Vishay vicharana) Committee. Doc.3/1975. Unpublished and undated document accessed from the central office of the Mumbai Meghwal Panchayat.

59 See Code 2000; Nedelsky 1989, 2003; Oshana 1998.

60 These additional economic responsibilities were not meant to deter these unions from taking place. Elsewhere, I have demonstrated that between 1975–2003 caste laws have evolved to balance the right to divorce and elopement with the runaway parties' responsibility towards the marital family in caste laws and practice (see Solanki 2011). The seed of this compromise was planted in this process undertaken between 1974–75.

REFERENCES

Agnes, Flavia. 1999. *Law, Gender, and Inequality: The Politics of Women's Rights in India*. Delhi: Oxford University Press.

Albuquerque, Teresa. 1992. *Bombay: A History*. New Delhi: Roshana/Pramila.

Basu, Srimati. 1999. *She Comes to Take Her Rights: Indian Women, Property and Propriety*. Albany: State University of New York Press.

Chowdhry, Prem. 2004. "Private Lives, State Intervention: Cases of Runaway Marriages in Rural North India." *Modern Asian Studies* 38 (1): 55–84.

Code, Lorraine. 2000. "The Perversion of Autonomy and the Subjection of Women: Discourses of Social Advocacy at the Century's End." In *Relational Autonomy: Feminist Perspectives on Autonomy, Agency, and the Social Self*, edited by Catriona MacKenzie, and Natalie Stoljar, 181–209. Oxford: Oxford University Press.

Cohn, Bernard. 1996. *Colonialism and Its Forms of Knowledge: The British in India*. Princeton: Princeton University Press.

Cook, Rebecca, ed. 1994. *Human Rights of Women: National and International Perspectives*. Philadelphia: University of Pennsylvania Press.

Crawford, Arthur. 1866. "Annual Report of the Municipal Commissioner of Bombay." Report submitted by Mr. Arthur Crawford, Municipal Commissioner for the City of Bombay.

Dave, Anjali, and Gopika Solanki. 2001. *Journal from Violence to Crime: A Study of Domestic Violence in the City of Mumbai*. Mumbai: Tata Institute of Social Sciences.

Derret, J. D. M. 1963. *Introduction to Modern Hindu Law*. Bombay: Oxford University Press.

Dirks, Nicholas. 2001. *Castes of Mind: Colonialism and the Making of Modern India*. Princeton: Princeton University Press.

Diwan, Paras. 1985. *Modern Hindu Law*. 6th ed. Allahabad: Modern Book House.

Friedman, Marilyn. 2003. *Autonomy, Gender, Politics*. New York: Oxford University Press.

Griffiths, John. 1986. "What Is Legal Pluralism?" *The Journal of Legal Pluralism and Unofficial Laws* 24: 1–55.

Harijano Matena Sri Lakshmi Narain Temple no Report. 1935. 23–4.

Holden, Livia. 2008. *Hindu Divorce: A Legal Anthropology*. Aldershot: Ashgate.

Kapila, Kriti. 2004. "Conjugating Marriage: State Legislation and Gaddi Kinship." *Contributions to Indian Sociology* 38 (3): 379–409.

Mehta, B. H. 1936. "The social and economic conditions of the Meghwal Untouchables of Bombay City (with special reference to the community centre at Valpakhadi)." Parts I (volumes i and ii), II and III. Unpublished M.A. thesis submitted to School of Economics and Sociology. University of Bombay.

Menski, Werner. 2003. *Hindu Law: Beyond Tradition and Modernity*. New Delhi: Oxford University Press.

Moghadam, Valentine, ed. 1994. *Identity Politics and Women: Cultural Reassertions and Feminisms in International Perspective*. Boulder: Westview Press.

Morris, Morris David. 1965. *The Emergence of an Industrial Labor Force in India*. Berkeley: University of California Press.

Mukhopadhyay, Maitreyi. 1998. *Legally Dispossessed: Gender, Identity and the Process of Law*. Calcutta: Stree.

Mulla, Dinshah. 1966. *Principles of Hindu Law*. Bombay: N.M. Tripathy.

Nedelsky, Jennifer. 1989. "Reconceiving Autonomy: Sources, Thoughts, and Possibilities." *Yale Journal of Law and Feminism* 1 (1): 7–36.

– 2003. "Laws, Boundaries, and the Bounded Self." In "Law and the Order of Culture," special issue, *Representations* 30: 162–89.

Nijjar, Manjit Singh. 1994. *Nullity of Marriage Under Hindu Law*. New Delhi: Deep and Deep.

Nussbaum, Martha, and Jonathan Glover, eds. 1995. *Women, Culture and Development: A Study of Human Capabilities*. Oxford: Clarendon Press.

Okin, Susan. 1999. "Is Multiculturalism Bad for Women?" In *Is Multiculturalism Bad for Women?*, edited by Joshua Cohen, Matthew Howard, and Martha Nussbaum, 7–26. Princeton: Princeton University Press.

Oshana, Marina. 1998. "Personal Autonomy and Society." *Journal of Social Philoso-phy* 29(1): 81–102.

Parashar, Archana. 1992. *Women and Family Law Reform in India: Uniform Civil Code and Gender Equality*. New Delhi: Sage.

Parashar, Archana, and Amita Dhanda. 2008. *Redefining Family Law in India: Es-says in Honour of B. Sivaramayya*. New Delhi: Routledge.

Parry, Jonathan. 2001. "Ankalu's Errant Wife: Sex, Marriage and Industry in Con-temporary Chhattisgarh." *Modern Asian Studies* 35 (4): 783–820.

Phillips, Anne. 2007. *Multiculturalism without Culture*. Princeton: Princeton Uni-versity Press.

Rajan, Rajeswari S. 2003. *The Scandal of the State: Women, Law, Citizenship in Post-colonial India*. Durham: Duke University Press.

Rao, Anupama. 2009. *The Caste Question: Dalits and the Politics of Modern India*. Berkeley: University of California Press.

Ray, Tinku. 2007. "Indian Wedding Registration Ruling." *BBC News*. Last Modi-fied October 25, http://news.bbc.co.uk/2/hi/south_asia/7062098.stm.

Solanki, Gopika. 2011. *Adjudication in Religious Family Laws: Cultural Accommo-dation, Legal Pluralism, and Gender Equality in India*. New York: Cambridge University Press.

Sri Meghwal Gnati Bandharan. 1953. Unpublished Document. Mumbai.

Stevens, Jacqueline. 1997. "On the Marriage Question." In *Women Transforming Politics*, edited by Cathy Cohen, Kathleen B. Jones, and Joan Tronto, 62–83. New York: New York University Press.

Sugarman, David, ed. 1983. *Legality, Ideology and the State*. New York: Academic Press.

Woodman, Gordon. 1999. "The Idea of Legal Pluralism." In *Legal Pluralism in the Arab World*, edited by Baudouin Dupret, Maurits Berger, and Laila Al-Zwaini, 3–20. Boston: Kluwer Law International.

Zelliot, Eleanor. 1995. "Learning the Use of Political Means: The Mahars of Ma-harashtra." In *Caste in Indian Politics*, 5th edition, edited by Rajni Kothari, 27–65. Hyderabad: Orient Longman.

Legislation

Family Courts Act, 1984.
Hindu Adoptions and Maintenance Act, 1956.
Hindu Marriage Act, 1955.
Hindu Minority and Guardianship Act, 1956.
Indian Penal Code, 1860.

Conclusion

SONIA SIKKA AND LORI G. BEAMAN

We take the opportunity in this conclusion to draw out some of the broader implications that have emerged from these chapters for managing religious diversity as relevant to the cases of Canada and India, to reflect on what may be learned from comparing the two nations, and to identify areas that need further research. Let us return to the questions posed toward the end of our introduction, and ask how we might answer them in light of the foregoing analyses and reflections.

The first question we raised was: What are the principles of political secularism, and do they conflict with the recognition of religious identity within a multicultural framework? In retrospect we can see that the segregation of secularism into political, social, and institutional segments may be of limited use. First, as we pointed out in the introduction, the separation of church and state in Western nations is made complex by the differences between doctrinal pronouncements and what happens on the ground. Further, as Beyer's chapter makes clear, the relationship between church and state is dynamic, shifting and changing over time, taking shape according to social and cultural variables. Here, though, we pause to consider the sort of critical self-reflection that a comparative anlaysis with India requires, and which has been, for the most part, only superficially engaged with in scholarship. Western scholarship has focused on the idea of church-state relations as a beginning place for analysis of religious freedom and religion in society generally. But, the notion of "church" has little purchase in the Indian context, and simply changing the words to "religion and state" would not quite meet the sort of conceptual renovation that a deep engagement with the comparative enterprise requires. Bhargava's idea of principled distance, then, requires a drilling down into the fabric of Indian society to reveal the multiple ways in which such an idea plays out in the messy contours of day-to-day life. This is also in large measure the contribution of Deepak Mehta's detailed discussion of law's response to the Ayodhya dispute. Although Mehta focuses on the legal process, we can begin to see through this discussion the ways in which the relationship between the state and religion plays out both in civil society and social institutions. In fact, Mehta's contribution pushes us to ask questions about the boundaries between these categories and about the ways in which their construction reflects particular power relations. And, of course, even when particular religious hegemonies exist, there is resistance to them that may shift the status quo. In other words, the re-deployment and re-constitution of the status quo is met with resistance from groups who, through their resistance, may eventually reshape the status quo itself. One would not wish to be unduly optimistic, but awareness of the influence of hegemonies, indeed their very naming, can at least begin the process of reconstitution.

As a number of the chapters in this volume demonstrate, acknowledgment of the power of religious histories can dramatically shape the ways in which the religious present is understood, and pragmatically affect responses to religious diversity at all levels of society. Thus, Lefebvre's contribution illuminates the influence of the Roman Catholic history of Quebec, and points to the paradox of preserving that history through a crucifix on the walls of the National Assembly at the same time as Quebec moves toward a model of secularism that resembles French laïcité. This paradoxical state of affairs is not unique to Quebec, and illustrates the importance of our project more generally, which seeks to reflect on the complexity of responses to diversity. The paradox of denial and reinforcement of religious hegemony is manifest in the case of China as well as India. While such a broad comparative statement may seem overly general, in our opinion there is a dire need for scholarship that moves into comparative analysis. The end result may be the confirmation of difference, or the affirmation of limited commonalities. To be sure, we are not seeking universal formulae or approaches to religious diversity. Rather, we are interested in exploring the varieties of approaches to secularism, whether the disestablishment of the United States, the ambiguous constitutional arrangement of Canada, or the Indian model of engagement with religion. With this knowledge in hand we can begin to raise questions about justice and fairness in new ways.

Most urgently, we argue that it is time to move beyond standard generalizations to undertake a critical engagement with approaches to religious diversity in order to identify profound injustices. Thus, for example, Laliberté's chapter engages with the China "problem" in a refreshing way that is both critical yet considered. Laliberté introduces the possibility that much of the standard analytical tool kit we use to assess responses to religious diversity may not work especially well for the Chinese case. The discourse of multiculturalism, for example, does not work in this context. However, as European rejection of multiculturalism becomes more pronounced, we are pressed to ask questions about the move toward a valorization of "our culture" that may well resemble the Chinese approach. And where, then, we wonder, does India fit in this discussion? Puri's exploration of Gandhi's model of the engagement of politics and religion offers some insight into possible alternative directions that force an open engagement with "the good" rather than the application of a model that is presented as neutral but that loses, in this very representation, its credibility. In other words, the claim to neutrality should be subject to scrutiny as an impossibility. Instead, as Puri suggests, discussion and negotiaton of what constitutes the good is essential. How, though, to engage in these explorations of the "good"? These are the sorts of exploratory questions for which we hope we have laid some groundwork in this volume.

Another question raised in our introduction was: What is required for the appropriate inclusion of religion within the paradigm of multiculturalism? There is no one single model of multiculturalism, of course; the basic commitment to some kind(s) of political recognition of group identity that defines multiculturalism can be interpreted and implemented in a myriad of ways. The groups to which such recognition may be extended are also not fixed, but subject to ongoing negotiation, as Gurpreet Mahajan points out in her chapter. Acknowledging that multiculturalism, in its original incarnation and development, was not intended to cover religious identities, she notes that in fact religious communities have employed multicultural arguments to support their case for protection and accommodation of their difference. Moreover, while the political accommodation of group identity has often been criticized, in both India and Canada, Mahajan points out reasons why the available alternatives – principles focused purely on equality, for instance, or on the protection of individual conscience – are insufficient for genuinely accommodating religious difference. What Canada can learn from the Indian approach, her analysis suggests, is that genuine respect for religious diversity requires providing space for the public articulation of religious identities. Mahajan notes that the emphasis placed in India on respect for communities has been accompanied by a relative neglect of individual liberty, a serious failing that needs to be remedied. But it is not obvious that these two principles come into serious conflict in relation to the issues that have in recent years caused so much anxiety in Canada and other Western nations: the public display of religious markers, signs, and symbols, or the building of places of worship or public prayer or accommodation for non-Christian religious holidays. It remains an open question whether these anxieties are primarily related to religion as such, or to the religions of "others" perceived as profoundly different. One suspects that the latter is at least an important factor. In that case, India's long history of dealing with deep religious diversity, to which Bhargava and Mahajan make reference, can provide some important lessons, and multiculturalism, with its emphasis on recognizing and respecting diversity is the appropriate model to pursue.

But in what form? Much of the concern about multiculturalism these days revolves around the worry that it encourages the formation of rigidly separate communities that do not interact with one another. An additional common worry is that multiculturalism implicitly endorses relativism, the view that all beliefs and practices are equally good, which would rule out the possibility of evaluation and criticism. These worries can only be exacerbated by the inclusion of religion within the identities recognized by multiculturalism, given widespread suspicions about the dangerously dogmatic and irrational character of religious beliefs in particular.

Sikka has these concerns in mind when she argues in favour of providing public education about religion in religiously plural societies, in a manner that encourages knowledge and discussion about different religious traditions, as well as critical theological and ethical reflection. This is an area in which, Sikka suggests, India can learn from Canada, and specifically from the principles on which Quebec's Ethics and Religious Culture (ERC) program are founded. The design and implementation of education about religion is, to be sure, no easy task. This is especially the case in India, where the subject of religion can easily provoke violence (often through the manipulation of actors with political or other power-based agendas), and where the provision of even a basic level of education for all citizens remains an enormous challenge. There are obstacles in Canada, too, of course, in the form of opposition by denominational groups and non-religious persons, as is evident from reactions to the ERC program in Quebec. Designing the curriculum for such programs of education, moreover, is a complicated and fraught business, and debates continue about what is the right level at which to introduce compulsory education on this topic. These topics require further research and investigation, but it is important to find ways to educate citizens in countries like Canada and India about the multiple religious traditions to which they and their neighbours subscribe. A further benefit of such education is that it can help to counteract the artificial freezing of religion as a marker of exclusivist identity, and the related (historically false) view that religious beliefs are by their very nature insusceptible to reasoned evaluation and revision.

Allowing religious discourses and perspectives within public dialogue also serves these ends, as well as being desirable for other reasons. Ashwani Peetush points out that the distinction Rawls draws between "political" and "comprehensive" reasons is not neutral in practice, as excluding comprehensive reasons, including religious reasons, from public discussion and debate inevitably disadvantages the perspectives of minorities. It also shuts out significant moral resources, as Peetush and Mayaram note with reference to the relation between human beings and the land within the religio-cultural imaginaries of indigenous/tribal peoples in Canada and India. In addition, Peetush rightly stresses the need, in the long term, to works toward a real moral and political consensus, at both the domestic and the global levels, where doing so requires engagement with substantive ethical, metaphysical, and religious views.

These arguments for permitting religious discourse, including the presentation of religious reasons, in the public sphere are equally valid in the contexts of Canada and India. This issue about the place of religious reasoning in public reasoning, much discussed in North American literature on religion and politics, has not usually been connected with multiculturalism. But in fact it needs to be included in discussions about what an appropriate multiculturalism requires, if this model's commitment to respect for diversity is to involve coming to understand one another, as it surely should. There are risks, admittedly, and some constraints may need to be imposed on religions as they are on other forms of speech, depending upon the dangers in a particular context. In India, for instance, there are restrictions on appeals to religion that promote enmity between groups in the course of electoral campaigns. "Public reasoning" is a broad category, moreover, comprising discussions in parliamentary debates, comments and speeches by both political and religious actors, and the language and modes of reason employed in judicial decisions. These will need to be assessed separately in normative analyses, in each case balancing the reasons for favouring inclusion of religious reasoning and expression against the risks of excessively inflammatory and divisive rhetoric. There is no simple formula here, for either Canada or India, but the chapters in this volume make a strong case against the principled exclusion of religion from public life, and suggest that such exclusion undermines the goal of achieving the kind of mutual understanding and convergence on essential matters that is crucial for long-term social harmony.

Yet one does have to ask whether all forms of religious belief are compatible with this goal, or whether there are some that are so profoundly at odds with it and with other basic commitments of multiculturalism that they should not be eligible for the forms of recognition and support that multicultural policies typically extend to groups. Davis' chapter raises this issue in relation to religious groups whose belief structure includes the belief that members of other groups are excluded from salvation. While one would have to be careful in drawing conclusions about behaviour directly from such beliefs, examining the available empirical evidence, Davis' chapter does raise an important issue. Expanded to include religious groups, multicultural recognition requires considerably more from the state than do policies grounded in respecting freedom of conscience. Should states extend such recognition to groups whose beliefs promote dispositions that are disrespectful of people with other religious affiliations, rejecting precisely the respectful relations between diverse groups that multiculturalism takes as its aim? A related empirical question is whether nations culturally shaped by religions that have been exclusivist form less hospitable bases for respecting religious diversity than do nations whose dominant religious traditions have been more pluralistic. These questions have serious ramifications for the development of multicultural policies extending to religion, and they are not easy to answer. Advancing hypotheses in response to them here would be premature; they indicate avenues where further comparative research is needed.

We asked also how the existence a majority religion in a nation impacts on the state's decisions, and those of communities attempting to negotiate their religious identities in relation to the state. A number of our authors reflected on the impact of majority religious presence and history, including its influence on the ways in which communities negotiate their identities. The acknowledgement of the presence of religious majorities is fraught with complication – as religious landscapes change, religious majorities sometimes become defensive and unwilling to acknowledge their historical if not continuing privilege. This can result in a limited range of possible claims that can be either practically or legally made by minority religious communities.

Especially important in discussions of religious minorities and majorities is paying attention to the tension between historical dominance and present day diversity. Once again, dynamic processes and shifting social landscapes are at play. Conceptually, the dynamic nature of social life presents perhaps the single greatest challenge to understanding the problems we have explored in this volume. Disciplines within the social sciences and humanities often pay lip service to the need to be attentive to the dynamic nature of social life, but analytical engagement with these processes often freezes in time and space. Yet, as Winter points out, religious groups themselves, along with the social processes in which they are engaged and embedded, must be understood as dynamic. The post-Westphalian process outlined by Beyer acknowledges both historical change and the shifting nature of post-Westphalianism itself. Puri's chapter raises the question of what happens if the believer retains the right to make decisions in private. But what if the believer is one of many who make up a majority? At what point does the "private" spill over into the "public" and affect majority-minority dynamics, or, are public and private ever really separate at all? Further, how are these concepts defined in different social contexts? In other words, does the public or private materialize differently in India than it does in Canada?

Whether described as the status quo, hegemony, establishment, or majority, an acknowledgement of past dominance by a religious group or groups is a necessary part of understanding religious diversity in the present. Moreover, as Beaman's chapter indicates, shifting political, legal, and social landscapes mean that response to diversity can change from being based on substantive equality to a much more formal equality approach. These shifts occur often due to a combination of local, national, and global forces. Thus, for example, a focus on securitization has meant that legal responses to a religious minority request have taken a rather sudden and narrow turn in many countries.

How to address power relations between majorities and minorities is an intriguing question, and one not easily answered. One possibility, suggested by Sikka, is to develop religious education programs that can provide the basis for engaged and respectful interaction and understanding. Bhargava's advocacy of principled distance points to the importance of developing principles of engagement which, following from Sikka's approach, begins with an assumption that some religious groups are disadvantaged and may require state intervention. Similarly, multiculturalism may also offer another principle of engagement that sets the stage for respectful negotiation and dialogue.

A final set of questions posed in our introduction concerned the dangers posed by definitions of religious identity for the purposes of legal and political recognition, where one central danger is the possible threat to gender and other forms of intra-group equality.

The latter danger is especially grave in India where, as Mahajan notes, judicial policy in independent India was oriented toward ensuring equality between religious communities, with relatively little attention given to the authority of religion over individuals and to individual liberty. This is not to say that the Indian constitution fails to enshrine respect for individual rights. On the contrary, the wording of many of its articles, including those dealing with freedom of religion and conscience, is directed toward securing the rights of individuals rather than groups. But in practice, legislative and judicial reasoning in independent India has given precedence to recognition of religious communities over the rights of individuals (SriRanjani 2011).

This contrasts sharply with Canada, where courts and lawmakers have been extremely careful to ensure that provisions designed accommodate the distinct beliefs, practices, and ways of life of religious and cultural groups accord with the individual protections set out in the *Canadian Charter of Rights and Freedoms*. Unlike India, the political culture in Canada heavily favours individual autonomy and equality. Perceived threats to these values in the name of multiculturalism provoke sharply negative reactions from large segments of the population, especially when the group being accommodated is positioned as foreign. Witness the public outcry in Ontario over the idea of Muslims being allowed to use an *existing* arbitration act to settle family law matters according to sharia principles (Bakht 2005). Undoubtedly, in certain respects the Canadian approach is more successful than the Indian one in protecting individual autonomy and intra-group equality. However, in practice it can sometimes harm the interests of members of religious groups, including even the most vulnerable members, whose everyday lives are profoundly shaped by their embeddedness within a given religious community.

At the same time, while we may agree that in India greater respect has to be given for individual rights against the inegalitarian practices of religious communities, particularly vis-à-vis women, there are serious obstacles to state-imposed measures aimed at equality. The employment of principled distance that Bhargava describes as a virtue of the Indian model has been compromised by the need to be sensitive to the fears and insecurities of minority communities, in a situation where direct state intervention into the religious affairs of these communities can be perceived as majority domination.

Given these various difficulties and considerations, both nations need to reflect on alternative means of improving the status of women within religious communities fostering intra-group equality more generally.

Here, close study is needed of the ways in which state and religious actors can and do interact to produce particular outcomes for religious individuals and communities, and to the agency of women in such processes. Solanki provides an excellent analysis of how this has worked in a given Indian case, pointing to conditions that enabled women in this case to participate in enacting change, and in producing a "law from below" that prioritizes their autonomy. These conditions included exposure to movements and organizations directed toward social justice, as well as a vibrant civic sphere within the religious group itself. The findings based on Solanki's case study may be generalizable, as she suggests, but more research on different cases in Canada and India would also be helpful in identifying the factors that enhance or diminish the agency of women within community decision-making processes, and promote or retard internal democratization.

Solanki notes that the conditions described in her study have also helped enable members of this community to resist the imposition of rigid categories of definition by the state and to craft hybrid religious identities for themselves. Thus, Solanki's analysis points out some means by which another serious hazard of the political recognition of group identities – the production and enforcement of essentialist categories of group identity – may be resisted and countered. The chapters in this volume by Mayaram, Mukherjee, and Vallely nicely highlight aspects of this hazard through an examination of instances where it has been realized in India. The two instances on which Mayaram focuses, Kashmir and the Dongaria Kondh tribal community, reveal the violence done to people's lives by state policies based, in one way or another, on division and recognition according to preconstituted and mutually exclusive categories of religious identity. While these cases are specific to India, the larger concerns Mayaram raises are not. Interpreted and applied in a certain manner, multiculturalism can lead to "de-cosmopolitanism," where "cosmopolitanism" refers to processes and habits of interaction favouring fluidity across indefinite and constantly shifting identity borders. Moreover, recognition extended to religion does tend to leave out of account communities whose beliefs and ways of life do not fit the categories of "world religions."

Mukherjee's chapter shows how liminal sects like the Sahebdhani, who challenge boundaries between Hindu and Muslim, are also left out of account by policies of recognition. Her study, like Mayaram's, points to the potentially tragic consequences of such recognition. Vallely's chapter on the functioning of identity politics within contemporary Jain self-constructions invites us to consider the role of relative power and historical grievance in quests for identity recognition. These quests, Vallely points out, are often not about self-definition in terms of existing characteristics. Rather, they seek to stake out a position within the political arena of recognition, as reflected in the varying alignments of contemporary Jain sects.

These chapters are ostensibly descriptive, but they contain a critical and normative element as well. If we find positive religious, moral, and social value in religious cosmopolitanism, in the expansive ecumenism of sects like the Sahebdhani, and in the indifference to identity categories of Jains at an earlier time in history, then we must not allow the politics of identity to monopolize the spaces in which religious conceptions of self and other are negotiated. It may be that here, too, state policies on their own cannot solve the problem. We may need to examine and nurture other spheres in which religious identity is expressed and reflected upon: literary and aesthetic works, forums for inter-faith dialogue, and public media, to name just a few sites.

Thus, although this volume has focused primarily on the state and its role in responding to diversity, many of the studies and analyses presented here point to the limits of constitutions, laws, and courts in bringing about social harmony across religious differences, and in ensuring the protection of vulnerable minorities. We see, for example, the extent to which law and social policy in both Canada and India inevitably reflect majoritarian attitudes and fears, however many legal and constitutional protections there might be in the nation. We also see the perverse effects of policies of recognition for religious groups, in cases where these policies incentivize the formation of rigid identities while marginalizing communities that end up being liminal or excluded in relation to the categories recognized by the state.

These difficulties suggest that state responses are only one aspect of a broader conversation that needs to happen. We are convinced of the need to look beyond exclusively state-oriented solutions to the management of religious diversity, to consider the role other levels of society play in fostering respectful, non-violent, and (ideally) welcoming religious relations between religious communities that have come to identify themselves as distinct from one another. This still requires attention to the role of the state, but in its interactions with civil society, religious organizations and individuals, with a view to understanding the way various actors participate in the negotiation of religious diversity. More research is needed, for instance, about how religious and state actors collaborate to create particular models of religious behaviour in various states. It is also worth inquiring further into the kinds of conditions within religious communities that help to foster gender and other forms of intra-group equality, under legal regimes where these communities are granted different forms and degrees of autonomy. Another focus for future research could be the potential role of publicly-funded schools and universities in educating citizens about religion. On this subject, it would be helpful to conduct more detailed work on the feasibility of providing non-sectarian education about religion in different countries, the different forms such education can take, and the possible benefits and hazards. We might also look at other measures that could help to counter tendencies toward exclusive, rigid, and hostile definitions of identity, including ones that draw on the internal resources of religious traditions.[1]

Our hope is that this volume has contributed to building the foundation required to foster such research directions and engage in broader comparative explorations of religious diversity in multicultural societies.

NOTE

1 Some of these subjects were the focus of a follow up seminar held at the India International Centre in Delhi in February of 2013 (see www.livingwithreligiousdiversity.com).

REFERENCES

Bakht, Natasha. 2005. "Were Muslim Barbarians Really Knocking on the Gates of Ontario? The Religious Arbitration Controversy – Another Perspective." *Ottawa Law Review, 40th Anniversary* Summer: 67–82.

SriRanjani, Vasanthi. 2011. "Constitution of Religious Identity: Constituent (Assembly) Debates and Beyond." In *Accommodating Diversity*, edited by Gurpreet Mahajan, 118–39. Delhi: Oxford University Press.

Contributors

PETER BEYER is professor of religious studies at the University of Ottawa, Canada. His work has focused primarily on religion in Canada and on developing sociological theory concerning religion and globalization. His publications include *Religion and Globalization* (Sage, 1994); *Religions in Global Society* (Routledge, 2006); and *Religion in the Context of Globalization* (Routledge, 2013). Since 2001 he has been conducting research on the religious expression of second generation immigrant young adults in Canada. From this research, he is principal author of *Growing Up Canadian: Muslims, Hindus, Buddhists* (McGill-Queen's, 2013).

LORI G. BEAMAN is the Canada Research Chair in the Contextualization of Religion in a Diverse Canada and professor in the Department of Classics and Religious Studies at the University of Ottawa. Her publications include *Defining Harm: Religious Freedom and the Limits of the Law* (UBC Press, 2008); "Is Religious Freedom Impossible in Canada?" (*Law, Culture, and the Humanities*, 2010); "'It was all slightly unreal': What's Wrong with Tolerance and Accommodation in the Adjudication of Religious Freedom?" (*Canadian Journal of Women and Law*, 2011); "Religious Freedom and Neoliberalism: From Harm to Cost-Benefit" (in *Religion and Neoliberal Policy and Governance*, 2012); and "Battles over Symbols: The 'Religion' of the Minority Versus the 'Culture' of the Majority" (*Journal of Law and Religion*, 2012). She is co-editor, with Peter Beyer, of *Religion and Diversity in Canada* (Brill Academic Press, 2008). She is principal investigator of a thirty-seven member international research team whose focus is religion and diversity (religionanddiversity.ca).

RAJEEV BHARGAVA received his BA (Honours) in economics from the University of Delhi and MPhil and DPhil from Oxford University. Currently, he is a senior fellow and director of the Centre for the Study of Developing Societies, Delhi. Bhargava has taught in many universities abroad and has been a visiting fellow at Harvard, Columbia, Belfast, Bristol, and Jerusalem. He has also been a fellow at the Wissenschaftskolleg, Berlin and Institute of Human Sciences, Vienna. His publications include *Individualism in Social Science* (Clarendon Press, 1992); *Secularism and Its Critics*, ed. (Oxford University Press, 1998); *The Promise of India's Secular Democracy* (Oxford University Press, 2010); and *What is Political Theory and Why Do We Need it?* (Oxford University Press, 2010). His contributions to political theory particularly in debates on secularism, constitutionalism and reconciliation between communities, have received international recognition.

GORDON DAVIS is chair of the Department of Philosophy at Carleton University, and author of several articles in political philosophy, ethical theory, and comparative philosophy, including most recently "Traces of Consequentialism and Non-Consequentialism in Bodhisattva Ethics" (*Philosophy East and West*, 2013) and "Moral Realism and Anti-Realism Outside the West: A Meta-Ethical Turn in Buddhist Ethics" (*Comparative Philosophy*, 2013). He is currently working on several projects regarding conceptions of human rights, mutual respect, and inter-faith respect in Asian religious and philosophical traditions.

ANDRÉ LALIBERTÉ is full professor at the School of Political Studies, University of Ottawa, where he teaches on the politics of China and comparative politics, and research affiliate to the Center on Religion and Chinese Society at Purdue University. He has done research in the People's Republic of China and Taiwan on democratic transition, issues of identity, and the regulation of religion. He has co-edited with Rajeev Bhargava and Bruce Berman *Secular States and Religious Diversity: Toleration and Accommodation* (UBC Press, 2013) as well as articles on the role of religious and philanthropic organizations on the politics of democratic transition in Taiwan and in Cross-Strait relations.

SOLANGE LEFEBVRE is member of the Royal Society of Canada, research chair in Religion, Culture and Society, and professor in the faculty of Théologie et de Sciences des Religion at the Université de Montreal, where she was also the founding director of the Centre for the Study of

Religions (2000–2008). She has been working on religion in the public arena for many years. Her most recent publications include the edited collections *Religion in the Public Sphere: Canadian Case Studies* (with L. Beaman; University of Toronto Press, 2014); *Le programme d'éthique et culture religieuse* (with M. Estivalèzes; Presses de l'Université Laval, 2012); *Les religions sur la scène mondiale* (with Robert R. Crépeau; Laval, 2010); *Le Patrimoine religieux du Québec: Éducation et transmission du sens* (Laval, 2009); and *Cultures et spiritualités des jeunes* (Bellarmin, 2008).

GURPREET MAHAJAN is professor at the Centre for Political Studies, School of Social Sciences, Jawaharlal Nehru University, India. She has published widely on issues relating to cultural diversity and minority rights, secularism, and civil society. Her publications include *Explanation and Understanding in the Human Sciences* (OUP, 1992, 1997, 2011); *Identities and Rights: Aspects of Liberal Democracy in India* (OUP, 1998); *The Multicultural Path: Issues of Diversity and Discrimination in Democracy* (Sage, 2002); and *India: Political Ideas and the Making of a Democratic Discourse* (Zed Books, 2013).

SHAIL MAYARAM is senior fellow at the Centre for the Study of Developing Societies, Delhi. Her publications include *Against History, Against State: Counterperspectives from the Margins* (Columbia University Press, 2003); *Resisting Regimes: Myth, Memory and the Shaping of a Muslim Identity* (OUP, 1997); and she co-authored with Ashis Nandy, Shikha Trivedi, Achyut Yagnik *Creating a Nationality: The Ramjanmabhumi Movement and the Fear of Self* (OUP, 1995). Recent edited volumes are *The Other Global City* (Routledge and Yoda, 2009/2012) and *Philosophy as Samvad and Svaraj: Dialogical Meditations on Daya Krishna and Ramchandra Gandhi* (Sage, forthcoming). She co-edited *Subaltern Studies: Muslims, Dalits and the Fabrications of History*, Volume 12 (Permanent Black, 2005). A forthcoming book is titled *Israel as the Gift of the Arabs: A Tel Aviv Diary* (Yoda). She is interested in the sub-altern pasts and moral imaginations of peasant and pastoral communities, cosmopolitanism and the city, and in *swaraj* in ideas or the enterprise of decolonizing knowledge.

DEEPAK MEHTA is associate professor in sociology at Delhi University. Dr. Mehta's research interests center on the study of material culture, the sociology of Muslim groups in India and the sociology of violence. He has published various articles on Hindu-Muslim violence in India and is presently completing a monograph on the afterlife of the demolition of the Babri mosque in 1992. Publications include: "Words That Wound: Archiving Hate in the Making of Hindu and Muslim Publics in Bombay" (in *Beyond Crisis: Re-evaluating Pakistan*, 2010); *Living with Violence: An Anthropology of Events and Everyday Life* (co-author, 2007); and "Circumcision, Body, Masculinity" (in *Violence and Subjectivity*, 2000).

SIPRA MUKHERJEE is associate professor at the Department of English, West Bengal State University. Her research interests are religion and identity, local cultures, tribal and syncretic religious sects, South Asian literature and European Modernism. Her current projects are on Bengal's Dalit literature and on folklore in East India.

ASHWANI PEETUSH is associate professor of philosophy at Wilfrid Laurier University in Waterloo, Ontario. He has published papers on human rights, cultural diversity, and topics in legal and political philosophy, as well as Indian philosophy. Some of his publications include "Justice, Diversity, and Dialogue: Rawlsian Multiculturalism" (forthcoming); "Indigenizing Human Rights: First Nations, Self-Determination, and Cultural Identity" (in *Indigenous Identity and Activism*, Shipra Press, 2009); "Kymlicka, Multiculturalism, and Non-Western Nations" (*Public Affairs Quarterly*, 2003); and "Cultural Diversity, Non-Western Communities, and Human Rights" (*Philosophical Forum*, 2003).

BINDU PURI teaches philosophy at the Department of Philosophy, University of Delhi. She has recently been appointed as an assistant editor for the journal of philosophy *Sophia*. Dr. Puri is interested in problems of moral and political philosophy and has been seriously engaged in attempts at articulating and recovering the Gandhian legacy. Her recent publications include *"The Importance of Being Reasonable; Interrogating Rawls"* (*Sophia*, forthcoming); *"The Self and the Other: Liberalism and Gandhi,"* (*Philosophia*, 2011); and *"Freedom and the Dynamics of the Self and the 'Other': Re-constructing the Debate between Tagore and Gandhi"* (*Sophia*, May 2012). She is the author of *Gandhi and the Moral Life* (Mittal, 2004), and editor of *Mahatma Gandhi and His Contemporaries* (Indian Institute of Advanced Study, 2001). She co-edited *Reason, Morality and Beauty: Essays on the Philosophy of Immanuel Kant, Volume 1*, and *Terror, Peace and Universalism: Essays on the Philosophy of Immanuel Kant, Volume 2* with Heiko Seivers for Oxford University Press (2007).

SONIA SIKKA is professor of philosophy at the University of Ottawa. Her primary areas of research are philosophy of religion, philosophy of culture, and continental philosophy. In addition to works on Heidegger, Levinas, and Nietzsche, she has written on Johann Gottfried Herder's thought in light of contemporary debates about race, identity, relativism, and multiculturalism. Her current research focuses on aspects of religious identity in a number of countries including India. Recent publications include "Moral Relativism and the Concept of Culture" (*Theoria*, 2012); "The Perils of Indian Secularism" (*Constellations*, 2012); "Untouchable Cultures: Memory, Power and the Construction of Dalit Selfhood" (*Identities*, 2012); *Herder on Humanity and Cultural Difference* (Cambridge University Press, 2011); and "Liberalism, Multiculturalism and the Case for Public Religion" (*Politics and Religion*, 2010).

GOPIKA SOLANKI is associate professor of political science at Carleton University. She is the author of *Adjudication in Religious Family Laws: Cultural Accommodation, Legal Pluralism, and Gender Equality in India* (Cambridge University Press, 2011) and the co-author of *Journey from Violence to Crime: A Study of Domestic Violence in the City of Mumbai* (Tata Institute of Social Sciences, 2001). Her research interests include multiculturalism and citizenship, indigeneity and politics, law and society, religion and politics, and feminist theory.

ANNE VALLELY's work falls within the field of the anthropology of religion, with a focus on South Asian religion, especially that of Jainism. Her research interests include death rituals and mourning, spirit possession, human/non-human boundaries, and religion and animals. Methodologically, she approaches these fields with a particular interest in the aesthetics of religious experience and phenomenology. She is the author of *Guardians of the Transcendent: An Ethnography of a Jain Ascetic Community* (University of Toronto Press, 2002) and *Animals and the Human Imagination* (Columbia University Press, 2012).

ELKE WINTER is associate professor of sociology at the University of Ottawa and research director of the thematic focus Migration, Ethnic Pluralism and Citizenship at the University of Ottawa's Centre for Interdisciplinary Research on Citizenship and Minorities (CIRCEM). Her scholarship is concerned with issues of migration, ethnicity, multiculturalism, and national identity in Canada/Quebec and Europe. Her most recent book, *Us, Them, and Others: Pluralism and National Identity in Diverse Societies* (University of Toronto Press, 2011) deals with the formation of pluralist group identities. It was awarded the Canadian Sociology Association's John Porter Best Book of the Year Award (2012).

Index

9/11, 189, 276, 334

Abdullah, Noman, 279–80
Abdullah, Sheikh, 283–7, 289, 296n9, 297n11
Abdullah, Sheikh Farooq, 286, 289, 297n10
Aboriginal: communities, 155, 157, 160–1; identity, 34, 44, 161; indigenous groups, 282; indigenous people, 4, 55–6, 59, 159, 161, 281, 295, 385; indigenous religions, 7, 126, 129; Royal Commission on Aboriginal Peoples (RCAP), 161; spirituality, 45. *See also* First Nations
abortion, 57, 175, 177, 342
accommodation, 5, 19, 25n5, 26n8, 45, 55, 58–61, 63, 65, 66, 69–72, 72n1, 73n4–5, 74n9, 88, 92, 109, 165, 189, 192, 200, 202, 204, 238, 246–7, 250n6, 254, 261, 311, 338, 344, 361, 383–4; reasonable accommodation, 5, 36, 59–60, 192, 246, 253, 261, 263, 338
acharyas, 320, 322, 329
Adams, Michael, 334–5
Adivasis, 24, 282, 291
Advaita, 98, 312
Afghanistan, 77, 280, 282

afterlife, 175, 185n5
agency, 22, 65, 114–15, 158, 160–2, 208, 212, 256n6, 287, 293, 310, 354–5, 370, 389
agnosticism, 183, 350n10
agnostics, 133, 246–7
ahimsa, 319
Alberta v. Hutterian Brethren of Wilson Colony (2009, Canada), 246–8
Allen v. Renfrew (Corp. of the County) (2004, Canada), 265–6
Ambedkar, Bhimrao Ramji, 291, 311, 359, 375n33, 375n39
ancestor, 100, 123, 127, 134
animals, 158, 160, 165, 193, 319, 360
animism, 293–4
anthropocosmic view, 123, 135
anti-caste discrimination movements, 366, 369
anticlericalism, 80
anticolonial politics, 355
anti-conversion laws, 24
Appiah, Anthony, 16
Archaeological Survey of India, 213
assimilation, 96, 200–1, 337, 339, 348
atheism, 5, 128, 130, 183, 261, 350n10
atheists, 64, 133, 137, 246–7, 261, 366
Ayodhya dispute, 17, 211–15, 222, 228–9,

382; Ayodhya Acquisition Act, 218; *White Paper on Ayodhya*, 218, 222–4, 228

Babri Masjid (BM), 211, 213–18, 220, 225–8, 230n10, 231n16, 231n18, 232n18, 232n23
Bader, Veit, 343
Bairagi Sadhus, 214, 230n6
Bakht, Natasha, 335
Bandyopadhyay, Sekhar, 308–10
Bangladesh, 46, 77, 280, 301, 308
Barry, Brian, 155, 165
Baubérot, Jean, 257, 264, 270n8
Beaman, Lori G., 3, 17–18, 25n1, 236, 267, 269n3, 275, 381, 387
Beckford, James, 8, 10, 239–40
Bengal, 24, 284, 301–2, 304–6, 310, 312, 315n2; East, 311; West, 301, 312, 329
Berlin, Isaiah, 114, 184n2
Beyer, Peter, 11–14, 33, 267, 381, 387
Bhagavad-Gita, 98
bhajan mandala, 363–4
Bhargava, Rajeev, 11, 13–14, 17, 23, 26n17, 76, 107–10, 112–14, 117
Bihar, 226, 233n34, 234, 282, 321
bilingualism, 44–5
Bill 94, 92, 250n6, 350n7
Bissoondath, Neil, 334
Bombay, 358, 374n28; Bombay Municipal Corporation (BMC), 358–9, 347n29, 374n31, 376n41. *See also* Mumbai
Bose, Subhas Chandra, 311
Bouchard-Taylor Commission, 10, 19, 246, 254, 257, 259, 263, 269n3; Report, 12, 19, 60, 70, 256–9, 262–4, 338, 350
boundary: ethnic, 199–201; external, 199–200
Brahmans, 198
British East India Company, 305

Buddhism: Chinese, 126, 130; Japanese, 40; Mahayana monks, 130, 137; Sri Lankan, 40; Thai, 40; Theravada, 130; Tibetan, 130
Buddhist Association of China, 130
burial, 64, 69, 80
burka, 259, 281
Byapari, Manoranjan, 311–12

Canada: Canadian Armed Forces, 240, 249n2; Constitution, *1867*, 65; government of, 161; Multiculturalism Act, 1985, 238; Royal Canadian Mounted Police (RCMP), 55, 259; Supreme Court of, 236–37, 242, 245, 249, 253, 267, 349n5
Canadian Charter of Rights and Freedoms, 1982, 6, 9, 238, 240, 242, 248, 254, 295, 388
Canadian values, 236, 240, 246, 335
caste: caste constitution, 358, 360–4, 366, 369, 376n45, 377n48–9, 377n52–3; caste-councils, 354; discrimination, 310, 359, 366, 369; formation, 354–5, 358, 361, 370, 371n9, 374n26; laws, 354, 358, 361–70, 372n10, 376n43, 378n60; reforms of, 363; reformist youth, 360; scheduled castes, 291, 312; system, 198, 206n7
Carrithers, Michael, 325, 331n6
cemetery, 63, 78, 214
chabutara, 364
Chaitanya, 304–5, 315n6
Chakraborty, Sudhir, 305–6, 315n2
Champion, Françoise, 255, 258
chawls, 358, 364, 374n32
China: Administration of Religious Affairs, 144; Chinese Communist Party (CCP), 120–2, 128–9, 136–41, 143; Committee for the Christian Three-Self Patriotic Movement of Protestant Churches of China, 131; Ministry of

the Interior, 140, 142; Nationalist Party of China, 128; Peoples Republic of China (PRC), 15, 39, 120–5, 129-30, 132–4, 136–7, 139–40, 143, 144n1; Public Security Bureau, 138; Republic of China (ROC), 15, 45, 51, 121–24, 130, 133, 134, 140, 142–5, 144n1, 144n3; United Front, 137

China Christian Council, 131

Chinese Catholic Patriotic Association of China, 131–2

Chinese Catholics, 137

Christian: holidays, 6; missionaries, 304, 310, 360, 375n33

Church of England, 34, 40, 62, 80

Church of Sweden, 40

clergy, 78, 126, 130, 131, 135

closure of social relations, 195–6

collective action, 194, 196, 204, 308

collective discrimination, 197, 204

collective identity, 142, 193–4, 203

collective life, 200, 265

colonialism, 7, 42, 153, 159, 164, 200–1, 206n9, 287, 292

colonization, 195, 199

communal violence, 66–7, 170, 223, 311

community: cultural, 55–7, 174, 184n3; membership, 57; religious, 12–4, 17, 23–4, 25n5, 55–9, 62, 67, 69, 80, 83–4, 97–105, 112–13, 116, 127, 135, 170–2, 174, 179, 182, 185n4, 291, 319, 324, 328, 330, 348, 353, 355, 383, 386, 388, 390–1

Confucianism, 128–9, 132, 135, 137–9

Congress Party (India), 363, 366, 376n41, 359

conjugal family, 22, 354–56, 358, 369, 371n9, 369, 371n9

Connolly, William, 239

conscience: freedom of, 12, 59–60, 65, 67, 142, 155, 265, 337–8, 386; individual, 63, 383; liberty of, 111, 114, 155

conservatives, 366–7

constitutionalism, 107, 155, 294

cosmopolitanism, 16, 23, 276, 281, 389, 390, 395

crucifix, 19, 60, 260, 268, 382

cults, 125, 128, 137, 183

Cultural Revolution, 15, 122, 130, 138, 145n10

customs, 195, 204, 309, 334, 338, 344, 360, 368, 377n48

Dalit Panthers, 363, 366

Dalits, 24, 187n18, 312, 359, 374n31, 375

Das, Raghubar, 214, 220, 229n1

Das, Ramchandra, 215, 299n1

Davis, Gordon, 16–7, 169, 386

Declaration on the Rights of Indigenous Peoples, 2007 (United Nations), 161

deep diversity, 17, 21, 204, 276

deep equality, 18

Delgamuukw v. *British Columbia* (1997, Canada), 161

demography, 11, 127

Denmark, 8, 10, 80

denominational: religions, 39, 106, 110; system, 11, 35

desecularization, 42

desertion, 357, 365, 367

Dher, 358, 374n29

differential treatment, 86–7, 109, 112, 114

diktats, 71

divinity, 175, 276

divorce (India), 362

Doctrine of Order (China), 140

Doctrine of Reason (China), 140

Dongaria Kondh, 289–90, 389

Dravidians, 124, 144n6, 198

Dundas, Paul, 320, 325

Dutta, Akshaykumar, 295n1, 302, 304

Dworkin, Ronald, 86, 109, 113

economic: development, 176, 285, 289; growth/prosperity, 140, 182, 187n18, 298n19; power, 197, 311, 359; rights, 275, 291, 367; stagnation, 182; well-being, 106

education: charter schools (Canada), 181; curriculum (Canada), 174, 344; parochial school/ing (Canada), 254, 260; school system (Canada), 255–6, 263–4, 350n6; teachers (Canada), 255, 339, 341

educational institutions (India), 67–8, 70, 78, 83–4, 291, 326

Eisenberg, Avigail, 56, 65, 349n1

Enlightenment, 63, 85, 103, 110, 112, 116, 198; post-Enlightenment, 108, 111

epochality, 219

equality: formal, 18, 72n1, 78, 155, 339, 387; group, 13, 68–9, 287, 288, 291; individual, 15; of man, 302, 308, 310, moral, 12, 59, 60–1, 69; social, 21, 87, 109; substantive, 18, 245, 287. See also gender equality

eschatology, 175

essentialism, 20, 22, 347–8

ethical norms, 156–7, 163

Ethics and Religious Culture (ERC) program (Canada), 22, 336–9, 344, 346, 349, 349n5, 350n6, 384

ethnic diversity, 190, 203

ethnicization, 193, 195, 202

ethnology, 143

ethnonationalism, 7

Europe: religious biases, 77; secularization, 80, 255

European Court of Human Rights, 18, 246–7

Evangelical Lutheran Church, 62

exclusion: ideological, 21, 320; inclusion/exclusion, 17, 108, 169; mutual, 81, 83, 90, 107; nationalist, 203, 205; one-sided, 79, 83, 85, 107; of religion, 58, 338, 385

exclusionary soteriology, 17, 169–71, 174–6, 178–81, 185n5, 186n11–12, 186n14

face covering, 350n7. See also niqab

Faizabad, Uttar Pradesh, 213–16, 220, 222, 227

Falun Gong, 124–5, 129, 132, 137–8

family: conjugal, 22, 324–6, 358, 369, 371n9; marital, 361, 363, 378n60; natal, 361, 363, 365, 367; religious, 22, 192, 353–5, 371n2

family laws, 22, 353–6, 366, 371n3, 388

Fédération des femmes du Québec, 254

female genital mutilation, 61, 73n9, 191, 240, 250n4

festivals, 5, 99, 115, 172, 191, 305, 363

feudal superstitions, 136

First Nations, 16, 35, 44–5, 153–4, 164, 295, 396. See also Aboriginal

Flügel, Peter, 322, 324

France, 77, 80, 83, 90, 257–8, 264–65, 269, 335

French Canadians, 46, 190, 262

fundamentalism, 6, 77, 180, 199

Gandhi, Mahatma: conception of God, 98; conversion, 110, 115, 117n1; the good life, 101; morality, 98–9, 101, 104, 106; position on secularism, 14; true politics vs power politics, 106

Geelani, Syed Ali Shah, 287, 295, 297n12, 298n20

Gemeinsamkeit, 194

Gemeinsamkeiten, 193

Gemeinsamkeitsgefühl, 194

gender: equality, 12, 22–3, 58–60, 64–5, 70, 72n3, 73n4, 74n9, 255, 353, 355, 370; ethno-gender identities, 22, 353; gender-just laws, 71, 74; inequali-

ty/injustice, 70, 83, 353, 368, 374n27;
role, 22, 353–5
geomancy, 121, 123, 134
Germany, 62, 77, 80
Globalization, 38, 40–1, 77, 156
gnats, 359
Goossaert, Vincent, 121, 131
Griffith, John, 354, 371n4
group formation, 17, 192–95, 200–2,
204, 372n10
group marriage, 356
Gujarat, 89, 277, 282, 321, 329, 358–9

Habermas, Jürgen, 8, 10
Hadj-Abdou, Leila, 241
Hakka, 126, 134
Han Chinese, 124, 131, 144n5
Harijan Sevak Sangh, 359
Harvey, Graham, 293
headscarf. *See* hijab
health care, 11, 59, 157, 175
heritage: military, 249n2; multicultural,
238, 249; religious, 49, 257–60, 263,
265
hijab, 58, 255. *See also* veil
Hindu Adoption and Maintenance Act
(HAMA), 1956, 357
Hinduism, 7, 9, 17, 46, 48, 78, 82, 87,
109, 112–14, 117n1, 118n5, 124–5,
127–8, 139, 174, 185n5, 187n18, 276,
281, 292, 301, 303–7, 313, 315n1,
323–5, 327–31, 360, 375n36, 375n339;
adoption, 357; Brahmins, 303, 305–6;
Hindu gods, 279, 325, 360; Hinduization, 14, 328; marriage, 356–7, 371,
373; nationalism, 44, 377n53; personal laws, 9; shared adjudication, 354–5,
358
Hindu Marriage Act, 1955, 354, 356–7,
371n5, 372n1, 372n16–17, 373n19
Hizb-ul Mujahidin, 287
Hobbes, Thomas, 111, 261

Holocaust, 191
homogenization, 21, 76, 80, 314
honour: killings, 191, 240, 250n4; social,
195, 198
Hui, 126, 131, 137
human dignity, 110, 112, 114, 163
humanism, 110, 166
human rights, 24, 44, 141, 155–7, 159,
162–3, 165–6, 244, 255, 277, 288
Hutterites, 246–8

identity: caste, 309, 312–13; collective
/shared, 142, 193–94, 196, 203; cultural, 5, 34, 67, 164, 290; European, 34;
group, 383, 389; heterodox, 361; linguistic, 313; minoritarian, 197, 199;
national, 5, 44, 190, 245, 262, 313; politics, 21, 199, 318, 320, 330, 389; religious, 3–6, 22–5, 55, 99, 145n9, 180,
190, 192, 316, 329, 330, 354–5, 357–8,
361, 375n36, 381, 387, 389; self-identity, 97, 100; shared, 194, 196
idolatry, 105, 107n1, 280
idols, 99, 222, 231n2, 322
illiberal practices, 191
immigrants, 35, 46, 72n1, 190–1, 206n8,
296n2, 334–5, 349n3
immigration, 4, 11, 13, 34–6, 46, 172,
200, 240, 242
Indian Act, 1876 (Canada), 34
individual freedom, 80, 356–7, 369
India: Communist Party of India, 282,
369; Constitution, 7–9, 70, 74n10,
83–3, 89, 95, 107, 224, 275, 283–5, 291,
302, 312, 315n1; essential practices
test, 112; post-colonial India, 292,
302, 356; secularism, 14, 42, 82–4, 87,
89, 91–2, 95–7, 107–13, 116; Supreme
Court of, 213, 328
individual rights
Indo-Aryan, 124, 144n6
Indonesian Pancasila, 42

industrial workers, 358–9
inheritance, 57, 66, 193, 232n22, 354, 367
Inquisition, 121
interculturalism, 23, 51, 192, 238, 262–3, 246, 296n2, 337–8
intercultural fluidity, 21
interethnic relations, 17
inter-religious marriage, 354
Iran, 40, 42, 77, 104, 129, 388
Islam, 7, 26n12, 46–8, 77, 81–2, 87, 123, 125–6, 131–2, 136–7, 139–40, 145n7, 191, 230n8, 255, 275–6, 279, 292, 296n4, 305, 307, 313, 323, 335, 348, 360, 366
Islamism, 281
Islamophobia, 80
isomorphism, 39–40
Israel, 42, 77–8, 294, 395

Jacobi, Hermann, 324
Jade Emperor, 127
Jaganath yatra, 68
Jainism, 7, 21, 98, 124, 276, 301, 318–28, 330–1; Council of Valabhi, 321
Jains, 9, 21, 180, 315n1, 318–31, 332n9, 356, 370, 390; Digambara, 320–3, 325–30, 331n1, 331n4, 332n9; Pro-National Minority Status (NMS), 327–8; Svetambara, 320–3, 327, 329–30, 331n1, 331n3–4
Jammu Kashmir Liberation Front (JKLF), 286–7
Japan, 44, 140, 143, 144n4
Jehovah's Witnesses, 242
Jinnah, Mohammad Ali, 99, 281–3
Juteau, Danielle, 199–201

Kant, Immanuel, 186n10
karma doctrine, 198
Kartabhaja sect, 303–7, 315n7; Ghoshpara, 304, 306
Kashmir, 21, 24, 127, 145, 230n8, 275, 277–89, 294–95, 296n1, 296n4, 297n11–2, 298n20, 327, 371n5, 389; Azad Kashmir, 280, 287; Kashmiriyat, 279–80, 283, 295n1
Kathiawar, 358–59, 374n28, 374n31
Kazakh, 137
Khuman, Devji, 365, 367, 376n48, 378n55
kirpan, 55, 244–5
Kokkinakis v. Greece (1993, ECHR), 246–47
kotwal, 359–60
Kumbh, 68, 311
Kuomintang (KMT), 128, 136, 140–1, 143, 145n11
Kymlicka, Will, 5, 25n2, 26n8, 56, 153–6, 184n3, 204, 237–8, 240, 333–34

laïcité/laicity, 10, 18–19, 36, 44, 50, 58, 91, 136, 189, 250n6, 253–60, 262–5, 269, 270n5, 270n8, 338, 350n8, 382. *See also* secularism
laïcité ouverte, 10, 19, 45, 256, 258–60, 262–3, 270n8
laïcité positive, 257
Laliberté, André, 11, 15, 120, 383
Land Acquisition Act, 1894 (India), 225
language, 19, 21, 34, 37, 56, 68, 102, 124, 131, 144n4, 144n6, 156, 192, 195–6, 200–4, 206n8, 218, 228, 237, 245–6, 248, 250n5, 255–6, 262, 281, 283, 294, 307, 322, 340, 347, 385: common, 195, 201, 204; legal, 227–8; of multiculturalism, 23, 63; official languages, 44, 57, 190, 334; rights, 21, 72n1, 171
Latour, Bruno, 212, 221, 293
Lautsi and Others v. Italy (2011, ECHR), 268
Lautsi v. Italy (2009, ECHR), 268
law: common, 113, 115–16, 291; religious family laws, 22, 353–5, 371n2
Lefebvre, Solange, 10, 17, 19, 253, 382

legal pluralism, 22, 354, 370, 371n3–4
Leroux, George, 338–9, 344
Levirate, 362, 365–66
liberalism, 110–11, 154–6, 163, 175, 177,
    179, 308, 368; classical, 92;
    contemporary, 111; ethical, 179;
    political, 157, 177–9, 184; Western,
    108, 111
Lutheranism, 10, 37, 62

Mahars, 359, 374n31, 374n33
Mahavira, 320–2, 331n1
majority: communities, 62, 67, 73n4;
    culture, 5, 70, 244, 339; religions, 13,
    22, 26n8, 62, 260, 265, 386; religious
    majority, 17, 73n4, 268; religious pres-
    ence, 10, 386; rights, 268
Manipur, 282–3
Maoist insurgents/cy, 21, 275, 282
marginalization, 63, 196, 305, 307, 312
Maritain, Jacques, 163
marriage: bride price, 361–2, 365–8,
    377n49; child marriage, 356, 361, 366,
    373n20; and divorce, 354, 356, 359,
    365–7; elopement, 361, 365–6,
    378n60; forced, 191; by insistence,
    361; intermarriage, 279, 329, 334;
    legally binding, 87, 109; love, 365;
    monogamy, 356; polyandry, 356,
    372n17; polygamy, 61, 72n1, 73n4;
    polygyny, 356–7, 362, 365, 367,
    372n13; rape within marriage, 357,
    376n21; remarriage, 365–7, 377n49
Marxist critiques, 10
Master Kong, 129. See also Confucianism
Matua sect, 21, 301–2, 308, 312
Mayaram, Shail, 20, 275, 348, 349n1,
    385, 389
Meghwals, 354, 358–61, 365–6, 372n10,
    374n31, 375n36, 375n39, 376n41,
    377n53
Mehta, Deepak, 17–18, 211, 295n1

Mehta, Pratap Bhanu, 100–1
Mennonites, 39
Messianism, 175
metaphysics, 98, 328, 349
Methodists, 39, 133; Methodist Episco-
    pal Church, 358
military-paramilitary, 129, 141, 233n29,
    249n2, 286, 288
Ming Dynasty, 127, 130
minority: community, 5, 58, 61, 69–71,
    280, 326, 333, 353, 386, 388; culture,
    48, 72n1, 238; national, 336; religions,
    7, 22, 62, 83, 336; religious, 34, 247,
    329, 348, 387; religious group, 5, 18,
    78; rights, 44, 268; status, 44, 48, 318,
    327, 329
Mir Baqi Isfahani, 214
missionaries, 136, 304, 308, 310, 360
missionary efforts, 115
modus vivendi, 66, 163, 166
moksha, 99, 319
Moore, Diane, 336, 341
moral equality, 12, 59–61, 69
moral life, 99–101, 103, 105–6, 116
mosques, 63, 80, 103, 288
motivations, 196, 204, 231n12
Mukherjee, Sipra, 20–1, 23, 301, 348, 389
Multani v. Commission scolaire Marguerite-
    Bourgeoys (2006, Canada), 244–5
multiculturalism: 35, 240; against, 20,
    170, 333; in Canada, 16, 35, 172, 181,
    191, 204, 237, 335, 337, 339; civiliza-
    tional, 276, 294; and diversity, 11, 123,
    239, 242, 244–5, 248; ethos of, 190,
    333; in India, 21, 275–6, 283, 291, 302;
    liberal, 153, 204; limits of, 21, 275;
    model of, 4, 8, 25n3, 383; normative
    paradigm/principle, 15, 190, 192, 203,
    205; as/and policy, 35, 120–2, 134, 137,
    142, 144, 170–2, 189, 190–2, 204, 237,
    301, 307; program, 179–82, 186n13;
    recognition of, 11, 17, 114; and reli-

gion, 5, 17, 22, 179, 189; and religious
  identity, 4; and secularism, 12–3, 15,
  294, 318–19; support for, 191, 205n1,
  237, 301, 334; theory/ists of, 55–8
Mumbai, India, 354, 358, 365, 372n10,
  374n31, 376n41, 377n49
Muslim League (India), 93n1, 96, 283
Muslims: Bengali, 305, 310; in Canada,
  334; in India, 18, 211; youth, 46, 48
mutual respect, 170–1, 175, 178–9,
  182–3, 186n10, 186n13
mutual understanding, 105, 159, 163,
  165, 349, 386
myths, 99, 102, 121, 124, 127, 262–3

Nanda, Meera, 345
Nandy, Ashis, 96–7, 102, 106, 291, 345
narrative, 11, 18, 37, 156, 204, 219, 244,
  279, 293
National Assembly (Québec), 19, 60,
  257, 259–60, 350n7, 382; crucifix, 19,
  60, 260
National Commission of Minorities
  Act, 1992 (India), 326
nationalism, 44, 46, 74, 89, 91, 96, 140,
  189, 246, 275, 283–4, 377n53; binationalism, 45
nationalization, 38, 291; trans-national-
  ization, 11, 42–3
national religions, 11, 42
Naxalites, 282
nazism, 191
nazul land, 215, 230n10
Nehru, 95, 283, 286–87; Nehruvian era,
  66; Nehruvian origins, 95
neoliberalism, 6, 242
Netherlands, 44, 77
neutrality: liberal, 57, 162; state, 12, 57,
  59, 630–1, 259–60; strict, 83, 86–7, 109
new religious movements, 43, 123, 138,
  140
niqab, 250n6, 350n7

Nirmohi Akhara, 213–15, 227, 229n1
Noman, Abdullah, 279–80
Nuruddin, 278
Nussbaum, Martha, 346

Oddie, Geoffrey, 305–6
Odissa, 24
Okin, Susan Moller, 58, 73n4
Orissa, 89, 282, 289
Orthodox churches, 40
Orthodox Jews, 70
ossification, 22, 370
Overmyer, Daniel, 121

Pakistan, 46, 67, 77–8, 280–2, 284, 286–7,
  294–95, 311
Palestine, 294
Palmer, David, 121
panch, 359, 364, 368; tana, 359; vada, 359
Panchayat, 279, 292, 294, 297n11, 354,
  360, 361, 364–5, 371n7, 375, 376n75,
  377n48, 377n55. See also caste
Pandey, Umesh Chandra, 216, 231n14
Parekh, Bhikhu, 26n9, 72n1, 156, 314
Parsi, 354, 356
partition, 7, 93n1, 281, 284, 311
Pateliya, 359–60, 362
Patil, Bal, 327–28, 331n9
Peetush, Ashwani, 16, 153–4, 157, 385
Philippines, 77, 139
philosophy, 3, 63, 111, 118n5, 129, 138,
  156, 177, 261, 328, 341, 346–7
Pietists, 39
pilgrimage, 229n4; Haj, Amarnath,
  Mansarovar, 67
pluralism, 236, 239–40, 247, 315, 37; cultural, 34; diversity and, 238, 240, 348;
  legal, 22, 354, 370, 371n3–4; reasonable, 111; religious, 9, 33, 36, 48, 262,
  269, 318–19, 330
poet/ry, 277, 312, 315n8, 363–4, 376n42,
  377n42